Axelle Germanaz, Daniela Gutiérrez Fuentes, Sarah Marak, Heike Paul (eds.)
To the Last Drop – Affective Economies of Extraction and Sentimentality

I0095687

Editorial

The **Global Sentimentality** series conceives of the sentimental as a distinctive code to be examined in literature, popular culture, political rhetoric, and cultural practices of all kinds. The book series offers a platform for reflection on the sentimental – both in terms of its cultural specificity and its transcultural adaptations on a global scale. Located in cultural studies, the series simultaneously invites an interdisciplinary engagement with the sentimental at the intersection of literary, cultural, and social studies. The series will include volumes of essays and survey works on the sentimental as well as monographs.

The series is edited by Heike Paul.

Axelle Germanaz (M.A.) is a doctoral researcher in American studies at Friedrich-Alexander-Universität Erlangen-Nürnberg. Her research interests include environmental humanities, far-right extremism, affect studies and sentimentalism, and critical race theory.

Daniela Gutiérrez Fuentes (M.A.) is a Chilean political scientist and journalist whose research interests include environmental humanities, decolonial theory/praxis, social justice, and post-development critique. She is a doctoral researcher at Friedrich-Alexander-Universität Erlangen-Nürnberg in Germany and Universidad Austral de Chile.

Sarah Marak (M.A.) is a doctoral researcher in American studies at Friedrich-Alexander-Universität Erlangen-Nürnberg. Her research interests include popular culture, discourses on terrorism, U.S.-American myths and ecocriticism.

Heike Paul (Prof. Dr.) is chair of American studies at Friedrich-Alexander-Universität Erlangen-Nürnberg and director of the Bavarian American Academy in Munich. She is project leader of the Global Sentimentality Project and spokesperson of the research training group on "The Sentimental" at FAU. In 2018, she received the Leibniz Prize of the German Research Foundation.

Axelle Germanaz, Daniela Gutiérrez Fuentes, Sarah Marak, Heike Paul (eds.)

To the Last Drop – Affective Economies of Extraction and Sentimentality

[transcript]

Printed with generous support of the German Research Foundation

Bibliographic information published by the Deutsche Nationalbibliothek

The Deutsche Nationalbibliothek lists this publication in the Deutsche Nationalbibliografie; detailed bibliographic data are available in the Internet at http://dnb.d-nb.de

First published in 2023 by transcript Verlag, Bielefeld
© Axelle Germanaz, Daniela Gutiérrez Fuentes, Sarah Marak, Heike Paul (eds.)

Cover layout: Maria Arndt, Bielefeld

https://doi.org/10.14361/9783839464106
Print-ISBN 978-3-8376-6410-2
PDF-ISBN 978-3-8394-6410-6
ISSN of series: 2751-1006
eISSN of series: 2751-1014

Contents

Preface

Stephanie LeMenager

In the volume, the editors ask us to consider "what extraction feels like" and how its feeling-states and bodily sensations are tentatively captured in representational media from television series to novels, film, visual and performance art. At "the nexus of affect studies and the environmental humanities," *To the Last Drop* challenges the energy humanities, in particular, to take seriously how affects associated with fossil fuels converse with ideologies, politics, and social movements. Affects can unstick us from dangerous attachments, such as automobility, cathect us to more sustainable hegemonies, such as the Green New Deal, and contribute in a multitude of scarcely traceable ways to atmospheres of resistance or transition. But affects do not, cannot, lead directly into any determinate behavior—and therein lies the rub for some politically committed scholars in the era of climate crisis, where the need for systemic and structural change is so urgent, so *yesterday*. No wonder that "affect studies" has been "marginalized in energy studies" whose focus tends toward development, as Cara Daggett insightfully notes in this volume.

The political scientist Deborah Gould has argued that "affective states can shake people out of deeply grooved patterns of thinking and feeling and allow for new imaginings"—yet "affect is an effect of being affected, and an effect that is itself a preparation to act in response, but in no preset or determined way" (Gould 32; 26). The inchoate quality of affect, as pre-emotional, un-narrativized feeling, opens the study of affect to critical contempt ("dithering while the planet burns," Hornborg) in our crisis times, especially for Marxists who overlook Raymond Williams' *Marxism and Literature*. In that classic analysis of the cultural dimensions of hegemony and revolution, affects persist in excess of hegemonic contracts; they are the structures of feeling "at the very edge of semantic availability" that may seed social change (Williams 134). How many symposia have I attended where the "environmental humanities" is elided with caricatures of the new materialisms, to which affect studies contributes, while the "energy humanities" is announced, with equal simplicity, as a desolate Marxism where cultural expressions never surmount the machinic means of production, which run on oil? In this cartoonish debate, the environmental humanities appear as frivolous and feminine, the energy humanities masculine and relentlessly economic.

Fortunately, such heteronormative hyperbole rarely mars the scholarly writing that laid the groundwork for this volume—and it has no place in the volume itself. Lauren Berlant's concern for "waning genres" and especially the psychoeconomic con of cruel, neoliberal optimism (235), Stacy Alaimo's notion of the transcorporeal exchange of toxins and other industrial effluents across porous bodies, and Karen Barad's insistence, from her background in physics, on relationality as foundational to the performance of identities, are among those new materialist ideas which influenced first and second-wave energy humanities scholarship by Imre Szeman, Jennifer Wenzel, Kathryn Yusoff, Cymene Howe, Patricia Yaeger, Dominic Boyer, and myself, to name a few. NB some in the aforementioned group also are avowed Marxists. Meanwhile Indigenous scholarship and activism, some of it explicitly connected to anti-extractivist social movements like Idle No More or #NoDAPL, have checked both Eurocentric Marxisms and new materialisms for their blindness to the persistence of colonialist violence in the Americas, Australia, and other settler regions which only recently began to appreciate Indigenous epistemologies. Zoë Todd and Vanessa Watts, among others, call out some strains of new materialism for cultural appropriation, in their attempts to express relationality without acknowledging the Indigenous ontologies for which relationality always has been central (Todd, "An Indigenous;" Watts, "Indigenous Place-Thought"). Several authors in this volume specifically frame their analyses as a critique of settler sentiments, signaling contemporary efforts to decolonize the energy humanities.

The environmental humanities, too, has undergone decolonial reckonings, as we recognize that even our foundational terms ("environment," "humanities") reflect the bourgeois, Eurocentric biases that Sylvia Wynter describes as foundational to hegemonic humanisms. Self-reflection in regard to colonialism and its collateral injuries, including racism, has long been an attribute of American studies, which owes much of its critical acumen to race and ethnic studies. The same influences, especially from Black thought, flash at crucial junctures of affect studies with cultural studies. Berlant's critique of sentimentality's unfinished business could be said to begin in James Baldwin's searing insights about the spectacularization of anti-Black racism and to engage

Saidiya Hartman's early analyses of "scenes of subjection" across abolitionist media (book of the same title), while more recently Christina Sharpe's lyrical critique of the affective "weather" of anti-Blackness (102), like Stefano Harney and Fred Moten's descriptions of the "feels" of Black fugitivity (97–99), correct affect studies' sometimes tacitly white assumptions about "ordinary" feelings and lives. The contributors to this volume who "track the neoliberal present, in which affective life and structural conditions are often out of step" (Staiger et al. 11)[1]—in Ann Cvetkovich's words—do so with a keen eye towards the ways in which hierarchies of race, ethnicity, class, ability, and gender impress feelings upon bodies and spaces.

References to Sara Ahmed's "affective economies" by many authors in this volume and in the book title as well ensures its sensitivity to how social hierarchies, including racism, generate feelings. Moreover, several chapters address 18th and 19th century genres that betray the historic entanglements of racial capitalism, extractive sentiments, and fossil fuels. One of the great pleasures of *To the Last Drop* resides in its sharp reimagining of earlier critical insights into the identities and mythemes generated by settler colonialism in North America. Manifest domesticity (Amy Kaplan), regeneration through violence (Richard Slotkin), beset (white) manhood (Nina Baym), and other scholarship of the 1990s, when American studies recognized itself as the study of empire, are redeployed here, within the material contexts of fuel. From "petro-masculinity" to "extractivist nostalgia" to "the melancholy of extraction," authors throughout this volume approach the conflicted identity performances of the era of climate crisis and U.S. imperial decline, which in so many respects feels like, and perhaps is, a referendum on petromodernities within the long project of Euroamerican empire.

Scholars here propose terms for socioecological transition, making this volume kin to other Anthropocene era-making lexicons, such as Matthew Schneider-Mayerson's and Brent Ryan Bellamy's *An Ecotopian Lexicon*. The volume is also kin to earlier explorations of petroemotionality and petrogender, as in my own "petromelancholia," Alaimo's "carbon-heavy masculinities" (95–96), and Yusoff's "coal subjectivities" (780). Such critical concepts function as proto-genres—keys to transition narratives, to new patterns of expectation and self-scripting in an era of the unexpected, if not unthinkable. Attending to the microdynamics of affect is a scholarly knowledge practice rather than a social movement, to be sure. Yet such practice approaches the "unthought

---

1   Ann Cvetkovich in *Political Emotions* 11.

known," as Berlant called the condition of "being historical in the present" (235). Being historical in the present implies being forced to think about feeling as a mode of world-making within social atmospheres of almost inexplicable change, where feeling, left unthought, might swerve toward violent retrotopia—as we are reminded by Heike Paul's close reading of the rhetoric of Donald Trump.

Near the end of *To the Last Drop*, Daggett offers that "there is a pedagogical moment in recognizing how one's feelings are attached to certain stories, even stories we no longer believe. This means having a kind of affective intelligence about our bodies and selves, one that learns how to develop our capacity for new sensibilities."

Let me add that ecological sensibilities and desires for post-oil living must be cultivated across discourses, practices, and movements, against the inertia of habit as well as the overt propaganda and violence of fossil capital.

References

Alaimo, Stacy. 2016. *Exposed: Environmental Politics and Pleasures in Posthuman Times*. Minneapolis, MN: University of Minnesota Press.

Berlant, Lauren. 2010. "Thinking about Feeling Historical." In *Political Emotions*, edited by Janet Staiger, Ann Cvetkovich, and Ann Reynolds, 229–45. New York, NY: Routledge.

Gould, Deborah. 2010. "On Affect and Protest." In *Political Emotions*, edited by Janet Staiger, Ann Cvetkovich, and Ann Reynolds, 18–44. New York, NY: Routledge.

Harney, Stefano, and Fred Moten. 2013. *The Undercommons: Fugitive Planning and Black Study*. New York, NY: Minor Compositions.

Hartman, Saidiya. 1997 *Scenes of Subjection: Terror, Slavery, and Self-making in Nineteenth-Century America*. New York, NY: Oxford.

Hornborg, Alf. 2017. "Dithering While the Planet Burns: Anthropologists' Approaches to the Anthropocene." *Reviews in Anthropology*, vol. 46 (2–3): 61–77.

LeMenager, Stephanie. 2011. "Petro-Melancholia: The BP Blowout and the Arts of Grief." *Qui Parle* 19 (2): 25–55.

Sharpe, Christina. 2016. *In the Wake: Blackness and Being*. Durham, NC: Duke University Press.

Staiger, Janet, Ann Cvetkovich, and Ann Reynolds (Eds). 2010. *Political Emotions*. New York, NY: Routledge.

Staiger, Janet, Ann Cvetkovich, and Ann Reynolds. 2010. "Introduction: Political Emotions and Public Feelings." In *Political Emotions*, edited by Janet Staiger, Ann Cvetkovich, and Ann Reynolds, 1–17. New York, NY: Routledge.

Todd, Zoë. 2016. "An Indigenous Feminist's Take On The Ontological Turn: 'Ontology' Is Just Another Word For Colonialism," *Journal of Historical Sociology*, vol. 29: 4–22.

Watts, Vanessa. 2017. "Indigenous Place-Thought & Agency Amongst Humans and Non-Humans (First Woman and Sky Woman Go on a European World Tour!)," *Re-visiones (Madrid)* vol. 7: n.p.

Williams, Raymond. 1977. *Marxism and Literature*. New York, NY: Oxford University Press.

Yusoff, Kathryn. 2013. "Geologic Life: Prehistory, Climate, Futures in the Anthropocene." *Environment and Planning D: Society and Space*, vol. 31 (5): 779–95.

Introduction

The Editors

In a 2013 installation called *Give us, Dear*, artists Matthias Böhler and Christian Orendt confront us with the dehumanizing and predatory processes that have defined and continue to define resource extraction as part of a global modernity. *Give us, Dear* is a 6.5-meters-long sculpture made of paper, wire, wood, glue, metal, rubber, ink, and acrylic paint. It represents a creature, "ambivalently human and/or animal" ("A Reference Companion") laying on the floor of an exhibition room. The creature is not alone. Around five hundred "anthropomorphic beings" (ibid.), made up of wires and hot glue, are harvesting the multiple materials that compose the beast: from its skin, nails, teeth, and hair/fur to its blood, mucus, and excrement. The sculpture contrasts starkly the immobility and powerlessness of the creature with the imaginary mobility and business of those besieging it, who are using industrial and pre-industrial objects such as cranes, ladders, scaffoldings, pumps, carts, bridges, to extract and exploit the creature's body and fluids. Two holes have seemingly been punched out in a wall of the exhibition room to transport the resources away and bring new workers to the extraction site.

In *Give us, Dear*, extractivism is depicted as an all-encompassing, cannibalizing enterprise. It not only critiques the notion that the human and more-than-human world is solely here to "give us" raw materials and sources of energy but it also humanizes that same object of extraction. The installation creates discomfort in the audience for it is faced with its own demise: The anthropomorphic quality of the creature and the fact that its human exploiters are made from the same materials, highlight that what is being extracted and what is being consumed are, ultimately, we ourselves. The fate of extractive industries' workers is also questioned by the installation as it highlights the intergenerational and enduring aspects of extraction: New workers and new machinery will replace old workers and their tools.

Give us, Dear *by Böhler & Orendt, 2013 (multi-part sculptural installation, 1,4 x 2,2 x 8m, black copied and shredded DIN A4 paper, newspaper, wallpaper paste, chicken wire, wood, hot glue, metal, rubber rings, ink, acrylic paint).*

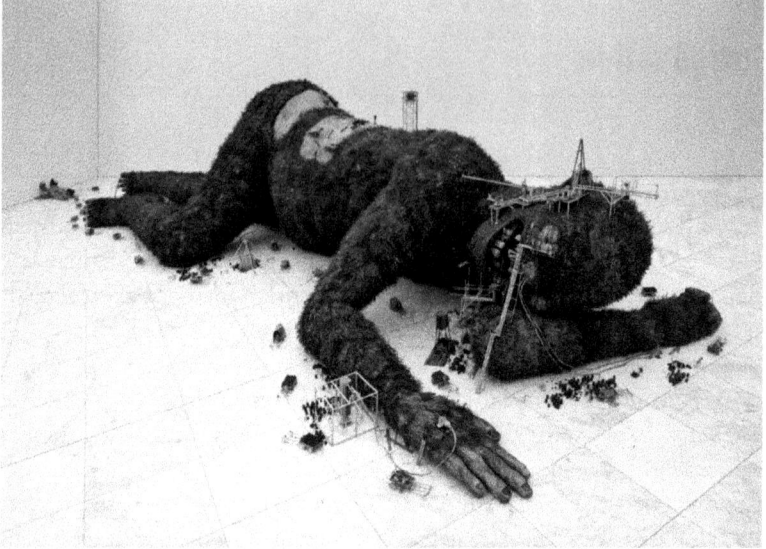

Collection of Neues Museum Nürnberg in cooperation with Elke Antonia Schloter and Volker Koch. Image courtesy of Böhler & Orendt.

The sculpture may seem repulsive at first glance, yet it is also deeply sentimental as spectators are made to empathize with the strangely human creature and its suffering. Indeed, as it is laid on its side in a recovery position—its head resting on one arm and the palm of its hand seemingly feeling the ground—the creature suggests helplessness and defeat, but also exhaustion, despair, and hopelessness. *Give us, Dear* requires viewers to feel what extractivism might feel like: from the violence of mining, drilling, and logging of the Earth to the pain and trauma that the extractive enterprise inflicts on its own workers. It is through the sentimental mode that the art installation renders the ordinariness and opacity of global extraction as a spectacular and embodied experience: extraction as intrusion, violation, and disruption of the planet(ary). The title of the work plays on the contradictory relations at the core of modernity: (Western) societies value, even treasure, the Earth and its components but consume it wholly through extraction and exploitation. The noun "Dear" seems to be used as an affectionate name for the creature, perhaps as *pars pro toto* symbolizing humanity and the planet, to emphasize its beloved and treasured quality. In somewhat oxymoronic fashion, "Dear" also clashes with the command "give us," which dictates that something should be transferred or handed over voluntarily and therefore highlights the 'toxic relationship' that humans entertain with the planet through extractivism. What happens, the installation seems to ask, when Earth provides us with its very last drop of (fossil) fuel? *Give us, Dear* raises key questions and concerns that the contributors of this volume address. It can be read as exemplifying the conditions and processes that highlight why extractivism has such a firm grip on societies in the Western hemisphere. The installation makes viewers consider the complex entanglement of resource extraction and affect by evoking the sentimentalization involved in the exploitation of a seemingly benevolent and always giving "Dear" Earth.

Practices of extraction—as shown in *Give us, Dear*—have long been entwined with narratives of economic growth and technological progress and can be considered part and parcel of the history of Western modernity and its regimes of exploitation: of bodies, resources, and land. Extractive colonization in its various forms has often been legitimized with a rhetoric of civilizational superiority and entitlement ("white man's burden"), at times along with pseudo-scientific notions of natural hierarchies that "stripped [nature] of activity and rendered [it] passive" in order to "be dominated by science, technology and capitalist production" (Merchant 514). As early ecofeminist Carolyn Merchant (*The Death of Nature*, 1980) and Americanist Annette Kolodny (*The Lay of the Land*, 1975) have shown, the rationalized destruction of nature often appears in heavily gendered—and we might add racialized—narratives.

Despite the scientific language and focus on technological processes as well as the more recent 'techno-fix' rhetoric regarding climate change, resource extraction is only seemingly a sober and rational affair (cf. Matthew Huber's notion of an "addiction" to fossil fuels). There are, in fact, deep affective attachments and dependencies that have long undergirded these developments. With rising critique of extractivism in a decolonial vein, both on a local and a global scale, these attachments become more contested and difficult to sustain. At the same time, they also become more visible and more explicit as they weaponize a defense of the status quo and a way of life dependent on extractivism that has long been simply taken for granted and that is made to appear as being without alternative. While this volume focuses on the romance with extraction and the romancing of extractivism in the sentimental mode firmly lodged into, at least, Western cultural imaginaries, it also addresses what Lauren Berlant have called "countersentimental narratives" (2011, 55). For Berlant, these narratives are part of "a resistant strain within the sentimental domain" (ibid.) and "are lacerated by ambivalence: they struggle with their own attachment to the promise of a sense of unconflictedness, intimacy, and collective belonging with which the U.S. sentimental tradition gifts its citizens and occupants" (ibid.). As some contributions in this volume make clear then, sentimentality—and the political feelings it can give rise to—has also been deployed to produce a sharp critique of extractivism.

To grasp the full force and intensity of such "affective economies" (Sara Ahmed) of extractivism, in which emotions "align individuals" with others "through the very intensity of their attachments" (119), it is important to look for the myriad forms of entanglements and complicities of what is considered "the good life" with extractivist practices and lifestyles; to bring into view the displaced, latent, and tacit forms of attachment to extractive practices and fantasies; and to analyze them with a view to their underlying implications regarding race, gender, class, and region. Inspired by a large body of scholarship by eco-feminist writers who have emphasized the parallels between extractivism and gender, notably in the feminization of nature and the romanticization of resource extraction in settler-colonial societies (see Kolodny, Merchant, Daggett), we consider the intersection of extractivism and sentimentality a meaningful site to interrogate the mechanisms behind the lasting power of extractive systems.

Moving away from a heavily gendered conceptualization of the sentimental (in the U.S. dating back to the 19th century), we conceive of the sentimental as a communicative code that works to establish relations, for example between the individual and the community, or the state. In *The Queen of America Goes to Washington City* (1997), Lauren Berlant, for example, have conceptualized and problematized the "intimate public sphere" as a space of convergence of the private and the public, the personal and the political. More recently, and regarding the genre of melodrama, political scientist Elisabeth Anker has identified in *Orgies of Feeling* (2014) the formula of political melodrama in U.S. politics following 9/11—a formula that relies on the specific affective features of melodrama in order to create national unity in the face of crisis. Similar phenomena can be seen elsewhere in times of political crisis. Judith Butler has pointed to practices of mourning that show the limits of what and who can or cannot be sentimentalized—and hence grieved (*Precarious Life*, 2004).

In the context of extractivism, ideological uses of the sentimental often run on a form of denial of the violence extractivism causes, at home and elsewhere, and attempt to obscure its larger consequences. In the U.S., for example, with the move towards climate-related regulations, some have expressed resentment and feelings of nostalgia about what has been considered a vanishing lifestyle rooted in "cheap energy"—LeMenager diagnoses these responses, among others, as symptomatic of a contemporary "petromelancholia" (*Living Oil*, 2013). Likewise, the regressive and defiant narratives of fossil fuel (hyper-)consumption analyzed by Cara Daggett in "Petro-masculinity: Fossil Fuels and Authoritarian Desire" seem to be often tinted with sentimental overtones—in plots of (male) victimization, displaying an extractive heroism that (re-)affirms the hegemony of extractivism.

At the nexus of affect studies and environmental humanities, this volume offers readings that expose and de-sentimentalize, as it were, the romance with extraction. It also points to instances where an eco-critical re-sentimentalization takes place. In fact, the volume aims to introduce more ambivalent approaches to the sentimental in new narratives of environmental stewardship. Case studies draw on literature (diaries, novels, personal letters), film, television series, video games, and other forms of public discourse as well as institutional politics; they examine the links between forms of extractivism and racialized and gendered discourses of sentimentality and the ways in which cultural narratives and practices deploy the sentimental mode in plots of (familial) attachment, sacrifice, and suffering to promote or challenge extractivism.

This volume consists of ten scholarly essays, two interviews, one with a scholar, Cara Daggett, one with a writer of fiction, Jennifer Haigh, and an artist's account of the multi-component project "Oil Ancestors: Relating to Petroleum as Kin." Some of the publications in this volume have developed out of conference papers delivered at an international workshop the editors hosted at Friedrich-Alexander-Universität Erlangen-Nürnberg in October 2021.

Katharina Fackler's contribution introduces the practice of 19th century whaling as an enterprise of extractive capitalism. She specifically valorizes the perspective of a whaling wife, Mary Brewster, who joins her husband on his tours and hence becomes a widely traveled woman whose journals grant us insights into the formation of an early "extractivist imagination." Fackler's reading shows how Brewster's perspective is informed by extractivist logics and profit seeking and thus effects a thorough commodification of the Pacific, its human and non-human inhabitants, and schemes of how to exploit them. In "Ecologies of Docility and Control," **Sophie Hess** examines

the role of a 19th century elite women's boarding school in Maryland, U.S.A.,
The Patapsco Institute, in (re-)producing and legitimizing the beginning of
an extractive culture. Through analyses of the writings of both teachers and
students (in poetry, journals, and correspondences), Hess argues that the
school's community manifested a gendered, classed, and racialized space of
ecological control, which rationalized early extraction (industrial metal production and agro-industrial grain processing) and romanticized the country's
territorial expansion. **Amy Fung**'s paper offers a critical appraisal of Canada's
National Day of Truth and Reconciliation, which became a federal holiday in
2021. According to her, the rhetoric of grief and mourning recently adopted
by political leaders rings hollow as it aims to primarily provide closure for
a history of dehumanization of Indigenous peoples and a gigantic, rarely
acknowledged land theft. Rather than to face the implication of its genocidal
and extractive past and ongoing inequality and racism, the wish for "reconciliation" appears to be a lip service paid to the victims of extractive colonization
while a pervasive settler sentimentality continues to exist unchallenged in
Canadian politics and society. **Gesa Mackenthun** discusses a set of novels by
Native American women writers Linda Hogan, Louise Erdrich, and Diane
Wilson to shed light on the subtle entanglement between the use of sexual
violence against Indigenous women and the extractive violence used against
the land. In a critical reading of these novels, Mackenthun shows how the
affective intimacies evoked in the literary texts present a viable alternative
to the extractive intimacies of colonization. Moreover, these texts contribute
to the survival and revival of Indigenous plant cultivation, validates women's
intimate knowledge of seeds and plants, and suggests an alternative land use.
In this scenario, it is not the proverbial American farmer but the Indigenous
gardener who is tilting—and protecting—the land. **Verena Wurth**'s contribution focuses on "extractivist nostalgia" in the successful TV series *Mad Men*
(2007–2015) as it romanticizes forms of extractivism. Analyzing the series as
an example of "petro-TV," which she conceptualizes as a televisual form of
Ghosh's "petrofiction," Wurth's reading of *Mad Men* makes visible the ways
the show tends to hide the sites and sights of extractivism behind a nostalgic
aestheticization of consumer culture and (some) modes of transport, while
negatively representing other, more sustainable alternatives. **Brian Leech**'s
article, entitled "Feeling Senti-Metal," examines the nostalgic and romantic
representations of gold mining in the U.S. popular tough-guy television shows
Gold Rush and its spin-off, *Parker's Trail*. He connects these representations to
U.S. American frontier myths of rugged masculinity, boundless riches, and

emptied (hostile) landscapes. His analysis shows how the series hides theat
times catastrophic consequences of mining and extractivism behind a nostalgic—and hence largely pleasurable—portrayal of small, family-led mining
operations that ultimately belong to the past. In "Sentimentality, Sacrifice,
and Oil," **Katie Ritson** zooms in on two recent novels—one from Norway
and the other one from Great Britain—to analyze how they contribute to the
memorialization of offshore oil extraction and its man-made environmental
disasters in the cultural imaginary of North Sea coastal states. Her readings
of Atle Berge's *Puslingar* (2019) and Iain Maloney's *The Waves Burn Bright* (2017)
examine how the novels unfold their affective power through sentimentality and "strategic empathy" in plots of intergenerational and environmental
conflict. **Kylie Crane** turns to discourses of nuclear extractivism in an article
entitled "On Some Absent Presences of Nuclear Extractivism." She examines
how the latter has been legitimized within a logic that locates scenarios of
danger and of threat "elsewhere" and "elsewhen," even as its consequences can
hardly be contained in such a manner. Her discussion of Bethesda Softworks'
2015 video game *Fallout 4* problematizes its cast of characters, its retro-futurist
aesthetics, and its atmosphere of nostalgia as reiterating such a false sense of
containment—or contain-ability—of nuclear risk. **Heike Paul**'s essay delves
into foundational American mythology and its concomitant extractivist imaginary. The latter still figures prominently in political and popular culture. To
illustrate this, she juxtaposes an analysis of a key appearance and speech of
former President Trump in front of representatives of the oil lobby to a reading
of Jennifer Haigh's novel *Heat & Light*, which tells the story of fracking in small-
town Pennsylvania. As the contrast shows, the somewhat simplistic rhetoric
of the treasure hunt that Trump promises to be successful and rewarding, is
undercut by the narrative in which Haigh shows individual hopes and dreams
to become unraveled and ultimately destroyed through the impact of fracking.
As a case of "cruel optimism" (Berlant) fracking leaves people not only without
their most valuable resource, the land, but also robs them of their future. In
an interview with the author, Heike Paul speaks with **Jennifer Haigh** about
growing up in a mining town, about masculinity, nostalgia, and about recent
ideological shifts and realignments in rural Pennsylvania. **Axelle Germanaz
and Sarah Marak** discuss how the 2012 movie *Promised Land* resolves the
controversy about fracking through a narrative of "agrarian sentimentality"
that romanticizes small-town rural life as an antidote to extractivism. As
a narrative with topoi and settings typical of a culturally specific "fracking
formula," the film partly deviates from other cultural artifacts on fracking in

that it presents a version of the Jeffersonian agrarian myth as an ostensible solution to questions of both economic and environmental sustainability and safety. **Axelle Germanaz**' and **Daniela Gutiérrez Fuentes**' conversation with **Cara Daggett** examines the intersections between affect, sentimentality, and extractivism in an era of climate emergency. The discussion addresses an array of relevant issues for better understanding the depth of societies' attachments to fossil fuels and the challenges that prevent them from moving away from extractive practices and ways of life. Finally, **Fereshteh Toosi**'s contribution introduces and describes their art project, *Oil Ancestors: Relating to Petroleum as Kin*, based on a series of interactive experiences about the affective relationship between people and the products of (mineral) extraction. Readers will be able to engage first-hand with the project in practicing a meditation centered on the materiality of petroleum extraction.

We would like to express our gratitude to all the contributors to this volume for their inspiring, thought-provoking, and disciplinarily diverse work. We also owe special thanks to Susen Faulhaber. She has, as always, been a superb and exceptionally thorough proofreader. Her assistance in all matters concerning bibliographic precision and consistency has been invaluable. We would also like to thank the Office for Gender and Diversity at FAU for generously funding the virtual workshop that ultimately led to this publication with a "Promotion of Equal Opportunities for Women in Research and Teaching" grant in 2021.

We are grateful to the artists Matthias Böhler and Christian Orendt for the permission to reprint an image of their work of art.

With generous permission from Campus, Heike Paul's article has been updated, translated, and reprinted here.

This book is the second volume in the "Global Sentimentality" book series. It is published with the generous support of the German Research Foundation.

References

Ahmed, Sara. 2004. "Affective economies." *Social Text* 22 (2): 117–39. DOI: https://doi.org/10.1215/01642472-22-2_79-117.

Anker, Elisabeth R. 2014. *Orgies of Feeling*. Durham, NC: Duke University Press.

Berlant, Lauren. 1997. *The Queen of America Goes to Washington City*. Durham, NC: Duke University Press.

Berlant, Lauren. 2011. *Cruel Optimism*. Durham, NC: Duke University Press.

Böhler, Matthias, and Christian Orendt. 2018. *A Reference Companion*. Vienna: Verlag für moderne Kunst.

Butler, Judith. 2004. *Precarious Life: The Powers of Mourning and Violence*. New York, NY: Verso Books.

Daggett, Cara. 2018. "Petro-masculinity: Fossil Fuels and Authoritarian Desire." *Millennium* 47 (1): 25–44. DOI: https://doi.org/10.1177/0305829818775817.

Huber, Matthew T. 2013. *Lifeblood: Oil, Freedom, and the Forces of Capital*. Minneapolis, MN: University of Minnesota Press.

Kolodny, Annette. 1975. *The Lay of the Land: Metaphor as Experience and History in American Life and Letters*. Chapel Hill, NC: University of North Carolina Press.

LeMenager, Stephanie. 2013. *Living Oil: Petroleum Culture in the American Century*. Oxford: Oxford University Press.

Merchant, Carolyn. 1980. *The Death of Nature: Women, Ecology, and the Scientific Revolution*. New York, NY: Harper & Row.

Merchant, Carolyn. 2006. "The Scientific Revolution and *The Death of Nature*." *Isis* 97 (3): 513–33. DOI: https://doi.org/10.1086/508090.

Whaling Wives, Life Writing, and Sentimental Extraction in the 19th Century Pacific

Katharina Fackler

Introduction

After waiting almost four years for the return of her captain husband to Stonington, Connecticut, Mary Brewster had had enough. She decided to join
him on his next years-long voyage. In December of 1845, she embarked on
the whaleship *Tiger*. Along with her husband and thirty male crew members,
Mary Brewster circumnavigated Cape Horn and made her way into the Pacific,
landing on the Sandwich Islands (today called Hawai'i) and then sailing on
to the whaling grounds off the Northwest Coast and Baja California. When
William Brewster decided to try his luck in the Arctic over the summer of
1847, Mary Brewster spent a season among American missionaries on Maui,
exploring the Hawaiian Islands on horseback and encountering "Yankees,"
missionaries, and Kānaka Maoli (Indigenous Hawaiians). In 1849, she would
even accompany her husband to the Arctic. Throughout her travels, she kept
extensive journals. While Brewster was not the first or the only captain's wife
on a whaler, her journals are some of the earliest and most comprehensive of
their kind. They testify to 19th century Euro-American women's maritime mobility—and they provide a unique female take on one of the largest extractive
enterprises of the United States in the first half of the 19th century.

This article brings together theories from postcolonial ecocriticism, the
energy humanities as well as gender and affect studies to explore how Mary
Brewster represented the Pacific Ocean and the extractive business of whaling.
It considers her journals a distinctly gendered, classed, racialized, and speciated contribution to a large body of 19th century cultural representations that
negotiated the early United States' dependence on raw materials and energy
extracted from whales, along with its imperialist tendencies. Among others,

whale oil was needed for illumination and as a lubricant for machines (Burnett 374). Substituting for tallow, which had been extracted on a small, domestic scale, whale oil radically broadened "energy's social, spatial, end ecological relations" (Wenzel 7; Shannon).[1] As whale populations on the Atlantic seaboard were exhausted, whalers ventured ever-further into the Pacific, where they became "an advance maritime guard for U.S. imperial goals" (Igler 103–4).[2] Ecological exhaustion also facilitated specific formal features of American whaling literature, such as plots revolving around long maritime voyages and adventures in distant places. These narrative structures usually helped evoke a notion of heroic national masculinity that presented a maritime complement to the ideal of "American husbandmen and craftsmen who produced valuable goods for the consumption of their fellow citizens" on land (Schell 12, 15). Women often remained invisible in these maritime "producerist phantasies" (Schell 16). Mary Brewster's writings, this article argues, expose how whaling's extractive and imperialist logics were built around White feminine consumption and domestic sentimentality.

Focusing in particular on the journals of her first voyage, I suggest that her writings slightly revised the gender norms of the era at the same time as they helped impose an extractive view onto the Pacific, including its human and non-human inhabitants as well as whalers laboring aboard the *Tiger*. This view "sees territories as commodities, rendering land [and sea life] as for the taking, while also devaluing the hidden worlds that form the nexus of human and nonhuman multiplicity" (Gómez-Barris 5). By doing so, it "facilitates the re-organization of territories, populations, and plant and animal life into extractible data and natural resources for material and immaterial accumulation" (ibid.). In other words, I contend that Brewster's journals helped erase and devalue a wide range of entanglements between human and non-human Pacific worlds in order to make them imaginatively compatible with logics of accumulation steered from and toward the Eastern seaboard. Her narrative, addressed

---

1   Whale oil only lost relevance with the watershed discovery of liquid fossil fuels, aka petroleum, which is said to have saved whales from extinction (Jones 193–94).

2   The Hawaiian Islands became highly frequented stop-over points for whalers in the first half of the 19th century. Whaleships also brought missionaries and other Euro-American settlers, who pushed the erosion of Kānaka Maoli culture and drove the appropriation of Indigenous land by non-Indigenous land holders. This restructuring of Hawaiian economies and land ownership, in turn, facilitated the expansion of extractive monocrop agriculture. In other words, whaling was instrumental in bringing colonial capitalism to the Pacific.

to an intimate audience back home, thus helped fuel an imagination of the Pacific as a vast reservoir of resources waiting to be exploited. Along with images of the North American continent as "virgin land," such representations helped sustain the "fantasy of unlimited resources" that drove the expansion of U.S. extractive capitalism (cf. Paul 159, in this volume).

To do so, Brewster adapted narrative strategies that activated deeply gendered, classed, racialized, and speciated structures of feeling (cf. Hendler 10–11). Strategically integrating a whaleship in the Pacific into the sentimental language of domesticity, she imagined the Pacific as a place where White women belonged. The notion that she is "feel[ing] right," as Harriet Beecher Stowe put it (385), is central to Brewster's endeavor. Feeling right in this sense means highlighting certain attachments while imaginatively severing others, producing figurations that regulate who can and should be cared for and who will not. Brewster's intense emphasis on the sanctity of heteropatriarchal marriage, the bourgeois home, and women's moral and emotional superiority, I suggest, coheres with a pronounced detachment from the suffering of laborers, whales, and Pacific Islanders, whose bodies are needed to sustain the bourgeois home but whose lives and attachments have no value *per se*. Extractive violence is thus justified through and for White feminine consumption. Disaffection emerges as a necessary strategy to legitimize large-scale resource extraction.[3]

Brewster thus articulated a specific oceanic variant of what Amy Kaplan calls manifest domesticity. This variant throws into relief the intimate connection between the ideology of separate spheres, the trajectory of national expansion, and extractive capitalism in the 19th century Pacific. It complements an approach that Alice Te Punga Somerville links with the term "Pacific" used by so-called Western "discoverers." To them, this ocean "was only sea, only water, only liquid, only empty space over which people would travel in order to get to real places he imagined might be sitting at its edges." Somerville contrasts this view with Epeli Hau'ofa's Indigenous notion of "Oceania," which "is a gigantic, connected, ever-traversed space through, in, and across which islanders have lived and moved for millennia" (Somerville 26; Hau'ofa). As Mary Brewster imagined the Pacific for her peers back on the Eastern seaboard, she

---

3   This article explores the patterns of disaffection built into dominant structures of feeling. For the ways in which unfeeling can serve as a "survival tactic for marginalized subjects," see Xine Yao's recent theorization of disaffection as "the unfeeling rupture that enables new structures of feeling to arise" (Yao, blurb, 6).

followed in the footsteps of the earlier "discoverers" who called the same ocean the "Pacific" or "El Mar del Sur" (cf. Braun).

Gender, Life Writing, and Whaling Wives' Intimate Publics

Mary Brewster was one of a number of women who defied the maritime gender norms of their time. The ship was widely considered a men's world, and all the more a whaler (Creighton/Norling ix–x). Jennifer Schell argues that writers and politicians of the early Republic appropriated the figure of the (male) whaler for nationalistic purposes, portraying him as a heroic and hard-working model of American masculinity (2–3). Women, in turn, have played a rather marginal role in the cultural imagination of whaling to this day. Lisa Norling points out that women's "substantive absence […] from maritime culture then and from most maritime history now" belies their "symbolic importance" as a foil for maritime masculinities (1).[4]

When captains' wives did begin to join their husbands in increasing numbers from the mid-19th century onwards, they at the same time resisted and reinforced dominant gender norms. Entering the masculine sphere of the ship, they usually occupied a narrowly defined and strictly gendered position on board. Far removed from their domestic networks and duties, they were neither engaged in the business of whaling nor responsible for other domestic duties such as cooking and cleaning. Living in the better part of the ship, they usually remained isolated from the crew (Schell 140). Margaret Creighton argues that common sailors feared that the captain's family affairs would take precedent over the demands of the whaling business and that women would undermine the sense of collectivity among the crew, often described as a "brotherhood" of sailors. Moreover, captains' wives represented feminine attributes, including "delicacy, sentimentality, and tenderness" that sailor culture forbade its members, as sailors' masculinity was usually tied to the ability to suppress or sublimate sentimentality and emotion (Creighton 164–68). Instead, male crew members often indulged in alcohol consumption and sexual encounters that seemed incompatible with normative White feminine

---

4   Norling also highlights the substantial interconnections between women's supposedly domestic lives on land and the maritime world. On the domestic importance of the oceanic in 19th century women's writing, see Melissa Gniadek's *Oceans at Home: Maritime and Domestic Fictions in Nineteenth-Century American Women's Writing* (2021).

sensibilities (Druett 1991, 11). Norling contends that, as captains' wives often had less agency over their own lives at sea than they had when they stayed at home, going to sea was "the more daring—but ultimately more conservative" choice (261). They were "essentially opting for sensibility over sense," as they strove to live up to the ideals of the dominant culture of domesticity that were so utterly incompatible with the inherent mobility of the whaling business (261).

Whaling wives left few officially published documents. Yet a number of them were prolific journal writers, among them Mary Brewster.[5] Brewster's journals were only published in 1992, in the context of a feminist revision of maritime history. To this day, they represent some of the most extensive documents of their kind. The fact that they were not officially published does not necessarily mean that they were not read by anyone besides Brewster herself. Even unpublished, 19th century women's travel journals were often circulated in the semi-public sphere of family, friends, or certain intellectual circles (Thompson 134, 141; Kinsley). Brewster explicitly describes her intended audience in the first paragraph of her journal, when she writes that the goal of her writing is that "my friends [...] by reading this form some correct ideas as regards my feelings while absent" (12). While the journals of later voyages are more fragmentary and unfiltered with regard to conflicts and tensions on board, those of her first voyage seem to have been written with much care, staying neatly within the frames of New England femininity on both the formal and the rhetorical level. It seems likely that the journals of her first voyages were presented to and read by family and friends in Stonington, Connecticut, and beyond after her return, shaping other New Englanders' ideas of the Pacific. In a certain sense, these readers may have constituted what Lauren Berlant calls an "intimate public," which is organized around "an expectation that the consumers of its particular stuff already share a world-view and emotional knowledge that they have derived from a broadly common historical experience" (viii).

Indebted to extensive scholarship on women's life writing, I approach these journals not to gain access to Mary Brewster's presumably authentic self. Rather, I consider them as performative acts that "constitute [...] interior-ity" (Smith 109). Such "expressions of interiority are effects produced through the action of public discourses" (Smith 109). As verbal constructs shaped by conscious and unconscious processes of selection and arrangement of detail,

---

5   For an overview and introduction to these writings, see Joan Druett's *Petticoat Whalers*.

they warrant a more "literary" line of inquiry (Culley 217). Kathryn Carter highlights that women's diaries have routinely been subjected to external editing and censorship, undermining their trustworthiness as sources of female experience. More subtly, and more importantly for my analysis, "the exigencies of imagined audiences exerted a compelling internal effect" on women's diaries (Carter 42). Taking seriously Brewster's implied audience and its impact on "what is said and how it is said" (Culley 218), I ask how Brewster fashions her maritime female subjectivity for a New England audience that, on the one hand, expected women to be domestic, pious, and submissive and that, on the other, depended on the resources extracted from the Pacific while habitually erasing the violence of extraction.

I argue that women's journals offered formal and rhetorical possibilities that squared well with both demands. In contrast to the logbook, which registers external factors such as the weather and the ship's location, the journal format allowed Brewster to evoke a distinct sense of interiority revolving around conventional sentimental tropes and themes, most notably the "idealized intimate bond [...]" between husband and wife and the "emphasis on women's virtue and their capacity to feel" that is so central to domestic ideology (De Jong 2–3). Spatially and socially far removed from her home on the U.S. East coast, Brewster used sentimental rhetoric to inscribe whaling wives into domestic modes of belonging. Brewster's journals thus extend and slightly revise the intimate connection between sentimentalism, the ideology of separate spheres, and the "cult of true womanhood" in the 19th century (Gerund/Paul 18) into the Pacific and toward the extractive business of whaling. Within this logic, the exploitation of both laborers and whales is sublimated as it provides the necessary material basis for the production of domesticity. If classic sentimental novels, such as *Uncle Tom's Cabin* (1852), evoked a "fantasy of experiential equivalence" between their readers and oppressed subjects (Hendler 7), Brewster's sentimental language first and foremost was to make readers empathize with herself and captain's wives in general. Sentimental appeals to the ideal of domesticity provided a sense of legitimacy without fundamentally challenging dominant gender norms, thereby offering a variant of 19th century women's "pragmatic feminism" (Baym 18).

Therefore, I suggest that Brewster's journals can be read as an extractivist variant of Amy Kaplan's manifest domesticity within a logic of expansionism. She uses the double meaning of "domestic," denoting both the familial household and the nation, to carve out how "the representation of domesticity and female subjectivity simultaneously contributed to and were enabled by narratives of nation and empire-building" in the 1830s and to the 1850s (2002, 19). While the ideology of separate spheres suggested a clear separation between the gendered separate spheres of the (feminine) private home and the (masculine) public, the ideology of domesticity was profoundly entangled with the U.S.'s supposed project of "Manifest Destiny," i.e., imperial expansion. Kaplan focuses her chapter on the territories "from the Rio Grande to Africa" (2002, 19). Brewster's journals demonstrate that this manifest domesticity extended far into the Pacific already in the 1840s, where it subjected both humans and non-humans to an extractive logic whose emotional center is the bourgeois home (only seemingly displaced in a cabin on a ship) and White women's right to consumption.[6]

As Brewster's journals refrain from explicitly questioning the connections between the exploitation of nature and of women's bodies and labor, they present a contrast to the 19th century women's writing analyzed in notable ecofeminist scholarship of the last decade. For instance, many of the writers analyzed in Karen Kilcup's *Fallen Forests: Emotion, Embodiment, and Ethics in American Women's Environmental Writing, 1781–1924*, harnessed affective approaches and a putatively feminine sentimental rhetoric in order to further environmentalist concerns (4). Like Mary Brewster's journals, these writings, such as Caroline Kirkland's *A New Home, Who'll Follow*, provide a case in point for 19th century women's mobility and their complicity in the erasure of Indigenous dispossession and genocide (Ganser 470). Yet, unlike Brewster, Kirkland highlights the interconnections between presumably masculine values and extraction. And while Kirkland's *A New Home* blends the genre of the migration narrative and the travelogue (Ganser 470), Brewster's story firmly remains anchored in the genre of the travel account, whose ultimate telos always remains the return to the point of departure, i.e., the New England home.

---

6   Anita Duneer makes a related argument in her analysis of published journals by two other captain's wives, Abby Jane Morrell and Mary Wallis. Duneer argues that their writings both reinforced and resisted domestic ideals. Their language of domesticity feeds into popular imperialist tropes of their day at the same time as it "also indicates that these voyaging women grappled with issues of race, class, and gender in ways they could not have imagined had they stayed home" (195). Duneer's emphasis, however, is less on the ecological and extractivist dimensions of imperialism than on its cultural implications.

"I feel quite at home": Maritime Femininity in Brewster's Journals

Aiming to convince her readers of the rightness of her feelings, Mary Brewster makes regular recourse to a sentimentalized language of domesticity. Commonly, 19th century maritime literature highlighted adventure and exploration. Brewster's journals, in contrast, imagine the whaleship as a place of home and containment for a White middle class woman that remains imaginatively tied to her landed home in New England. In her first journal entry, she explains how her decision to go to sea all but uprooted her link to the domestic sphere, along with its emotional bonds. As friends and even her stepmother tried to dissuade her from embarking on the voyage, she writes that "few had to say one encouraging word" (12). Her stepmother even tells her that "[h]er house would never be a home for me again if I persisted in coming" (12). This initial framing might have suited a story of female rebellion against landed domestic norms. And it seems that Brewster's experience would have offered ample material for a female adventure tale. However, her narrative choices take her into a somewhat different direction. Brewster assures herself and her readers that, while going to sea may seem like a rejection of domestic norms, it is eventually a truer form of devotion to the sentimental norms of domestic life, as it allows her to be with the person she truly belongs with: "Well thank Heaven it is all past and I am on board of the good ship Tiger and with my dear Husband" (12). Although she has been suffering seasickness for weeks, she asserts, "I feel quite at home and think I shall never regret this voyage" (12). As the presence of her husband renders the ship her home, Brewster sets out to rewrite the ship in ways that align it with the ideology of domesticity.

Throughout her journal, Brewster regularly highlights the supposedly right forms of attachment to home and husband. All while she is voyaging the deep blue sea amid over two dozen men who were slaughtering countless whales, Brewster imagines the whaleship as the place where she can perform her womanly duties.[7] She offers regular excursions to the state of her inner life that af-

---

7   All in all, Mary and William shared the *Tiger* with 30 mariners, consisting of four mates, four boatsteerers, a cook, a steward, a carpenter, a cooper, a "boy," four seamen, and twelve greenhands (Druett 1992b, 9). As was customary in the whaling business, the sailors hailed from diverse backgrounds, including a number of Anglo-American New Englanders from whaling families, two young men from rather privileged backgrounds who hoped to improve their physical constitution at sea, two African Americans, and a steward described by Brewster as a "pleasant looking" "Mullato" (13). As Nancy Shoemaker has demonstrated in her work on Native American whalemen, racial categoriza-

firm her conformity to the emotional norms of femininity as she is traversing the Pacific. The holiness of home and matrimony and the moral superiority of women are cornerstones of this performance of respectable feminine maritime mobility. In a prominent passage, Brewster recommends lines from a book called *Woman's Mission*, which is attributed to Sarah Lewis.[8] It states that "All woman had a mission to perform and in all circumstances in life it should be their aim to establish peace and love and unselfishness, to be achieved by any means and at any cost to themselves, in the cultivation first of themselves then in all over whom they have influence" (108). Her journal leaves little doubt that she seeks to put these ideals into practice as a devoted wife to her husband. Her marriage, her husband's well-being, and her responsibilities as a wife are the narrative and emotional centerpiece of her journal. She presents herself, in her own words, as "a soother of woes, a calmer of troubles and a friend in need, a sharer of his sorrows as well as of his joys" (79, punctuation as in the original). Brewster fulfills her feminine duties by serving as her husband's moral and emotional compass, imagining herself as a much-needed feminine influence on the masculine order of the ship.

Brewster thus aligns herself with a rather moderate position in the era's debates about the role of women in society. The author of *Woman's Mission* rejected other feminists' calls for women's political rights, countering demands for a reconsideration of the separate spheres' ideology, along with the inequality built into marriage law. In the absence of "mental and *physical*" equality between the sexes, she argued, only men belonged in the public sphere, which she calls the sphere of "power." Women, in contrast, belonged in the sphere of "influence," i.e., the private sphere (Lewis 45–46). From there, they could be "moral agents" (51), wielding influence on men, by which they would ultimately shape a better political and social order. Women and men were to function as "coadjutors" in this endeavor (45). While this contribution to the debate hardly furthered women's social and political self-determination, Lewis's take on gender roles provided a compelling argument for a woman's presence on a whaler and for

---

tions proved somewhat contingent at sea, as rank often trumped landed racial hierarchies—until, of course, it didn't (Shoemaker 5).

8   The volume *Woman's Mission* was based on a translation of a book by the Rousseauist thinker Louis-Aimé Martin, "in which he presented a view of woman as man's spiritual guide. Men, he averred, were sensual by nature, naturally profligate, and the baseness of the male character could only be moderated by the moral example of women." Sarah Lewis shortened the book, sharpening its focus on "the all-important maternal role, making it [...] much more of interest to [English] women" (Druett in Brewster 109).

women's maritime mobility in general: Making a home at sea, they could significantly expand their moral influence.

On the formal level, the regularity of Brewster's entries in the journals of her first voyage affirms her performance of a reliable, constant return to the modes of feeling and thinking interpellated by the genre and its imagined audience. Brewster's daily entries assure her readers that she, unlike countless deserters, maroons, and beachcombers, remains committed to her New England home. When entries are missing, she justifies these absences, for instance by mentioning illnesses (12). Yet, the violence that it takes to extract the resources that make this life possible from the Pacific barely registers in her account. As the remaining paragraphs in this section will show, Brewster's intimacy with her husband stands in a striking contrast with her detachment from the crew of the ship and from Indigenous islanders. Her perceived moral mission, it seems, included only minor degrees of care for workers, racialized subjects, or animals.

In Brewster's journals, the ship seems to have two strictly separate spheres. One belongs to men and is dedicated to whaling, the other belongs to Mary and stays clear from business. In contrast to other crew members, who usually only had a filthy bunk to themselves, Brewster has two cabins, one "to sleep in the other to sit in" (13). For meals, she shares a table with her husband and the four officers (Druett 1992b, 6). She has a cabin boy who is employed to wait on her and for whom she sews clothing (13). Otherwise, she mentions hardly any significant interaction with the crew. Even her daily routines are out of step with her laboring shipmates, at least as long as they are on whaling grounds. "The others have breakfast at 5 and half past 4," she writes on May 14, 1846, "which gives them time to whale it when light, but I do not wish to have so long a day, therefore rise at 7, and eat my meal alone" (81). Both her gender and her elevated social position set her apart from the crew. This detachment plays out spatially and emotionally, and most strikingly when it comes to labor.

In *The View from the Masthead*, Hester Blum argues that sailors in their journals often theorized the ship and the sea as a place of labor, making a connection between manual labor and the life of the mind. Mark Kelley, in his dissertation, analyzes the affective dimensions of such representations of maritime labor. Kelley's "sentimental seamen" are emotionally invested in "sailors' embodied unity" in ways that channel their energies toward productive and cohesive labor (2018, 11). Like Brewster, sentimental seamen narrate certain normative forms of sentimental attachment in order to "secure their respective claims to domestic interiority in a watery expanse" (Kelley 2018, 3). They articulate a "terraqueous domesticity" that integrates the ship into the imagined community of the (continental) nation (Kelley 2018, 2).

Yet, unlike Kelley's sentimental seamen, Mary Brewster is exempt from the harsh discipline and labor of whaling. Instead, she affirms dominant binary gender logics by assuming the position of the observer and consumer. As Lori Merish argues in *Sentimental Materialism*, female consumption became the 19th century complement to male production (18, 1). Accordingly, Brewster is spared the tactile interactions and physical dangers of manual laborers. On Wednesday, June 17, 1846, she notes: "After [the whale] was secured alongside I went to see it. The idea I had was good, I found, which from what I had heard I was not disappointed save as to the head which is the most singular part. When they began to cut it I seated myself in the boat and spent the whole afternoon in looking on" (93). In other words, what was often a deadly encounter for whales and hard, dangerous work for whalers constituted an entertaining spectacle consumed from a distance for the whaling wife. Whereas she found the cutting of the whale visually pleasing, the soil and grease of whaling were hardly compatible with Brewster's notion of domesticity. On Monday February 8, 1847, she wrote: "The oil is all coopered and tomorrow they clean ship which I shall be glad to have in better condition, for when whaling business is carried on I keep below as the decks are oily and I like to keep my apartments clean" (188). While both Brewster and Kelley's sentimental seamen thus created sentimental visions of productive labor and extraction by erasing the violence and contradictions of extractive capitalism and imperialism, Brewster sets the bourgeois, domestic White feminine subject apart from the sailors' embodied unity. White feminine visual and material consumption emerges as the telos of mariners' labor.

Another journal of the same voyage, kept by the foremast hand John Perkins, put into question Mary Brewster's representation of a harmonious maritime home. It rather confirms what maritime historians have written about life and work aboard 19th century whaleships. Multiethnic crews may have offered opportunity for some. Yet for most, they also meant harsh living and working conditions, filthy bunks, unsavory food, hard labor, strict discipline, high risks, and usually low, unreliable pay.[9] Many were disillusioned and driven onto whaleboats by dire need and a lack of other options (Busch). As

---

9   On the working conditions of whalers and the so-called lay system, which granted whalers a certain share of the profits of the journey, from which many other expenses were deducted, see Dolin 313–15.

Perkins put it succinctly, "[m]ost all wish themselves out of the ship" (134). On May 2, 1846, the day Mary Brewster wrote elatedly about her ability to be with her husband, Perkins, a common sailor, noted: "We weighed anchor without a song all feeling to [sic] bad at departing from summer islands to the cold Norwest sure of hard labor, absolute suffering & danger" (148). In his journal, crewmates scrabble over food and many other items of daily life (126–27, 143). Perkins's melancholy outlook foreshadows his own fate. Having gone to sea to improve his eyesight and having repeatedly complained about his inability to see enough to go whaling (Perkins 128), he dies in a whaling accident on June 15, 1846.

Perkins's death presents one of the few moments in which the violence of extraction becomes visible in Brewster's journals. Brewster reports:

> Early this morning the boats put off for whale, after clearing sometime the bow boat got fast when the whale struck the boat and stove it, also hit a young man by the name of John Perkins and killed him instantly, supposed to have been hit by the flukes of the whale. One of his companions kept him up till the boat filled and to save himself from drowning was obliged to relinquish his grasp when he sank, the waves closing over him forever concealing his form from our view. (90)

This intrusion of death into Brewster's shipboard home somewhat changes her course as she takes up, as she puts it, "the office of the ship's nurse. The lame the sick and bruised all come to me. Doctoring done free of all expense" (98). She extends feminine services to the crewmembers, expanding, somewhat, the circle of her domestic care, but does not presume that workers have the same rights to women's unpaid reproductive labor as the male head of the middle class heteropatriarchal family.

When Mary Brewster arrives on the Hawaiian Islands, her ideals of domesticity are easily compatible with established imperial tropes. Relations between American missionaries and whalers were often fraught with tensions (Dolin 339–40), but Brewster, as a pious New England wife, gets along well with the missionaries. In her portrayals of the Kānaka, she describes Indigenous lifeways as "savage" and "backward" in comparison to Western civilization and domesticity, writing that she "had expected to see them much farther advanced" (57). She expresses dismay when Kānaka Maoli do not seem to live up to her standards of diligence, industry, and cleanliness, especially when they cross the boundaries of Brewster's speciesist sensibilities: "They are very filthy and the places I saw was [sic] better fitted for their dogs than for human beings and it is quite usual for them to dip in their finger in the Poi Calabashes and hold it for their dogs to lick and then the same for their own palate" (60). Emphasizing the presumed lack of hygiene in the context of interspecies contact, Brewster resorts to the strategy of "animal-linked racialisation," which uses other cultures' different treatment of animals to marginalize subordinate groups (Elder/Wolch/Emel qtd. in Huggan/Tiffin 153–54). Amy Kaplan theorized the domestic as "related to the imperial project of civilizing" when "the conditions of domesticity [...] become markers that distinguish civilization from savagery" (1998, 582). Brewster's journals speak to the important role of speciesism in the imperialist notion of domesticity. In this context, it seems particularly ironic when one considers that the dangerous germs and diseases that had killed Kānaka Maoli by the thousands did not come from close interspecies contact but from human Euro-American travelers.[10]

Unsurprisingly, Brewster is much more contented when she visits a school that instills what she describes as "order" and "neatness" in Kānaka children (58). Her narrative foreshadows what this form of discipline would lead to. Right after the school, she visits a sugar factory (59), a foreboding of the extractive monocrop plantation economy that would soon take hold of Hawai'i, enriching the children of American missionaries, among others, and exploiting uprooted and disowned Kānaka Maoli as wage laborers (Silva 48–51). Brewster's journals thus speak to the tensions between the empire's desire to absorb new territories, subjects, and resources and its perceived need "to control and manage their disruptive potential" (Kaplan 2002, 11–12). As Brewster imagines the ship as a domestic sphere, she is forced to manage and contain the contradictions between her vision of harmony and belonging and the exploitative, extractive realities of shipboard life and U.S. imperialism in Hawai'i. She ensures her fiction of harmony through erasure, both on the narrative and the material level.

---

10   "Conservative estimates of Hawai'i's population in 1778 range from 400,000 to 1,000,000; just forty-five years later that number was reduced to about 135,000" (Silva 24). For a more comprehensive account of the devastating impact of diseases on Kānaka health and society, see Seth Archer's *Sharks Upon the Land: Colonialism, Indigenous Health, and Culture in Hawai'i* (2018).

"I long to count thousands": Brewster's Extractive View

While Brewster's journals lend a certain value to living sailor and Kānaka bodies as long as they labor for extractive economies, whales only hold affective value as a material resource. After all, turning living whales into tons of blubber and whale bone to be sold in the market was the goal of the *Tiger*'s journey. Eventually, it was a ship's hold filled with blubber that would allow Brewster to return home and to lead a bourgeois domestic life in New England.

The basic logic of extraction, Elizabeth Miller argues, "presumes the ability to withdraw one component from the 'receptacle' of nature" without tending to the ecologies in which it is embedded (4). After the resource has been withdrawn and, likely, exhausted, the extractivist subject moves on. On an affective level, extraction thus is incompatible with long-term attachments to certain places and beings. It also involves the erasure of other, pre-existing forms of care or kinship.[11] In Brewster's case, imposing an extractive view onto whales in the Pacific required the material and discursive work of extricating them from the wide range of biological and cultural ecologies they had been embedded in. Among these "submerged perspectives" erased by the extractive view (Gómez-Barris 1) are vibrant human-non-human networks of interdependence.

Contrary to the ideology that shaped Brewster's worldview, many Indigenous cultures in the Pacific and the Arctic, including the *Māori*, the Makah, and the Iñupiat, have traditionally asserted a sense of kinship between humans and whales. This interspecies kinship is based on the belief in a common past, present, and future, which entails a sense of interdependence, reciprocity, and mutuality between humans and non-humans (Steinwand 185–86). Chie Sakakibara relates how the Iñupiat of Arctic Alaska foster "an emotional kinship among the people, the land, and the whales," which is founded, among others, on a shared myth of origin (1005). Joshua Reid, in turn, documents how the Makah in the Pacific Northwest successfully adapted a 2000-year-old whaling tradition in order to cope with settler-colonialism. And yet, commercial non-Native overhunting so depleted Northwestern whale populations that the Makah determined "[i]n 1928, nineteen years before non-Natives decided to suspend the hunt of gray whales [...] to suspend the active practice of whaling until populations had rebounded." "Makahs," Reid argues, "took their responsibilities to nonhuman kin such as whales seriously, and this tough decision

---

11   On kinship as a critical idiom in oceanic studies see Fackler and Schultermandl.

made sense" (167–68, 175–76).[12] In other words, they displayed less the "non-reciprocal, dominance-based relationship with the earth, one purely of taking" that defines extractivism but quite the opposite, a relation of "stewardship, which involves taking but also taking care that regeneration and future life continue" (Klein 169).

When Mary Brewster and the *Tiger*, along with thousands of other U.S. whaling ships sailed into the Pacific, they imposed extractivist logics that erased and violently ruptured such forms of kinship, along with the existing ecological balance in the region. Brewster's journals expose how domesticity and sentimentality sometimes bolstered such extractivist logics at the expense of other attachments. Her writings display an emotional distance from whales as living beings and an intense desire for blubber that add a significant extractivist dimension to her maritime manifest domesticity. Brewster places whales at the bottom of what Mel Chen calls "animacy hierarchy, which conceptually arranges human life, disabled life, animal life, plant life, and forms of nonliving material in orders of value and priority" (13). While Brewster recognizes whales as living bodies with certain attachments among their own kind, their death and suffering are validated as necessary for the production of Brewster's own domesticity. Whales remain firmly located on the other side of the great divide between animal and human, between nature and culture that has characterized Western thought.

It is the desire for whale oil that aligns Brewster's feelings most prominently with those of the *Tiger*'s crew. Tempers on board are frayed when they cannot seem to find a whale. On Saturday 25 [of July] 1846, Brewster writes: "For my part I am glad with anything in the shape of a whale, let it be small it will add something. I long to count thousands knowing that we must before we go home" (108). When they finally kill a whale, she asserts to her readers: "I saw the whole transaction from the ship and think this is the first time I could willingly see blood shed so freely" (93). Spirits on board rise even more when

---

12   Importantly, Reid points out that this decision was not only necessitated by environmental factors, i.e., the depletion of whale stocks, but also by federal policies and assimilationist agents who were too intent on transforming the Makah into farmers to provide them with modern equipment for off-shore whaling (176–77). When the Makah decided to resume whaling, renewing their traditional hunting rights, in the 1990s, they faced the "overt racism" built into certain "environmental discourses" (Roos/Hunt 12; Russell 162).

they approach 1000 barrels: "Men all singing and bawling [...] as this will certainly make us 1000 bbls" (108). With the reference to bloodshed, Brewster, to a certain extent, acknowledges the livingness and the suffering of whales. She also seems to imply a certain incompatibility of the slaughtering of living beings with feminine sensibilities. Yet, these are overruled by the yearning for a domesticity that is materially and ideologically sustained by extraction. While she does not condone violence *per se*, the slaughter and suffering of whales is legitimated for the production of domesticity. This domesticity is organized through a quantifying capitalist logic that values whales as numbers, in barrels of blubber and whalebone. Accordingly, the plot structure of the journal of her first voyage evokes the linearity of accumulation: Every barrel of whale oil brings her closer to her actual home on the Eastern seaboard.

Brewster's tone remains matter of fact even when she describes a particularly gruesome method of hunting whales which uses whale calves as bait to attract and kill their mothers:

> A plenty of boats stove every day and they all say these are the worst whale to strike they ever saw. The only way they can get fast is to chase the calf till it gets tired out then they fasten to it and the whale will remain by its side and is then fastened too. Brother James has been in the boats a few times. he [sic] said he saw a calf fastened to and the whale came up to it and tried to get the iron out with her fin and when she could not she took it on her back and endeavored to get it away. frequently [sic] the iron will kill them. when [sic] this is the case the whale when finding her young one dead will turn and fight the boats. (181)

David Igler describes Brewster's report as one characterized by "cool detachment" (101–2). Not even the smallest and most conventional unit of sentimental attachment, mother and child, compelled Brewster to frame this interspecies encounter in explicitly sentimental terms.

Brewster's detachment, I contend, stands out more from a present-day than from an early 19th century perspective and reveals the contingency of sentimental attachments. As Lawrence Buell argues, whales now are sentimental icons of an endangered Earth (201–3). Owing to their size, their intelligence and sociability, their "fascinating alterity" as well as their "increasing scarcity" (Buell 203), they emerged as "endangered charismatic megafauna of the sea" in environmentalist portrayals since the 1960s (Steinwand 183). This became possible, according to Buell, because they were no longer needed as resources to fuel modernization (203). This was not the case in the first half of the 19th

century, when whale oil lighted many homes and lubricated the industrial machinery that, for instance, was needed to process the large amounts of cotton
produced on slave plantations in the U.S. South. At this point, whales found
themselves among many other animals whose slaughtering was considered
a "non-criminal putting to death" in a Western anthropocentric world view.[13]
This world view "relies on the tacit acceptance that the full transcendence to
the human requires the sacrifice of the animal and the animalistic" (Derrida
qtd. in Huggan/Tiffin 5). It strictly separated the human from the non-human, routinely failing to acknowledge the entanglement of humans' and non-
humans' wellbeing and existence. Unsurprisingly, whaling narratives of the
day stressed "the daring, risks, dangers, and excitement of whaling far more
than the suffering of the whales" (Buell 208), though some of them did.

As more recent scholarship highlights, common sailors, too, displayed
complex emotional relationships with whales. Some compared their own
exploitative working conditions with the fate of the animals they were to
slaughter. Kyla Schuller argues that Herman Melville's *Moby-Dick* explores "the
deeply affective relationship that pre-industrial whaling ironically nurtured
between whales and whalers through the very intimacy of the hunt" (4). "By
animating the feeling animal," Melville represents both whales and whalers as
"deserving of empathy from the emerging middle classes who had voracious
appetites for sperm whale oil" (4). Jeffrey Bolster demonstrates that common
fishermen were often the most perceptive to the impact of overfishing on
animal populations (130, 140). Moreover, Ayasha Guerin even goes so far as
to discern a kinship between whales and minoritized 19th century sailors
who together became fugitives from extractive capitalism. As whales adapted
their migration routes in order to avoid areas of intense commercial fishing,
they also opened up new routes of escape for Black and Indigenous sailors
who joined the whaling industry in order to flee slavery and dispossession
in the continental United States. Thousands found refuge in the Kingdom of
Hawai'i, which "was not organized on the basis of race" (Guerin 54). Drawing
on Katherine McKittrick's work, Guerin advocates "methodologies of care"
that spotlight the "intimacies of survival at sea in the whaling industry" (46).

---

13   In this, their position differs significantly from those of shipboard animals, such as
      hens, which became the objects of sentimental attachments in the journals of other
      captain's wives, helping to reinforce these women's imaginative hold over the ship as
      a domestic sphere (Kelley 2021).

I suggest that Brewster's detached description of whales adds to this tableau of differently gendered, classed, and racialized 19th century perspectives. It asserts that, while 19th century women are conventionally associated with sentimentality and while Brewster herself certainly uses sentimental rhetoric when it comes to home and marriage, this does not have to be the case when it comes to animals or the natural world at large. While sailors who closely interacted with whales in the realm of production sometimes resorted to sentimental language, some captain's wives, who stayed clear from the realm of production, did not. Brewster's journals thus demonstrate that the language of sentimental domesticity not only linked up with U.S. imperialism but also with extractivist capitalism in the Pacific of the 1840s. Explicit affection for whales had no place in Brewster's performance of maritime femininity. When it comes to fellow feelings, the Pacific, along with all its inhabitants, needed to remain a site of detachment, not *terra nullius* but *aqua nullius*.

At the same time, I suggest that, from a narratological point of view, there is more to this scene. As Brewster could have erased this brutal hunting scene, just like the tensions between her husband and his crew, the fact that she *did* consider it worth telling is significant. While interspecies attachments had no place in her narrative, she did use language that acknowledges social bonds among whale mothers and their offspring and that renders mother whales' attacks on whalers in terms that were certainly emotionally comprehensible to her 19th century audience.[14] Whales thus acquire a degree of agency and sentience that gestures beyond their mere bodily existence as raw material. By doing so, I suggest, Brewster's journal provides set pieces that might potentially facilitate more affectively charged and more ambivalent readings in the future.[15]

---

14   Today, biologists assert that whales not only live in kin-based social units but they appear to have large networks of communication that, for instance, helped them exchange information about whalers and thus avoid lethal dangers (Whitehead/Smith/Rendell).

15   See, for instance, the journals of Eliza Williams, which chronicle Williams's time as a whaling wife ten years after Brewster, between 1858 and 1861. She writes that "[i]t was a pleasant sight to see" whales "playing about, so happy in their native element, all unconscious, it seemed, of danger" (138). She continues that "it made me feel very bad" to see the whales "tumbling and rolling about in the water, dying. I could not bear the sight, but it was soon over" (ibid.).

Conclusion

This article has examined how Mary Brewster's journals of her first voyage on board a whaleship in the late 1840s imagined the Pacific and female maritime mobility for a readership based on the Eastern seaboard. It has shown how Brewster legitimates her maritime mobility through the language of sentimental domesticity. She re-imagines the ship as a home, the place where she, as a wife, belongs and can further what she perceives as moral feeling, civilization, and order. By doing so, Brewster also articulates an oceanic and extractivist variant of what Kaplan calls "manifest domesticity." Different but related narrative strategies imaginatively prepare laborers, whales, and Kānaka Maoli for subjection to an extractive view. This view routinely erases the violence of labor exploitation, resource extraction, and imperialism. It partakes in dominant imperial and extractivist tropes that deny, albeit in different and unequal ways, the histories and entanglements of both humans and animals in Pacific ecologies. In other words, Brewster frames her own breaking out of gender conventions in and through the logics of empire and extraction. Her journal presents a case in point for the ways in which sentimentality revolves around a White, bourgeois, and heteropatriarchal center whose language of domesticity helps erase its own conditions of possibility.

As historian Joan Druett asserts, the material traces of Brewster's sentimental domesticity are visible to this very day. The wealth that the *Tiger* extracted from the Pacific, along with the gains of other voyages, allowed the Brewsters to eventually build a "large and commodious" home in Stonington, Connecticut, and to "retire [...] to a life of leisure" (Druett 1992a, 407). This mansion is still standing, providing a monument to the early entanglements between New England notions of domesticity and the "domestication" and violent appropriation of humans and animals in the Pacific. Along with this material trace, the extractivist imagination that Brewster helped create lingers on. As whale oil was substituted by petroleum, whales increasingly escaped the intense focus of extractive capitalism. Yet, the climate warming effects of contemporary petrocultures disproportionately affect Pacific Islanders. Recent research in biology, in turn, has begun to explore how whales contribute to the mitigation of climate change, as both their bodies and their excrements can trap large quantities of carbon dioxide (Pearson et al. 238). Whereas such research advises the further protection of whales and marine ecologies, resource-hungry nations are still vying to claim and extract submarine resources (DeLoughrey). As corporations have recently made considerable advances in their quest for permissions to start deep-sea mining, with unforeseeable effects for the current climate and biodiversity crises, the struggle over extractivist imaginations of the Pacific is bound to continue (Lyons).

References

Archer, Seth. 2018. *Sharks Upon the Land: Colonialism, Indigenous Health, and Culture in Hawai'i, 1778–1855*. Studies in North American Indian History. Cambridge: Cambridge University Press.

Baym, Nina. (1978) 1998. *Woman's Fiction: A Guide to Novels by and about Women in America, 1820–70*. Urbana, IL: University of Illinois Press.

Berlant, Lauren G. 2008. *The Female Complaint: The Unfinished Business of Sentimentality in American Culture*. Durham, NC: Duke University Press.

Blum, Hester. 2008. *The View from the Masthead: Maritime Imagination and Antebellum American Sea Narratives*. Chapel Hill, NC: University of North Carolina Press.

Bolster, W. Jeffrey. 2012. *The Mortal Sea: Fishing the Atlantic in the Age of Sail*. Cambridge, MA: Harvard University Press.

Braun, Juliane. 2018. "'Strange Beasts of the Sea': Captain Cook's Last Voyage and the Creation of a Transoceanic American Empire." *Atlantic Studies: Global Currents* 15 (2): 238–55.

Brewster, Mary. 1992. *"She Was a Sister Sailor": Mary Brewster's Whaling Journals, 1845–1851*. Edited by Joan Druett. The American Maritime Library 13. Mystic, CT: Mystic Seaport Museum.

Buell, Lawrence. 2003. *Writing for an Endangered World: Literature, Culture, and Environment in the U.S. and Beyond*. Cambridge, MA: Belknap Press of Harvard University Press.

Burnett, D. Graham. 2017. "Whaling." In Szeman, Wenzel, and Yaeger 2017, 373–75.

Busch, Briton Cooper. 1994. *"Whaling Will Never Do for Me": The American Whaleman in the Nineteenth Century*. Lexington, KY: University of Kentucky Press.

Carter, Kathryn. 2020. "Feminist Interpretations of the Diary." In *The Diary: The Epic of Everyday Life*, edited by Batsheva Ben-Amos and Dan Ben-Amos, 39–56. Bloomington, IN: Indiana University Press.

Chen, Mel. Y. 2012. *Animacies: Biopolitics, Racial Mattering, and Queer Affect*. Perverse Modernities. Durham, NC: Duke University Press.

Creighton, Margaret S. (1995) 2006. *Rites and Passages: The Experience of American Whaling, 1830–1870*. New York, NY: Cambridge University Press.

Creighton, Margaret S., and Lisa Norling. 1996. "Introduction." In *Iron Men, Wooden Women: Gender and Seafaring in the Atlantic World, 1700–1920*, edited by Margaret S. Creighton and Lisa Norling, vii–xiii. Gender Relations in the American Experience. Baltimore, MD: Johns Hopkins University Press.

Culley, Margo. 1998. "Introduction to *A Day at a Time: Diary Literature of American Women, from 1764 to 1985*." In Smith and Watson 1998, 217–21.

De Jong, Mary G. 2013. "Introduction." In *Sentimentalism in Nineteenth-Century America: Literary and Cultural Practices*, edited by Mary G. De Jong, 1–12. Madison, NJ: Fairleigh Dickinson University Press.

DeLoughrey, Elizabeth. 2017. "Submarine Futures of the Anthropocene." *Comparative Literature* 69 (1): 32–44. DOI: https://doi.org/10.1215/00104124-3794 589.

Dolin, Eric Jay. 2007. *Leviathan: The History of Whaling in America*. New York, NY: W.W. Norton.

Druett, Joan. 1991. *Petticoat Whalers: Whaling Wives at Sea, 1820–1920*. Auckland: Collins New Zealand.

Druett, Joan. 1992a. "Epilogue." In *"She Was a Sister Sailor": Mary Brewster's Whaling Journals, 1845–1851*, edited by Joan Druett, 405–9. The American maritime library 13. Mystic, CT: Mystic Seaport Museum.

Druett, Joan. 1992b. "Introduction to Part One." In *"She Was a Sister Sailor": Mary Brewster's Whaling Journals, 1845–1851*, edited by Joan Druett, 1–10. The American maritime library 13. Mystic, CT: Mystic Seaport Museum.

Duneer, Anita J. 2010. "Voyaging Captains' Wives: Feminine Aesthetics and the Uses of Domesticity in the Travel Narratives of Abby Jane Morrell and Mary Wallis." *ESQ* 56 (2): 192–230. DOI: https://doi.org/10.1353/esq.2010.0038.

Fackler, Katharina, and Silvia Schultermandl, eds. 2022. "Kinship as Critical Idiom in Oceanic Studies." *Atlantic Studies: Global Currents*. Special issue. DOI: https://doi.org/10.1080/14788810.2022.2079900.

Ganser, Alexandra. 2016. "From 'Wall-Flower' to 'Queen of the Forest': Frontier Migration, Nature, and Early Ecofeminism in Caroline Kirkland's 'A New Home, Who'll Follow?' (1839)." *Amerikastudien/American Studies* 61 (4): 469–88.

Gerund, Katharina, and Heike Paul. 2018. "Sentimentalism." In *Handbook of the American Novel of the Nineteenth Century*, edited by Christine Gerhardt, 17–33. Berlin: De Gruyter.

Gniadek, Melissa. 2021. *Oceans at Home: Maritime and Domestic Fictions in Nine-teenth-Century American Women's Writing*. Amherst, MA: University of Massachusetts Press.

Gómez-Barris, Macarena. 2017. *The Extractive Zone: Social Ecologies and Decolonial Perspectives*. Durham, NC: Duke University Press.

Guerin, Ayasha. 2021. "Shared Routes of Mammalian Kinship: Race and Migration in Long Island Whaling Diasporas." *ISJ* 16 (1): 43–61. DOI: https://doi.org/10.24043/isj.160.

Hau'ofa, Epeli. 2008. "Our Sea of Islands." In *We Are the Ocean: Selected Works*, 27–40. Honolulu, HI: University of Hawaii Press.

Hendler, Glenn. 2001. *Public Sentiments: Structures of Feeling in Nineteenth-Century American Literature*. Chapel Hill, NC: University of North Carolina Press.

Huggan, Graham, and Helen Tiffin. 2015. *Postcolonial Ecocriticism : Literature, Animals, Environment*. 2nd ed. London: Routledge.

Igler, David. 2013. *The Great Ocean: Pacific Worlds from Captain Cook to the Gold Rush*. Oxford: Oxford University Press.

Jones, Jamie L. 2017. "Fish Out of Water: The 'Prince of Whales' Sideshow and the Environmental Humanities." *Configurations* 25 (2): 189–214. DOI: https://doi.org/10.1353/con.2017.0012.

Kaplan, Amy. 1998. "Manifest Domesticity." *American Literature* 70 (3): 581–606. DOI: https://doi.org/10.2307/2902710.

Kaplan, Amy. 2002. *The Anarchy of Empire in the Making of U.S. Culture*. Cambridge, MA: Harvard University Press.

Kelley, Mark B. 2016. "When Species Meet...At Sea: The Animating Sympathy of Hen Frigates." Presentation at the American Studies Association's Annual Meeting, Denver, CO, November 17–20, 2016.

Kelley, Mark B. 2018. "Sentimental Seamen and Pirates of Sympathy: Antebellum Narratives of Terraqueous Domesticity." University of California San Diego. Retrieved from https://escholarship.org/uc/item/18n16828.

Kilcup, Karen. 2013. *Fallen Forests: Emotion, Embodiment, and Ethics in American Women's Environmental Writing, 1781–1924*. Athens, GA: University of Georgia Press.

Kinsley, Zoë. 2017. *Women Writing the Home Tour, 1682–1812*. London: Routledge.

Kirkland, Caroline M. (1839). 1990. *A New Home, Who'll Follow? Or, Glimpses of Western Life*. Edited by Sandra A. Zagarell. New Brunswick, NJ: Rutgers University Press.

Klein, Naomi. 2014. *This Changes Everything: Capitalism vs. The Climate*. New York, NY: Simon and Schuster.

Lewis, Sarah. 1839. *Woman's Mission*. 4th ed. London: John W. Parker. https://a rchive.org/details/womansmissionbyoochamgoog.

Lyons, Kate. 2021. "Deep-Sea Mining Could Start in Two Years After Pacific Nation of Nauru Gives UN Ultimatum." *The Guardian*, June 30, 2021. https: //www.theguardian.com/world/2021/jun/30/deep-sea-mining-could-sta rt-in-two-years-after-pacific-nation-of-nauru-gives-un-ultimatum.

Merish, Lori. 2000. *Sentimental Materialism: Gender, Commodity Culture, and Nineteenth-Century American Literature.* Durham, NC: Duke University Press.

Miller, Elizabeth Carolyn. 2021. *Extraction Ecologies and the Literature of the Long Exhaustion.* Princeton, NJ: Princeton University Press.

Norling, Lisa. 2000. *Captain Ahab Had a Wife: New England Women and the Whalefishery, 1720–1870.* Gender and American Culture. Chapel Hill, NC: University of North Carolina Press.

Pearson, Heidi C., et al. 2023. "Whales in the Carbon Cycle: Can Recovery Remove Carbon Dioxide?" *Trends in Ecology and Evolution* 38 (3): 238–249. DOI: https://doi.org/10.1016/j.tree.2022.10.012.

Perkins, John. T. 1934. *John T. Perkins' Journal at Sea, 1845: From the Original Copy Owned by Mrs. Grosvenor Ely.* 1 vol. 8. Mystic, CT: Marine Historical Association.

Reid, Joshua L. 2015. *The Sea Is My Country: The Maritime World of the Makahs, an Indigenous Borderlands People.* The Henry Roe Cloud Series on American Indians and Modernity. New Haven, CT: Yale University Press.

Roos, Bonnie, and Alex Hunt. 2010. "Introduction: Narratives of Survival, Sustainability, and Justice." In Roos and Hunt 2010, 1–13.

Roos, Bonnie, and Alex Hunt, eds. 2010. *Postcolonial Green: Environmental Politics and World Narratives.* Charlottesville, VA: University of Virginia Press.

Russell, Caskey. 2010. "The Makah Whale Hunt and Its Aftermath." In Roos and Hunt 2010, 157–76.

Sakakibara, Chie. 2010. "Kiavallakkikput Agviq (Into the Whaling Cycle): Cetaceousness and Climate Change Among the Iñupiat of Arctic Alaska." *Annals of the Association of American Geographers* 100 (4): 1003–12. DOI: https://doi.o rg/10.1080/00045608.2010.500561.

Schell, Jennifer. 2013. *A Bold and Hardy Race of Men: The Lives and Literature of American Whalemen.* Amherst, MA: University of Massachusetts Press.

Schuller, Kyla. 2010. "Specious Bedfellows: Ethnicity, Animality, and the Intimacy of Slaughter in *Moby-Dick*." *Leviathan* 12 (3): 3–20. DOI: https://doi.or g/10.1111/j.1750-1849.2010.01291.x.

Shannon, Laurie. 2017. "Tallow." In Szeman, Wenzel, and Yaeger 2017, 346–48.

Shoemaker, Nancy. 2015. *Native American Whalemen and the World: The Contingency of Race.* Chapel Hill, NC: University of North Carolina Press.

Silva, Noenoe K. 2004. *Aloha Betrayed: Native Hawaiian Resistance to American Colonialism.* American Encounters/Global Interactions. Durham, NC: Duke University Press.

Smith, Sidonie. 1998. "Performativity, Autobiographical Practice, Resistance." In Smith and Watson 1998, 108–15.

Smith, Sidonie, and Julia Watson, eds. 1998. *Women, Autobiography, Theory: A Reader.* Madison, WI: University of Wisconsin Press.

Somerville, Alice Te Punga. 2017. "Where Oceans Come from." *Comparative Literature* 69 (1): 25–31. DOI: https://doi.org/10.1215/00104124-3794579.

Steinwand, Jonathan. 2011. "What the Whales Would Tell Us: Cetacean Communication in Novels by Witi Ihimaera, Linda Hogan, Zakes Mda, and Amitav Ghosh." In *Postcolonial Ecologies: Literatures of the Environment*, edited by Elizabeth M. DeLoughrey and George B. Handley, 182–99. New York, NY: Oxford University Press.

Stowe, Harriet Beecher. (1852) 1994. *Uncle Tom's Cabin.* Edited by Elizabeth Ammons. Norton Critical Editions. New York: Norton.

Szeman, Imre, Jennifer Wenzel, and Patricia Yaeger, eds. 2017. *Fueling Culture: 101 Words for Energy and Environment.* New York, NY: Fordham University Press.

Thompson, Carl. 2015. "Journey to Authority: Reassessing Women's Early Travel Writing, 1763–1862." In "Journeys to Authority: Travel Writing and the Rise of the Woman of the Letters a Special Issue of Women's Writing." Special issue, *Women's Writing* 22 (1): 131–50.

Wenzel, Jennifer. 2017. "Introduction." In Szeman, Wenzel, and Yaeger 2017, 1–16.

Whitehead, Hal, Tim D. Smith, and Luke Rendell. 2021. "Adaptation of Sperm Whales to Open-Boat Whalers: Rapid Social Learning on a Large Scale?" *Biology Letters* 17 (3): 1–5. DOI: https://doi.org/10.1098/rsbl.2021.0030.

Williams, Eliza Azelia. 1964. "Journal of a Whaling Voyage to the Indian and Pacific Oceans, Kept on Board the Ship *Florida*, T. W. Williams, Master, Commencing September 7th, 1858." In *One Whaling Family*, edited by Harold Williams, 3–204. Boston, MA: Houghton Mifflin.

Yao, Xine. 2021. *Disaffected: The Cultural Politics of Unfeeling in Nineteenth-Century America.* Perverse Modernities. Durham, NC: Duke University Press.

Ecologies of Docility and Control: Environmental Fantasy and Extractive Economy at a Maryland Girls Boarding School, 1834–1868

Sophie Hess

Jane Smith thought she saw conquest in the sky. In 1850, the seventeen-year-old girl recalled an experience she had while standing on a cliff near her home in Virginia. First observing the "rippling" creeks and "azure" mountains of the natural landscape, Smith then looked above her at "the western sky." The clouds suddenly began to merge and transform into the shape of an eagle. "As I gazed upon it," mused Smith, "I thought of my country." Bathed in the red light of sunset, the bird reminded her of "blood spilled upon the plains of Mexico." With this violent imagery, Smith conjured memories of the Mexican-American War, which had ended two years earlier, expanding the United States' territory and sparking new enthusiasm among Americans for westward expansion. "When we see the crimson glow in the West," she wrote, "we know that night is approaching; so, wherever a nation exults in tyranny and bloodshed, it is a sure sign of downfall" (*Patapsco Young Ladies Magazine* Vol. 1 no. 4, 5–7). This nation was almost certainly Mexico, which many Americans saw as an enemy country, standing in the way of the United States' ability to possess the continent and realize a so-called Manifest Destiny (Adelman/Aron; Merry). In Smith's piece, "The Star of Empire," the landscape blessed and made natural the United States' occupation of the West, fantasizing an animate environment that condoned and encouraged the nation's imperialist expansion and its exploitation of the land's natural resources. Smith's text debuted not in a newspaper or magazine, but in the pages of a literary journal published by the elite all-girls boarding school she attended.

Smith's writing exemplified the prose produced by students at her school, the Patapsco Female Institute. The school was founded in 1834 by industrialists who had built fortunes extracting from the environment. Capitalizing on the hydrology of the Patapsco River, their businesses processed locally mined iron-ore in their furnaces and plantation-grown wheat and cotton in their mills, creating and exporting natural resources as lucrative commodities. As a site of production, the Institute was meant to create both material and cultural profits. It charged high tuition fees for an education that groomed young women to be part of the industrial economy as wives and teachers. While enrolled at the school, female students developed sentimental attachments to the natural world. In their writing, they imagined the landscape as nurturing, supportive, and full of emotional and physical beauty. Focusing particularly on the intellectual discourse circulated between teachers and students, this essay argues that the school cultivated an imagined environment, which was passive, gentle, and deeply empathetic to human emotions. Institutional and census records reveal that the women at the Institute benefitted from extractivism through their families' plantations and factories, and through their identities as enslavers, employers of domestic servants, and settler-colonial migrants. In their academic and personal writings, however, students and teachers repeatedly envisioned the environment through sentimental fantasy, as a space dedicated to serving their needs and desires. These writings emphasize the role of ecological fantasy in obscuring the harms of extractivism.

The domestic sphere remains a thorny construct for scholars of 19th century America. Once thought to imply a space to which all women belonged in contrast to masculine public life, the term now more commonly evokes the culture of elite white women, who were able and expected to opt out of the formal economy (Gómez-Reus/Usandizaga; Park/Wald). As Amy Kaplan has argued in her formative 1998 essay, "Manifest Domesticity," affluent white women deployed fantasies of domestic life to perpetuate imperialist and white supremacist projects, rendering domestic space as the center of civility and citizenship. Even as rich white women publicly embraced the cult of domesticity, however, they often did so while working within semi-political spaces, like schools, churches, and clubs that blurred the lines between public and private. In her study of early American women's schools, Mary Kelley (2012) further argued that women were overtly engaged in public and political life and that to fashion the school as a private space is to misread the deliberately and distinctively political activity that women engaged in within them.

Elite girls' schools like the Patapsco Female Institute embodied what Lauren Berlant have termed an "intimate public sphere," an affective social space in which shared discourse around emotion and feeling constituted a shared identity. Berlant argued that, beginning around 1830 with the publication of *Godey's*

Lady's Book and other publications marketed to women, one can see "the first subcultural, mass-mediated, market population of relatively disenfranchised people in the United States" (xii). Berlant's readings of *Godey's Lady's Book* and similar national periodicals, as well as novels like *Uncle Tom's Cabin* by Harriet Beecher Stowe, demonstrate how intimate public spheres cultivated supposedly universal concepts of "womanhood" (20–69). In reality, these publics largely represented the emotional and cultural lives of white, affluent women. I apply Berlant's intimate public to the social space of the boarding school, considering the literature created for and assigned to students, as well as the writings produced by students, in affective conversation. By reading, learning, and writing about their emotional and sensory experiences, female teachers and students modelled for one another feelings that rearticulated themselves in the women's lived experiences. I argue that the feelings and labor produced within the Institute manifested in the production of reproducible cultural ideas about women's relationship to the environment, ideas which lived beyond the school's formal existence as a cultural institution and which were porous to and consequential for people who lived outside of this intimate public space.

Merging Kaplan's contention that feminine domestic fantasy fueled extractive and imperialist projects with Berlant's theory of feminine social production, I demonstrate that within this boarding school, women produced an intimate public sphere of environmental thought and affect. Students and teachers generated, circulated, and internalized fantasies of pristine landscapes free from the consequences of industrialist and extractivist activities. Through an examination of the writings of teachers and students, this essay will demonstrate how women at the Institute used ecological fantasy to soothe their own extractive anxiety. In poetry and prose, the same environments which their families actively exploited could be recast as spaces of spiritual and emotional refuge. Through this sentimental attachment, these women thus upheld, reinforced, and reproduced the extractive culture and industrial production from which they profited.

Extractive Capitalism, Whiteness, and the Patapsco Female Institute

Most of the families of students enrolled at the Patapsco Female Institute gained capital through the extraction of environmental resources, whether in the monocrop farming of southern plantations, in the mining of stone and heavy metal, or in the processing of natural resources in industrial factories. The exploitation of human labor also fueled these profits, whether through the overt use of enslaved labor in plantation agriculture or by using coercive and undercompensated wage labor systems. The students at the Institute held stake in the upholding of environmental capitalism, as it funded their ways of life and senses of self. The Institute thus kept intact the capitalistic order by gatekeeping race and class boundaries, developing a community where affluence and whiteness were naturalized, and those who might deviate from this norm sought assimilation into its ranks.

Beginning in the mid-1700s, Maryland's Patapsco River Valley became a popular site for privately funded extractive projects. The valley's proximity to the river made it a convenient point of access to the Baltimore harbor and Chesapeake Bay. At the time, the river was deep and wide enough to accommodate sea-faring vessels. The area's forests and ore deposits made it an attractive site for iron furnaces, while its fertile soils provided land for both tobacco and wheat farming. The river itself also provided power for grist mills. By the 1830s, some families in the area had amassed several generations of extractive wealth. Using enslaved and convict labor as well as the exploitation of wage laborers, the area's industrial economy grew rapidly (Varle; Rockman; *Ellicott Family Deeds and Land Records*; *Caleb Dorsey & Co. Elk Ridge Furnace Journal*).

While this economic landscape provided managerial roles for men within these elite families, feminine roles within this ecosystem were less certain. The proliferation of elite all-girls' schools throughout the country in the Early Republic era, scholars have argued, came largely from a desire to formalize the training for women's future reproductive roles as wives and mothers who would encourage proper Republican values in their husbands and sons (Kelley 2012; Kerber 1988; Norton). The stockholders of the Patapsco Female Institute conceived the school in this image in 1834. A small trust of the area's most wealthy industrialists and planters founded the school as both a monetary and cultural investment. Through expensive tuition, the school would produce financial profit. Through education, it would produce female alumni capable of reinforcing the industrial market economy by way of reproductive and family labor.

Despite the lofty ideals of the school's founders, by 1840, the Institute was hemorrhaging capital. The trustees strategized that to keep the Institute (and their investments) afloat, they needed to enroll more students. To do this, they courted Almira Hart Lincoln Phelps to serve as the school's headmistress. At forty-seven, Phelps was a well-known figure in elite women's education, a textbook writer, headmistress, and the sister of Emma Willard, who had established one of the country's most influential boarding schools, the Troy Female Seminary. In 1841, Phelps signed a contract to lead the Institute. Her academic pedigree and public status proved to be brilliant marketing for the school, significantly boosting its enrollment (Baym; Bolzau; Mitchell; Rudolph).

Phelps was calculating, ambitious, and contradictory. A born-and-raised Northerner, she enslaved at least two people during her tenure at the Institute (U.S. Census 1850) but also maintained close relationships with abolitionists. She was devoted both to Christianity and to Linnaean natural sciences. She valued hierarchy in all things and believed fervently in the biological weakness of women, but also advocated for them to gain financial independence in becoming teachers and part of the work force. Over the course of Phelps' tenure, the school became significantly more Southern in terms of demographics. When she arrived, the population was equally split between Southern students and Northern students but by 1855, the school was made up of ninety percent Southerners and only ten percent Northerners (Mitchell). Phelps' identity as an enslaver doubtlessly influenced her sense of social and racial hierarchy and almost certainly led to the school's high rate of Southern students. A great many of the students' families enslaved people as well. The social order of the school was inextricably linked to the social order of slavery.

The student body was almost entirely white, apart from four Cherokee students. These young women, Mary Jane Ross, Amanda Ross, Cora Ross, and Henrietta Coodey all had blood connections to Cherokee Chief John Ross, and Coodey was the daughter of William Shorey, a writer and Cherokee leader (Preston 327–56). Theda Perdue has suggested that by sending their daughters to white boarding schools, Cherokee men sought both to assimilate them into white society and to subdue their power in traditionally matrilineal Cherokee culture. "Trained and treated like elite women in the non-Native South," writes Perdue, "these women had connections to the new locus of power in the Cherokee Nation, but they were the Cherokee women least likely to attempt an exercise of that power themselves" (146). As historian Tiya Miles has highlighted, many Cherokees themselves owned slaves, which could be interpreted as a further attempt to claim and perform whiteness. William Shorey, father of Henrietta, owned at least two slaves, and Chief John Ross owned at least twenty (Perdue 141; Ross 5). In this way, one might read the Cherokee families as seeking acceptance into the norms of whiteness, which included slave ownership.

The school also enforced rigid class gatekeeping through both its high tuition costs and attempts at subsidized scholarship. At $290 a year, the school was significantly more expensive than any other female academy in operation, which usually cost around $200 annually ("Female High Schools," *The Christian Advocate and Journal* 1847, 15). Beginning in 1835, the Maryland state government mandated that the Institute sponsor one student per year as a Free Scholar, allowing the student to attend the school free of charge. These students were to be "selected from the poor children" of the county, and the designation was appointed by the state Orphan's Court (*Patapsco Female Institute Records*). The Free Scholars, however, were the daughters of the area's emerging middle class, coming from the families of tailors, shoemakers, boardinghouse owners, and other middle-class service and artisan professions of the period (U.S. Census Records 1850–1870). That these students were designated as poor further points to the astronomical wealth likely held by students paying full tuition at the school.

The Patapsco Female Institute's trustees forged a feminine space from extractive capital and designed it to adhere to the race and class structures, which upheld that capital's steady growth. With Phelps at the helm, the school developed a culture, which also enforced a hierarchy of the natural world. Through curriculum, academic culture, and writing, students at the Institute would learn to envision an environment, which endorsed their desires and served their needs.

The Illusion of a Docile Environment

The school's education centered on hierarchical and highly regulated relationships to the environment, community, and self. Phelps closely monitored time and social hierarchy, teaching her students to be submissive to the structures of etiquette, family, and society. She considered her students as temporary daughters and saw it as her duty to parent them. Restraint, control, and moderation were central to Phelps' philosophy, undergirded by the idea that women were inherently more emotionally sensitive and fragile than men. For this reason, botany became a core part of the curriculum. Phelps believed that internalizing botanical order through the Linnaean system, which categorized all plant, animal, and mineral life based on visually observable traits, helped to encourage women towards order and regulation in their lives. She believed that Linnaean taxonomy mimicked the intelligent design of God. Students practiced rigorous observation of themselves and their surroundings through field observation and personal reflection. She took students on field trips to collect plant specimens that they dried in scrapbooks and touted the benefits of open air during observational excursions, which she viewed as "conducive to health and cheerfulness" (Phelps 1876, 159). Likewise, direct observation provided women with the opportunity to "strengthen" the muscle of their minds. "All our thoughts, by means of the senses, are originally derived from external objects," wrote Phelps, and thus engaging directly with natural objects rather than seeing them mediated through images in a textbook would better sustain and nourish the mind (Phelps 1838, 36).

The students seemed to enjoy field visits, at least as an aesthetic experience. Mary Stone, a student at the Institute, wrote to her mother of one such excursion, remarking that "we enjoyed ourselves very much, ascending the lofty hills, and gathering the beautiful flowers, which grew in great abundance" (*Mary Stone Letters*). Many students discussed flower collecting as a more pleasant part of the regular exercise the headmistress mandated. "Calisthenics, or female gymnastics," wrote Phelps in *The New York Mirror*, "is very properly becoming a branch of female education." The physical sciences, which could be viewed in the "wild and sequestered scenes," of the natural world, thus offered unique opportunities for girls to engage their bodies through walking, hiking, and breathing fresh air (1833). Phelps promoted the idea that engagement with the environment would physically improve the human body, an idea which, at some level, suggested a utilitarian relationship to the natural world. Within the school, exercise and environmental appreciation often went hand in hand.

If exercise was an ideal engagement with the natural world, it remained secondary to the performance of domestic labor Stone fixated on in her correspondence (*Mary Stone Letters*). "In reference to exercising in the open air," she wrote, "I must inform you, I scarcely ever have time, except a short time in the morning, when I am not Roomkeeper." Stone's reference to her work highlights the importance of household labor in the Institute's curriculum. "The rising bell has not yet rung," Stone reported to her mother, "but I have been up some time, and have made my toilet, and spread my bed, and am now seated in the school room, writing you a few hurried lines." Stone emphasized the time and energy that it took for her to be domestically virtuous, echoing instructions given by Phelps. "How much might be done by an energetic daughter in the family," Phelps wrote in *The Educator or Hours with My Pupils* (1876), her collection of lectures given to students at the Institute, "where servants sleep away the best hours of the day, and rise to lounge about." While servants could be expected to "indulge in idleness," ideal young women "should be seen to rise early, to walk about and notice what is going on" (Phelps 1876, 179). Scholars have observed that rhetoric like this served to create a moral boundary between the mistress, cast as refined and virtuous, and the servant, cast as lazy and untrustworthy. Thavolia Glymph and other scholars have shown that "mistresses" constantly found ways to assert moral differences over those they controlled to naturalize their positions of power (Branch/Wooten 169–89; Dudden; Glymph; Green). Mary Stone's family owned at least seventeen slaves (U.S. Census 1840). After emancipation, census records show that Mary Stone would go on to employ black servants for her entire life. Her letter demonstrates that at the Institute, Stone was instructed to naturalize the hierarchy of power upon which her family built wealth. Through her writing, she made invisible the domestic labor that fueled the extractive economy, which she lived in and benefitted from.

Stone's letter also highlights the corrective thinking and selective remembering that Phelps encouraged in students. A striking speech by Phelps epitomized these skills. She instructed students to write frequently to their parents, but also not to dwell upon the challenges of their experiences. She offered two sample letters by fictional students of her own creation. The first was written by a bad child who she named "Growlinda Snarl." In Snarl's letter, she wrote to her parents that "When we arrived in this dirty village of Ellicott's Mills, we were directed to get upon some narrow rocks, and climb up a narrow passage; in this way we proceeded for some miles [...] it was the worst climbing I have ever done" (Phelps 1876, 258–64). Phelps admonished Snarl's writing as an example of ungratefulness and complaint. In contrast, she offered the letter of "Agatha Goodchild," who wrote to her parents, "On reaching the romantic village of Ellicott's Mills, we were directed to the institute by a winding path which leads up a steep ascent, but were amply rewarded for our labor." In this fascinating fictional reimagination, Goodchild corrected the improper, but perhaps more honest, depiction of the natural state of the land surrounding the Institute. The negative details such as "dirty," "narrow" and "worst climbing" are replaced with "romantic," "winding," and "rewarded for our labor." Interestingly, Phelps herself wrote at length about her own arrival at the Institute and discussed the off-putting appearance of the school and the hike up to it, including brambles, jagged rocks, and "ill-favored swine rooting up the ground" at the entrance. "All around the mansion were heaps of unremoved stones which had been left there on the erection of the building." Her own words suggest that Growlinda Snarl's account of the ascent might still have held some truth.

The fable of Snarl and Goodchild exemplifies how women at the Institute encouraged one another to embellish and adjust their renderings of the natural world. Indeed, student writings focused on ecological beauty and sentimental experience, and hardly ever noted unpleasant or negative sensations or situations. In this way, they created an image of the environment which served their fantasies, rather than one which might be challenging to physically navigate, or which showed signs of extractive damage. The Patapsco River Valley was, in fact, a highly industrial environment. During this period, the valley was peppered with iron furnaces, grist mills, and cotton mills, which required environmental manipulation like river damming, deforestation, and roadbuilding. The environment would have showed significant sensory signs of extraction, including olfactory, auditory, and visual markers of industrial production. In students' writing, however, any markers of industrial activity were notably absent, suggesting that students were oblivious to them, minimized or misunderstood them, or that they had been expressly instructed not to focus on them. By ignoring signs of extraction within the landscape, students furthered an imagined environment where extractive consequences did not exist, and where the environment appeared as a bucolic and peaceful backdrop for their lives.

Students wrote constantly about environmental experiences in the *Young Ladies Magazine*, a quarterly journal produced and edited at the school. Flowers, climate and air, forests, mountains, and bodies of water all occurred as constant motifs in the students' writings and were often the direct subject of their pieces. 17-year-old student Kate D. Earle's "The Teachings of Wildflowers," (*PYLM* Vol. 1 No. 3, 14–15) for instance, envisioned flowers as a messenger of God. In the piece, a "sad and weary" young girl found a woodland glen to sit in and meditate on her troubles. As she sat, the flowers surrounding her came to life as a "fairy-like band" and spoke to her directly. "Their voices murmured softly: 'Maiden we are sisters from the spirit-land.'" The blossoms beseeched her to stop isolating and pitying herself and rejoin her community. "'Though hast wandered to muse in solitude and cherish thine own dark thoughts,'" they scolded. The flowers suggested to the narrator that her painful feelings were self-inflating, and that she should, instead, cultivate happiness and a sense of care toward others. This aspect of the fable, perhaps, reflected the values of Transcendentalism, which had become fashionable during this period. In particular, transcendentalists believed in nature's ability to foster virtue within the self and inspire greater care for the community. The flowers also exalted faithfulness and told Earle to serve God. "Live for Him," they sang, "bow humbly and meekly to His will and sadness shall no longer dwell with thee." In Earle's reading of nature, as in many of her peers', nature spoke the teachings of a Christian god, and embodied Christian principles. The flowers thus served human interests and existed primarily to enrich human life.

Earle's devout flower vision depicted nature as a messenger of Christianity. Phelps, a zealous Christian, also frequently referred to plants as connected with God. Part of her campaign to send students into the field for observation suggested that by doing so they might experience direct connection with God and suggested that by observing them directly rather than through the mediation of a textbook, students might sharpen all parts of their minds. She posited that by guiding students down "paths strewn with flowers," they would learn that "these beautiful creations of Almighty Power" exemplified "the goodness of God" (Phelps 1876, 11). References to God were frequent throughout the book, and often suggested that students see the aesthetic benefits of the botanical world, such as beauty and order, as evidence of intelligent design. The nature that Phelps and her students wrote about frequently embodied European and Neoclassical aesthetic traditions as well. Earle's piece was one of many to envision nature as "mild and beautiful spirits," with feminine qualities. "Nymphs and Naiads sprang lightly from the sparkling waters of the stream," wrote a student named Laura Bevan, and "mermaids glided with inimitable grace beneath the leaping fountains" (*PYLM* Vol. 1 No. 1, 8–9). Through both Christian and Greco-Roman imagery, the students envisioned natural environments which bared signs and symbols of Western cosmology. Like Phelps, their affective experiences of nature celebrated their own spiritual values.

In both its Christian and Neoclassical manifestations, the environment served as a spiritual allegory for feminine existential struggles. Writings often dealt with death, for instance, connecting seasonal change and botanical death cycles to the loss of people in their lives. The young women consistently noticed death within their natural environments. As Institute student Harriet Ryan wrote, "we see a tiny rosebud just opening its beautiful petals to catch the first faint rays of the morning sun, but ere we turn to look again, the withering blast has come, and swept the lovely bud to death" (*PYLM* Vol. 1 No. 3, 5). The flower illustrated the brevity and temporality of life, and the natural cycle of death. During this time, Phelps was also grieving the loss of her own daughter, Jane, killed in an 1855 train accident. In her eulogy for Jane, Phelps wrote that "in the beautiful seasons of youth, before the storms of worldly sorrow had swept over her—like a young and tender plant she is transplanted to a more genial clime, and in the garden of Paradise you will find her blooming with expanded and perfected nature" (1855). Through her writing, Phelps often found solace in the rhythm of seasons passing, discussing the autumn and winter as seasons of death, and spring and summer as seasons of birth.

Cycles of time seemed also to preoccupy students who neared adulthood, particularly relating to the pressures of marriage and reproductive obliga-tion. Eliza Dall Thomas, a student at the Institute from 1844–49, wrote about these concerns in her journal, in a piece titled "Sixteen." In it, she lamented her youth's passing, using natural imagery including landscape, animals, and flowers to recall innocence. "Light heart of my youthful years," wrote Thomas, "when rambling over the picturesque hills of my native land, or stalling by some romantic river in quest of sweet flowers to deck my sister's hair, I imagine myself as happy, as though the future would add no grief to my unsophisticated soul." Thomas used flowers to suggest a childlike femininity but also seems to be concerned with the temporality that flowers represent. In another piece titled "Flowers," Thomas began by waxing on beauty. However, as the piece progressed, her writing became darker and more anxious. She discussed how blossoms died with the passing seasons and likened human life to this process, writing, "we, like these frail flowers, remain but for a brief space [...] we pass away, and others occupy the space we once filled" (*Eliza Dall Thomas Commonplace Book* 44).

In some ways, student writings mirrored the interests of wider literary cul-ture at the time, which placed tremendous cultural and aesthetic importance in images of plant life, the environment, and its symbolism. The language of flowers served discreet and symbolic purposes in 19th century literary culture. Flower dictionaries were some of the era's most popular books, expressing the classical and symbolic meanings embedded within floral imagery. As Dorri Beam has convincingly argued, "the language of flowers" was a significant way in which notable 19th century female writers such as Margaret Fuller and Sarah Hale expressed desire and fantasy. The students would have been familiar with these writings through their consumption of novels, newspapers, and nationally circulated magazines. In this way, the students were following patterns of literary expression outlined by Beam and other scholars.

In writings from the Institute, flowers were treated as living, if not com-pletely autonomous, creatures. Flowers "trembled," "wept," "murmured," "wel-comed," and "sheltered." While the personification of flowers never rose to the level of full emotional sentience, the language surrounding flowers suggested them to be subjects with more agency than plants were traditionally endowed with. Rather, the souls of plants seemed to rest somewhere between child and spirit, acting with care but also on instinct rather than intention. The conceptualization of plants as living and acting creatures could also be informed by botanical instruction, which emphasized plants as having anatomies and behaviors, and being responsive to changes in the environment. This suggests that in the act of observing botanical life, women at the Institute felt and noticed emotions that lay at the intersection of actual plant behavior and their affective perceptions, evoking what the theorist Jane Bennett has called "vibrant materialism" (2010). While the students projected their own fantasies of plant behavior in their writings, they also inadvertently pointed to actual ways that plants can act in their own interests, such as through adaptive growth patterns and retreat from threatened soil. The tension between the agency which humans might project onto things and the agency which things themselves have reflects Bennett's idea that abstract concepts like nature or "the Wild" are attempts to "acknowledge a force that, though quite real and powerful, is intrinsically resistant to representation" (xv–xvi).

The nature that students and teachers imagined was, however, always sympathetic and deferent to feminine experiences. It could communicate for them, empathize with them, support them, speak to, and assist them. It was, in other words, the ally of the human world, and especially of affluent and 'civilized' white women. In the same way that Almira Phelps suggested to her students that they were suited to botany as women, the students seemed to suggest that nature itself was classically feminine: docile, mothering, empathetic, beautiful, gentle, and kind. What student experiences implied, however, was a situated and manipulated experience of nature, one that was designed to show them care, and one which belied their own settler role within the landscape. As Mark Rifkin has argued, white writers in the first half of the 19th century often utilized nature to conceptualize their own sense of "sovereign selfhood" against a passive landscape, a "purifying space" in which the Anglo-Americans could articulate their sense of self outside of the market economy (91–93).

For the students, nature was both passive and, at points, an active conspirator in the growth of capital. Jane Smith's "Star of Empire" literally guided Anglo-Americans towards control over the landscape, suggesting that not only did nature endorse the imperialism and extraction of resources that westward expansion wrought, but it would also actively assist in the project of expansion (*PYLM* Vol 1. No. 4). Smith described the star's flickering at the rise of non-western, non-white empires like "Persia," and the "rush of barbaric hordes" which caused the star to be obscured from sight. When she finally claimed to glimpse the star, it was at the end of the Mexican-American war, when the United States annexed Texas and continued its expansion. For Smith, glimpsing the star meant that the country was just in its decisions to continue to expand territory, thus acquiring the natural resources that would lead to continued wealth for elite families such as hers. In some of her writings, Phelps too refers to the school as a nation-building space, imagining the ways in which students from spaces at the peripheries of the Anglo-American empire, "Canada and the southern States, from the Atlantic and the Mississippi, and even the Cherokee nation," came to live "together as a band of sisters under the care of common parents" (1876, 34). This rhetoric harkens to Amy Kaplan's suggestion that women's writing in the 19th century used the domestic as a site in which to enact the imperial, and, to fantasize a space of white control over the landscape. The school, in this case, acted as a stand-in for the family itself. Phelps' writing and that of her students not only support Kaplan's thesis, but also affirm that for elite white women the school was a collective domestic space in which to manifest imperialist and extractivist fantasies of the land. Ideas of 'manifest domesticity' could circulate in lessons, writing, reading, and relationship-building between students and teachers.

After leaving the Institute, many students carried on this discourse as teachers themselves. Phelps had always contended that a major purpose of female education was to train future teachers. Teaching had given her financial stability after her first husband's death. Particularly in the students who came from less generational wealth, such as the free scholars, teaching offered a legitimate source of income throughout their lives. Teaching was also a source of public influence for some women, such as Mary Jane Ross, of Cherokee Nation, who established a prominent school for children orphaned in the Civil War. The school even produced a student publication, which mirrored *The Young Ladies Magazine* in its design.

The majority of students at the Institute, meanwhile, went on to become wives and mothers, enacting those domestic and reproductive labors so essential to the growth of the market economy. Fantasies of a passive and loyal environment were, in this way, passed on in the instructions that they gave their children and in the financial choices, which they helped to make about familial control of natural resources. Student Susan E. Bryant, for example, came from a wealthy slaveholding family of Louisiana and Kentucky origins (Johnson). After attending the Institute, Bryant moved to San Francisco, California, with her husband Isaac Thorne, also from Kentucky. The decision was likely the result of her family's need to restructure their financial assets in the aftermath of emancipation. It was perhaps also influenced by her time at the Institute and its fetishistic adoration of the environment. For many white Americans, migration to California evoked a fantasy of settling virgin land in the Eden-like imaginary of the far West. By 1900, Bryant, now Thorne, had birthed nine children in her adopted home of San Francisco, and employed at least one servant, a Japanese man named Oti Otero (U.S. Census 1900). Like many of her peers at the Institute, Susan Bryant Thorne's romantic visualizations of the environment thus played out in real life settler colonial actions, relocating to claim new American land to preserve and gain wealth, and continuing to exploit the labor of non-white people to sustain her and her family's lifestyle.

Bryant did make one observation about the valley's ecology while studying at the Institute, which hinted at the unsettling realities of the landscape. One day, wandering through the forest, she paused to notice "the troubled bosom of the Patapsco River," and listened to the "confused noise of the falls" (*PYLM* Vol. 1 No. 2, 5–6). These characterizations of the environment alluded, albeit gently, to the tremendous force of the river, and its uncertain relationship to the landscape. "Troubled," in particular, could have alluded to the river's history of flooding. Since its settlement, the Patapsco had several times flooded, resulting in destruction to residential and industrial property, and demonstrating the landscape's power over human life. As students like Bryant perched on the banks of the Patapsco, musing about the meaning of the landscape, the natural world was beginning to react negatively to years of industrial extraction.

In 1868, what began as an ordinary thunderstorm spiraled into a massive flood along the river. While moderate flooding was an inevitable event, decades of excessive damming and sediment runoff from iron and grain production greatly exacerbated the flood's intensity. The flood was catastrophic, destroying most buildings in the town, killing between thirty and sixty people, and permanently stunting industrial growth ("The Maryland Flood," *Harpers Weekly* 1868; Sharp). In this flood, the behavior of the river aggressively challenged the images of docility students had adorned it with, reflecting not a submissive or pristine ecology, but instead, one deeply affected by extractive capitalism.

The intimate public of the Patapsco Female Institute demonstrates how a collective fantasy of a non-threatening environment could rationalize and perpetuate extraction. Through visions of talking flowers, mothering forests, and magical guiding stars, women benefiting from ecological exploitation could ignore the dangers it posed. The sentimentality that women at the Patapsco Female Institute expressed towards the environment thus reflected a settler-colonial power relationship between humans and environment, a relationship which we should see as complicit with the causes of the river's flooding. While women at the school did not dam the river or fill its waters with sediment, they held intimate attachment to the executives who ordered these actions, and doubtlessly influenced the direct harms that extractive capital wrought. The sentimental writings of these women thus provide great insight as to how an extractive disaster could approach in plain sight, and yet remain unseen until the day that floodwaters began to rise.

References

Howard County Historical Society
Mary Stone Letters
Maryland Center for History and Culture
Eliza Dall Thomas Commonplace Book
Ellicott Family Deeds and Land Records
Patapsco Female Institute Records
Patapsco Young Ladies Magazine (PYLM) no. 1–4
Maryland State Archives
Caleb Dorsey & Co. Elk Ridge Furnace Journals
U.S. Census Records
1850–1900, Ellicotts Mills, Howard County, MD. Accessed through ancestry.com.
Virginia Center for History and Culture
Mary Jerdone Coleman Pressed Flower Album

Adelman, Jeremy, and Stephen Aron. 1999. "From Borderlands to Borders: Empires, Nation-States and the Peoples in Between in North American History." *The American Historical Review* 104 (3): 814–41.
Baym, Nina. 2002. *American Women of Letters and the Nineteenth-Century Sciences: Styles of Affiliation*. New Brunswick, NJ: Rutgers University Press.
Beam, Dorri. 2010. *Style, Gender, and Fantasy in Nineteenth-Century American Women's Writing*. New York, NY: Cambridge University Press.
Bennett, Jane. 2010. *Vibrant Matter: A Political Ecology of Things*. Durham, NC: Duke University Press.
Berlant, Lauren. 2008. *The Female Complaint: The Unfinished Business of Sentimentality in American Culture*. Durham, NC: Duke University Press.

Berry, Daina Ramey. 2017. *The Price for Their Pound of Flesh: The Value of the En-slaved, from Womb to Grave, in the Building of a Nation*. Boston, MA: Beacon Press.

Bolzau, Emma Lydia. 1936. *Almira Hart Lincoln Phelps: Her Life and Work*. Lancaster, PA: Science Press Printing Company.

Branch, Enobong Hannah, and Melissa E. Wooten. 2012. "Suited for Service: Racialized Rationalizations for the Ideal Domestic Servant from the Nineteenth to the Early Twentieth Century." *Social Science History* 36 (2): 169–89.

Bushman, Richard L. 1993. *The Refinement of America: Persons, Houses, Cities*. New York, NY: Vintage Books.

Daggett, Cara New. 2019. *The Birth of Energy: Fossil Fuels, Thermodynamics, and the Politics of Work*. Durham, NC: Duke University Press.

Dudden, Faye E. 1985. *Serving Women: Household Service in Nineteenth-Century America*. Middletown, CT: Wesleyan University Press.

Easton-Flake, Amy. 2013. "Harriet Beecher Stowe's Multifaceted Response to the Nineteenth-Century Woman Question." *The New England Quarterly* 86 (1): 29–59.

"Female High Schools," *The Christian Advocate and Journal* 22 (4), January 27, 1847.

Glymph, Thavolia. 2008. *Out of the House of Bondage: The Transformation of the Plantation Household*. New York, NY: Cambridge University Press.

Gómez Reus, Teresa, and Aránzazu Usandizaga. 2008. *Inside out: Women Negotiating, Subverting, Appropriating Public and Private Space*. Amsterdam: Rodopi.

Green, Keith Michael. 2015. *Bound to Respect: Antebellum Narratives of Black Imprisonment, Servitude, and Bondage, 1816–1861*. Tuscaloosa, AL: University of Alabama Press.

Jeffrey, Julie Roy. 2001. "Permeable Boundaries: Abolitionist Women and Separate Spheres." *Journal of the Early Republic* 21 (1): 79–93.

Johnson, E. Polk. 1912. *A History of Kentucky and Kentuckians: The Leaders and Representative Men in Their Commerce, Industry, and Modern Activities*. Chicago, IL: Lewis Publishing Company.

Kaplan, Amy. 1998. "Manifest Domesticity." *American Literature* 70 (3): 581–606.

Kelley, Mary. 2003. "'A More Glorious Revolution': Women's Antebellum Reading Circles and the Pursuit of Public Influence." *The New England Quarterly* 76 (2): 163–96.

Kelley, Mary. 2012. *Learning to Stand and Speak: Women, Education, and Public Life in America's Republic*. Chapel Hill, NC: University of North Carolina Press.

Kerber, Linda K. 1988. "Separate Spheres, Female Worlds, Woman's Place: The Rhetoric of Women's History." *The Journal of American History* 75 (1): 9–39.

Kerber, Linda K. 2000. *Women of the Republic: Intellect and Ideology in Revolutionary America*. Chapel Hill, NC: University of North Carolina Press.

Kerber, Linda K., et al. 1989. "Beyond Roles, Beyond Spheres: Thinking about Gender in the Early Republic." *The William and Mary Quarterly* 46 (3): 565–85.

Lasser, Carol. 2001. "Beyond Separate Spheres: The Power of Public Opinion." *Journal of the Early Republic* 21 (1): 115–23.

Merry, Robert W. 2009. *A Country of Vast Designs: James K. Polk, the Mexican War and the Conquest of the American Continent*. New York, NY: Simon and Schuster.

Miles, Tiya. 2015. *Ties That Bind: The Story of an Afro-Cherokee Family in Slavery and Freedom*. Oakland, CA: University of California Press.

Mitchell, Helen Buss. 1990. "The North and South Here Meet: Almira Hart Lincoln Phelps and the Patapsco Female Institute 1841–1856." Ph.D. diss., University of Maryland College Park.

Norton, Mary Beth. 1996. *Liberty's Daughters: The Revolutionary Experience of American Women, 1750–1800*. Ithaca, NY: Cornell University Press.

Park, You-me, and Gayle Wald. 1998. "Native Daughters in the Promised Land: Gender, Race, and the Question of Separate Spheres." *American Literature* 70 (3): 607–33.

Perdue, Theda. 1998. *Cherokee Women: Gender and Culture Change, 1700–1835*. Lincoln, NE: University of Nebraska Press.

Phelps, Almira Lincoln Hart. 1833. "Physical Education." *The New York Mirror, A Weekly Journal, Devoted to Literature and the Fine Arts* 10 (51), June 22, 1833.

Phelps, Almira Lincoln Hart. 1838. *Familiar Lectures on Botany.* New York, NY: A.S. Barnes & Company.

Phelps, Almira Lincoln Hart. 1844. *The Female Student; or, Lectures to Young Ladies on Female Education, For the Use of Mothers, Teachers, and Pupils.* London: Thomas Allman.

Phelps, Almira Lincoln Hart. 1855. "Tribute to the Memory of Jane Porter Lincoln, Printed for Private Circulation." Baltimore, MD: John D. Toy Press.

Phelps, Almira Lincoln Hart. 1876. *The Educator or Hours With My Pupils.* New York, NY: A.S. Barnes & Company.

Preston, Jr M. Lee. 2011. *Archaeology in Howard County and Beyond: What I've Learned in 40 Years About Its People and Sites.* Baltimore, MD: Chesapeake Book Company.

Rifkin, Mark. 2014. *Settler Common Sense: Queerness and Everyday Colonialism in the American Renaissance*. Minneapolis, MN: University of Minnesota Press.

Rockman, Seth. 2009. *Scraping By: Wage Labor, Slavery, and Survival in Early Baltimore*. Baltimore, MD: Johns Hopkins University Press.

Rosenberg, Anat. 2012. "Separate Spheres Revisited: On the Frameworks of Interdisciplinarity and Constructions of the Market." *Law and Literature* 24 (3): 393–429.

Ross, John. 1985. *The Papers of Chief John Ross*, edited by Gary Moulton. Norman, OK: University of Oklahoma Press.

Rotman, Deborah L. 2006. "Separate Spheres? Beyond the Dichotomies of Domesticity." *Current Anthropology* 47 (4): 666–74.

Rudolph, Emanuel D. 1984. "Almira Hart Lincoln Phelps (1793–1884) and the Spread of Botany in Nineteenth Century America." *American Journal of Botany* 71 (8): 1161–67.

Ryan, Mary. 1981. *Cradle of the Middle Class: The Family in Oneida County, New York 1790–1865*. New York, NY: Cambridge University Press.

Schuller, Kyla. 2018. *The Biopolitics of Feeling: Race, Sex, and Science in the Nineteenth Century*. Durham, NC: Duke University Press.

Scott, Joan Wallach, and Debra Keates. 2004. *Going Public: Feminism and the Shifting Boundaries of the Private Sphere*. Urbana, IL: University of Illinois Press.

Sharp, Henry K. 2017. *America's First Factory Town: The Industrial Revolution in Maryland's Patapsco River Valley*. Baltimore, MD: Chesapeake Book Company.

Snyder, Terri L. 2012. "Refiguring Women in Early American History." *The William and Mary Quarterly* 69 (3): 421–50.

"The Maryland Flood," *Harpers Weekly: A Journal of Civilization* XII (606), August 8, 1868.

Varle, Charles. 1833. *A Complete View of Baltimore: With a Statistical Sketch, of All the Commercial, Mercantile, Manufacturing, Literary, Scientific, and Religious Institutions and Establishments, in the Same, and in Its Vicinity ... Derived from Personal Observation and Research ... To Which Is Added, a Detailed Statement of an Excursion on the Baltimore and Ohio Rail Road to the Point of Rocks ... and an Advertising Directory*. Baltimore, MD: Samuel Young.

Wischermann, Ulla, and Ilze Klavina Mueller. 2004. "Feminist Theories on the Separation of the Private and the Public: Looking Back, Looking Forward." *Women in German Yearbook* 20: 184–97.

The Melancholy of Extraction: Settler Sentimentality in Canada's Ahistorical Era of Economic Reconciliation

Amy Fung

The original draft of this paper was presented on September 30, 2021, which coincidentally marked the first time in history that Canadians observed the National Day for Truth and Reconciliation.

September 30 has been known as Orange Shirt Day, a day of collective grief and mourning since 2013. The Orange Shirt grassroots campaign began with Phyllis Webstad from Stswecem'c Xgat'tem First Nation, then 46 years old, who publicly shared her story for the first time at a commemoration event.[1] A former student at St. Joseph's Indian Residential School in William's Lake, British Columbia, she recalled how her grandmother gifted her an orange shirt for her first day of school, and how upon entering the Mission, as it was known, she was stripped of her possessions, and her shirt was taken away by school administrators, never to be seen again. The memory of that loss from over forty years ago, however seemingly insignificant to distant observers and unempathetic ears, opened up a floodgate of compounded losses (Charleyboy).

St. Joseph's first opened in 1891 and ran until 1981. During its 90-year operation, the Mission was a notorious site of ongoing child abuse including physical, sexual, and emotional violence against Indigenous youth from as young as four to sixteen years old. Dangerous living conditions, inadequate nutrition, the disappearance of students, and other forms of gross negligence by its operators, the Oblates of Mary Immaculate, a Roman Catholic missionary, were

---

1   Specific nations will be named in this text, otherwise, "Indigenous" will be preferred except when referring to "Aboriginal" in the Constitutional sense or "Indian" in the legal sense of the Indian Act or residential schools.

long ignored by federal government officials. Canada's then Deputy Superintendent of the Department of Indian Affairs (DIA), Duncan Campbell Scott, who made school attendance compulsory, clearly stated in 1920 at a Special Committees hearing, "I want to get rid of the Indian problem [...] our objective is to continue until there is not a single Indian in Canada that has not been absorbed into the body politic and there is no Indian Question and no Indian Department" ("Until There Is Not a Single Indian in Canada").[2] A few years later, Scott would make it illegal for anyone under DIA's jurisdiction to hire their own legal counsel to challenge land claims without DIA's approval. Through a multi-pronged approach of colonial interference, the Canadian government, for the majority of its 155 years of existence, has pursued an aggressive policy direction of termination against Indigenous ways of life.

Phyllis Webstad's story is unfortunately not unique. The colonial force of assimilation began long before the establishment of residential schools and continues after the last school was closed. The purpose of residential schools was to remove Indigenous children from their families and communities and instill in them ideas of Western Eurocentric supremacy. Children were taught to be ashamed of who they were and where they came from. Webstad's story goes beyond the material loss of her shirt, which was a gift and therefore a relational bond to her grandmother. She spent 300 nights in the Mission, and her mother and grandmother each spent ten years in the Indian Residential School (IRS) system along with over 150,000 First Nations, Métis, and Inuit children. The erosion of Indigenous language, knowledge, and culture was three generations deep by the time Phyllis entered the Mission as a six-year-old. The significance of Orange Shirt Day and the subsequent slogan "every child matters" resonated with other IRS survivors, intergenerational survivors, their supporters, and settlers who were long overdue in learning about the extent of their country's difficult history from the perspective of survivors.

As a result of the largest class action settlement in Canadian history, the Indian Residential School Survivors Agreement (IRSSA) established its own Truth and Reconciliation Commission to document the experiences of survivors. Alongside the momentum of the Orange Shirt Day movement, a list of 94 recommendations came out of the Truth and Reconciliation Commission's (TRC) Final Report, with #80 stating:

---

2   Excerpt from the 1920 testimony of Duncan Campbell Scott, to the Special Parliamentary Committee of the House of Commons that was examining Scott's proposals to amend the sections of the Indian Act that focused on enfranchisement.

We call upon the federal government, in collaboration with Aboriginal peoples, to establish, as a statutory holiday, a National Day for Truth and Reconciliation to honour Survivors, their families, and communities, and ensure that public commemoration of the history and legacy of residential schools remains a vital component of the reconciliation process. (TRC 2015a, 291)

It would take another six years for the federal government to confirm September 30 as the National Day for Truth and Reconciliation. Its unanimous approval through the House of Commons came mere days after the Tk'emlúps te Secwépemc First Nation confirmed the discovery of 215 bodies, likely all of them children, in an unmarked mass grave on the site of a former residential school in Kamloops, British Columbia. Since then, over two thousand more bodies and counting have been identified across the country on the sites of former residential schools using ground penetrating radar technology. During the multi-year process of the TRC, the commissioners had requested a separate budget in excess of $1.5 million to work on what they called "the Missing Children and Unmarked Burials Project" when they began to realize the additional scope of work needed to find unmarked graves at former residential schools, but their request was denied.[3] Rather than search for missing children and bring some closure to their families, the scope of the TRC became focused on multi-day events of public ceremonies and survivors' testimonies for Indigenous and non-Indigenous people to bear witness as a step toward reconciliation, which as a term has taken on the weight of colonization's aftermath.

In the TRC Final report, the commission defined reconciliation as a process which must be about establishing and maintaining a mutually respectful relationship between Indigenous and non-Indigenous peoples in this country. In order for that to happen, "there has to be awareness of the past, an acknowledgement of the harm that has been inflicted, atonement for the causes, *and action to change behaviour*" (2015a, 6, my emphasis). I emphasize the last line, "an action to change behaviour" because the history of Canada's identity as first a British dominion and now a sovereign and wealthy G7 nation grew out of its foundation as an extraction-based colony. Resource extraction has been the driving motivation for past and ongoing colonial violence, from forced

---

3   For more information, see Volume 4 of *The Final Report of the Truth and Reconciliation Commission of Canada*, Canada's Residential Schools: Missing Children and Unmarked Burials, 6.

removals via court injunctions, child welfare, and disproportionate rates of incarceration to the establishment of residential schools, whose stated goals were to assimilate Indigenous people into the settler body politic including its laws, language, and a capitalist wage economy.

In trying to parcel out the political purpose of the new national holiday and understand how reconciliation discourse has been shaped by Canada's political economy, this chapter is not building toward a working definition of reconciliation or approaching reconciliation as its end goal. Rather, I am revisiting the study completed in the years after IRSSA and before the completion of the Commission's findings by Corntassel, Chaw-win-is, and T'lakwadzi's (2009) "Indigenous storytelling, Truth-telling, and Community Approaches to Reconciliation," where they define that

> [a]t its core, reconciliation is a Western concept with religious connotations of restoring one's relationship to God. Given that reconciliation is not an Indigenous concept, our overarching goal as Indigenous peoples should not be to restore an asymmetrical relationship with the state but to restory our communities toward justice. (5)

In centering justice as the goal, the authors also highlight the responses to the Common Experience Payments (CEP), the lump sum payments administered to IRSSA survivors. The responses to CEP were varied from recipients suffering depression, substance abuse, and even committing suicide after the process of tallying years of violence and trauma into a bureaucratic calculation. Also notably, these researchers showed that cultural loss including language and ceremonies can never be replaced with remuneration, but that their culture and knowledge must become accessible again for Indigenous communities if justice is the goal.

Attempts continue to be made to share space between Indigenous and non-Indigenous nations to listen and bear witness to the truths of their intertwined histories. In both of the aforementioned definitions of reconciliation and justice, there is an understanding that this is a dynamic process that is more than payments and lip service as it requires actual change in behavior. For Tkemlúps te Secwépemc Chief Rosanne Casimir, the act of coming together to bear witness is an "integral part of history making."[4] Casimir spoke these words on October 18, 2021, from the PowWow Arbour, an open-air gathering space along the bend of the South Thompson River and the present home to the Kamloopa

---

4   From the live address at Tk'emlúps te Secwepemc on October 18, 2021.

Pow Wow, one of the largest celebrations of Indigenous culture in Western Canada. While non-Indigenous people may observe Indigenous culture with curiosity, and even appropriation, what is important to acknowledge is how these cultural practices have survived through generations of genocidal policies. Casimir spoke about the importance of bearing witness as the Tkemlúps te Secwépemc had just hosted the first National Day for Truth and Reconciliation in this circular space that connects the past to the present. Casimir's words of coming together to bear witness were directed toward Prime Minister Justin Trudeau, who sat to her right in a mea culpa appearance for going surfing on September 30, 2021, instead of accepting the Tk'emlúpsemc's original invitation to bear witness to the findings of unmarked graves in their territory. Trudeau's decision to take a beach holiday exemplifies how many Canadians choose to observe the first National Day for Truth and Reconciliation, as a day off, completely divorced from the intentions to remember and mourn Canada's atrocities against Indigenous communities.

In this specific context, the reconciliation discourse is limited and only capable of performative grief. Settler sentiments fall into an ahistorical cycle of denial, apologies, and denial, once again. While dedicating a national day to remember and mourn the loss of Indigenous youth as a direct result of church- and state-run residential schools, the federal government does not actually address ongoing systemic violence against Indigenous lives. I interpret this performative grief as an extension of sentimental extraction where feelings of shame and regret in ecological destruction co-exist with an interminable reliance upon its ongoing devastation. I observe a parallel and reckless abandonment of Canada's genocidal history in its seemingly progressive stance to pursue "reconciliation" without any change in policy or behavior. In establishing a national memory to remember the state's past violence toward Indigenous ways of life, there is an incongruency in the unchanged methods of the federal government's continued expansion of its economic model based on extractivism that has always been and continues to be heavily dependent on forced access to Indigenous territories.

As a form of critical discourse analysis, I am closely reading the post-TRC rhetoric surrounding "reconciliation" as a substitute to address the gravity of residential schools. I question whether this affective shorthand to focus only on the atrocities of child abuse obfuscates the larger and more insidious political and economic motivations that led to their creation by the state in the first place. The forced removal of Indigenous people from their lands and the criminalization of their ceremonies, languages, and governance structures was to fulfill the colonial desire to secure the 'pristine wilderness' that has formed the backbone of Canadian identity and the fertile farmlands and rich deposits of precious minerals, lumber, and fossil fuels at the heart of its modern economy. The underlying bureaucracy to quell Indigenous resistance against colonial jurisdiction initiated the abusive system of IRS and continues to this day through the double-speak of achieving "economic reconciliation," which will be explored in the second part of this paper.

As a first-generation immigrant living and working in Canada, I believe there is an imperative to remember and honor the victims and survivors of Canada's residential schools by speaking the truth of what happened in those federally mandated institutions. It is ongoing work to connect these colonial logics back to the national narratives that drive extractive economies. For many, the violence of extraction and exploitation has never stopped. In observing the oftentimes callous apathy of my fellow Canadians, I see this inability to mourn the incalculable scales of violence against Indigenous life as an expression of settler sentimentality. My definition for settler sentimentality is indebted to Judith Butler's (2004) work on the politics of mourning. In Butler's analysis, the assumption of whose lives are "grievable" in the aftermath of September 11 is a broader critique of the role imperialism and nationalism play in shaping our parameters for mourning. Drawing from the philosophical foundation of Foucauldian biopolitical analysis, Butler questions the political role of grief and the act of mourning as justification for inciting war and violence—that other people must die in order to pay for *our* grief. By developing a philosophical treatise to challenge whose lives count as livable and whose deaths are grievable, Butler speaks back to Foucault's analysis of racism as one form of governmentality in determining who must live and who must die in the name of state sovereignty. Foucault originally wrote, "Racism is the indispensable precondition that allows someone to be killed, that allows others to be killed. Once the state functions in the biopower mode, racism alone can justify the murderous function of the state" (2003, 256). Expanding upon Canada's politics of mourning, this paper will also analyze the rhetorical emergence of "economic reconciliation" as well as the bridging of two opposing epistemologies toward remembrance and responsibility. Tracing how Canada chooses to officially recognize its own violent past when the violence has never stopped, the scope of this analysis takes aim at this hypocrisy of reconciliation discourse that ultimately benefits the settler state above all else.

The Melancholy of Extraction

It is near impossible to speak about melancholy without referring to Sigmund Freud, but 'the melancholy of extraction' is less about the Freudian subject or ego tinged with sadness or regret than it is a description of the pathological inability to move on from an idealized past. In my reading, Canada's extractive economy is unable to let go of its idealized past as a white British colony. As one of the settler Commonwealth colonies, along with Australia and South Africa, Canada also actively enforced exclusionary immigration policies against racialized people to protect its character as a "white nation" (Hage). The establishment of white supremacy as the law of the land determined who could live and prosper, which included the project of assimilating Indigenous communities while simultaneously limiting and containing non-white communities from settling. Even to this day, Canada continues to uphold the Doctrine of Discovery as its legal standing over Indigenous land. To affirm 15th century Papal Bulls as the reason for settler jurisdiction is to actively glorify European colonization over existing Indigenous laws and protocols. The melancholy of extraction is therefore an analytical framework that interprets Canada's recognition of its colonial violence against Indigenous communities and its simultaneous refusal to stop pursuing its colonial agenda as a result of the nation's idealization of its past as a white British colony.

In what Sara Ahmed calls "affective economies," where feelings are not only psychological or emotional but are also socially and politically produced and circulated as identities, the identity of Canadians is bound to settler colonial access to Indigenous territories. This access is rooted in entitlement, white supremacy, and heteropatriarchy. One only has to be reminded of the mythos of explorers and homesteaders being relevant to today's laborers in oil and gas industries, logging, and mining to get a sense of the connection between national identities and its foundation in settler colonialism.

As an example of this behavior of recognizing the harm but refusing to change, Canada is projecting more oil and gas extraction in 2050 than in 2019. Despite global trends in the past decade of moving away from fossil fuels and international regulations such as the United Nations Declaration on the Rights of Indigenous Peoples (UNDRIP) re-centering the rights of Indigenous people, Canadian policies remain tethered to colonial logics of extraction. The latest economic projections forecast an increase in Canadian fossil fuel production while its geopolitical allies in the G7 are moving to eliminate its use altogether.

This makes Canada the only country in the alliance to increase its carbon emissions since signing the Paris Agreement (Perez).

As another example of unchanged behavior, at the 2021 Climate Change Conference (COP26) in Glasgow, Trudeau made a Freudian slip when he referred to Canada as "a major oil and gas producing company" instead of "country." Either way, as country or company, Canada repeatedly demonstrated that it refuses to shift away from fossil fuels and other carbon-heavy economies, which relies on undermining Aboriginal title as defined by the Supreme Court ruling of Delgamuuk vs. British Columbia, in 1997, as well as infringing on Aboriginal and treaty rights as recognized and affirmed by Section 35 of the Canadian Constitution. In fact, this slip of the tongue proved more accurate than not, as former Conservative leader Erin O'Toole also repeatedly stated that in order to shift into a green economy, Canada must maximize its potential revenues from fossil fuels first (Tasker). The logic offered by the political leadership in Canada is that for any step the country makes towards a green economy, Canadians are to expect more, and not less, of fossil fuel extraction. This inability to imagine moving away from fossil fuels and other carbon-heavy economies directly relates to ongoing colonial violence through extraction and assimilation. As political leaders pay lip service to reconciliation, the ahistorical remembrance of colonial violence allows them to pursue the status quo rather than take concrete actions such as policy changes, bearing witness, and mending broken treaties.

By critically analyzing the affective dimensions surrounding the federal government's discourse of reconciliation including National Day for Truth and Reconciliation, I am scrutinizing the settler impulse for sentimental gestures and holding these intentions in remembrance of past and ongoing violence. Canada continues to press forward assimilative policies against Indigenous communities that extinguish Aboriginal title, neutralize constitutional status, and dismantle treaties through the development of alternative legal agreements (Diabo; Collis 9). Starting from the position that settler violence is an economic project against Indigenous communities and territories because "colonialism and capitalism are based on extracting and assimilating" (Simpson 75), I question the capacity of settler sentiments to acknowledge the harm of colonialism as long as a dependency on the extractive processes of reducing everything into exploitable resources is maintained.

Long Memory as Method

Using a methodology of a long memory approaches Canadian history as always being in relation to Indigenous history, I begin with the acknowledgement of this complicated new national holiday because the affectively powerful gesture of remembering Canada's genocidal history cannot be separated from the state's ongoing colonial policies to erode and evade Indigenous self-determination. More specifically, I am analyzing the narrative transformation of anti-racism, liberation, and mutual dignity into a neoliberal discourse of political and economic inclusion under so-called politically progressive rhetoric. I am defining neoliberalism via Jodi Melamed's definition of neoliberal multiculturalism, where the freedom of commerce has been collapsed with social freedoms to the point where economic rights become the most fundamental civil right for equality (16).

While there are national debates about the veracity of calling residential schools a "genocide," there remains a pressing agenda of militarized invasions into unceded and occupied Indigenous territory to uphold corporate interests.[5] The inherent rights of Indigenous jurisdiction includes immemorial rights over traditional territories including people, land, and what has been termed "resources" under the logic of settler colonialism.[6] My method of understanding the contradictions of Canada's socially progressive liberal rhetoric such as creating a statutory holiday to honor truth and reconciliation is to put them in relation to ongoing actions of extraction. By looking at the ideological differences between the Canadian government's words and actions, specifically this new national holiday and how reconciliation has been transformed into a discourse on economic reconciliation, I am closely reading the role of settler sentiments in political discourses and questioning the politics of mourning that only reinforce the jurisdiction of the colonial state.

---

5   The refusal to admit colonial violence towards Indigenous communities as genocide has been widely debated in Canadian press and politics, but more disturbingly an open letter dated August 9, 2021, against the Canadian Historical Association's Canada Day Statement of 2021 by academics has entered the fray. The open letter was signed by a long list of Canadian historians and appeared on the blog of the *Dorchester Review*, a self-described "non-partisan" history journal with right-wing tendencies on August 9, 2021. A further rebuttal appeared on Shekon Neechie, an Indigenous history site, a few days later on August 11.

6   Settler logic defines nature as private property, or resources in the form of water, trees, minerals, oil, gas, etc.

Understanding ongoing racism as a function of globalization, Achilles Mbembe's "necropolitics" has also informed how I understand settler sentimentality through a contemporary anti-colonial lens. For Mbembe, the role of violence cannot be understated in the making of a modern sovereign nation. Indeed, he writes the "ultimate expression of sovereignty largely resides in the power and capacity to dictate who is able to live and who must die" (66). In all of the G7 nations, sovereignty has been historically defined as the right to kill, where "the violence of civilization" is all but swept under the carpet (11). The circumstances in Canada are no different. Read together with Butler's philosophy on the politics of mourning, the concept of "necropolitics" creates a useful, though not always commensurable parallel for my own analysis of the politics of mourning in a settler colonial context. For the purposes of this essay, I define settler sentimentality in the Canadian context as a means of justifying past and ongoing violence against Indigenous lives in the name of securing the settler state's economic sovereignty. Turning towards an expansive remembrance of what is being grieved, how this loss is accounted for, and whom this remembrance serves, my analysis of the National Day of Truth and Reconciliation explores the initial loss as a complex site of remembrance that began in grassroots advocacy away from state recognition, before it was repurposed into a discourse of economic reconciliation.

The Rhetorical Turn to Economic Reconciliation

The appearance of "economic reconciliation" in mainstream political discourse has been years in the making.[7] Bridging capitalist extraction and progressive liberalism, the term "economic reconciliation" has been used in the context of 'achieving' reconciliation with Indigenous peoples as a palatable and profitable venture for all Canadians.

The earliest public use of the phrase "economic reconciliation" I could trace appeared in 2015 by a BC-based organization called Reconciliation Canada. In

---

7   Examples of "economic reconciliation" include Ottawa Mayor Jim Watson claiming Tewin, a land development project, with the controversial Algonquins of Ontario as a form of reconciliation. See Shady Hafez (2021) and Kate Porter (2021). More notably, with "reconciliation" as a priority for most voters in the federal election of 2021, Liberal and Conservative leaders Justin Trudeau and Erin O'Toole referred to""economic reconciliation" as the way forward. See Stephanie Taylor (2021) and the op-ed by Dawn Madahbee Leach and Chief Terrance Paul (2016).

its 2015 "Impact Report," the same year the organization was registered as a charitable organization, Reconciliation Canada notes that in partnership with Vancouver Island University, a series of dialogues on "economic reconciliation" were developed and facilitated to engage senior level business and First Nations leaders. This included former Assembly of First Nations (AFN) national chief Shawn Alteo, who was handpicked by outgoing BC Premier Christy Clark to promote dialogues between business, government, and Indigenous peoples (Shaw). Alteo was listed as the Chair of the Reconciliation Canada board in its 2015 "Impact Report" and according to its financial highlights section, the organization spent $87,413 to develop the program and over $43,790 on dialogue workshops in partnership with VIU's Centre for Pre-Confederation Treaties, who employed Alteo as their first Speaker for Indigenous Dialogue (26).

The following year in 2016, another federally funded group, the National Indigenous Economic Development Board (NIEDB), released its report, "Reconciliation: Growing Canada's Economy by $27.7 Billion" (Fiscal Realities Economists).[8] As a summary, the report suggests that there are significant financial gains to be made by reconciliation. Dawn Madahbee Leach, Vice-Chairperson of NIEDB, and Chief Terrance Paul, a member at large and CEO of the Waubetek Business Development Cooperation (for which Madahbee Leach also serves as General Manger), also co-authored an op-ed in the *Ottawa Citizen* titled "How helping Indigenous communities can boost the economy." The latter distilled the contents of the 2016 report on the potential benefits of economic reconciliation for a general mainstream readership in the nation's capital. From there, NIEDB hosted a three-part series to further develop what would become the contents of its 2019 *Indigenous Economic Reconciliation.* Four key areas are highlighted in the 2019 report as topics of ongoing discussions to be had with ministers and government officials, including "procurement, access to capital, capacity development, and wealth sharing" (9). I want to highlight that under wealth sharing, the recommendations endorse traditional economies and participation in environmental stewardship, but they also focus on expanding settler economies, namely, "to increase equity positions and involvement of Indigenous peoples in resource development" (ibid.). From a policy perspective, increasing Indigenous equity in extractive economies that have poisoned waterways and food sources and been the root

---

8   It may be worth noting that NIEDB also falls directly under the responsibilities of the Minister of Indigenous Services, whose department also funded the printing of the 2015 "Impact Report" from Reconciliation Canada.

cause of systemic violence against Indigenous nations does not signal that there is going to be any change to behavior in this particular path of economic reconciliation. Instead, Canada continues to pursue an assimilative direction, even in its approach to reconciliation.

As a counter policy direction, I turn to the Yellowhead Institute, an Indigenous-led think tank started in honor of the late great Secwepemc leader Art Manuel. Their most recent Red Paper, *Cash Back*, considers that economic restoration must go beyond talk and payments, but includes: "Redress for suppressing Indigenous values, Compensation for land theft based on principles of Indigenous laws and mechanisms of justice, and Restitution of Indigenous economies that challenge the exploitation of global capitalism" (14). The report also references Glen Coulthard's article "For Our Nations to Live, Capitalism Must Die," where he makes an argument against wealth sharing under the uneven power dynamic of settler colonial capitalism. Even if it provides short-term financial aid, this type of wealth sharing hooks people into "predatory economies that undermine the deep reciprocity of Indigenous economies" (Yellowhead Institute 60). At the same time, Coulthard notes that the choice to challenge settler colonial economies proves to be a difficult decision between improving socio-economic conditions through available revenues from extraction or exercising independence from the state. However, as exemplified by ongoing injunctions and paramilitarized operations against land defenders exercising their rights to protect their territories from destructive extraction, the definition of Indigenous economies is being narrowly defined by the state.[9]

The sowing and nurturing of the idea of "economic reconciliation" to promote Indigenous people's access to resource wealth reveals an epistemological divide. The Canadian state understands wealth in strictly capitalist terms of privatization of land and resources and its accumulation for monetary wealth. Indigenous laws that disallow individual ownership of non-human life including land and water and all living beings have been treated as dangerous, uncivi-

---

9   There are several Indigenous land defense groups who actively refuse assimilation, such as Tiny House Warriors (resisting the expansion of the Trans Mountain Pipeline), Land Back Lane (holding up Six Nations governance), Gidimt'en and Unist'ot'en clans (who are actively defending Wet'suwet'en life from the Coastal GasLink pipeline). These defenders are criminalized for practicing and remembering their rights to live on their land. That their resistance is met with state violence demonstrates Canada's unwillingness to shift away from carbon-heavy economies while pledging reconciliation is pathologically colonial.

lized, and therefore criminal under Canadian law. The settler colonial economy and its legal system has never honored the Indigenous legal provision that humans are also "Earth-Bound," which speaks to how human beings have been and will always remain tied to the health and abundance of the natural world we live in (Borrows 2018).

Two Worlds Colliding

To remember the truth is to acknowledge the hypocrisy of Canada's continuing attempts to assimilate Indigenous people and communities into extraction-based economies as the policy direction for reconciliation. Shifting reconciliation discourse into a neocolonial method of shared stakes in extraction-based projects, Canada's politics of mourning is smoke and mirrors for ongoing economic assimilation. In the few short years since the TRC issued its Final Report, the term "reconciliation" has already become a derisive concept amongst long-standing grassroots organizers and the next wave of youth-led movements (Ballingall; Hale). A core issue that arose from Canada's Truth and Reconciliation Commission was the chasm between two distinctly different ontologies, histories, public memories, and thus, two vastly different ideologies underpinning the narrative of this place called Canada. While the living conditions on reserves were never adequately funded by the federal government and children from these communities were being indoctrinated and severely abused in residential schools, the majority of the growing settler society directly benefited from this violent "clearing" of land. In order to make room for the arrival of European settlers across the interior, Canada actively targeted the herds of bison, a primary traditional food source, to the brink of extinction, forcing "the original inhabitants of the region into an increasingly desperate situation" (Daschuk 79). The starvation of communities led to the signing of the numbered treaties between First Nations and the Crown, a legal obstacle for Canada to proceed, but whose fiduciary responsibilities have atrophied. Canada pushed and segregated Indigenous communities away from white settlers, who were given large tracts of land to farm, and their growing households, and enforced this separation through the creation of the North-West Mounted Police, today's Royal Canadian Mounted Police (RCMP). In choosing to disconnect the violence of IRS from the state's desire for settler expansion, this ahistorical remembrance of Indigenous life falls short of taking responsibility for the scope of cause and effect when existing governance systems, legal protocols, and non-capitalist economies are criminalized and wholly replaced with European institutions. At the base of Canada's genocide is the core belief in Crown jurisdiction superseding Indigenous jurisdiction. This is the fundamental definition of settler colonialism where existing Indigenous legal, social, and economic authority are replaced with imported traditions from the settlers' origins (Stasiulis/Jhappan).

Canada's sovereignty is modeled upon its British predecessors which privileges Eurocentric viewpoints of private property. This approach to mastering the land through agrarian principles stands in opposition to what Shiri Pasternak calls "an ontology of care" (6). Canada existed in this type of "uneasy legal pluralism" where Indigenous networks of relational kinship as governance structures were vital to the establishment of trade and European survival prior to the formation of settler laws and the criminalization of these same Indigenous governance systems that allowed settlers to thrive. "As the stakes of territorial control began to override the values and necessity of legal multiplicity," the shift from legal pluralism to only colonial authority required the denigration of Indigenous justice and kinship systems (Pasternak 13).

Another important factor in regards to Indigenous stewardship in their own territories is what Tewa scholar Gregory Cajete calls the "ensoulment of nature" (qtd. in Alfred/Corntassel 609). Contrasted with Eurocentric worldviews rooted in Newtonian-Cartesian perspectives, Indigenous worldviews "understood that all entities of nature—plants, animals, stones, trees, mountains, rivers, lakes and a host of other living entities—embodied relationships that must be honored" (609). In this model of relational ontology, there is an ethical duty to care for every aspect of life within your kinship network because survival is dependent on it. In this relational model, it is also unethical to own, sell, and exploit your kin for individual profit. Keeping this epistemological and ontological difference in mind, it becomes evident how settler sentimentality and its capacity for grief are limited under white colonial supremacy.

Canadian cultural politics and identity are rooted in who the nation defined as a British subject. Under the British North American Act, the British subject explicitly did not include Indigenous people, racialized people, or even other British subjects if they came from colonies such as India or the West Indies. The white family homestead would construct a powerful mythology, especially one of man conquering nature that affirmed social notions of belonging, stability, and entitlement. This highly valued settler narrative has been entrenched into the cultural imaginary through the iconic paintings of early 20th century white Anglo-Saxon artists including The Group of Seven and Emily Carr. In their vividly modern paintings depicting vast tracts of 'empty' wilderness, Canada was visually and metaphorically portrayed as a site to be explored and developed (Watson). As a visual re-enactment of terra nullius, these settler mythologies are made possible only through the violent erasure and containment of Indigenous communities, a violence that has been both material and structural. Treaties, wampum belts, and covenant chains are more than acknowledgements and certainly more than museum artifacts. They are legal records of alliances, agreements, and diplomacy consensually agreed upon between various Indigenous nations such as the Anishinaabe and Haudenosaunee and their European counterparts to share the land peacefully (Borrows 1997; Alfred; Henderson).

Reserves and residential schools both physically, socially, politically, and economically segregated Indigenous communities from the development of settlements throughout the late 1800s and 1900s as immigration boomed and formed a new settler society. Canadian immigration up until the 1960s was largely composed of Western European subjects; white agrarian settlers were deemed by political leaders and immigration officers to be more assimilable to Canadian society. The creation of this predominantly white settler class was further enforced through exclusionary legislations and clauses aimed at Asians as well as hostile anti-Black measures that did not equate legal acceptance with social acceptance (Thobani; Walker; McKittrick). Only in the post-World War II order of global human rights did Canada begin to shift its blatantly racist and exclusionary immigration policies and adjust to the newly developed United Nations Refugee Convention of 1951. That same year, amendments were finally made to the Indian Act to decriminalize traditional ceremonies such as pow-wows and potlaches as well as the hiring of independent legal counsel by Indigenous individuals and communities to address land disputes against the Crown.

An analysis of powerful narratives such as national identities requires us to understand that it is "emotions that keep us invested in relationships of power" (Ahmed 2). In a settler colonial context, white supremacy was built into the laws and governments to uphold Eurocentric systems as morally superior. Canadians who emote regret or shame over past events of violence often still expect their settler colonial governments and officials to rectify the situation. The deferral of responsibility to government leaders not only upholds white supremacist power structures, but it also tries to hold onto the fantasy of

Canada's international reputation as a progressive democracy and defender of human rights.

The decimation of Indigenous cultures is now understood as an act of genocide by international standards, but in settler logic, settlers believed it was a charitable act by Church and state to create a labor pool for menial work to perpetuate income disparity. Residential schools were created following the Indian Act of 1876, which included the development of the reserves system that confined First Nations people to fractions of land largely removed from burgeoning urban centers, as well as the creation of the pass system that controlled their movements requiring the permission of government officials to leave their reserves. These 'schools' were designed by Egerton Ryerson, a Methodist minister and founder of Ontario's public education system, and John A. Macdonald, Canada's first Prime Minister, to instill Christian values as the de facto identity of a white settler nation. The Indian Act was also constructed on heteropatriarchal understandings of governance and lineage, which imposed a further layer of violence against traditional governance structures and leadership positions held by women and non-binary persons. The layers of extraction of lives, of labor, and of resources are intertwined histories that cannot be easily undone with words alone.

Building from Ahmed's concept of intensification, or how pain renders certain bodies legible and other bodies as less than human, the case of Canada's National Day for Truth and Reconciliation reveals the ways Indigenous pain has been instrumentalized by settler authorities (92). The ahistorical focus on abused youth outside of any socio-political context becomes the locus of politicized mourning. In centralizing and fetishizing this particular pain of a group that cannot speak back and is not perceived as a threat, settler emotions can project compassion and a moral benevolence for past wrongs while remaining disconnected to the present realities of resistance, often led by Indigenous youth who are demanding justice and who are in turn criminalized and targeted as terrorists against the state. The politics of mourning, especially in settler colonialism, "does not produce universalism or homogenous groups of bodies together in their pain," but it "produces unevenness" (Ahmed 22). It is this unevenness that propels the narrative of settler supremacy, even if expressed as sentimental sorrow, where Indigenous trauma can be consumed comfortably from a distance by the dominant majority because it supposedly belongs out of sight and out of time.

The emotional gravitas of painful narratives is what keeps power in its place. The circulation of trauma and pain, as opposed to willful resistance, helps fuel settler-centric narratives by reinforcing uneven relationships of power. The preference for a narrative rooted only in Indigenous pain rather than witnessing living communities defending themselves and their kinship networks by practicing cultural regeneration equals a denial of Indigenous life and strength. By privileging narratives of settler compassion over Indigenous joy, Canada, as a liberal state, can be free to remember and mourn on designated holidays while living every day based on extraction and assimilation.

Following critical Indigenous studies scholars and thinkers including Leroy Little Bear, Glen Coulthard, Leanne Simpson and the Yellowhead Institute's *Land Back* report, the centrality of land to Indigenous life, culture, language, and knowledge cannot be overstated. Coulthard and Simpson, specifically refer to this connection as "grounded normativity," a form of place-based solidarity based on the inherent intelligence of living in relation to non-human life forms that is so central to many Indigenous ways of knowing. Speaking back to the over-reliance of Western academic traditions, they write:

> In the context of Indigenous peoples' struggles in Canada and elsewhere, this has historically resulted in not only in a very shallow solidarity with respect to Indigenous claims and struggles (when it can even be said to exist) but more often than not a call on Indigenous peoples to forcefully align their interests and identities in ways that contribute to our own dispossession and erasure. (252)

I interpret their use of "shallow" as a critique of Marxism and other Western traditions of thought including settler colonialism. Western academia's penchant for delegitimizing non-Western epistemologies and methodologies, especially in regards to Indigenous worldviews, has had a long history in Canada of devaluing Indigenous knowledge as marginal at best (Kovach; Battiste). This strategy of elimination on the part of Canada is premised on alleviating its own legal obligations to First Nations as enshrined in the Indian Act, a divisive piece of legislation that legally acknowledges Canada's fiduciary duty towards First Nations. Through various strategies, from forced enfranchisement to misogynistic clauses against women and their children who marry non-status men, Canada has actively tried to diminish the number of legally recognized First Nations people through assimilative coercion into the colonial state. This is what I believe Coulthard and Simpson mean by "erasure," whereby the expectation is for Indigenous people to become more like settlers culturally, politically, and economically rather than be self-determining. Through ahistorical

mourning and rhetorical strategies such as promoting "economic reconciliation," the settler state continues to privilege colonial jurisdiction as the only
rule of law.

There has always been a before and an after to colonial capitalist law. Indigenous diplomacy and governance systems long predate contact and continue to be in operation. Though there is no pan-Indigenous legal order, individual nations, alliances, and confederacies regularly practiced diplomacy
with one another. Nation-to-nation diplomacy and the concept of reciprocity
have been established through an extensive history of Indigenous governance
protocols (Regan). Informing the earliest treaties signed between European
colonies and First Nations, multiple Indigenous and non-Indigenous representatives mutually agreed upon sharing the land based on Indigenous principles of diplomacy. This was not a one-time event but standard practice, including the gathering of over 40 Indigenous nations with over 1,300 ambassadors
at the Great Peace of Montreal in 1701, the signing of the Royal Proclamation
issued by King George III in 1763 and the subsequent Treaty of Niagara in 1764
between multiple Indigenous representatives and the British Crown, allowing further settlement only through an agreement that Indigenous jurisdiction
would be respected. Early colonists understood that the only way to move forward was to respect existing Indigenous governance, but every subsequent settler government has repeatedly and systematically broken these legally binding
agreements to pursue extractive development projects.

The centering of Indigenous diplomacy and governance is foundational for
counteracting Canada's zealous ambition to be a global energy provider. Combined with the intensity of state surveillance and criminalization of Indigenous and allied resistance, the nature of an extraction-based economy requires
the ongoing dispossession of Indigenous territory through militarized invasions. In the wake of the National Day of Truth and Reconciliation, from its
grassroots advocacy to bear witness to its politicized focus on economic reconciliation, this paper has critically reflected on the contradictory nature of national efforts to mourn past wrongs against Indigenous life, while continuing
to repeat the same colonial logics. Returning to the enigmatic power of grief
and accepting that one will be changed, possibly forever, by the transformative
power of loss, I believe the original intention of establishing a national holiday
to reflect on truth and reconciliation must include acknowledging the entanglements of extraction, capital, and violence within a long memory of mourning.

Conclusion

Only in the past decade has the scale of IRS violence been widely known, let alone acknowledged, by most Canadians. The large numbers of Indigenous and non-Indigenous people across Canada wearing orange, putting up signs in their street-facing windows, and participating in events to recognize and raise awareness about the history and legacies of the residential school system in Canada are still a recent phenomenon. With the conclusion of the TRC's findings in 2014, the narrative of abused and neglected Indigenous children has become the focal point of reconciliation, which, for some, meant bearing witness on a shared journey of healing. The willingness to witness and understand history from the perspective of those who have been most harmed is in and of itself not the completion of restitution, but only the first step. The power of emotions, not merely as circulating affects, but as social and politically-sanctioned modes of biopower, illustrates how nations shape their cultural identities. In Canada, the rhetorical expression of grief and desire for reconciliation have been adopted by political leaders and federal legislation, but the contradictions between words spoken and actions taken to address irreparable losses require deeper scrutiny.

The National Day of Truth and Reconciliation, when read through the long memory of mourning, fails to contextualize past dehumanization tactics as part and parcel of ongoing federal policies. Mourning colonial violence is impossible when the violence of settler colonialism has never stopped. This analysis critiques the hypocrisy in the politics of mourning where Canada can pedal its soft power as a global human rights defender by establishing a national holiday for truth and reconciliation for the dead while continuing to oppose the living rights of Indigenous jurisdiction. Tracking the discursive use of reconciliation as an assimilative tool in the decade after the TRC's Final Report and recommendations, I have articulated how the rhetorical shift went from mutual healing based in bearing witness to an overtly economic focus to encourage First Nations job creation through the expansion of oil and gas extraction. According to the Yellowhead Institute, Canada's claim to Indigenous territories can be understood at best as a "paper empire" based on one of the largest land grabs in global history.[10] At the end of the day, "colonization is an eco-

---

10   Demarcating the entire Hudson Bay watershed in 1869 as Rupert's Land for the use of trade under a Royal Charter issued by King George II, the subsequent sale of Rupert's Land, a vast territory that was never settled or even negotiated for, only adorned

nomic project based in land theft" and it continues to be a power dynamic that enriches the settler state through ongoing extraction economies (Yellowhead Institute 5)

In its attempts thus far to reconcile with its genocidal past, Canada appears unable to move on from its colonial foundations. Despite ongoing resistance that demand the honoring of treaties and Indigenous jurisdictions to be respected, the federal government continues to operate from a colonial position of domination, from domesticating a version of the United Nations Declaration of Indigenous Peoples to failing its international commitments to reduce carbon emissions. Federal decision-making against Indigenous nations reveals a domestic priority to secure the settler narrative at all costs. The continued negation of Indigenous laws and practices in favor of colonial authorities and recognition perpetuates an uneven relationship where terms of reconciliation and mourning are defined only by settler standards. In understanding the trajectory of settler expansion to economic sovereignty through extraction, let us not forget why Canada needed to establish a Truth and Reconciliation Commission in the first place.

References

Ahmed, Sara. 2014. *The Cultural Politics of Emotion.* 2nd ed. Edinburgh: Edinburgh University Press.

Alfred, Gerald R. 1999. *Peace, Power, Righteousness: An Indigenous Manifesto.* Oxford: Oxford University Press.

Alfred, Gerald, and Jeff Corntassel. 2005. "Being Indigenous: Resurgences against Contemporary Colonialism." *Government and Opposition* 40 (4): 597–614.

Ballingall, Alex. 2020. "'Reconciliation is dead and we will shut down Canada,' Wet'suwet'en supports say." *The Toronto Star*, February 11, 2020. https://ww w.thestar.com/politics/federal/2020/02/11/reconciliation-is-dead-and-w e-will-shut-down-canada-wetsuweten-supporters-say.html.

---

with trading posts, gave way to the Dominion of Canada with a land title spanning 1.2 billion acres of land. Canadian Rail companies acquired 56 million acres. Hudson Bay Company retained 7 million acres, but the consolidation of all First Nations reserves would fit into a mere 3 million acres, accounting for .5% of Canada's total land mass. See Yellowhead Institute's *Cash Back.*

Battiste, Marie. 2013. *Decolonizing Education: Nourishing the Learning Spirit*. Saskatoon: Purich Publishing Limited.

Borrows, John. 1997. "Wampum at Niagara: The Royal Proclamation, Canadian Legal History, and Self-Government from Michael Asch." In *Aboriginal and Treaty Rights in Canada: Essays on Law, Equity, and Respect for Difference*, edited by Michael Asch, 155–72. Vancouver: UBC Press.

Borrows, John. 2018. "Earth-Bound: Indigenous Resurgence and Environmental Reconciliation." In *Resurgence and Reconciliation: Indigenous-Settler Relations and Earth Teachings*, edited by Michael Asch, John Borrows, and James Tully, 49–82. Toronto: University of Toronto Press.

Butler, Judith. 2004. *Precarious Life: The Powers of Mourning and Violence*. London: Verso.

Charleyboy, Lisa. 2020. "Survivor: The Story of Phyllis Webstad." *Canadian Geographic*, September 30, 2020. https://www.canadiangeographic.ca/article/survivor-story-phyllis-webstad-and-orange-shirt-day.

Collis, Susan. 2021. "W(h)ither the Indian Act? How Statutory Law Is Rewriting Canada's Settler Colonial Formation." *Annals of the American Association of Geographers* 112 (1): 167–83. doi: 10.1080/24694452.2021.1919500.

Corntassel, Jeff, Chaw-win-is, and T'lakwadzi. 2009. "Indigenous Storytelling, Truth-telling, and Community Approaches to Reconciliation." *ESC: English Studies in Canada* 35 (1): 137–59.

Coulthard, Glen. 2013. "For Our Nations to Live, Capitalism Must Die." In *Unsettling America—Decolonization in Theory & Practice* (blog), November 5, 2013. https://unsettlingamerica.wordpress.com/2013/11/05/for-our-nations-to-live-capitalism-must-die/.

Coulthard, Glen, and Leanne Simpson. 2016. "Grounded Normativity / Place-Based Solidarity." *American Quarterly* 68 (2): 249–55.

Daschuk, James. 2013. *Clearing the Plains: Disease, Politics of Starvation, and the Loss of Aboriginal Life*. Regina: University of Regina Press.

Diabo, Russ. 2021. "With Bill C-15 (CANDRIP) and an Indigenous GG, Canada Spreads the Lie that It's Implementing UNDRIP." *Georgia Straight*, August 7, 2021. https://www.straight.com/news/russ-diabo-with-bill-c-15-candrip-and-an-indigenous-gg-canada-spreads-lie-that-its-implementing.

Fiscal Realities Economists. 2016. "Reconciliation: Growing Canada's Economy by $27.7 Billion Background and Methods Paper." November 2016. http://www.naedb-cndea.com/en/national-reconciliation-the-27-7-billion-argument-for-ending-economic-marginalization/.

Foucault, Michel. 2003. "Society Must Be Defended." *Lectures at the Collège de France, 1975–1976*. London: Picador.

Freud, Sigmund. (1915) 2007. "Mourning and Melancholia." In *On Freud's "Mourning and Melancholia,"* edited by Letitia Glocer Fiorini, Thierry Bokanowski, and Sergio Lewkowicz, with a foreword by Ethel Spector Person, 19–34. London: International Psychoanalytical Association.

Hafez, Shady. 2021. "Algonquin Anishinabeg vs Algonquins of Ontario: Development, Recognition, and Ongoing Colonization." *Yellowhead Institute*, February 8, 2021. https://yellowheadinstitute.org/2021/02/18/algonquin-anishinabeg-vs-the-algonquins-of-ontario-development-recognition-ongoing-colonialization/.

Hage, Ghassan. 1998. *White Nation: Fantasies of White Supremacy in a Multicultural Society*. London: Pluto Press.

Hale, Alan. 2020. "Reconciliation isn't dead it was never alive, Mohawk activist says." *The Whig*, March 4, 2020. https://www.thewhig.com/news/local-news/reconciliation-isnt-dead-it-was-never-alive-mohawk-activist-says.

Henderson, James Youngblood. 2002. "Sui Generis and Treaty Citizenship." *Citizenship Studies* 6 (4): 415–440. DOI: https://doi.org/10.1080/1362102022000041259.

Kovach, Margaret. 2009. *Indigenous Methodologies: Characteristics, Conversations and Contexts*. Toronto: University of Toronto Press.

Leach, Dawn Madahbee, and Chief Terrance Paul. 2016b. "Leach and Paul: How Helping Indigenous Communities Can Boost Canada's Economy." *Ottawa Citizen*, November 22, 2016. https://ottawacitizen.com/opinion/columnists/leach-and-paul-how-helping-indigenous-communities-can-boost-canadas-economy.

Little Bear, Leroy. 2000. "Jagged Worldviews Colliding." In *Reclaiming Indigenous Voice and Vision*, edited by Marie Battiste, 77–85. Vancouver: University of British Columbia.

Mbembe, Achilles. 2019. *Necropolitics*. Durham, NC: Duke University Press.

McKittrick, Katherine. 2006. *Demonic Grounds: Black Women and the Cartographies of Struggle*. Minneapolis, MN: University of Minnesota Press.

Melamed, Jodi. 2006. "The Spirit of Neoliberalism: From Racial Liberalism to Neoliberal Multiculturalism." *Social Text* 24 (4): 1–24.

Monaghan, Jeff. 2013. "Settler Governmentality and Racializing Surveillance in Canada's North-West." *Canadian Journal of Sociology* 38 (4): 487–508. DOI: https://doi.org/10.29173/cjs21195.

National Indigenous Economic Development Board. 2019. *Indigenous Economic Reconciliation: Recommendations on Reconciliation and Inclusive Economic Growth for Indigenous Peoples and Canada*. http://www.naedb-cndea.com/en/publications/.

Pasternak, Shiri. 2017. *Grounded Authority: The Algonquins of Barriere Lake Against the State*. Minneapolis, MN: University of Minnesota Press.

Perez, Eddy. 2021. "Canada's Next Climate Plan Must Address its Blind Spots." *Climate Change News*, June 21, 2021. https://www.climatechangenews.com/2021/06/28/canadas-next-climate-plan-must-finally-address-blind-spot-oil-gas-emissions/.

Porter, Kate. 2021. "Watson support Algonquins of Ontario Taggart Development." *CBC*, January 27, 2021. https://www.cbc.ca/news/canada/ottawa/watson-support-algonquins-of-ontario-taggart-development-1.5890474.

Reconciliation Canada. 2015. *Impact Report. Reconciliation Canada—A New Way Forward Society*. https://reconciliationcanada.ca/impact-report-2015/

Regan, Paulette. 2010. *Unsettling the Settler Within: Indian Residential Schools, Truth Telling, and Reconciliation in Canada*. Vancouver: UBC Press.

Shaw, Rob. 2014. "Christy Clark Enlists Shawn Alteo to Improve Aboriginal Relations." *Vancouver Sun*, October 29, 2014. https://vancouversun.com/news/metro/christy-clark-enlists-shawn-atleo-to-improve-aboriginal-relations.

Simpson, Leanne. 2017. *As We Have Always Done: Indigenous Freedom Through Radical Resistance*. Minneapolis, MN: University of Minnesota Press.

Stasiulis, Daiva, and Radha Jhappan. 1995. "The Fractious Politics of a settler Society: Canada." In *Unsettling Settler Societies: Articulations of Gender, Race, Ethnicity and Class*, edited by Daiva Stasiulis and Nira Yuval-Davis, 95–131. New York, NY: SAGE Publications.

Tasker, John Paul. 2021. "O'Toole Defends Climate Plan While Promising to Revive Oil Pipeline Project." *CBC*, August 30, 2021. https://www.cbc.ca/news/politics/otoole-climate-plan-northern-gateway-1.6158384.

Taylor, Stephanie. 2021. "O'Toole Supports Building Dead Northern Pipeline, Cites Indigenous Benefits." *The Canadian Press*, August 30, 2021. https://www.cp24.com/news/o-toole-supports-building-dead-northern-gateway-pipeline-cites-indigenous-benefits-1.5566977.

Thobani, Sunera. 2007. *Exalted Subjects: Studies in the Making of Race and Nation in Canada*. Toronto: University of Toronto Press.

Truth and Reconciliation Commission of Canada. 2015a. *Honoring the Truth, Reconciling for the Future: Summary of the Final Report of the Truth and Recon-*

ciliation Commission of Canada. https://irsi.ubc.ca/sites/default/files/inline -files/Executive_Summary_English_Web.pdf.

Truth and Reconciliation Commission of Canada. 2015b. *Canada's Residential Schools: Missing Children and Unmarked Burials. The Final Report of the Truth and Reconciliation Commission of Canada. Vol. 4.* https://publications.gc.ca/collec tions/collection_2015/trc/IR4-9-4-2015-eng.pdf.

"Until There Is Not a Single Indian in Canada." 2020. *Facing History & Ourselves Canada*, July 28, 2020. https://www.facinghistory.org/en-ca/resource-libr ary/until-there-not-single-indian-canada.

Walker, Barrington. 2017. *The African Canadian Legal Odyssey: Historical Essays.* Toronto: University of Toronto Press.

Watson, Scott. 2007. "Race Wilderness, and the Origins of Modern Canadian Landscape Painting." In *Beyond wilderness: the Group of Seven, Canadian Identity and Contemporary Art*, edited by John O'Brian and Peter White, 277–81). Montreal-Kingston: McGill-Queen's University Press.

Yellowhead Institute. 2019. *Land Back. A Yellowhead Institute Red Paper.* https://r edpaper.yellowheadinstitute.org/wp-content/uploads/2019/10/red-paper -report-final.pdf.

Yellowhead Institute. 2021. *Cash Back. A Yellowhead Institute Red Paper.* https://c ashback.yellowheadinstitute.org/.

"Mute Endurance": Precarious Planting and Affective Ecologies in Native American Novels

Gesa Mackenthun

Soil and Oil

This paper attempts to shed some light on the subtle entanglement between the use of sexual violence against Indigenous women and the extractive violence used against the land. The connection between land theft-cum-soil abuse and cross-cultural sexual relations is the topic of a set of novels by Linda Hogan (*Mean Spirit*, 1990), Louise Erdrich (*Tracks*, 1988 and its sequel, *Four Souls*, 2004), and Diane Wilson (*The Seed Keeper*, 2021). My discussion of these texts' representations of 'affective extractivism' is coupled with a glimpse at these novels' representation of quite another kind of intimacy—that between plant cultivators and their plants, seeds, and the soil. The counterhegemonic, ecofeminist discourse of *non*-extractive intimacies—encapsulated in the role of Indigenous women gardeners—shows these literary women not only as pawns in appropriative land deals but also as keepers of plant knowledge and agents of food security. I suggest that the reality behind the semantics of feminizing the land in colonial discourse rests on the tacit knowledge that women possessed a more intimate familiarity with the complex organic entanglements between plants and soils than extractive colonial agriculture would ever achieve (Merchant 17–19). The long history of women's work with seeds and plants, it seems, remains as yet largely unwritten with regard to what is today the United States.

This volume focuses in large part on the 'affective' aspects of fossil and nuclear forms of extraction—an important topic, given the need to phase out of these energy sources as quickly as possible. Yet there are also organic entities that became subject to violent extractive practices: The focus here will be on soil and seeds, which have been manipulated by an increasingly extractive and omnivorous form of agriculture, purportedly with the purpose of feeding a growing world population.[1] The novels in discussion suggest a critical attitude to this practice.

The Domesticity of Colonial Extraction

In *Mean Spirit*, Linda Hogan fictionalizes the historical case of the Osage murders, an uninvestigated spree of killings of members of the Osage tribe on whose lands oil had been discovered in 1920s Oklahoma. The novel addresses the nexus between the systematic legal dispossession of Native Americans during the Allotment era, itself shown as a continuation of the Indian Removal of the 1830s, and the beginnings of the oil industry. Non-Indian settlers made and still make strategic use of sexual relations—in addition to murder and intimidation—to bring themselves into the possession of land formerly considered useless for farming but now strongly desired for its resource wealth. The novel shows the micropolitics of land transactions conducted in the shadow of the General Allotment Act (1887), which transformed commonly held reservation lands into private allotments, threatening to evict and dispossess Indigenous title holders who did not comply with the requirement of practicing European-style agriculture on their land (Justice/O'Brien). The novel's central focalizer, respected Osage woman Belle Graycloud, is apprehensive of the danger of sharing the fate of a murdered cousin, Grace Blanket, who became wealthy through oil. Grace had inadvertently picked a piece of "barren" land inadequate for farming. "With good humor, she named her property 'The Barren Land.' Later, after oil was found there, she called it 'The Baron Land,' for the oil moguls" (Hogan 8). Her daughter Nola, who had witnessed the persecution and murder of her mother by two men in a black Buick, is adopted by Belle to protect her from sharing her mother's fate. Meanwhile, Belle gets under a more and more dangerous siege herself after oil is discovered in her garden. All kinds of legal tricks and violent intimidation are used by white settlers to deprive the Osage of their valuable land. Marriage is one of these

---

1   Obviously, deforestation, especially in the pre-coal age, is another example of extraction, the romanticization of trees in song and poetry its sentimental counterpart. Other examples are the quasi-extinction of beaver and other animals by the fur trade, the sperm whale for candle wax, and the bison for factory leather (and taking away subsistence food from Plains tribes). These ecocidal activities, I suggest, also belong to the larger complex of 'affective extractivism.'

tricks, resulting in an atmosphere of suspicion in cross-cultural relationships. In search of protection, Nola ends up marrying a seemingly unsuspicious white man but feels ambivalent about him. She makes the mistake of asking him to look over her finances:

> She wanted to see what she could spare for her friends so that they would not be forced to lease more of their land. But the news he brought back was that his father had squandered much of her money investing in companies that were now going broke. And her old fears returned to her and she again suspected her young husband. She believed he would murder her one day. Not while she was pregnant. The child was her safeguard, but later, or maybe he would wait for another child as others had done. (Hogan 263)

Both out of fear and being caged in by her marriage, Nola ends up killing her husband.

Hogan articulates a common settler colonial practice: territorial appropriation through marriage.[2] This plot line is paralleled by that of Belle herself, whose cornfield is constantly visited by unseen disturbances: Holes are dug in her garden at night; the white neighbor's fence mysteriously moves closer and closer onto her land; her beehives are disturbed by her neighbor's cattle. Finally, her house burns down of an unknown cause, and she has to join her ancestors' example in leaving her home and garden.

Mean Spirit is a particularly good example of how Native American literary works explore the kinship 'economy' of "tense and tender ties" between colonialism's exploitative attitude toward the land and the role of human, especially sexual, intimacy within the colonial extractive dispositif. "Tense and tender ties" is Ann Laura Stoler's metaphor for the sociopolitical and discursive entanglement of asymmetrical colonial and conjugal relations of power—including the articulation and enactment of colonial abuse through physical abuse. Inspired by the work of Sylvia Van Kirk, Stoler discusses the ways in which the macropolitical "regimes of truth" (Foucault) are enacted on the "microsites" of imperial governance (Stoler 24). The regime of truth considered in this essay is the colonial structure of resource exploitation of oil and soil in the United States. Conducted on Indigenous land, this extractive practice was rational-

---

2   Louise Erdrich also addresses the topic of territorially invasive intimacies, without reference to extractive resources, in her novel *The Round House* (2012).

ized and legitimized by a network of legal and domestic constructions of human relationships, many of them enacted on the bodies of Indigenous women.

Wastelanding

Recent critical reflection on the cultural consequences of the extraction economy focuses on the fossil and nuclear energy cycles.[3] In *The Birth of Energy*, Cara Daggett explores the formation of "petro-subjectivities" and "petro-humanities" in conjunction with the burgeoning fossil fuel-based economy. She traces the discourse of "energy" and thermodynamics throughout the Anglophone literature of the industrial age. In *Living Oil*, Stephanie LeMenager discusses the aesthetics of petroleum in American literature. Her reading of Upton Sinclair's novel *Oil!* (1927), an early critique of petromodernity, reinforces Rob Nixon's discussion of that novel as an example of "slow violence"—the gradual and almost invisible encroachment of the violent effects of ecocidal practices on the lives of people. In mixing the petroleum plot with the emergence of Hollywood culture and international socialism, Sinclair draws a global picture of the massive changes brought about by the fossil age, which deprives some people of their farmland while enabling the more privileged Hollywood society to go love cruising in fancy cars along the California coast. In its critical representation of the entanglement of these various economic and cultural forces, the novel stands as a fine example of literary dialectics.

In *Wastelanding*, her account of the destruction of Diné land by the uranium industry, Traci Voyles carves out the ideological subtexts of the connection between resource extraction and the cultural characterization of the land to be exploited. She explains that the very meaning of "Navajo" emerged from a semantic shift in relation to the land the tribe inhabits. While "navahu" in the language of the Tewa-speaking Pueblo tribes meant "large areas of cultivated fields," the meaning subsequently degenerated into the Spanish-derived

---

3   For a magisterial treatment of the emergence and representation of the fossil fuel industry see Malm. Among many other insights into the workings of fossil capital, Malm reminds us that both the fossil industry and the Anthropocene, which it fuels, are neither the work of nature nor of the human species (as some theorists of the Anthropocene suggest) but the work of a tiny "clique" of white and originally British men who "employed steam power as a literal weapon against the best part of humankind" (Malm 267).

"a large, more or less worthless, flat piece of land" (Voyles xi). "The social construction of the high, arid landscapes of the Southwest as 'more or less worthless'," Voyles writes,

> has been a fundamental component of colonization of the Diné, as well as
> other southwestern and Great Basin tribes. In fact, the inhabitation of dry,
> arid landscapes by native nations was used as evidence of their low status
> on the Western hierarchy of civilization, following a kind of environmen-
> tal determinism that posited that "barren" landscapes supported villainous
> and savage peoples. (xi-xii)

The semantic transition from "fertile" to "barren," with the latter's association of wickedness (xii), confirms my overall impression that Indigenous
agricultural practices and plant knowledges were and still are systematically
effaced—not least because these practices and knowledges lay primarily in the
hands of women.

At the beginning of her book, Voyles describes the wanton destruction of
over four thousand fruit-bearing peach trees and more than eleven acres of
corn and beans as part of a U.S. military operation in 1864. Diné peach trees
and other food plants even continued to be destroyed after the tribal people
had surrendered. Quoting historian Stephen Jett, Voyles wonders "what it was
about these peach trees, corn stalks, and bean plants that invited such unneces-
sary violence, such 'systematic eradication' of fruits, grains, and legumes" (viii).
Historian Peter Iverson's assumption that "perhaps the army simply wanted to
remove evidence that contradicted the image of Navajos as full-time nomadic
wanderers" seems convincing, as evidence for Indigenous agriculture has been
removed alongside the tribes throughout American history (Voyles viii). While
the removal of people has been a central topic of American studies discourse,
from colonial discourse analysis to settler colonial studies, the historical and
historiographical effacement of Indigenous agriculture has apparently hardly
been tackled. Daniel Heath Justice and Jean O'Brien's recent edition *Allotment
Stories* (2021), containing many examples of the effects of what Theodore Roosevelt called approvingly a "mighty pulverizing engine" (Voyles xiii), is a laud-
able exception to the rule. The invisibilization of Native American land tenure
works in tandem with the effacement of the extractiveness and "slow violence"
(Nixon) of settler agriculture, which is one of the most vicious motors of climate change and species extinction to this day.

Colonial Intimacies in North America

In her classic study *The Lay of the Land* (1975), Annette Kolodny documents the discursive feminization of the land in colonial texts, suggesting a connection between the subjugation of the land and its original inhabitants and the subjection of women. In particular, she refers to the "pastoral paradox" by which settler writers at once praised the 'feminine' beauty and desirability of the land while advocating its defloration by 'husbandry.' This contradictory set of desires, Kolodny writes, led to a tension within the discourse of the American pastoral, forcing an impossible extension of its semantic range, "from a healthy sense of intimacy and reciprocity to the most unbridled and seemingly gratuitous destruction" (27–28). In the patriarchal-colonial imagination, "mastery over the landscape" was gained "at the cost of emotional and psychological separation from it" (ibid.). The rhetoric of rape and ravishment, found in numerous descriptions of the unknown land, had its practical equivalent in an exhaustive treatment of the soil: an issue that early American writers (like Jefferson) noted but did not problematize. After all, if a field was degraded due to overuse and/or under-fertilization, one could just move further west (Kolodny 29).

Within the colonial discursive formation, the metaphorical liaison between land theft and sexualized violence reaches from Sir Walter Raleigh's famous "maidenhead" passage[4] and the seizure of Pocahontas (romanticized into America's "Indian princess" in love with Captain John Smith) all the way to the scandalous disappearance and murder of Indigenous women in both the U.S. and Canada throughout the 20th and into the 21st century (Razack; Martin; "Missing and Murdered Indigenous Women"). Observers assert a correlation between the murder and disappearance of Indigenous women and near-by "man camps" inhabited by men working for fossil fuel extraction companies (Martin). Sexual violence and colonial resource extraction converge in this particularly appalling aspect of racial capitalist 'intimacy.' There is nothing sentimental about it. Raped and murdered women and stolen lands

---

4   "Guiana is a country that hath yet her maydenhead, never sackt, turned, nor wrought, the face of the earth hath not bene torne, nor the vertue and salt of the soyle spent by manurance, the graves have not bene opened for golde, the mines not broken with sledges, nor their Images puld downe out of their temples. It hath never bene entered by any armie of strength, and never conquered or possessed by any christian Prince" (Ralegh 428).

are realities which romantic sentimentalism struggles in vain to convert into comfortable stories.

As Carolyn Merchant and other ecofeminist scholars have shown, colonial land management frequently led to the degradation and erosion of soils. The modern rationalistic ideal of agriculture rests on the notion of intense farming with a limited amount of fallow periods during which the exhausted soil could regenerate. This is a departure from former medieval practices. In medieval times, when the distance that had to be covered to reach a community's fields exceeded the walking limit, new settlements were created (Merchant 104).[5] With the destruction of the commons by enclosure and the "imparking" of land beginning in the late Middle Ages (Way), these traditional land use practices receded. The Lockean ideal of enclosure was carried to America. John Winthrop explains the classic distinction between a "civilized" and a "non-civilized" relationship to the land: "The natives in New England, they inclose no land neither have any settled habitation nor any tame cattle to improve the land by, and so have no other but a natural right to those countries" (73). This natural right, which Winthrop associates with the common use of the land, had long been superseded in more developed countries (he claims) "by enclosing and peculiar manurance" which gave its practitioners a "civil right" (ibid.). Early settlers were perfectly aware of the land tenure practices there but regarded Indigenous land tenure, with its shifting planting sites and seasonal choice of accommodation, as nomadic "wandering" and "vagrancy," reducing the complex agricultural practice to a hunting economy (Mackenthun 165–73). As Carolyn Merchant and others suggest, this misreading of the evidence is related to the gender order in these diverse cultural groups. Control of the planting cycle lay in the hands of women; consequently, "'civilizing' the Indians meant converting their female-dominated shifting horticultural production into male-dominated settled farming. Despite the power of women in production, colonial fathers dealt only with Indian males" (Merchant 92). The colonial land-grab thus not only brought about a degradation of the soil but also led to the disempowerment of Indigenous women.

---

5   Native American agricultural societies acted similarly, moving their settlements according to the requirements of their fields (Trigger 133–34).

Deferred Garden

The paradox involved in the continuing "lay of the land"—its celebration as a pastoral ideal concurrent with its ongoing exhaustion not only by the obvious activities of mining, drilling, and fracking, but also by monoculture—has been addressed by American historians and writers for quite some time, such as Frank Norris in *Octopus* (1905) and John Steinbeck in *Grapes of Wrath* (1939). Chemical fertilization was added to organic manure after World War II all the while the Little House on the Prairie iconography continued undisturbed. While settler agriculture asserts to 'improve' the soil, it actually contributed to its degradation and depletion right from the start. In *Grapes of Wrath*, Steinbeck deploys and counters the American political myth of the search for a pastoral paradise by giving a historically precise analysis of the reasons for the economic dilemma of the New Deal period: For him, the cause of human and ecological misery is a fatal combination of a speculative finance industry and a misguided and ignorant agricultural policy, directly leading to the environmental catastrophe of the Dust Bowl.

In *Dust Bowls of Empire*, historian Hannah Holleman describes the Dust Bowl as a global environmental phenomenon, critiquing the historiographical consensus that regarded it as an exclusively natural catastrophe. This view, Holleman asserts, was made possible by scholars ignoring the larger economic and environmental context. The outcome of this ignorance is a Dust Bowl denialism that served the national (mythical) narrative of settler agriculture, counteracted the New Deal narrative of rationalistic reforms, and still serves the purposes of agricultural extractivism (Holleman 40–46). She identifies an ideological competition between the officially accepted version of the event based on an article written for NASA, which completely excludes consideration of the social factors leading to the catastrophe, and concurrent empirical scholarship that proved the relevance of those factors. Holleman shows how science-based interventions by soil experts calling for a reform of agricultural practices in the 1930s and earlier were systematically ignored (46). Soil erosion had been identified as a "world problem" by the 1930s and it was related to the expansion of cash crop agriculture (Holleman 47). Yet, published as recently as 2004, the NASA report flies in the face of both previous and more recent studies (e.g., Worster) and of a modern understanding of the entanglements of human and non-human factors in the production of climate-related events. Environmental historian Donald Worster identifies the cultural assumptions underlying both the economic mismanagement and settler colonial arrogance responsible for the disaster: "The attitude of capitalism—industrial and pre-industrial—toward the earth was imperial and commercial; none of its ruling values taught environmental humility, reverence, or restraint" (Worster 97). Holleman goes one step further when she demands to regard the Dust Bowl as the manifestation of an ongoing extension of "white territorial control," ideologically inspired by white supremacism (45). It is this "'new imperialism' of the late 1800s and early 1900s, which violently transformed societies and the land, entrenching the ecological rift of capitalism on a global scale and the related patterns of unequal ecological exchange that persist to this day" (ibid. 47).

In his reading of *Grapes of Wrath* and speaking from an Indigenous perspective, novelist Louis Owens expresses his puzzlement about "the American phenomenon of destroying the Garden in the search for the Garden" (53). As we have seen with the instance of the destruction of the Diné peach trees, the search for the mythical garden—a crucial element in Jefferson's narrative of the agrarian republic—regularly coincided with the destruction of the gardens already in place. Owens identifies the search for the eternally deferred Promised Land as the ideological core of the problem leading to the 20th century's agro-ecological disasters: "There is no Promised Land and nowhere else to go [...] The American myth of the Eden ever to the west is shattered, the dangers of the myth exposed" (Owens 55). The present commitment will have to be not to some elusive mythical space but "to making *this* place, *this America*, the garden it might be" and to arrive "at a new understanding of the place [the people] inhabit *here and now*" (ibid.; my emphasis).

Extractive and Affective Intimacies

Domestic micropolitics of exploitation and property transfer in conjunction with affective regimes are also addressed in Louise Erdrich's *Tracks* and its sequel, *Four Souls*. Both novels center on the Anishinabe woman Fleur Pillager, an allotment landowner endowed with special powers, who, in *Tracks*, reciprocates her rape by non-Indian men and the clearcutting of her oak trees by causing deadly storms. In *Four Souls*, however, now displaced from her land, she enters into an intimate relation with the owner of the logging company, Mauser, sharing his home built from the stems of her beloved trees. Mauser goes bankrupt and disappears to the East, and with the help of their smart son, Fleur is able to retrieve her land in a poker game with the man who bought up Mauser's forfeited property. She returns to her land, adopting her mother's name Four Souls.

In *Tracks* we learn that Fleur Pillager entertains a special relationship with natural forces, in particular the mythical lake creature Misshepeshu: "Men stayed clear of Fleur Pillager [...] Even though she was good-looking, nobody dared to court her because it was clear that Misshepeshu, the water man, the monster, wanted her for himself" (Erdrich 1988, 11). The unreliable narrator of this passage, her enemy Pauline, claims that Fleur was messing with "half-forgotten medicine," that the tracks of her feet changed into the tracks of bear paws, and that her laugh resembled that of a bear (ibid., 12). Like Hogan's mysterious female landowner Nola, Medea-like Fleur is the object of male desire and fear, her defiance and solitary life in the forest a constant provocation in the eyes of settler society.

Novels like *Mean Spirit*, *Tracks*, and *Four Souls* link sexual intimacy and property theft. They also comment on the abuse of the land by colonial extractive economies like clearcutting, oil drilling, and cash crop agriculture. Hogan and Erdrich are less articulate about *Indigenous* forms of land tenure and their significant difference from colonial practices. Leslie Marmon Silko's novel *Gardens in the Dunes* (1999), in contrast, provides a particularly informative and poetic description of Indigenous women's stewardship of soil and food plants which amounts to a very different kind of intimacy from that of the "tender ties" forced upon female landowners within the colonial extractive social formation. Silko contrasts Indigenous agrarian practices with the scientifically guided plant management of colonial society—not just the tending of plants but also the art of seed selection, propagation, and breeding.[6] Before her death at the beginning of *Gardens*, the elder Grandmother Fleet instructs the protagonist Indigo and her sister, Salt, in the art of tending to the foodplants in the Sand Lizard tribe's dune gardens. She teaches them to grow corn, squash, beans, pumpkins, amaranth, cornflowers, and apricot trees in a way that stresses a companionship between the seedlings and the children:

> After the rains, they tended the plants that sprouted out of the deep sand; they each had plants they cared for as if the plants were babies. Grandma Fleet had taught them this too. The plants listen, she told them. Always

---

6   Steinbeck, in *Grapes of Wrath*, notes the gender displacement also evidenced in Europe: He characterizes plant breeding as an activity conducted by "men of understanding and knowledge and skill" (chapter 25).

greet each plant respectfully. Don't argue or fight around the plants—hard feelings cause the plants to wither. (Silko 1999, 14)

The girls learn that the dune gardens had been initiated a long time ago by the tribe's ancestor Sand Lizard, a mythical female who also established cultural rituals in relation to the plants:

> The first ripe fruit of each harvest belongs to the spirits of our beloved ancestors, who come to us as rain; the second ripe fruit should go to the birds and wild animals, in gratitude for their restraint in sparing the seeds and sprouts earlier in the season. Give the third ripe fruit to the bees, ants, mantises, and others who cared for the plants. A few choice pumpkins, squash, and bean plants were simply left on the sand beneath the mother plants to shrivel dry and return to the earth. Next season, after the arrival of the rain, beans, squash, and pumpkins sprouted up between the dry stalks and leaves of the previous year. Old Sand Lizard insisted her gardens be reseeded in that way because human beings are undependable; they might forget to plant at the right time or they might not be alive next year. (Silko 1999, 15)

Grandmother Fleet is a gardener who passes on her ancient tribal knowledge to her grandchildren shortly before her death and the girls' absorption into colonial society. Her ritual giveaway of part of the harvest testifies to her respect for companion species. She knows how to coax the plants into flowering in the complex ecotope between sand dunes and floodplains, knowing "which floodplain terraces were well drained enough to grow sweet black corn and speckled beans" (Silko 1999, 47). During colonial times, which interrupt traditional patterns of food production, Fleet creatively collects the seeds for her plants from the local town dump (Silko 1999, 22) and then plants them in the ancient dune gardens—a dismissal of colonial ideas of purity reminiscent of Silko's placement of the sacred man Betonie's abode in view of the city dumps of Gallup (in *Ceremony*). When her death draws near, Fleet remains in a grove formed by her apricot tree seedlings, her dead body to be eventually absorbed by the soil which feeds the trees (Silko 1999, 50).

As Ellen Arnold remarks, Silko contrasts Fleet's nurture of spiritual ties between plants and humans with "the extravagant formal gardens of the New England Robber Baron estates, transplanted and forced to bloom at obscene cost," thus exemplifying

> the flowering of capitalism in the Americas, the reshaping of the land for power, profit, and display, that builds on the exploitation and destruction of its native human, animal, and plant inhabitants, and the creation of economic dependencies that prevent subsistence outside the system. (103)

Yet, Arnold continues, Silko's novel resists the seduction of simplistic oppositions between Indigenous and colonial attitudes to the land and its beings. Rather, her novel allows readers to identify capital-driven economic competition as well as patriarchal Western societies' inherent extractivist stance toward "women, indigenous peoples, animals, and earth," imagining possible alliances between these subaltern groups to resist this kind of exploitation (Arnold 103). The novel's avoidance of the notorious colonial binary (Europe vs. its 'Others') and its disclosure of the deep structure of socio-ecological exploitation joins forces with its poetic and sensuous language of transcultural and interspecies friendship.

The fatal embrace of extraction-oriented sexuality on which some of the novels reflect is coupled with representations of interspecies intimacy between Indigenous women and their more-than-human companions. Grandmother Fleet is an iconic traditional knowledge keeper who passes on survival-related information to the younger generation and prepares to have her dead body merge with the soil, feeding her beloved apricot trees with herself. Hogan's *Mean Spirit*, too, includes female characters possessing special knowledge of gardens, rivers, and bees.

Diane Wilson continues this theme with her novel *The Seed Keeper* (2021) which entangles the history of colonial dispossession of land with the politics of cultural disenfranchisement by the disruption of family lines due to poverty, racial violence, and systematic 'reeducation' in boarding schools. In spite of its individualist title, the novel deals with a whole lineage of Dakhóta seed keepers and their efforts in saving their tribe's vegetable seeds from destruction. The protagonist Rosalie Iron Wing is the youngest member of a family who, after having been estranged from her tribe and relatives, manages to reconnect with an elderly aunt waiting to pass on the seeds and knowledge about them before her death. It is not quite certain whether the tradition of plant knowledge, whose earliest keeper survived the traumatic experience of Little Crow's War in 1862, including the execution of 38 Dakhóta men at Mankato, will be passed on to future generations.

The Seed Keeper is also a story about cross-cultural complications: In the 1980s, Rosalie marries a non-Indian farmer whose mother still possessed the knowledge of vegetable gardening but who feels pressured to join a contract with a company promising exorbitant harvests with its combination of chemical fertilizers and GMO-manipulated patent seeds. Wilson traces the social consequences of this encroachment of an extractive form of agriculture on the local level: the ways in which the new economic scheme, which dictates its conditions to the farmers and prohibits them from using their own seeds, disrupts communities, families, and friendships.[7]

Wilson represents seeds as bearers of life and transmitters of intimacy between humans and more-than-human life. During the Indian wars the Dakhótas' fields and gardens are systematically destroyed to quicken their defeat; Rosalie's ancestor teaches her children how to hide the precious seeds and gardening implements and to memorize the correct planting and harvest times from observing the astronomical constellations. When Rosalie finds the seeds of her husband's deceased mother, she starts planting corn, beans, peas, potatoes, squash, and tomatoes in her house garden, feeling a special "connection" to the woman she never met and "who had kept these seeds to feed her family and left them neatly organized and labeled for the next gardener to care for them" (Wilson 135). She explains to her Dakhóta activist friend the difference between European-style farming and Indigenous gardening while her friend fills her in on the scientific evidence for the causes of groundwater pollution by chemical fertilizers (ibid. 169–72). Rosalie mentions the emotional returns she receives from her interaction with plants:

> I needed the comfort of plants around me, the language of their mute endurance, their ability to survive and thrive and adapt. My father had once pointed out a chokecherry tree that had dropped most of its leaves, while a young tree nearby was thriving. The mother tree had chosen to sacrifice its own health for its offspring, sending its share of nutrients to help the other tree battle a fungus. The young tree recovered and, over time, the mother tree also regrew its leaves. (Wilson 187)

This little description of a tree's "mute endurance," whose resilience goes unnoticed by most humans, transculturates Indigenous plant knowledge with Western knowledge about tree-fungus interaction first described in the 1990s by Canadian forest expert Suzanne Simard, to whose concept of the "mother tree" the passage refers. The scientist in the novel is Rosalie's father who was

---

7   The company named "Mangenta" is easily identifiable as Monsanto, now part of German Bayer.

dismissed from his job as a school instructor for teaching "Native science" (Wilson 197).

Surrounded by the disastrous effects of the agroindustry on both her social and natural environment, Rosalie retreats into her garden as into a sanctuary:

> Everywhere I looked, I saw how seeds were holding the world together. They planted forests, covered meadows with wildflowers, sprouted in the cracks of sidewalks, or lay dormant until the long-awaited moment came […] Seeds breathed and spoke in a language all their own. Each one was a miniature time capsule, capturing years of stories in its tender flesh. How ignorant I felt compared to the brilliance contained in a single seed. (Wilson 238)

Wilson depicts Rosalie as someone who instinctively develops a natural affection for her vegetable garden in the midst of her husband's extractive field economy. Her aunt Darlene practices her plant knowledge even in the unlikely space of an elderly home and lives long enough to pass on her wisdom about heirloom seeds to her niece. *Seed Keeper* perfectly captures the two very different meanings of "intimacy" discussed in this essay: the total disruption of American farmers' lives by the introduction of ever more extortionary forms of agriculture; and the loving care invested in the growing of food plants. While the community once depended on the thriving of the plants for their physical survival, the plants now allow their modern descendants to reconnect with their cultural roots.

When she entrusts Rosalie with her last traditional seeds, the aged relative tells her to "'Love them like your children, the way you love your son'" (Wilson 327). Unfortunately, the son is rather fascinated with the idea of having the heirloom seeds patented to turn them into money—thus following the modern commercial practice of treating seeds as property. But a tribal elder is sure the seed will work its magic and make the young man change his mind.

The Hum of a Thousand Conversations

The novels analyzed here alert us to the fact that the agricultural and horticultural labor of Indigenous women has received little attention in historical accounts of Indigenous land tenure in North America (and beyond). The discursive hegemony of the colonial hunting trope is indebted to its strategic function as a legal justification of removal and dispossession, as well as to the

physical ephemerality of crop cultivation: Historical descriptions of Indigenous gardens are rare, and if they exist, they mostly refer to the destruction
of food crops. The bioarchaeological reconstruction of the former agricultural
landscape of the Americas has produced evidence of a much more intense pre-
Columbian land tenure than formerly thought (Doolittle; Safier). More work
is required to arrive at a realistic assessment of the scope and character of
historical Indigenous plant cultivation before and after the Columbian moment, including the decisive role of women within that economy.[8] The novels
discussed here contain selective glimpses of that female economy, including
its ecological aspect: a recognition of the intimate ties and dependencies
between humans and other creatures.

While Erdrich, Hogan, and Silko focus on women as plant experts and
knowledge keepers, Wilson also includes seeds themselves in her chorus of
voices. In an introductory poem, the seeds speak:

> We surrendered our wildness to live in partnership
> with the Humans.
> Because we cared for each other, the People and
> the Seeds survived. (Wilson n.p.)

The seeds as magic communicators and gardens as sanctuaries of interspecies
survival may seem, to a Western rationalistic reader, a slightly esoteric take of a
gardener-writer.[9] Yet, many Indigenous writers and gardeners (such as Robin
Wall Kimmerer) stress the sacredness of their seeds, which are part of a whole
cluster of sacred meanings. I would like to once more return to Louise Erdrich's

---

8   Robin Wall Kimmerer describes Indigenous planters as "essential partner[s]": "It is she
     who turns up the soil, she who scares away the crows, and she who pushes seeds into
     the soil. We are the planters, the ones who clear the land, pull the weeds, and pick the
     bugs; we save the seeds over winter and plant them again next spring. We are mid-
     wives to their gifts [...] Corn, beans, and squash are fully domesticated; they rely on us
     to create the conditions under which they can grow. We too are part of the reciprocity.
     They can't meet their responsibilities unless we meet ours" (139–40). For the role of In-
     digenous women in agriculture see also Merchant. For the historical disarticulation of
     women in agriculture more generally see Federici. For the current global significance
     of female gardeners see Shiva.
9   Diane Wilson does have a garden. She plants the vegetables in a slightly different
     order than the classical "three sisters" arrangement, as she reveals in various online
     videos. Wilson is also the former executive director of the Native American Food
     Sovereignty Alliance.

Tracks whose fantastic finale consists of Fleur Pillager causing the oak grove surrounding her hut to collapse in a sudden storm probably created by herself: her last gesture of defiance against the powerful logging company waiting to take possession of her land. Nanapush, the narrator of this sequence, witnesses the scene. Just before the final showdown, he is surprised to find that Fleur had tended a garden plot near the lakeshore. The pumpkins and squash now "flourished madly," spreading their leaves and blossoms "almost in defiance" (Erdrich 1988, 218). There are also peas and rhubarb (ibid. 222), a full-grown garden. In reaching her cabin, Nanapush has to pass through an area already clearcut. All that is left of the former forest is a circle of high oaks around Fleur's home. As Nanapush enters her place, he is overwhelmed by the presence of a multitude of living beings:

> I heard the hum of a thousand conversations. Not only the birds and small animals, but the spirits in the western stands had been forced together. The shadows of the trees were crowded with their forms. The twigs spun independently of wind, vibrating like small voices. I stopped, stood among these trees whose flesh was so much older than ours, and it was then that my relatives and friends took final leave, abandoned me to the living. (Erdrich 1988, 220)

Nanapush meets his deceased relatives whose spirits are all crowded into that small space of Fleur's home. Erdrich here imagines a complete collapse of the space-time continuum, a chronotopical clash caused by colonial extractive violence. Fleur's garden is a sacred site, a sanctuary of all spiritual and more-than-human life to be erased: connected to each other by their shared and ancient "flesh."

The intimacy evoked by Hogan, Erdrich, Silko, and Wilson radically differs from the extractive intimacies discussed above. In addition to shedding a critical light on how the members of a patriarchal colonial society gain access to land property by taking possession of Indigenous women's bodies, these novels contain the literary groundwork of an older, companion-species intimacy and its survival throughout the destruction wrought by removal, allotment, and termination policies, as well as colonial 'reeducation.' These texts contribute to the survival and current revival of Indigenous plant cultivation; they form a counterpoint to the colonial discursive and practical deformations of land tenure.

Survival Seeds

In spite of the daily importance of food on the plates of all people, including urban academics, the extractive practice of food production has received relatively little attention from cultural and literary studies discourse. We munch our organically grown bean and cashew burgers without thinking too much about the conditions of their production, nor those of the less healthy conventional foodstuffs many of us can afford to ignore. Plant cultivation and food production are disproportionately controlled by internationally operating corporations using combinations of GMO organisms and chemical fertilizers, which endanger soil and seed health. Food is also the subject of stock market speculation. Yet, the cultural discourse about food more often than not ignores this political dimension, maybe because it is not considered cultural enough or maybe these things range beyond the cognitive horizon of urban academics. The importance of food production flares up in moments of danger—for example, in the Russian war against Ukraine whose blockade of wheat exports threatens to cause a global humanitarian catastrophe. Risking their own lives, Ukrainian farmers managed to sow new seeds in spite of their fields being torn up by tanks and missiles. This truly heroic action demonstrates the importance of these food workers and the necessity to keep food production independent from corporate, speculative, and geopolitical calculus.

The American monopolistic system of monocrop agriculture, with its degradation of soils and seeds, began in the early 20th century, its impact reaching all the way to the U.S.S.R. As Uta Ruge shows in her eye-opening book *Bauern, Land*, U.S.-made industrial agriculture lay the foundation for the modern global food system in conjunction with the socially incompetent post-Czaristic and Stalinist land management (chapters 33 and 37). In both cases, imperial agriculture depended on population control, including, in the United States, the theft of fertile soils by means of Indian Removal, allotment privatization, and termination. These policies led to the disenfranchisement of Indigenous women from their function as food producers. The result, as Christina Gish Hill contends, was a "profound loss of knowledge and [...] [a] damaged seed stock" (93). Today, there are efforts to unmake some of the effects of this policy. Local food sovereignty initiatives are a response to the fatal hegemony of extractive food production. Rural and urban garden projects are sprouting around the globe. They testify to a reawakening of the half-forgotten intimacy between humans and plants, and they provide future generations with a knowledge that may be decisive for their health and survival. Indigenous garden projects in North America also give the lie to the popular discourse of Indian nomadism that still frequently serves as a rationalization of dispossession. These projects are reminders of the fact that seeds are not only food but also, as Hill writes, "relatives, ancestors, and sacred entities" (98). Gardens are not only places for food production but works of art in their own right, offering the gardener a great potential for aesthetic creativity.[10] In addition to their potential for art, seeds are a natural archive, holding genetic knowledge, and are tied to cultural and cultivation-related knowledges. As both seed sovereignty and food sovereignty depend on the control over land, the repurchase of fertile land is therefore one of the principal activities toward Indigenous cultural survival.

To refer to the heirloom seeds' "mute endurance" (Wilson 187) is to mark their invisibility within the colonial episteme as well as their resilience. Indeed, they may just owe their "endurance" to their very "muteness" or invisibility, their ability to range below extraction agriculture's possessive radar. Every now and then, a plant believed to be extinct shows up again because its seed was pre-served by an Indigenous gardener. The image (fig. 1) of Tiana Suazo from Taos cradling her heirloom pumpkin with unadorned tenderness resonates with the power of an epic story yet waiting to be fully told.

---

10   Formal flower gardens or landscape gardens are accepted as aesthetically pleasing, if not outright works of art—the culmination of a culture of taste whose historical rise was concurrent with that of European expansion. Vegetable gardens are less fre-quently the subject of aesthetic attention—wrongly so, as the creativity invested in the shaping of contemporary organic gardens shows. My favorite is in Klein Jasedow, a vil-lage near the island of Usedom, which is tended by members of the European Academy of Healing Arts. Each year it has a different shape, due to the necessarily changing ar-rangements of flower and vegetable plants. See Europäische Akademie der Heilenden Künste—EUROPEAN ACADEMY OF HEALING ARTS (https://eaha.org).

Figure 1: Tiana Suazo of Taos Pueblo cradling a squash that had been gone from the community for many years, but whose seeds were found in the Seed Savers Exchange collections, where Rowen White (red shawl) serves as chair of the board and has endeavored to return as many of the seeds originating from Native communities back to their original homes. Henrietta Gomez, in the yellow shawl, is a respected seed keeper in the Taos Pueblo community.

Text and photo by Elizabeth Hoover, October 2018 (Hoover 2021).

References

Arnold, Ellen. 1999. "Review of Leslie Marmon Silko, *Gardens in the Dunes*." *Studies in American Indian Literatures* 11 (2): 101–04.

Daggett, Cara New. 2019. *The Birth of Energy: Fossil Fuels, Thermodynamics, and the Politics of Work*. Durham, NC: Duke University Press.

Doolittle, William E. 2000. *Cultivated Landscapes of Native North America*. Oxford: Oxford University Press.

Erdrich, Louise. 1988. *Tracks*. New York, NY: Harper & Row.

Erdrich, Louise. 2004. *Four Souls*. New York, NY: Harper Perennial.

Federici, Silvia. 2019. *Re-Enchanting the World: Feminism and the Politics of the Commons*. Oakland, CA: PM Press.

Hill, Christina Gish. 2017. "Seeds as Ancestors, Seeds as Archives: Seed Sovereignty and the Politics of Repatriation to Native Peoples." *American Indian Culture and Research Journal* 41 (3): 93–112. DOI: https://doi.org/10.17953/aicrj.41.3.hill.

Hogan, Linda. 1990. *Mean Spirit*. New York, NY: Ballantine.

Holleman, Hannah. 2018. *Dust Bowls of Empire: Imperialism, Environmental Politics, and the Injustice of 'Green' Capitalism*. New Haven, CT: Yale University Press.

Hoover, Elizabeth. 2021. "Sky Woman's Daughters." *TheCommonTable.eu*, May 13, 2021. Accessed June 20, 2022. https://thecommontable.eu/sky-womans-daughters/.

Justice, Daniel Heath, and Jean M. O'Brien, eds. 2021. *Allotment Stories: Indigenous Land Relations Under Settler Siege*. Minneapolis, MN: University of Minnesota Press.

Kimmerer, Robin Wall. 2013. *Braiding Sweetgrass*. Minneapolis, MN: Milkweed.

LeMenager, Stephanie. 2014. *Living Oil: Petroleum Culture in the American Century*. Oxford University Press.

Mackenthun, Gesa. 1997. *Metaphors of Dispossession: American Beginnings and the Translation of Empire, 1492-1637*. Norman, OK: University of Oklahoma Press.

Malm, Andreas. 2016. *Fossil Capital: The Rise of Steam Power and the Roots of Global Warming*. London: Verso.

Martin, Nick. 2019. "The Connection Between Pipelines and Sexual Violence." *The New Republic*, May 19, 2019. https://newrepublic.com/article/155367/connection-pipelines-sexual-violence.

Merchant, Carolyn. 1989. *Ecological Revolutions: Nature, Gender, and Science in New England*. Chapel Hill, NC: University of North Carolina Press.

"Missing and Murdered Indigenous Women." *Wikipedia*. https://en.wikipedia
.org/wiki/Missing_and_murdered_Indigenous_women#cite_note-RCAA
NC_20160422-16. Accessed May 3, 2022.

Nixon, Rob. 2011. *Slow Violence and the Environmentalism of the Poor*. Cambridge,
MA: Harvard University Press.

Owens, Louis. 1996. *The Grapes of Wrath: Trouble in the Promised Land*. New York,
NY: Twayne/Simon&Schuster.

Ralegh, Sir Walter. 1904. "The discoverie of the large, rich, and beautifull Empire of Guiana." In *The Principal Navigations Voyages Traffiques and Discoveries
of the English Nation*, edited by Richard Hakluyt. Vol. 10. 1598–1600. Reprint,
Glasgow. 338–431.

Razack, Sherene H. 2002. *Race, Space, and the Law: Unmapping a White Settler Society*. Toronto: Between the Lines.

Ruge, Uta. 2020. *Bauern, Land: Die Geschichte meines Dorfes im Weltzusammen-
hang*. München: Antje Kunstmann.

Safier, Neil. 2015. "Fugitive El Dorado: The Early History of an Amazonian
Myth." In *Fugitive Knowledge: The Loss and Preservation of Knowledge in Cultural
Contact Zones*, edited by Andreas Beer and Gesa Mackenthun, 51–62. Mün-
ster: Waxmann.

Shiva, Vandana. 2016. *Who Really Feeds the World? The Failures of Agribusiness and
the Promise of Agroecology*. Berkeley, CA: North Atlantic Books.

Silko, Leslie Marmon. 1977. *Ceremony*. New York, NY: Viking Press.

Silko, Leslie Marmon. 1999. *Gardens in the Dunes*. New York, NY: Scribner.

Simard, Suzanne. 2022. *Finding the Mother Tree: Uncovering the Wisdom and Intelligence of the Forest*. New York, NY: Penguin.

Steinbeck, John. (1939) 2014. *The Grapes of Wrath*. New York, NY: Penguin.

Stoler, Ann Laura. 2016. "Tense and Tender Ties: The Politics of Comparison in
North American History and (Post-) Colonial Studies." In *Haunted by Em-
pire: Geographies of Intimacy in North American History*, edited by Ann Laura
Stoler, 23–67. Durham, NC: Duke University Press.

Trigger, Bruce. 1987. *Children of Aataentsic. A History of the Huron People to 1660*.
Montreal: McGill-Queen's University Press.

Voyles, Traci Brynne. 2015. *Wastelanding: Legacies of Uranium Mining in Navajo
Country*. Minneapolis, MN: University of Minnesota Press.

Way, Twigs. 1997. *A Study of the Impact of Imparkment on the Social Landscape of
Cambridgeshire and Huntingdonshire from c. 1080 to 1760*. Oxford: BAR.

Wilson, Diana. 2021. *The Seed Keeper*. Minneapolis, MN: Milkweed.

Winthrop, John. (1629) 1985. "Reasons to be Considered." Reprint in *The Puritans in America*, edited by Alan Heimert and Andrew Delbanco, 71–74. Cambridge, MA: Harvard University Press.

Worster, Donald. (1979) 2004. *The Dust Bowl: The Southern Plains in the 1930s*. Oxford: Oxford University Press.

Pains, Planes, and Automobiles: Extractivist Nostalgia in *Mad Men*

Verena Wurth

In "The Gold Violin," a season two episode of the period drama series *Mad Men* (2007–2015), created by Matthew Weiner, protagonist Don Draper leaves his office in the advertisement agency Sterling Cooper on Madison Avenue, New York, to take his family for a ride in his new Cadillac and have a picnic on a green. Upon their departure from their outing, Don throws his beer can towards the end of the park into the shade of the trees, and his wife Betty clears the picnic blanket by shaking it out, leaving a pile of food wrappers behind. Before getting into the car, Don orders Betty to check the children's hands for dirt—ironic, considering the pile of rubbish they leave behind (S2E7). While the family drives off, the camera continues to direct our view to the abandoned detritus, leaving the audiences with great discomfort—a discomfort that is created through the clash of the pastoral image and the Drapers' environmentally harmful behavior. The scene thus also leaves the audience questioning and criticizing the family's "(and thus, an entire generation's) utterly laissez-faire attitude to littering and the environment" (Dean).

This picnic scene is one of the most memorable instances when watching the AMC drama from an ecocritical perspective. This scene has been mentioned only in passing in a few journalistic texts (cf. Dean; CBS News), and it is striking that also in scholarly texts, discussions of environmental issues in *Mad Men* in general, and the picnic scene in particular, are rare, despite the scene's strong affective impact. One exception is an essay by Brenda Cromb, who argues that the "disjunction" depicted in the scene "does not necessarily reflect a major social upheaval, but it is still a shock that jars viewers into remembering that the past was *different*" (70). Another example is the article "The Shock of the Banal," in which Caroline Levine argues that compared to other shows from the same era, *Mad Men* puts the technique of televisual pleasure "to the best political use" (134). She contends that this pleasure is achieved through shocking the audiences in depictions of the banal—like seeing Don's daughter Sally playing with a dry cleaner plastic bag over her head or the Draper family's garbage dump after the picnic. Levine maintains that such shocking images do not necessarily show viewers how much society has supposedly progressed since the 1960s; rather, they raise the question of whether change is possible at all and if so, how it happens (138f.). I agree with this claim about the complications of social progress and with her assertion that

> the show does not distance us from this past altogether, but always and significantly maintains the play of sameness and difference: after all, the impulse to exploit and vandalize the natural world remains strong, and thus the uncannily tranquil, relaxed, familiar feeling of this [picnic] scene may serve to evoke at once our own ecological habits and the ones we have left behind (Levine 142).

Mad Men, especially in the picnic scene, holds up the mirror to its audience to show how little has changed in regard to human ecological habits, in particular when it comes to littering and plastic pollution, which is an environmental problem that continues to grow in our present day.

The entire episode surrounding the picnic scene marks one of the rare moments when *Mad Men* displays some degree of critical awareness of human-made environmental destruction at the individual level. *The Guardian* critic Will Dean observes that there is a "tiny subplot" of unsustainability that runs through the episode, in which some Sterling Cooper executives think of how to "market the relatively new disposable Pampers," which are "just one of thousands of consumer goods marketed in the mid-20th century whose convenience trumped their terrible environmental impact." The fact that this observation only appears in the "Notes" section at the end of Dean's article marks it as an afterthought, which is consistent with the relatively small amount of ecocritical work on *Mad Men*, and in fact on New Golden Age TV series more generally.[1] This article seeks to begin to close this gap.

When watching the series through an ecocritical lens, it becomes apparent that there are a few subplots in the show that deal with environmental issues, but these are indeed sub-, as in minor plots. This marginalization is initially somewhat surprising, considering the often proclaimed and appraised

---

1   There are some exceptions, like Leyda's and Negra's article "Television In/of the Banal Anthropocene: Introduction," MacDuffie's "Seriality and Sustainability in *Breaking Bad*," and Palatinus' "Humans, Machines and the Screen of the Anthropocene."

historical accuracy of the series (Rosenheck 161). One would think that such an at-the-time nascent—if undervalued—topic would be spotlighted more in a show set during the 1960s that, over the course of its seven seasons, broaches so many other historical developments in considerable detail.[2] For example, Earth Day in 1970, a landmark event of the modern environmental movement, does not appear in the show itself, but in the DVD set paratexts for the seventh season, which teases only very committed viewers to buy the DVD and watch these extra materials "to dig deeper about the Earth Day to find its relevance to the present" (Baruah 138). Moreover, while season two is set in 1962, and while the series literariness is well known,[3] it does not reference Rachel Carson's *Silent Spring*. The book, released in June 1962, is often said to have sparked the modern environmental movement (cf. Griswold). In season three, Carson is indeed mentioned—albeit only in one line—when Betty Draper joins the all-women non-profit organization Junior League to campaign against a water tank that would drain the local water reservoir ("Seven Twenty Three," S3E7).[4] Betty's neighbor's naïve-sounding comment in response to one of the Junior League women's explanation for why such a water tank poses dangers to the local environment and community ("Well said!") ridicules and plays down the issue's importance. Moreover, the storyline is overshadowed by Betty's flirt with Henry Francis, who is 'the person she knows' in the office of Republican governor Nelson Aldrich Rockefeller, and whom she offers to contact to support the women's organization's cause. This plotline narratively downplays her environmental work, suggesting that her true motivation is to fulfill her personal, romantic desire of getting closer to Henry, who becomes her second husband later in the series.

The fictional Governor Rockefeller, whose family "owns half the land" ("Seven Twenty Three," S3E7) in the area where *Mad Men* is set, apparently later agrees to Francis' appeal to support Betty's and the Junior League's conservational efforts. What this portrayal of the political figure erases from the

---

2   Especially the instances in which environmental matters are romanticized or ridiculed in the show, discussed later on, suggest that the marginalization of environmentalism is a not a deliberate narrative or meta-narrative choice by the creators.

3   Cf. The New York Public Library's reading list with the works read by the protagonists, including then topical releases like Frank O'Hara's *Meditations in an Emergency* (1952) (cf. Parrott).

4   Adam Rome remarks that water pollution was also a much-discussed issue in major women's magazines of the early 1960s (538)—a very minor historical parallel that the show draws.

narrative is the fact that in real life, the Rockefeller family's immense wealth is built on the large-scale extraction of oil. The historical Rockefellers' success in the industry started in 1911 with the founding of Standard Oil of New Jersey, a predecessor of ExxonMobile—a company that spread misinformation about fossil fuels and their impact on the climate (cf. Union of Concerned Scientists), and which, just like Chevron Oil, is one of Sterling Cooper clients in the series. While we do not learn much about Rockefeller beyond his extensive real estate dealings, the love story with Henry that drives this subplot, and the glamorous depiction of the show's New York setting obscure the Rockefellers' harmful extractivist history. To put it differently, this focus erases their environmental impact while it glorifies and sentimentalizes the material goods and lifestyle(s) they produced.[5]

Another major aspect in petroleum history that *Mad Men* leaves out in its later seasons is the Santa Barbara Oil Spill that occurred in 1969 in the Santa Barbara Channel and which had devastating effects on the surrounding ecosystems, akin to the Deepwater Horizon disaster in 2010. Deepwater Horizon happened during the airing of the fourth season and could have served as a historic event that parallels the show's diegetic event. Yet, the catastrophe seems to have been forgotten about by the time *Mad Men*'s season seven was written: the season, released in 2014 and set in 1969, makes no mention of an oil spill—despite its significance and even though it enlivened the environmental movement in California, especially as it "offered a [radically different] reinterpretation of oil extraction as death-making" and not as an optimistic "realization of modern life," to quote environmental humanities scholar Stephanie LeMenager (69). Other than that, season seven only briefly touches upon the theme of environmentalism during the period. For example, Roger Sterling's daughter Margaret flees wedlock and motherhood to join a farm commune ("The Monolith," S7E4) and nominatively restyles herself as a

---

5   The show's audience is also not presented with any Chevron Oil ad campaigns, but one could only assume that such an advertisement would look like the one Geoffrey Supran and Naomi Oreskes list in their article on "The Forgotten Oil Ads That Told Us Climate Change Was Nothing," where the authors describe how a Humble Oil (now ExxonMobil) ad from 1962 subverts the devastating warning to American oil bosses that "burning fossil fuels could lead to global heating 'sufficient to melt the icecap and submerge New York'" into the power-professing slogan that "Each day Humble supplies enough energy to melt 7 million tons of glacier!" (Supran/Oreskes) The ad was originally released in *Life Magazine*, which is frequently mentioned in *Mad Men*, and the offices of which are in the same building.

flower by changing her name to Marigold. Also, Don Draper is cast as a fair-weather hippie in the series' finale, finding enlightenment through meditation in a more 'natural,' outdoor environment than his offices and homes. Yet, unlike the picnic scene, which cinematographically comments on the protagonist's lack of awareness of and involvement in environmental matters, Margaret's story is depicted with a certain amount of ridicule and insincerity.[6] Don's spiritual salvation and portrayed oneness with the environment does not escape the capitalist ideals that (parts of) the environmental movement sought to dismantle. His enlightenment goes hand in hand with creating the popular Coca-Cola 'Hilltop' ad—which is aimed at growing profit for him and his company, rather than growing "apple trees and honey bees," as the lyrics go in the ad's song. Moreover, the narrative strands remain individualistic depictions of a developing ecological consciousness, while more large-scale, systemic environmental problems and the movement as a whole are not addressed. Consequently, interpretations of environmental history that would be constructive in our current eco-crisis are not easily drawn when watching the show and would have to be accounted for by the viewer.

Such missed opportunities to engage, such brief thematizations of environmentalism in *Mad Men* call for deeper investigations of the (mis-)construction of the environmental movement's history in the show.[7] In the following, however, I focus on the inverse, namely on the question of how the series does depict structures and actions that are detrimental to the environment. Before doing so, I introduce the genre I call petro-TV as a televisual form of the literary genre of petrofiction. With *Mad Men* as an exceptional example of petro-TV, I frame the notion of an extractivist nostalgia, which denotes a form of nostalgia that romanticizes, obscures, or celebrates past forms of extractivism and from which negatively connotated affects, such as grief or guilt, are absent. In my analysis, I ask how the series represents extractivism, especially of steel, which is made from mined iron and other raw minerals, oil, and the modes of mobility fueled by oil like planes and automobiles. In contrast to these, I also examine how the series depicts a less oil-intensive mode of transport, the train. I argue that *Mad Men*'s depictions of extractive materials like steel and more refined products like cars points to such an extractivist nostalgia for the 1960s.

---

6   Aly Semigran, for example, interprets Marigold's escape as ridiculous.

7   Cf. Rome, who notes the marginalization of the environmental movement in historical discourse (526).

I aim to show how the series celebrates extractivism through visual aestheticizations of such 'indispensable' extractive products like steel, oil, planes, and
automobiles, while a less extractivist, more collective mode of transport like
the train is frequently portrayed as tedious, even painful.

Petro-TV

If one were to ask whether *Mad Men* could be considered a typical example of
petro-TV, as the televisual equivalent of the literary genre that Amitav Ghosh
calls "petrofiction,"[8] one would have to negate this question. The series does
not deal as openly with oil as petrofictional works such as Upton Sinclair's *Oil!*
(1926)—adapted for the screen as *There Will Be Blood* (2007)—, Abdelrahman
Munif's *Cities of Salt* (1987), or the graphic novel *Oil and Water* (2011) by Steve
Duin and Shannon Wheeler that negotiates the BP oil catastrophe. Nor, to
name a televisual example, does *Mad Men* have the crude, rusty, dark aesthetics
of *True Detective* (2014–19), the first season of which Delia Byrnes examines as
a representation of petroculture. Despite the lack of direct oil thematization
in *Mad Men*, I deem it important for petrocritical analyses to also examine cultural representations that do not as openly or visibly deal with oil, but rather
do it in symptomatic ways. My approach thus aligns with Patricia Yaeger's
notion of an "energy unconscious" (309), that is inspired by Frederic Jameson's
"political unconscious," and Julia Leyda's concept of a "climate unconscious."
Leyda too draws from Jameson, but also refers to Lawrence Buell's idea of an
"environmental unconscious," both of which she uses to discuss the medium
of television specifically (Leyda/Negra 78). I argue that petro-TV can appear
in shiny, celebratory, and glamorous aesthetics that somewhat cover up the
crude, conflictual, and exploitative connotations of oil's materiality and the
processes and crises involved in its extraction, and thematically (and visually)
deal with issues other than extractivism, pollution, or socio-ecological crises.
If oil is kept mute (Ghosh 30) within petrotexts and is deferred through aestheticizations, like the nostalgic ones in *Mad Men*, the petroleum bases of such
cultural artefacts must be made conscious through a petrocritical analysis.

---

8   Popular seriality studies often draw comparisons between TV series and literature. See
Winckler, Reto, and Víctor Huertas-Martín, *Television Series as Literature*, for a discussion
of TV as literature.

My approach to petrocultural criticism is also based on Imre Szeman's strategy of interrogating "the energy-demanding structures and categories of modernity" (146), and apprehends that "[d]espite being a concrete thing, oil animates and enables all manner of abstract categories, including freedom, mobility, growth, entrepreneurship, and the future in an essential way" (ibid.). Szeman explains that "[i]t may be reductive to position oil as the *ur*commodity that fuels" the imaginaries of capitalism and socialism, but he also stresses that it is a highly significant substance "fully deserving [of] a prominent role" (ibid. 162). Despite the high political and cultural relevance of oil in *Mad Men*, it does not surface in its material form—except in one small instance mentioned later. Instead, it is mediated, appearing only through extractive end-use products such as planes and automobiles. In this way, Szeman's framing of oil as an *ur*commodity does convince, especially if we read "*ur*" as a primordial point of origin that is veiled or forgotten—a fundament (ibid. 147) that needs to be uncovered if one is to understand the past "within which our ideas of labour and capital were born and shaped into forms on which we still rely" (ibid. 162). To put it differently, in accordance with the notion of an energy unconscious, *Mad Men* narratively buries oil either under a romantic love story between Betty and Henry as mentioned in the introduction, or under the depiction of shiny cars and glamorous planes, which will be elaborated in the following.[9] For the characters, especially for protagonist Don Draper, these petro-objects often signify freedom, mobility, or entrepreneurial and personal success (ibid. 146). In its abstract, mediated way, oil does not presented "both as problem and possibility" (ibid.), but leans heavily towards the latter—or rather, the objects fueled by oil are generally framed positively as "possibility," while the train, as a collective, lower emission means of transport is presented with negative, that is, constricting and traumatic connotations—to use Szeman's word, it appears as "problem." In the following, I will examine the celebratory depiction of 1960s petroculture and extractivism in *Mad Men*, arguing that its aestheticization of extractive materials can create an extractivist nostalgia for the period for a 21st century audience.

---

9   Another example for such petro-TV in which extractivism is mediated through celebrations of petrocultural objects is *Sons of Anarchy*, in which motorcycles are revered by viewers and critics. See for example Philip Etemesi, "Sons of Anarchy: Top 10 Bikes Owned by SAMCRO Members, Ranked."

Extractivist Nostalgia

As a historical drama, *Mad Men* is often perceptibly as nostalgic about the past. This nostalgia manifests itself in the detailed interior designs, the fashion, the music, the media, the abundance of food and cocktails in fancy restaurants, or in referencing of historical events (cf. Bevan). The series does not always sentimentalize the past, however. As Trisha Dunleavy argues, the show oscillates between "deployment and critique of nostalgia" (51). Critique of nostalgia for the 1960s and early 70s, she explains, occurs especially when it comes to "social prejudices and inequities" (ibid.), for instance regarding gender or race,[10] or regarding individual actions that harm the environment, as can be seen in the picnic scene. Yet, when it comes to the larger topic of extractivism, its end-use products, and their advertisement, the TV show strongly leans towards a deployment of nostalgia for the era. The show thus projects an extractivist nostalgia that affirms fossil fuel reliance.

I develop the term 'extractivist nostalgia' out of several definitions of extractivism and nostalgia. Maristella Svampa defines extractivism as "the pattern of accumulation based on the overexploitation of generally nonrenewable natural resources, as well as the expansion of capital's frontiers toward territories previously considered nonproductive" (66). According to Jeffrey Insko, such nonrenewable resource extraction has always been facilitated by advancements in technology and includes actions ranging from "the harvesting of salt and stone to fishing; logging; the mining of precious metals like silver and gold; the extraction of hydrocarbons like coal, oil, and natural gas through a variety of techniques" (173). Ben McKay, who coined the term "Agrarian Extractivism," explains that extractivism can also entail the agricultural exploitation of resources up to the point where the soil's fertility is exhausted.[11] Insko describes the logic of extractivism as a "form of taking without giving in return" (173). Extraction, he further maintains, has "produced the modern world" with its toxic wastes and destroyed landscapes and ecosystems, while at the same time having "yielded remarkable wealth (for some)" (174). *Mad Men* prominently

---

10   Regarding race and racism in *Mad Men*, see Sarah Nilsen, "'Some People Just Hide in Plain Sight': Historicizing Racism in *Mad Men*."

11   McKay coined the term to describe "the dominant soy agro-industrial complex" in Latin America (see also Cristóbal Kay's foreword in McKay). For more information on global agro-extractivism, see also James Petras and Henry Veltmeyer, "Agro-Extractivism: The Agrarian Question of the 21st Century."

features this capitalist logic, as it is set in an advertisement agency that deals with clients from different extractive and producerist industries, and as it depicts the unequal distribution of the monetary "benefits of extractive practices" (ibid.) through its focus on protagonists from the white middle- and upper class. I argue that such focalization contains an element of social commentary in the way that *Mad Men* purposefully highlights this wealth and marginalizes inequality and social justice issues to also match 1960s history. However, the series still celebrates wealth, especially when it stems from, or is connected with, extractivism, as in the case of Bethlehem Steel, or the aestheticized planes and automobiles.

Such celebratory reminiscing about the 1960s expresses a form of extractivist nostalgia. In this connotation, 'extractivist nostalgia' provides a twist on Robin Murray's and Joseph Heumann's notion of "environmental nostalgia," which they define as "a nostalgia we share for a better, cleaner world" (196). Already the picnic scene suggests that the 1960s are neither better nor cleaner, and, as Carson's *Silent Spring* reveals, it is already an era of anthropogenic environmental destruction, pollution, and large-scale extraction of resources. If we take the definition of the Anthropocene as having only *started* in 1950 (National Geographic Society), then *Mad Men* begins twelve years into the Anthropocene, a temporal setting in which the fast and "dramatic increase in human activity affecting the planet" (ibid.) and this 'Great Acceleration' starts to become palpable.[12] Still, at the time in which *Mad Men* is set, agricultural and fossil fuel extractivism had not yet progressed as much as it has today. In other words, in the 1960s, the environment was considerably less burdened with the effects of extractivism, and in particular, with greenhouse gas emissions as the major driver of our current climate crisis. According to this logic, there *is* an element of going back to a "better, cleaner world" depicted in the series, to an earlier time, to an earlier stage of the Anthropocene, when much of the depletion of

---

12   I use Eugene Stoermer's and Paul Crutzen's term of the Anthropocene here but want to acknowledge the controversies and criticisms surrounding it. Some scholars have challenged the concept, for example regarding its white- and maleness, for instance Giovanna Di Chiroor and Kathryn Yusoff. Moreover, while I use the National Geographic Society's starting point of the Anthropocene, I also want to highlight the larger debate about its onset and stress that the extractive economies under colonialism and slavery laid the foundation for the post-World War II wealth depicted in *Mad Men*. For the first mentioning of the Plantationocene, see Haraway et al., "Anthropologists Are Talking: About the Anthropocene."

resources and much of the profit that resulted from it during the Great Acceleration largely still lie ahead. Many of its negative consequences are still far enough in the future in *Mad Men* so that, in the show's temporal setting, extractivist products and practices can be enjoyed, both diegetically by the characters and extra-diegetically by the show's audience.

Extractivist nostalgia, as I use it, bears similarities to Stephanie LeMenager's concept of "petromelancholia," which she defines in *Living Oil* as the "the grieving of conventional oil resources and the pleasures they sustained" (102). One parallel between the two concepts is that they function as "mode[s] of preserving the happier affects of the U.S. twentieth century," while the "activism" (ibid.) that LeMenager argues petromelancholia can incite is not necessarily inherent in extractivist nostalgia. Extractivist nostalgia does not entail the "conditions of grief" that were set up in the 20th century due to our "[l]oving oil" so much that its "resources dwindle" (ibid.). It is not a mourning over the loss of the oil resources and the "pleasures they sustained" (ibid.), but a nostalgia for a time when the use of these resources could still be enjoyed without reservation. Such enjoyment without reservation is also part of nostalgia. According to Svetlana Boym, "[n]ostalgia (from *nostos*–return home, and *algia*–longing)" does not just mean "a longing for a home that no longer exists or has never existed" and a "sentiment of loss and displacement," but also "a romance with one's own fantasy," a love that "can only survive in a long-distance relationship" (xiii). With reference to Michael Kammen, Boym calls nostalgia a "guilt-free homecoming" (xiv). The extractivist nostalgia, then, allows viewers to come home or go back to a "better, cleaner world" where extractivism and its products can be enjoyed guilt-free when watching *Mad Men*.

The absence of guilt in extractivist nostalgia in comparison to (petro)melancholia also impedes the "incitement to activism" (102) that LeMenager describes. In the series, the depiction of petroculture does not call for activism to end extraction through feelings of grief or guilt. Quite the opposite: Petroculture and its objects are celebrated in the narratives and depicted for the viewer to nostalgically long for and enjoy without reservation, at least on screen. In comparison to petromelancholia then, extractivist nostalgia points to absences in texts rather than to presences and serves especially as a tool to analyze works that do not as openly deal with (oil) extractivism and environmental issues.[13]

---

13   Petromelancholia on the other hand seems to be useful for works that address petroleum more directly (cf. LeMenager, especially chapter 3).

In *Mad Men*, depictions of 'natural' or 'exterior' environments are rare, which also means that the series does not present its viewers with images and sites of extraction. In accordance with its televisual genre, much of *Mad Men* is filmed in studios and the cast, especially in earlier seasons, usually roams through the smoky offices of Sterling Cooper or stuffy suburban family homes. In some rare instances, we see Betty outside, horseback riding or driving her car to the supermarket, but she is mostly confined to the inside of her home. There, it seems like the furthest she can break out is her impeccably kept, Lynchian suburban lawn, as she does in "Shoot" (S1E9), where, in lieu of taking up her modeling career again and starring in a Coca-Cola campaign—which features a family having a picnic—she shoots the neighbor's pigeons dead.

Scenes that could cause feelings of guilt or grief in the show's audience, for example of ruined landscapes or sick workers, are left out. Another reason why such petromelancholic affects are not (necessarily) evoked in the viewer is that the violence of the Anthropocene that is depicted in the series can be too banal to be noticed. In her article on "The Banality of the Anthropocene," Heather Anne Swanson explains that

> [f]or many living in precarious situations, the Anthropocene is already life-altering, life-threatening, and even deadly. It comes in the form of a massive flood or a rising tide that takes their homes away. Or as an oil well that poisons the river on which they depend. But for others, especially the white and middle-class of the global North, the Anthropocene is so banal that they *do not even notice it*. It is the green front lawn, the strip-mall parking lot, the drainage ditch where only bullfrog tadpoles remain. (n.p. italics mine)

While Swanson discusses the Anthropocene in its contemporary manifestation here, the negative effects of extractivism, anthropogenic destruction, and climate change were already palpable in (and before) the 1960s, with the synthetic pesticides that Carson discusses, oil spills, or the pollution that "exacerbated [...] structural inequalities [...] along racial and ethnic lines" (Insko 174). As mentioned before, these effects are conspicuous in very few instances in *Mad Men*, for example when plastic pollution occurs or when the Junior League women try to stop the draining of three million gallons of water from the local reservoir for industrial purposes. Generally, however, the large-scale and relational effects of the Anthropocene and the concomitant extractivism are not flagged as problematic by the series, let alone by the characters themselves. More detailed environmental storylines could have the potential to raise the audience's awareness of extraction and its disastrous effects, but because of the scarcity of such storylines, the audience's environmental awareness or feelings of petromelancholia are not easily raised when watching the show and demand further cognitive and analytical labor.

Aestheticization of Extractivism

Don's pitch for his proposed Bethlehem Steel advertising campaign illustrates this unawareness of extractivism and ecological destruction. In a meeting with the boss of the Pennsylvanian company, Don explains that "we," meaning the modern citizens of the 1960s "take for granted the things we need the most: water, oil, electricity [...] steel" ("New Amsterdam," S1E4). Here, Don lists extractivist products of the Anthropocene, the greenhouse gas emission drivers, which go hand in hand with the "massive amounts of toxic waste, destroyed local ecosystems, [and] degraded landscapes" (Insko 174). Like the fictional inhabitants of New York in the series, who never actually take notice of the Bethlehem Steel out of which their city is built, the audience also does not get to see the real urban landscape and the raw materials that Sterling Cooper advertises, nor their sites of extraction. These non-fictional places that are part of the series' larger ecosystem, like the cityscape or the Bethlehem Steel mines, are not presented. Only the stylishly furnished Madison Avenue high-rises, which are constructed from this steel, are shown from the inside, as well as the further-mediated depiction of Bethlehem Steel in Sterling Cooper's advertising artwork. The underlying extractivist basis of this built environment is perceived as a given, disregarded, and it disappears under the selective historical narration. This narration of extractivist nostalgia creates, through blinkered aestheticizations, a longing for a place or past in which Anthropocene destruction does not seem to exist (yet).

Moreover, the things "we" need the most that are taken for granted—so much so, that they are not even mentioned by Don—are clean air and intact ecosystems that sustain human existence and ways of living. Instead, *Mad Men* often focuses on the things that suggest the "concentrated wealth in the hands of the few" (Insko 174), generated through extractivism, rather than depicting or referencing anthropogenic destruction or the cataclysmic and interconnected effects of extractivism. What we do see is a capitalist, extractivist aesthetics; a nostalgia for unhalted 'progress,' a linear, capitalist accumulation of wealth that builds upon the exploitation of resources, feeding into U.S. American mythologies of expansion and extraction. In the series, this extractivism is disguised through an aestheticized representation of the material wealth and lifestyle it enables. The Rockefeller's extractivist operations are hidden behind the romance plot between Betty and Henry that takes place in the wealthy, sub-urban setting. In the case of Bethlehem Steel, it is the product of extractivism itself, steel, that is aestheticized through advertising and that aims at increas-ing Sterling Cooper's and Bethlehem Steel's profit, and thus at further pushing and legitimizing the extraction of natural resources.

One instance when oil makes an appearance on the show occurs in "The Better Half" (S6E9), as Don runs into his now ex-wife, Betty, at an Esso (a Stan-dard Oil/ExxonMobil) gas station. In this scene, petroleum does not emerge in its liquid form and we do not see any of the protagonists getting gas, but it ap-pears as black stains on the shirt of the station attendant. Not only is the greasy substance placed into the background because it is mixed with the blueness of his fabric, but it also merely serves to highlight the attendant's sleazy behav-ior, as he lecherously stares at Betty leaning over her car window. His harassing stares at Betty's body as well as the more incredulous ones by Don who takes up the same viewpoint, and the camera's slow move up her naked legs, are a classic example of the male gaze that also directs the viewer to adopt the men's objec-tifying perspective. The presence of oil—already muted through its appearance in stain-form—is obscured by the clichéd way in which Betty is presented and almost vanishes because of the filmic centralization of her sexually aestheti-cized body.

Modes of Transport: Train

Another facet of such aestheticization of extractivism relates to its end-use products, in particular, to the modes of mobility represented in the show. The audience is not presented with images of extraction itself, but it sees prod-ucts that rely on extraction, namely the end-use products which Heather Anne Swanson would view as ubiquitous in the banal Anthropocene of the 21st cen-tury, but which were often reserved for members of the white middle class in the 1960s. The show presents these products, these fossil-fueled cars and kerosene-powered planes, through a form of nostalgic aestheticization that celebrates the luxurious products and individualized modes of mobility, which are detrimental to environmental well-being. It presents the audience with extractivist-nostalgic sets, and with denigrating depictions of more collective, lower emission modes of transportation, like the train.

Especially in the earlier seasons, Don Draper does not take the car, but the train to work, which is a more environmentally-friendly transport modality than the car or the plane. Yet, the train is used less and less frequently throughout the later seasons, the reasons being not just his move to the city, his increasing wealth and social status, or the historic reality in the early 1960s, when train passenger numbers declined and the number of passenger trains dropped by half between 1950 and 1970 (Britannica). The train holds negative connotations for Don in the early seasons, which are expressed in multifarious ways: It is depicted as restrictive, it threatens Don's identity, and it is a site of the reemerging trauma of his agricultural past. All these observations lead to the conclusion that the retrospective depiction of the train is far from nostalgic in Boym's sense of longing but agrees more with the protagonist's own definition of nostalgia.

The first, most obvious function of the train is that it takes Don to and from work. As such, this man-in-the-gray-flannel-suit mode of transport robs Don of his individuality. On the train, he meshes into the army of uniformly dressed businessmen who travel with him on this parochial connection between the office in the glamorous city and the stuffy family homes in the commuter belt. For Don, this home is located in Ossining, Westchester County, a small village that also serves as the fictional location in the stories of John Cheever. Cheever apparently inspired *Mad Men* creator Matthew Weiner, who once remarked that he chose the village for the same reason the short story author and novelist did: because of the maximum-security prison Sing Sing (Scholl). Against this institutional background, the train to Ossining becomes a symbol of confinement for Don, a forced return to a suburban nightmare that he flees so frequently. This implication of the train as (a threat of) imprisonment—in comparison to the car signaling freedom—is made manifest in episode three, when Don's train journey to work is interrupted by an unwelcome person from his past. Larry Kryszinski, a former army buddy, calls upon the protagonist repeatedly, but does not use the name familiar to the viewer and instead identifies him as Dick Whitman—the identity he has set aside to be able to escape his past and start a new, more successful life under the name of Don Draper. After Kryszinski repeatedly shouts out Don's bygone name, Don finally agrees to take up a short chitchat, but keeps looking around nervously during their talk, making sure nobody notices him being 'misnamed.' Don is clearly affected by paranoia during this occurrence, as it could put his rags-to-riches narrative, his professional success, and, ultimately, his freedom at risk. In this way, the train does not only literally connect the city with Ossining but could also figuratively lead Don straight into Sing Sing. Thus, it also serves as a site that reminds him of committing identity theft, the central crime on which his new life, and the series' narrative is based.

While Don's (mis)naming as Dick Whitman in this instance does not disclose his criminal offense to anyone familiar on the train, his unease about public transportation is repeated in the series. The train is not just immuring, but also a site of shame and trauma for Don, as it is a reminder of Dick Whitman's Depression adolescence in both psychological and historical terms—two implications that are intertwined in this context. Seeing it as an icon of a bygone era, the train reminds the protagonist of his poverty-stricken agricultural life in 1930s Illinois, where he had grown up as the son of a deceased prostitute and an alcoholic farmer, and had spent an unhappy, violent childhood full of loss and displacement. When he was ten years old, his father was killed by a kick from his own horse, which meant that his stepmother Abigail could not keep the farm and had to move into a brothel with Dick and his younger brother. These memories, manifested in fragmented flashbacks, do not address the precise course of events that lead to the family's eviction—after all, a young child would not know much about its family's exact financial circumstances. Although leaving the farm is not directly linked with the larger agricultural and economical changes in the run up to and after the Great Depression (the primary reason being the death of father Archibald), and despite the lack of information given about the era, the flashbacks do reference the dire socio-economic realities that many farmers faced in the 1930s due to the higher demands in produce and the concomitant rise in extractivist, industrial, and agricultural practices.[14] In other words, the Whitman family in *Mad*

---

14   Robin Fanslow explains that the recession after World War I led to a decrease in farm crop prices, which forced farmers to "increase their productivity through mechanization and the cultivation of more land. This increase in farming activity required an increase in spending that caused many farmers to become financially overextended" (n.p.)—a situation further aggravated by the stock market crash in 1929. As a result, many independent farms had to be given up, and "tenant farmers were turned out when economic pressure was brought to bear on large landholders" (ibid.). Simultaneously, heightened farming activities, such as intensified agricultural extraction, put a great "strain on the land"—a development that resulted in devastating dust storms during the Dust Bowl (ibid.). Moreover, the many small-scale farms were incorporated by larger, more productive, and mechanized farms, so that the percentage of work-

Men are not directly forced to leave their farm due to the financial overexten-sion then common amongst other farmers (Fanslow) resulting from industri-alization, mechanization, and other extractivist developments in agriculture. Still, with the depiction of the father as a destructive alcoholic and the gen-eral storyline of dispossession, this personal tragedy expresses the often-dev-astating situation of farmers in the 1930s. Again, we do not learn many details about what life at the farm was like during the Great Depression, except about Archibald's hostility towards a "hobo" who is taken in, fed, and given work by Abigail. The critical economic situation is alluded to—the family's visitor is "embarrassed to ask" for food, considering "we all have it hard right now" ("The Hobo Code," S1E8)—but the more substantial narrative point of these flash-backs is to explain that the self-designated "gentleman of the rails" from New York City plants the seed of the idea of a free life in young Dick Whitman. Like for this gentleman, the train becomes Don's opportunity of escape and freedom from his adolescent hardships, but it also remains a reminder of his murky per-sonal history, even in his new life.

The train is also the site where Don last sees his younger brother Adam, the only beloved member of his family, after his return from the Korean War and his concomitant adoption of a new identity. The fact that Adam also sees *him* from the train station platform, and thus realizes that Dick Whitman is not dead in the casket that had just been delivered to the family but continues to live as someone else, makes Don's identity change shameful: deception with respect to the law *and* to his loved one ("Nixon vs. Kennedy," S1E12). Adam's recognition only temporarily spoils Don's journey towards starting a new life of his own—a lady on the seat next to him urges him to "[f]orget that boy in the box" (ibid.) and buys him a drink, thus marking the beginning of his sexual

---

force employed in agriculture halved from 1900 to 1930, and the number of farms de-creased by 63 percent, while the average size of farms rose by 67 percent between 1900 and 2000. These few large farms have also shifted towards becoming more "special-ized," to use the U.S. Department of Agriculture's phrasing (Dimitri/Effland/Conklin 2). In other words, these industrial farms practice extractivist, monocultural agriculture and only produce one commodity in the 21st century, compared to five different goods in 1900—a development towards monoculture that reflects the "production and mar-keting efficiencies gained by concentration on fewer commodities" (ibid.). Moreover, "farm price and income policies [...] have reduced the risk of depending on returns from only one or a few crops," such as the Agricultural Adjustment Act (AAA) in 1933, which regulated "commodity-specific price supports and supply controls" (ibid. 2, 9).

sprees. Yet, the memory of this moment at the train station hurts Don and continues to do so up until the later seasons: The gaze on the platform comes back as a flashback to haunt Don's new life, and the memory of his brother reappears in person, as Adam accidentally comes across Don's picture in a magazine and tries to invade and harm his carefully developed new life by tracking him down at his office ("5G," S1E5). Read in this way, Don's etymological error of defining nostalgia as a "pain from an old wound" ("The Wheel," S1E13) later in the show has some truth to it, but also Boym's framing of the concept clarifies the scene. Don misses his brother but does not long for returning home to him, because he knows that this fraternal home that Adam imagines never existed. Moreover, he does not long for his past life that is signified by the train in the series, because he knows that his way of life—and the story in general—depends on a "[n]ostalgic love" that "can only survive in a long distance relationship" (Boym xiii). If the home from the past that "no longer exists" (ibid.), and the people that belong to it creep into the present, Don's survival cannot be ensured. Also, the cinematography of the scene at the train station expresses nostalgia in Boym's sense, as the two frames outside and inside of the train can be read as a "double exposure, a superimposition of two images—of home and abroad, past and present, dream and everyday life" (xiv): The audience sees the "past" Dick Whitman in the coffin outside taken "home," and the "present" (xiii f.) Don Draper on the train. If the one invaded the other, Dick's new life as Don would be harmed.

To sum up, the train takes Don back to his yesteryears as Dick Whitman, who is caught in the tight structures of a family that has never really been his own, with a father figure that seems to despise him and leaves him little room for personal growth or developing individual interest. This personal lack of individuality is not just reflected in Don's flashbacks of his provincial history in which freedom of opportunity seemed hard to reach, but also in the train's structure itself, as a collective, uniform mode of transportation. The scene in which Kryszinski bumps into Don on the train portrays well this double function of the train as both a place where Don is haunted by his past life and as a place that structurally disallows individuality. Before Kryszinski approaches him, Don studies a successful ad from his business rival in a magazine: the famous Lemon VW ad that casts the German cars ironically as flawed vehicles ("Marriage of Figaro," S1E3). What the encounters with both Kryszinski and the ad that embitters Don during his following work meetings highlight is not the competition between Sterling Cooper and other advertising agencies, but the competition between collective travel on a train and the more individualized and individualist mode of travel in a car. Similar to Don's childhood living in poverty with his restrictive family, no individual decisions of direction are possible on a train which runs on pre-configured rails, suggesting that there is no room for individualism, whereas the popularity of the automobile mode of transportation is grounded in its individual autonomy when it comes to reaching one's destination. Moreover, petrocultural commodification plays an important role here: When roads "replaced train tracks as the nation's circulatory system and in its metaphoric vocabulary," personal mobility was made into "a form of consumption" (Marling 58). Marling's remark also feeds into the U.S. American capitalist ideology that *Mad Men* often affirms: Trains are not a prestigious commodity you can buy or own like a car—and therefore also do not fit into the advertising logic that Don follows.

Modes of Transport: Planes and Automobiles

The chic airplanes with luxurious interior designs, and the streamlined, now vintage, automobiles that are frequently used by the characters in the show are modes of mobility that better fit into the capitalist ideology of commodity consumption than the train. In Julia Leyda's words, these petrocultural products rehash a kind of All-American "geographical mobility [...] [that] comes to symbolize a particularly modern, American, and 'Western' freedom" (25). Yet, as Dipesh Chakrabarty explains, such a "mansion of modern freedoms stands on an ever-expanding base of fossil-fuel use" (208). As mentioned before, the resource extraction and the oil that is necessary to fuel these petrocultural products is, to borrow Don's expression, "taken for granted" and remains largely invisible in the series. We never see the oil refineries—not even in the flashbacks to Don's past in Illinois, the state with the fourth highest capacity in refining crude oil (U.S. Energy Information Administration). This lack of visibility and thematization in the show conceals the Anthropocene to especially those white and middle class Americans who use these petrocultural products, and whose ignorance Heather Anne Swanson laments. Moreover, extractivism is disguised through a blinkered, even glorifying focus on the aircrafts and automobiles from the era, which are presented by means of nostalgic aestheticization.

Mad Men does contain some stories of harmful, even fatal aviation accidents, however. One example to be mentioned here is the story of account executive Peter Campbell, whose father died during the crash of an American Airlines flight ("Flight 1," S2E2). Despite the death of a family member, Pete does not grieve but uses this tragedy to convince the American Airlines executive to hire the agency, as he knows how prestigious the national airline would be on Sterling Cooper's client portfolio. More generally, aviation is presented as highly esteemed, in accordance with its apprehension of the time: Commercial aviation increased in the 1950s and remained an extremely luxurious and "stylish experience" (Bilstein) in the 1960s. Accordingly, flying is highly embellished in vintage aesthetics in the series and depicted as a departure into a modern world. This celebration is well visible in the promotional campaign for the seventh season, which is, according to the AMC clip, "all up in the air," and where the cast members are all photographed in bright, gaudy colors at the airport, looking polished, chic, and relaxed (Ockenfels and Guardian staff).

In season three, the celebration and aestheticization of aviation and air travel, although presented in a slightly different fashion, is even more prominent. The business trip to Baltimore that Don takes with Salvatore Romano (Sterling Cooper's art director) seems more like leisure time than work. The two drink and smoke on a plane that is tinted in friendly sunlight, which seamlessly fits into the chipper atmosphere on their descent into Friendship (sic) International Airport. They carelessly joke around, while the (stereotypically sexualized) stewardess waits on them with extra dedication and personal care. She asks them if they would like a refill before the landing, to which Salvatore responds: "Don't you need something to run the plane?" ("Out of Town," S3E1). With this joke, Salvatore equates the fossil-fuel powered machine with their alcoholized bodies, suggesting that both run on the same combustible. Thus, he humanizes the machine—comparable to Pete's favoring of having an airline on the portfolio rather than grieving his deceased father. The conflation of the plane and the men's identity in this scene is, moreover, reminiscent of Cara Daggett's concept of petro-masculinity, which suggests that "fuels mean more than profit; fossil fuels also contribute to making identities" (25)—in this instance, not a social, but a very much corporeal identity.

Such a connection between fossil fuel's end-use products and petro-masculine identity is also frequently apparent with regard to automobiles. When Dick Whitman begins his new life as Lieutenant Don Draper, he first works in a used-car dealership, trying to solidify his new identity. Soon, however, Anna, the wife of the real Don Draper, discovers her husband's impersonator there and confronts him with identity theft ("The Gold Violin," S2E7). Five episodes later, we find out that his strategy of consolidating his new life was to use Anna's late husband's serial number to get a driver's license ("The Mountain King,"

S2E12). Again, harking back to the concept of petro-masculinity, this marks an instance where Don's identity relies heavily on automobility: Without a driver's license, without being able to drive, the new Don Draper would not be able to attain his full-fledged personhood and would not be on his way to becoming a successful businessman.

The flashback to Anna's discovery occurs in response to Don's visit at a car dealership, where he takes a first look at his 1962 Cadillac Coupe de Ville—a scene that is hard to surpass when it comes to fetishizing petrocultural objects. It starts with a close-up of the shiny wheel, after which the camera moves right towards the back fender in rhythmic accord with Don's slow footsteps. Don almost dances around the car accompanied by a soft string-quartette Muzak melody, and the camera moves back left to follow him, granting the viewer an extra-long look at the car's smoothly shaped, shiny wings. Then the frame cuts to a wider angle, to enable us to see the spotless car in its full, cornflower blue bloom. The car salesman strikes up an aphoristic conversation with Don and tells him that the Dodge he drives at the minute is "wonderful if you want to get somewhere," but that the Coupe de Ville is "for when you've already arrived" ("The Gold Violin," S2E7). In relation to the protagonist, this line suggests that the car would further solidify both his position and his identity; he doesn't have to escape anymore and doesn't have to prove himself anymore—a surety that is also signified by the slowness of Don's footsteps, suggesting he has indeed arrived and does not have to go anywhere. To use Bert Cooper's words, who is one of the founders of Sterling Cooper's and Don's senior, Don can simply "take [his] seat" amongst "the few people who get to decide what will happen in our world" (ibid.) and enjoy his stolen life as Don Draper—an identity that this car enables and consolidates.

The car dealer also promises that Don would "be as comfortable in one of these [Cadillacs] as [he] would in [his] own skin." This assurance again humanizes the machine and conflates the man's identity with the petro-object, thus once more confirming Daggett's notion of petro-masculinity, that fossil fuels and the objects that rely on them make (human) identities. This verbal comparison of the car as a second skin is also confirmed visually later in the episode. Despite the aesthetic, flirtatious presentation, Don only buys the car upon his second visit, in which we see him sitting in the driver's seat, with his hands resting naturally on the wheel as if he was driving. Without taking a test drive, but with absolute assertiveness, he lets the car dealer know he would like to buy the car. The camera zooms in, so that he is perfectly embedded in the window frame of the car, his second, chrome skin. With the purchase, Don's "oil desires" are fulfilled (Daggett 32). He now owns the car that is proof of his achievement of the American Dream, for which more generally, cheap energy and "fossil fuel consumption became necessary" (ibid.). In this way, for Don, the individualized use of fossil fuels has an extra meaning in comparison to the train, namely that of achieved upward social mobility. Moreover, in accordance with the concept of petro-masculinity, which purports that "burning fuel was a practice of white masculinity, and of American sovereignty, such that the explosive power of combustion could be crudely equated with virility" (ibid.), the car ignites Don's virility as well. This is reflected in Betty's reaction to Don showing her the new car, when she tells him that the kids won't be home for an hour and asks if Don wants to take 'her,' this new metal mistress, around the block—her breathy tone and the long kiss following her remark insinuating her desire for a sexual encounter. The female personal pronoun used by Betty moreover proves the synonymity between women and cars as objects of desire that Cecily Devereux discusses in her article "'Made for Mankind': Cars, Cosmetics, and the Petrocultural Feminine," showing how our

> relations and our gendered relationships to commodities and the identity tropes they embody have been figured as the natural outcome of oil and progress, when in fact they form a complex series of socio-cultural entanglements in the West over the last two centuries, culminating in neoliberal politics and economics (Szeman/Wilson/ Carlson 10f).

The scene with the Drapers that follows is the family picnic scene, which, aesthetically, does not contrast this petrocultural intermezzo. On the contrary, both the automobile and the picnic scene have an idyllic, sunny feel, but only the latter is depicted as an environmentally deleterious action.

Conclusion

The use of fossil fuel is not marked as environmentally deleterious in the show, but the extractivism of the 1960s is celebrated through an aestheticized depiction of the end-use products of resource extraction that, for an environmentally aware viewer in the 21st century, are the mobility products of the banal Anthropocene. In this way, the petro-TV show *Mad Men* points towards uncomfortable societal issues of the past, but to modify Amitav Ghosh's words, oil does not stink in the series. He explains that

> [t]o a great many Americans, oil smells bad. It reeks of unavoidable overseas entanglements, a worrisome foreign dependency, economic uncertainty, risky and expensive military enterprises; of thousands of dead civilians and children and all the troublesome questions that lie buried in their graves [...] And to make things still worse, it begins to smell of pollution and environmental hazards. It reeks, it stinks. (30)

While the sexual harassment by the gas station attendant stinks to high heaven, the oil stains on his shirt are backgrounded against Betty's sexualized body. Neither do other extractivist products stink—Bethlehem Steel is framed as crucial for 'modern' citizens in the 1960s and is aesthetically advertised accordingly—while a more sustainable life on a farm, be it Marigold's or young Dick Whitman's, is depicted as dirty, improper, unhygienic, and thus a little titter-worthy, and environmental endeavors like Betty's are buried under the storyline of a romantic affair. By romanticizing, disguising, and celebrating 1960s fossil fuel extraction and consumption in these ways, the series creates an extractivist nostalgia, with an element of 'going back' to a fictional 'better, cleaner world'. In this world, the Anthropocene has not progressed as much, which is why the audience is still able to enjoy the luxurious aspects of modern petroculture. *Mad Men* does not suggest the obvious—that actions should have been taken back then could have prevented today's large-scale environmental destruction, which is becoming a more and more excruciating pain from a wound created in the middle of the 20th century.

References

Baruah, Debarchana. 2021. *21st Century Retro: Mad Men and 1960s America in Film and Television*. Bielefeld: transcript.

Bevan, Alex. 2013. "Nostalgia for Pre-Digital Media in Mad Men." *Television & New Media* 14 (6): 546–59. DOI: doi:10.1177/1527476412451499.

Bilstein, Roger E. "History of Flight–the First Airlines." N.d. *Britannica.com*. Accessed on September 25, 2021. https://www.britannica.com/technology/history-of-flight/General-aviation.

Boym, Svetlana. 2001. *The Future of Nostalgia*. New York, NY: Basic Books.

Britannica, The Editors of Encyclopaedia. 2021. "Amtrak: American Railway System." Accessed December 22, 2021. https://www.britannica.com/topic/Amtrak.

Byrnes, Delia. 2015. "'I Get a Bad Taste in My Mouth Out Here': Oil's Intimate Ecologies in HBO's *True Detective*." *The Global South* 9 (1): 86–106. DOI: doi:10.2979/globalsouth.9.1.07.

CBS News. 2010. "11 Ways Living Like 'Mad Men' Could Kill You." *CBS News*, July 27, 2010. Accessed December 17, 2021. https://www.cbsnews.com/pictures/11-ways-living-like-mad-men-could-kill-you/12/.

Chakrabarty, Dipesh. 2009. "The Climate of History: Four Theses." *Critical Inquiry* 35 (2): 197–222. DOI: doi:10.1086/596640.

Cromb, Brenda. 2011. "'The Good Place' and 'The Place That Cannot Be': Politics, Melodrama, and Utopia." In *Analyzing Mad Men: Critical Essays on the Television Series*, edited by Scott F. Stoddart, 67–78. Jefferson, NC: McFarland.

Daggett, Cara. 2018. "Petro-Masculinity: Fossil Fuels and Authoritarian Desire." *Millennium* 47 (1): 25–44. DOI: doi:10.1177/0305829818775817.

Dean, Will. 2009. "Notes from the break room: The Gold Violin.". *The Guardian*, March 25, 2009. Accessed on September 22, 2021. https://www.theguardian.com/culture/tvandradioblog/2009/mar/24/mad-men-television-review-s2e7.

Di Chiro, Giovanna. 2017. "Welcome to the White (M)Anthropocene? A Feminist-Environmentalist Critique." In *Routledge Handbook of Gender and Environment*, edited by Sherilyn MacGregor, 487–505. London: Routledge.

Dimitri, Carolyn, Anne Effland, and Neilson Conklin. 2005. "The 20th Century Transformation of U.S. Agriculture and Farm Policy." *United States Department of Agriculture: Economic Information Bulletin*, no. 3. https://www.ers.usda.gov/publications/pub-details/?pubid=44198.

Dunleavy, Trisha. 2019. "*Mad Men* and Complex Seriality." In *The Legacy of Mad Men: Cultural History, Intermediality and American Television*, edited by Karen McNally et al., 47–62. Cham: Palgrave Macmillan.

Etemesi, Philip. 2020. "*Sons of Anarchy*: Top 10 Bikes Owned by SAMCRO Members, Ranked." *Screen Rant*, October 1, 2020. Accessed on December 19, 2021. https://screenrant.com/sons-anarchy-top-samcro-member-bikes/.

Fanslow, Robin A. 1998. "The Migrant Experience: Voices from the Dust Bowl: The Charles L. Todd and Robert Sonkin Migrant Worker Collection, 1940 to 1941." *Library of Congress*, June 4, 1998. Accessed on December 13, 2021. https://www.loc.gov/collections/todd-and-sonkin-migrant-workers-from-1940-to-1941/articles-and-essays/the-migrant-experience/.

Ghosh, Amitav. 1992. "Petrofiction: The Oil Encounter and the Novel." *The New Republic*, March 2, 1992, 29–34.

Griswold, Eliza. 2012. "How 'Silent Spring' Ignited the Environmental Move-
    ment." *The New York Times*, September 21, 2012. Accessed on December 18,
    2021. https://www.nytimes.com/2012/09/23/magazine/how-silent-spring
    -ignited-the-environmental-movement.html.

Haraway, Donna, et al. 2015. "Anthropologists Are Talking: About the Anthro-
    pocene." *Ethnos* 81 (3): 535–64.

Insko, Jeffrey. 2021. "Extraction." In *The Cambridge Companion to Environmental
    Humanities*, edited by Jeffrey Cohen and Stephanie Foote, 170–84. Cam-
    bridge: Cambridge University Press.

Kay, Cristóbal. 2020. "Foreword." In McKay, 2020. n.pag.

LeMenager, Stephanie. 2014. *Living Oil: Petroleum Culture in the American Cen-
    tury*.Oxford: Oxford University Press.

Levine, Caroline. 2013. "The Shock of the Banal: *Mad Men*'s Progressive Re-
    alism." In *Mad Men, Mad World: Sex, Politics, Style, and the 1960s*, edited by
    Lauren M. E. Goodlad, Lilya Kaganovsky, and Robert A. Rushing, 133–44.
    Durham, NC: Duke University Press.

Leyda, Julia. 2016. *American Mobilities: Geographies of Class, Race, and Gender in US
    Culture*. Bielefeld: transcript.

Leyda, Julia, and Diane Negra. 2021. "Television In/of the Banal Anthropocene:
    Introduction." *Screen* 62 (1): 78–82. DOI: doi:10.1093/screen/hjab006.

MacDuffie, Allen. 2020. "Seriality and Sustainability in *Breaking Bad*." *Cultural
    Critique* 106 (1): 58–89. DOI: doi:10.1353/cul.2020.0002

Marling, William. 1995. *The American Roman Noir: Hammett, Cain, and Chandler*.
    Athens, GA: University of Georgia Press.

McKay, Ben M. 2020. *The Political Economy of Agrarian Extractivism: Lessons from
    Bolivia*. Black Point: Fernwood Publishing.

Murray, Robin L., and Joseph K. Heumann. 2009. *Ecology and Popular Film: Cin-
    ema on the Edge*. Albany, NY: State University of New York Press.

National Geographic Society. 2019. "Anthropocene." Accessed on September 24,
    2021. https://www.nationalgeographic.org/encyclopedia/anthropocene/.

Nilsen, Sarah. 2014. "'Some People Just Hide in Plain Sight': Historicizing
    Racism in *Mad Men*." In *The Colorblind Screen: Television in Post-Racial Amer-
    ica*, edited by Sarah Nilsen, 191–218. New York, NY: New York University
    Press.

Ockenfels, Frank, and Guardian staff. 2014. "*Mad Men* Season Seven: New
    Photos Show Bright Future—in Pictures." *The Guardian*, March 14, 2014.
    Accessed on September 25, 2021. https://www.theguardian.com/tv-and-r

adio/gallery/2014/mar/14/mad-men-season-seven-new-photos-bright-fu
ture-gallery.

Palatinus, David L. 2017. "Humans, Machines and the Screen of the Anthropocene." *Americana E-Journal of American Studies in Hungary* 13 (2), http://am
ericanaejournal.hu/vol13no2/palatinus.

Parrott, Billy. 2012. "The 'Mad Men' Reading List." *The New York Public Library*,
February 27, 2012. Accessed on November 6, 2022. https://www.nypl.org/
blog/2012/02/27/mad-men-reading-list.

Petras, James, and Henry Veltmeyer. 2014. "Agro-Extractivism: The Agrarian
Question of the 21st Century." In *Extractive Imperialism in the Americas*,
edited by James Petras et al., 62–100. Leiden: BRILL.

Rome, Adam. 2003. "'Give Earth a Chance': The Environmental Movement and the Sixties." *Journal of American History* 90 (2): 525–54. DOI:
doi:10.2307/3659443,

Rosenheck, Mabel. 2013. "Swing Skirts and Swinging Singles: *Mad Men*, Fashion, and Cultural Memory." In *Mad Men, Mad World: Sex, Politics, Style, and
the 1960s*, edited by Lauren M. E. Goodlad, Lilya Kaganovsky, and Robert A.
Rushing, 161–80. Durham, NC: Duke University Press.

Sannwald, Daniela. 2014. *Lost in the Sixties: Über MAD MEN*. Berlin: Bertz + Fi-
scher.

Scholl, Diana. 2009. "Live Like a Mad Man." *Westchester Magazine*, October 20,
2009. Accessed on December 13, 2021. https://westchestermagazine.com/l
ife-style/history/live-like-a-mad-man/.

Semigran, Aly. 2014. "Why Roger's Daughter Margaret on 'Mad Men' Could
Prove the Deadly Megan/Sharon Tate Theory Right." *Bustle*, May 5, 2014.
Accessed on December 18, 2021. https://www.bustle.com/articles/23346-w
hy-rogers-daughter-margaret-on-mad-men-could-prove-the-deadly-me
gansharon-tate-theory-right.

Supran, Geoffrey, and Naomi Oreskes. 2021. "The Forgotten Oil Ads That
Told Us Climate Change Was Nothing." *The Guardian*, November 18, 2021.
Accessed on December 06, 2021. https://www.theguardian.com/environ
ment/2021/nov/18/the-forgotten-oil-ads-that-told-us-climate-change-w
as-nothing?utm_source=instagram&utm_campaign=oilads.

Svampa, Maristella. 2015. "Commodities Consensus: Neoextractivism and Enclosure of the Commons in Latin America." *South Atlantic Quarterly* 114 (1):
65–82.

Swanson, Heather A. 2017. "The Banality of the Anthropocene." *Society for Cultural Anthropology*, February 22, 2017. Accessed on July 28, 2021. https://culanth.org/fieldsights/the-banality-of-the-anthropocene.

Szeman, Imre. 2013. "How to Know About Oil: Energy Epistemologies and Political Futures." *Journal of Canadian Studies/Revue d'études canadiennes* 47 (3): 145–68. https://muse.jhu.edu/article/542312.

Szeman, Imre, Sheena Wilson, and Adam Carlson, eds. 2017. *Petrocultures: Oil, Politics, and Culture*. Montreal: McGill-Queen's University Press.

Union of Concerned Scientists. 2007. "ExxonMobil's Disinformation Campaign." *Smoke, Mirrors & Hot Air: How ExxonMobil Uses Big Tobacco's Tactics to Manufacture Uncertainty on Climate Science*. Union of Concerned Scientists. http://www.jstor.org/stable/resrep00046.7.

U.S. Energy Information Administration. 2021. "Illinois State Energy Profile." Accessed on December 14, 2021. https://www.eia.gov/state/print.php?sid=il.

Weiner, Matthew, creator. 2007–2015. *Mad Men*. New York, NY: AMC.

Winckler, Reto, and Víctor Huertas-Martín, eds. 2021. *Television Series as Literature*. Springer eBook Collection. Singapore: Springer Singapore.

Yaeger, Patricia, et al. 2011. "Editor's Column: Literature in the Ages of Wood, Tallow, Coal, Whale Oil, Gasoline, Atomic Power, and Other Energy Sources." *PMLA* 126 (2): 305–26. DOI: doi:10.1632/pmla.2011.126.2.305.

Yusoff, Kathryn. 2018. *A Billion Black Anthropocenes or None*. Minneapolis, MN: University of Minnesota Press.

Feeling Senti-metal: Frontier Nostalgia, Mining Masculinity & Corporate Landscapes in the U.S. American Reality TV Series *Gold Rush*

Brian James Leech

When it comes to mining, U.S. American popular culture remains stuck in the past. Video games showcase low-tech mining with picks and axes. Country songs mourn tough times in company towns. Western films tell stories about 19th century gold rushes. YouTube videos examine abandoned mines. Environmental historian Jessica DeWitt argues that one reason for this tendency can be found in Dean MacCannell's 1976 book *The Tourist: A New Theory of the Leisure Class*. In that book, MacCannell argues that tourist destinations and historic sites enact a "museumization" of pre-modern jobs and their workers for the benefit of tourists. Doing so ensures that the popular image of industrial work remains stuck in the past because it is more comfortable for tourists to consume it that way (1). Historian Steven High agrees that North Americans still love to "museumify" former industrial landscapes despite worries that this act can "sanitize and romanticize" an often-uncomfortable past (423; High/Lewis 8).

Despite its present-day setting, reality television similarly sanitizes and romanticizes industrial work—although they do so for the sake of couch-bound, not wandering, tourists. Just like those tourist sites, they often rely on reenactments of the past. This approach figures prominently in the popular U.S. series *Gold Rush*, which, since it began in 2010, has often served as the U.S. Discovery Channel's top-rated show. Its multiplying spin-offs, like *Gold Rush: South America*, *Gold Rush: Whitewater*, and *Gold Rush: Winter's Fortune* have proven similarly lucrative for the network. In March 2020, the *Gold Rush* franchise featured four of the top five cable series amongst all American viewers ages 25 to 54, with men in particular driving its ratings up (Rumer). The show ostensibly provides viewers with a window into modern-day mining; yet, *Gold Rush* relies on long-standing, nostalgic tropes about resource extraction and settler colonialism.

Gold Rush is part of the reality genre described as "Macho TV," "Real Men at Work," or "Tough Guy TV" (Soviak 3). Among the most popular of these shows are *Ax Men*, *Bering Sea Gold*, and *Deadliest Catch*, all of which, just like *Gold Rush*, feature mostly hetersexual white men, joining in small bands, braving extreme conditions, and practicing the tough work of natural resource extraction. The long-running *Gold Rush* franchise has perhaps received the most scholarly attention. For Diane Negra, *Gold Rush* represents a peculiarly masculine reaction to the Great Recession in the U.S. because the original series featured a number of men who lost jobs in the Great Recession from 2007–2009 and hence sought new fortune in the Alaskan gold fields (123–9). Susan Alexander and Katie Woods, on the other hand, focus on the show's hypermasculinity, claiming that shows like this convince men to enact a somewhat anachronistic hegemonic masculinity in the present. For the authors, the show is about men being able to succeed today (149–68).

Most others, however, emphasize the show's depiction of a "rugged frontier" as the key to its continued success. For these scholars, *Gold Rush* provokes a romantic nostalgia for North America's "frontier"—a fraught term that wrongly implies adventure and exploration when, in North America's case, white settlement during the 18th and 19th centuries too often meant a violent conquest of the land from its original inhabitants (Limerick). For Shannon Eileen Marie O'Sullivan, *Gold Rush* hides the working class status of its main characters by instead validating them as ideal, authentic examples of a white masculinity undergoing crisis. Facing women's emancipation and calls for racial equality, white men responded positively to a show that offered an escape to the past—a frontier for white men to conquer (129–45). For William Trapani and Laura Winn, the show provides a masculine frontier in which all others, whether they be the protagonists' families, indigenous peoples, or modern society itself, disappear, leaving only white men's freedom and mastery (183–200).

This article will emphasize another function of *Gold Rush*'s frontier nostalgia: It obscures the modern mining industry while simultaneously justifying its continued extractivism. As a concept, nostalgia describes the common feeling of a longing (an *algia*) to return home (the *nostos*). Typically, this home no longer exists because of the passage of time, or it exists only as a myth; hence, a person experiencing nostalgia cannot truly return to this home despite their emotional attachment to it (Boym 543). Robert Solomon argues that nostalgia is a "form of sentimentality"—one that edits out "unpleasantness" to present a warm narrative about the past (19). Solomon defends this kind of editing, and it may contain virtues. As David Lowenthal suggests, nostalgia may "shore-up self-esteem," enable "enduring association," and "buffer social upheaval" (8–13); and yet, on a collective level, Lowenthal argues that pervasive nostalgia can also be harmful, hiding the truth about the past and present. *Gold Rush* practices its sentimental nostalgia by embracing an imagined American mining past—a time when life was supposedly simpler, risk-taking was celebrated, and white men primarily performed tough work in nature, not behind a desk. *Gold Rush* does so by replaying old colonial gold rushes as contemporary adventures in which white men conquer exoticized—and often quite cold—places. The show's stories focus on small-scale prospecting and mining, suggesting they are a gamble that small groups of tightly-bonded, enterprising men can successfully undertake, just like their forebears supposedly did during the 19th century. For the prospectors in *Gold Rush*, white men's resourceful toughness and the location of small specks of gold are the true pathway towards mining success. *Gold Rush* portrays its mostly frozen landscapes as a challenging back-country, ready to be conquered, and not what they, in fact, are: long-inhabited places of modern industrial development.

The mining adventure stories told by shows like *Gold Rush* therefore continue to be used to justify extraction *in* and the exoticization *of* far-away lands. Indeed, reality television seems to have made older colonial narratives more palatable to some segments of the contemporary audience even as they might make other viewers uncomfortable with the colonialist heritage of mining. The show's sentimental portrayal of small groups of men obscures the fact that mining today is actually a highly-capitalized industrial affair, run by massive global corporations, all of whom have a larger impact on the environment than the tiny operations celebrated by *Gold Rush*. *Gold Rush* instead provides viewers with a landscape unburdened by supposedly modern trappings like global capital, a diverse workforce, industrial unions, or environmental concerns. Viewers come to believe that modern-day miners are simply continuing the nostalgic practices of the past, not enacting an extractive present.

Stories from North America's 19th Century Gold Rushes

The *Gold Rush* franchise draws upon a plethora of old colonial stories about the role of mineral wealth in driving white colonization. In particular, *Gold Rush* harks back to the global era of 19th century gold rushes. That era began with California in the United States in 1848, but people struck with "gold fever" also traveled to new mining sites across the Pacific Rim, particularly Australia and New Zealand, and then continued their search across parts of Africa. In North America, the U.S. West and both western and northern Canada became targets for gold seekers, with each new discovery triggering a new rush. Gold brought people from around the world to North America's mining areas, but Anglo, white settlers came to dominate the social, political, and legal systems (Mountford/Tuffnell 3–41; S. Johnson). Mining hence continued—and sometimes initiated—a process historians call "settler colonialism," a form of colonialism that demanded the permanent, often violent, replacement of the original inhabitants with a new society of settlers (Lahti).

Gold rush narratives in North America soon justified colonization in the name of gold. They often recounted miners' individual success in the face of arid lands and contentious natives. Historian Christopher Herbert explains that the mid-19th century conception of "white manliness" required itinerant miners to showcase their "bravery, emotional control, and self-reliance" (7). Facing great uncertainty in these unfamiliar lands, white men celebrated their supposed independence, juxtaposing this feature of their lives with the non-white peoples they encountered along the way. Whether done through letters home or newspaper stories back East, mining's "triumphalist stories," as literary scholar Janet Floyd calls them, came to emphasize American individualism and white men's triumph over a harsh environment (1–31).

These themes became especially prominent at the turn of the century. In Canada, just as in the United States, "the pursuit of mining riches" had long "played its part in fostering dreams of a transcontinental nation," as historians John Sandlos and Arn Keeling recently explained (38). Mineral exploration proved just as, if not more, central to Canadian colonization as it had in the United States (Zeller). The last rush of North America's Gilded Age happened in the Klondike region of Canada's Yukon Territory. A widespread depression coupled with an emerging mass media to turn this rush into a global phenomenon. Between 1896 and 1899, the Klondike "stampede" drew at least 100,000 prospectors, many from the United States, to a previously remote area in northern Canada.

The Klondike Gold Rush also became one of the most romanticized rushes in world history. Historian Ken Coates points out that it fit well with the era's fascination with adventure novels and rags to riches stories (21–35). Many also sensed that the Klondike would be "democratic"—anyone supposedly could make their own fortune with a bit of luck—an appearance that contributed to the wide reach of Klondike culture (Coates 26–28). *The San Francisco Call*'s edition from January 23, 1898, provides a good example of the rhetoric surrounding the rush north. A large spread titled "Picking Up Millions in Alaska" featured tales from "successful Klondike gold hunters." Miner George Clancy, for instance, noted his "discouraging trials" and the "biting cold," but still celebrated his "luck when I picked up a fortune on the Klondike one day." Another miner, D. Barnes, played up his triumph over typhoid and a winter unlike anything he had ever experienced. Another writer claimed to have "scratched $10,000 out of the earth with a little stick." One of the wives interviewed believed Alaska and the Yukon "a hard country for a woman." She wrote that "[I] would not take responsibility of advising any of my sex to go to the Klondike" ("Picking Up Millions"). This kind of narrative omitted the very real presence of women in northern mining areas, including both indigenous women and migrants who worked their own claims (H. Green; Porslid; Zanjani; Spude; Nystrom).

Jack London's *The Call of the Wild* remains the most famous literary representation of the Klondike gold rush. In this tale, a dog named Buck is stolen from his idyllic southern California home and brought to the supposedly uncivilized Klondike. Buck becomes the best of the sled dogs through learning to physically dominate them. Experiencing the harsh environment leads Buck to become progressively feral. When the Native American Yeehats murder his owner, Buck kills several of them in vengeance. Hearing the "call of the wild," Buck joins a wolfpack at the end of the short novel, which was originally serialized for the *Saturday Evening Post* in 1903 (London 2009). Here London presents the trope of a white hero—but in the form of a dog—who learns the ways of the unforgiving environment and then comes to dominate the indigenous dogs and peoples (Higginson 317–32). The book moved away from the "emotional control" idea that had been prominent in the original gold rushes, suggesting that men sometimes had to become violent to protect or revenge their families. In dismissing the indigenous people who lived in areas that European-Americans planned to conquer and extract from, this expansionist discourse supported empire-building projects in the North and justified the violence that made those projects possible. Although Jack London and the letter writers of *The San Francisco Call* had all traveled to the Klondike, the public rhetoric they shared romanticized the triumph of white manliness over the extreme environment. Little thought was given to the original inhabitants of the land, except as obstacles to overcome. For instance, the village of the Tr'ondëk Hwëch'in was forcibly relocated away from the Klondike's new mining center, Dawson City, following the Gold strike (Sandlos/Keeling 69).

This public discourse also omitted letters and journals from men and women who returned from the Klondike broke and sometimes broken. Examples include a letter from the Klondike trail by Anna J. Rickenback back to her home in California. Distraught, she explained that a snow slide had buried many of her traveling companions and a blizzard had almost killed the rest. Edward C. Sharpe also traveled to the Klondike gold region. Sharpe's first diary recounts an exciting adventure towards fortune—both in drama and comedy—of a trip up the Klondike. It was published in the Seattle *Argus* in 1897. Sharpe's second diary describes a painful, grueling trip back south, absent any wealth, all while suffering from a tuberculosis that would soon take his life. This second diary was not published, perhaps because it failed to fit the public romanticization of the Klondike rush. The lessons taught by this public rhetoric were simple: The cold North would be conquered by respectable white men willing to endure its hardships. The common experience of failure was typically omitted entirely from the discourse.

Why were stories about the Klondike gold rush so disconnected from reality? One reason is a long-standing association in both Canada and the U.S. between their less-populated areas and individual freedom. By the middle of the 19th century, the emerging idea of a "Wild West" had connected historical figures like Daniel Boone and mythical creations like the characters in James Fenimore Cooper's *Leatherstocking Tales* to male "adventure and comradeship in the open air," as one classic analysis put it (Smith 52). Reliant on their own backcountry skills, male characters could make and re-make themselves because they lived far away from the centers of power.

Another reason is that these Klondike stories were created at the same time that many North Americans had become quite anxious about the loss of their "frontier." For historians like Frederick Jackson Turner, Americans' encounter with a supposedly unpopulated "frontier" as they moved West made them distinct from Europeans. Turner has labeled his ethno-centric frontier as the "meeting point between savagery and civilization" (38). As many critics have since pointed out, Turner pretended that indigenous people were part of a "savage" environment, while white people represent the coming "civilization." (Limerick 17–32). For Turner, white Americans' struggle to make a new life amidst an often-unforgiving environment shaped them into a "stalwart," "rugged," and "restless" folk who were truly paragons of resourceful "individualism" (37–62). He even claimed that the frontier experience had similarly created American institutions, including democracy. Like many of his generation, Turner worried that white people now inhabited much of this former frontier—hence, America and its Americans might lose their distinctive qualities (Wrobel).

Once Americans became convinced that this imagined frontier had, indeed, closed, frontier anxiety soon became frontier nostalgia. Theodore Roosevelt, for instance, expressed the increasingly common belief that Americans needed to preserve elements of the frontier experience. Roosevelt celebrated his "strenuous life" out West in the Dakotas because it provided him with hardships. In overcoming the West's challenges, he had learned the value of hard work, gained physical prowess, and learned the importance of bold action. Many Americans agreed that the lack of a frontier would feminize American men. The saving of purportedly "wild" spaces through the conservation movement grew partly out of an attitude that saving the frontier backcountry would similarly save white people—especially men. At the same time, a new cultural emphasis on physical fitness, organizations like the Boy Scouts, and even increased American involvement in global affairs all intended to provide men with experiences that could test and hence renew their masculinity (Wrobel; Etulain 5–30; Slotkin 29–62).

Klondike stampeders in the 1890s had clearly imbibed this hinterland mythos. Their initial letters home, before so many of them experienced failure, often expressed a rejection of industrial, urban life and an embrace of adventure. Historian Kathryn Morse explains that Klondike miners wanted more than just gold out of their participation in the rush. They also "looked to gold mining for other things that they felt to be absent from industrial life: adventure, simplicity, freedom, independence, satisfaction, a connection between hard work and wealth, and an invigorating, physical engagement with the natural world" (Morse 117). In their accounts, the remote North represented a fresh start and a mythic adventure for many of the men and women who joined the trail.

By the early 20th century, this settler colonial view had become codified in the Western—an important genre in novels, film, and, by the middle of the century, TV shows. As historian Richard Etulain puts it, the Western's frontier myth portrayed underpopulated places as "in need of double doses of civilization," forcing its "strong masculine heroes" to "conquer the demanding landscapes and challenging natives of the New Country" (30). In an altered form, many of these same elements—including risky exploration, the challenges of the natural environment, nostalgia, and white masculinity—have shown up in what Kristin Jacobson calls the "adrenaline narrative." This popular kind of writing (and filmmaking) presents its audience with adventurous journeys into nature and protagonists who experience heightened, extreme forms of risk. Among Jacobson's examples is a popular 1990s book about an attempt at summiting Mount Everest, *Into Thin Air* (Krakauer), but many other examples can be found in television, including spinoffs from the *Gold Rush* franchise.

The Hidden Corporate Landscapes of *Gold Rush*

The reality TV series, *Gold Rush: Alaska*, reiterates many of these "frontier" ideas about white men, suggesting that they can rejuvenate both their masculinity and their pocketbooks through hard mining work in harsh environments. It began its run in 2010 by portraying Oregon father and son Jack and Todd Hoffman as average, but now unemployed, men who want to better provide for their families. They decide to gamble on their future by venturing to Alaska to find gold. In true Fiedleresque fashion, Todd leaves behind the women in his family but takes along his sons, making this a multi-generational male challenge (*Gold Rush: Alaska*, S1E1). In season one, Alaska proves unforgiving for the inexperienced gold hunters. Their hard work is valorized, but the Hoffmans have underestimated how much work it will take to get a small gold mining operation off the ground. The end result? Not quite fifteen ounces of gold—certainly not enough to have funded their operation (*Gold Rush: Alaska*, S1E11). They also received money from the network to be on the show, which made the enterprise worth their time and energy. The Hoffmans therefore return in season two, more confident in their mine; yet they fail once again and hence head to the famous mining region of the Klondike (*Gold Rush*, S2E2).

In this second season, we meet new characters, most of whom continue to be white men seeking to exploit the northern landscape, just as in 19th century mining stories. One of the new cast members is Parker Schnabel, who, at age 16, takes over his grandfather John Schnabel's Big Nugget Mine (*Gold Rush*, season 2). The series soon splits into parts, following the Hoffmans in some sections, "Dakota" Fred Hurt and his crew in others, Tony Beets and his crew in yet others, and Parker Schnabel and his foreman Rick Ness in still others. In September 2021, the show kicked off its twelfth season, but at this point the Hoffmans had left the main show (doing so in 2018) (*Gold Rush*, S8E23). New miners have become important cast members, including Rick Ness, who has started his own mining operation. Likely because his family-owned good property and he already had a background in mining, the aforementioned Parker Schnabel is among the most successful miners on this show. Starting in season three, Schnabel has typically made more money from mining than the other featured cast members.

As might be expected for a show titled *Gold Rush*, the show spends much of its time focusing on the actual gold mined in the show but the gains are often quite small, especially in the early seasons. In season two, we learn that if the Hoffmans do not make a hundred ounces this mining season, their investors will pull out (*Gold Rush*, S2E18). In that same season Parker Schnabel needs to make a "last ditch effort" to find gold at another property (*Gold Rush*, S2E17). These rhetorical elements play up the drama, even if it is unclear if anyone is truly in danger of complete failure—especially given the complementary income from the TV network. Indeed, the low amounts of gold mined help to increase the tension, as there are constant concerns that the miners will not hit their expectations.

The mined amounts are a pittance when compared to the large enterprises that make up the modern mining industry. For example, Alaska's Fort Knox Gold Mine, an open pit, run by the Toronto-based Kinross Gold company, is a massive operation that pays $80 million in annual wages to 650 employees. In 2018, Knox employees poured 255,000 ounces of gold (Lasley). The biggest gold mines in Canada create even more revenue. The Canadian Malartic Mine, for instance, fed its mill with 55,000 tonnes/day of ore, producing around 569,000 ounces of gold in the shortened 2020 season (Bosov). These totals dwarf the figures on *Gold Rush*. The largest amount of gold mined by any of the crews on *Gold Rush* so far came from Parker Schnabel's crew, which achieved 7,500 ounces of gold in season 11 (*Gold Rush*, S11E21). Other crews have been much less successful. In season seven, Todd Hoffman completely failed at a site in the state of Oregon, and then his crew barely reached break-even at a Colorado site (*Gold Rush*, S7E14 and E21). In other words, the crews practicing small-scale mining on *Gold Rush* are not representative of how most of the mining industry and its profit work today.

The small scale of each enterprise on *Gold Rush*, however, makes it possible to celebrate miners as resourceful entrepreneurs, just as earlier gold rush stories celebrated their own protagonists. Parker Schnabel, for instance, is treated as a gold mining prodigy because of his young age, despite the fact that he had been handed a successful mining operation by his grandfather. The show's narration continually tells viewers about the industriousness and resourcefulness of the crews as they try to manipulate old mill technology, build treacherous roads, and dig water-filled glory holes. In the view of the show, these small teams are successful due to their own skills, not due to their reliance on the knowledge and technological advances of a global extractive industry. The show therefore draws upon older ideas about the West and the North—as places where self-made men prove their worth without others' help.

Indeed, no one on the show is portrayed as working for anyone else. Rick Ness serves as the foreman for Parker Schnabel in many episodes, but his lower place on the totem pole barely received a mention. He is even allowed to disagree with his boss as a way to increase tension on the set. Having proven his masculinity and mining prowess, Ness obtains his own crew and sets off to run his own operation in later seasons (*Gold Rush*, S9E1). When we do meet other crew members, they appear as roughly equal members of a camaraderie, not as workers trying to earn a paycheck. When a crew member leaves, it is often in a dramatic way. Cast member Dave Turin, for instance, left the show after a fistfight with another crew member (Pruitt-Young). Viewers of *Gold Rush* are not supposed to think about employer-worker relations at a modern workplace but about "adventure and comradeship in the open air," just as in 19th century frontier narratives (Smith 52).

The small scale of the mining operation also hides any environmental damage produced by extractive industries. At worst, we see small "glory holes" or tiny mills in *Gold Rush* episodes. The massive scale of an operation like the Canadian Malartic never appears. We do not learn about the environmental agencies' concerns about mine cleanup, nor problems related to property ownership. One 2018 article discusses what happened in Park County, Colorado, where some members of the *Gold Rush* show operated a dredge near a rural area called Fairplay. The show's presence caused local consternation. There was a re-zoning of land favorable to mine development by the *Gold Rush* show, followed by major concerns about contamination when the dredge dug up old tailings that likely contained mercury (Queen). State regulators in Alaska similarly feared that the show gave the wrong impression of the state. As one article puts it, "some worry about the message that's being sent to roughly 3 million American viewers who've tuned in: The Last Frontier is a land where anything goes" in terms of extraction (A. Green).

This utilitarian view of natural resources stands out—the earth is only important because it might provide the protagonists with gold. Even though the show often relies on sweeping shots of beautiful, supposedly uninhabited landscapes, it also portrays the environment as simply being there to serve people. Because the mining sites are remote, the show implies that mining them causes no real harm to society. In the show, miners and mining companies are portrayed as never having to think about their environmental impact, which is clearly not the case in an industry that, partly due to the demands of governmental regulators, employs specialists to plan for and manage environmental mitigations.

Another industry obscured by the filming techniques is the entertainment industry, from which most of the cast is making their money. The TV network pays stars like Schnabel a rumored $25,000 an episode. That amount becomes multiplied by at least 20 episodes in a season, plus episodes for a number of spin-offs. There is a good reason why Schnabel's net worth is in the millions, and it has less to do with his actual mining prowess than with his outspoken nature on a reality show (Hamilton; Mitra). Furthermore, these frontier-based shows never reveal the large camera crews who are obviously present behind the scenes. We never learn who the people on the crews are or what role they play. The goal is instead to emphasize the supposed independence and loneliness of the "rugged" miners. This franchise therefore acts much like other shows that play with frontier nostalgia and the adrenaline narrative. *Man vs. Wild*, with Bear Grylls, is a show that pretends the protagonist is completely alone when he is, in fact, operating with a large production crew. In *Gold Rush*'s portrayal, Alaska and the Yukon remain an empty wilderness bereft of "civilization," beyond the somewhat antiquated mining technology we see. The globalized entertainment machine that creates and promotes the show thus hides amongst images of trees, mountains, mines, and the protagonists' masculine posturing.

Replaying the Gold Rush through *Parker's Trail*

The frontier nostalgia and colonialist view practiced by *Gold Rush* goes to extremes in the spinoff series, *Gold Rush: Parker's Trail*. Rebecca Weaver-Hightower and Janne Lahti have suggested that settler colonial films allow "descendants of settlers to relive the experiences of first-generation settler ancestors to better appreciate their 'sacrifice' and legacy" and, through repetition, to remind "viewers that settlement is far from accomplished" (3). This kind of portrayal "offers viewers a recreation of the historic events of settlement," then connects that celebrated past to the present (Weaver-Hightower/Lahti 3). *Gold Rush: Parker's Trail* fits this framework. Instead of showcasing modern mining, this spinoff spends even more of its time promoting a settler colonial view of the North, as it repeatedly connects Euro-American colonizers of the 19th century to rugged white people in the present. The show presents a literal "recreation of the historic events of settlement" by re-playing the Klondike Gold Rush of the 1890s in the present-day (Weaver-Hightower/Lahti 3).

The 2017 season of *Gold Rush: Parker's Trail* involves Parker Schnabel, his foreman, Rick Ness, his filmmaker friend, James Lavelle, and a female wilderness guide, Karla Charlton. They all decide to honor Parker's grandfather, who recently passed away, by attempting the 600-mile Chilkoot trail from the Alaskan coast to Dawson City in the Yukon. They plan to follow the same trail that many of the 100,000 stampeders on the first rush followed to get to the Yukon Territory. It is not clear exactly how this trek will honor his grandfather, who, despite being labeled a "pioneer," did not arrive in the North until 40 years after the 1890s Klondike gold rush. Still, there is obvious emotion expressed by protagonist Parker Schnabel, who deeply mourns his role-model grandfather, the first miner in his family. In the show, Schnabel's sentimental attachment to his grandfather quickly funnels into nostalgia for a by-gone era of supposedly "rugged" miners and their conspicuous extraction.

The first episode begins by considering the difficulties facing the modern-day crew. Karla Charlton criticizes "these alpha males," who have not prepared for the trip properly, having done no real training for an expedition that will involve intense climbing and extensive canoeing. Nor are they doing the trip at an appropriate time—as the narrator emphasizes throughout, winter is closing in on the Klondike, and they are leaving a couple of months later than the "pioneers" before them. Now they have to face what the narrator calls "the cold hard reality of the frozen North." We learn that for much of the trip, they will be alone and so they have to actually "film themselves" this time. They are going to prospect along the way, the narrator tells us, picking up gold that the original rushers missed (*Gold Rush: Parker's Trail*, S1E1). Just like the older colonial stories about mining, *Gold Rush: Parker's Trail* drives home the idea that white people are meant to struggle through an uncomfortable environment on their path to riches and success. Although Charlton's early comments about "alpha males" pokes fun at the masculinity involved in this mythos, the two men's lack of physical fitness, in the narrator's portrayal, quickly becomes just another hurdle that they have to overcome in "the frozen North" rather than a full-fledged critique of the exaggerated masculine roles the men are playing.

Viewers soon learn that the four travelers are going out of their way to make the trip as hard as possible, largely because doing so emphasizes their sentimental kinship with 1890s travelers. As Lavelle puts it in episode 1, "[w]e want it to be as authentic as possible. It should be as tough for us as it was for the old timers" who hit the trails in 1897 and 1898 (*Gold Rush: Parker's Trail*, S1E1). Authenticity therefore becomes their preferred measurement of success—partly because the nostalgia driving the trip makes the three men believe they can enact a return to a famous place. They don't recognize that the Klondike trail itself no longer exists as it did in the 1890s because it radically changed over time. For instance, later episodes feature our intrepid team having to move their canoes around modern dams. Hence, the men have to continually deny themselves the many advantages contemporary travelers would have. Self-inflicted suffering serves as the pathway to authenticity. When Parker Schnabel later remarks that early miners "were some damn tough guys," the viewer is clearly meant to connect "old timers" to the white men currently undertaking a perilous journey (*Gold Rush: Parker's Trail*, S1E3).

Authenticity also becomes their measurement for success because being "authentic," in their view, allows them to imagine themselves as mining men who are individualistic, tough, and resourceful. During the first part of their trip, the crew climbs a mountain range, including a steep ascent called the "golden staircase" that the narrator tells us "broke" many original "pioneers." Yet today's crew learns to follow Schnabel's admonitions of "Yukon or bust" and "never give up," with one hiker yelling into the air that he will defeat nature. Finally, they reach the summit of "the toughest hike I've ever done," Schnabel tells us (*Gold Rush: Parker's Trail*, S1E1). By playing pioneer, the protagonists want to point out the "sacrifice" of people involved in the original colonial project. The end result is a sentimental justification of continued domination of mining in the area; it is supposedly part of these white people's hard-earned legacy.

By enacting an "adrenaline narrative," the show portrays nature as the main challenge the crew must overcome. Nature poses a heightened risk to every one of their actions. After their big hike in the first episode, Parker's crew faces tough winds on a lake they are supposed to canoe. After waiting for the winds to subside, some members of the crew want to take a train line around the lake. Schnabel, however, refuses to use "modern technology" like engines to pay ode to the original Klondike stampeders. Instead of "cheating," the crew finds a wagon on the rails, and then move their canoes on the train line by pushing it around the first lake (*Gold Rush: Parker's Trail*, S1E2). It is not clear why using rails without an engine somehow made their solution more true to the "authentic" trip they intend, but viewers are reassured that the crew has not broken any of the imagined rules Parker has set. They are still able to accurately play pioneer.

By episode two, the crew is running out of food. As with many adrenaline narratives, the show's narrator tries to exaggerate the danger, telling us our crew would otherwise starve. The four protagonists therefore have to go fishing and hunting, we are told, just like the "original pioneers" did. Yet both hunting and fishing prove tough to successfully complete in the November frost. Viewers also hear about bears and wolves seen along the trail, with the narrator noting what dangers this part of nature might pose (*Gold Rush: Parker's Trail*, S1E2). Each episode also reminds viewers of the great distance—600 miles total—for this trip, while cast members often explain that the crew is continually falling behind schedule if they are going to beat the icing over of the waterways. The heightened danger posed by nature thus provides viewers a reason to stay tuned and the protagonists with an ability to appear virtuous in facing off against the "wilderness" in each episode.

Despite this spin-off sharing the name *Gold Rush*, little actual mining happens. The small amount of prospecting the crew does mostly becomes another way for them to play pioneer. It is only in episode 3 that Schnabel decides to prospect for gold—changing the schedule in case they fail to make it all the way to the Klondike Region, where they had originally planned to prospect. With 362 miles still left to Dawson City, they find an old creek channel, dig out dirt, and use a pan to look for gold flakes. Seeing some promise, the crew crafts a make-shift rocker box out of a canoe paddle, a wool shirt, and some nearby trees, using it to help separate gold from gravel. They find a few flakes of gold and then decide to stake a claim for that spot—likely more for the sake of the show than as an actual prospect to later mine. The protagonists name their claim "Perseverance" in honor of the trawler boat that Rick Ness's grandfather operated, the grit shown by the Klondike's original rushers, and their own determination during the present-day journey (*Gold Rush: Parker's Trail*, S1E3). Just like the trip itself, which connected Schnabel's personal mourning to his nostalgia for the mining past, the name of their new claim connects Ness's personal mourning to this frontier myth. Viewers are meant to believe that members of the crew are therefore meant to mine the Yukon—their mourning justifies their mining. They are persevering in the same way as their ancestors.

During this episode, viewers only see old mining techniques, which the crew portrays as the "authentic" way to prospect. When Parker Schnabel finds a few flakes of gold in his pan, he tells viewers that "this isn't the motherlode but we found it just like the old timers did" (*Gold Rush: Parker's Trail*, S1E3). Hence, the show glorifies small-scale mining as exempt from the growing criticism the extractive industries face. It is a move akin to Clint Eastwood's Western

Pale Rider, which criticizes the environmental destruction caused by a massive mining enterprise. Yet, that 1985 movie sentimentally presents an alternative to corporate mining: a loving, cooperative community of small-scale tin-panners who are just trying to provide for their families, not trying to amass great wealth like the hydraulic corporation upstream (Murray/Heumann 57–8). *Gold Rush: Parker's Trail* similarly waxes nostalgia for miners living the "strenuous life." In doing so, it portrays small-scale mining as a long-standing part of the region, making mining and its practitioners seem like a natural feature of the landscape.

This representation of small-scale mining as the "authentic" form of mining also does not match the reality of the late 19th century Klondike. No matter how democratic shows like *Gold Rush* make the Klondike out to be, "as a mining phenomenon, the Klondike was also emblematic of the decisive shift away from individual and small-scale mining and toward highly-capitalized, technology-intensive extraction methods" (Sandlos/Keeling 67). During the initial stages of the rush (1897–1898), so many people took small claims in the Yukon that they completely denuded the landscape. By 1899, miners had already begun mechanizing their operations by steam thawing the tundra, which led to steam engines running hoists, steam shovels digging up creek beds, and some hydraulic mining systems, all of which employed wage labor, not truly independent producers (Sandlos/Keeling 74). In other words, even during the original Klondike rush, mining practices quickly became labor- and capital-intensive and miners rapidly became wage workers. That true story becomes yet another aspect of the rush obscured by the show's romanticization of small-scale mining in both the past and present.

Despite proclamations of "Yukon or Bust," the crew's journey to the Klondike ends abruptly in the third episode. While attempting to disembark from his canoe, Parker Schnabel slips on ice and then falls into the freezing water. The crew quickly builds a fire and gives him dry clothes, thereby staving off the danger of hypothermia, but they all remain quite worried about the rivers icing up. They decide to abandon the trip with hundreds of miles yet to travel. Schnabel calls for a plane to take the group to Dawson City by air (*Gold Rush: Parker's Trail*, S1E3). We are told by the cast members and narrator that they have made a valiant effort on this true frontier mission. It is not a failure because they showed grit and determination. Parker Schnabel admits that nature's opposition to his trip is sadly out of his control and that his goal is probably not "worth dying for." Schnabel explains that "a lot of the old timers died," noting that only one in three "old timers" who set out for Dawson City actually made it there (*Gold Rush: Parker's Trail*, S1E3). The narrator concludes, "Parker, Karla, Rick, and James have tested themselves against the old timers of 1897. The freezing river forced them to complete the journey by plane but otherwise they've achieved their ambition" (*Gold Rush: Parker's Trail*, S1E3).

Like *The Call of the Wild* and like many Westerns, *Gold Rush: Parker's Trail* thus treats nature as the enemy—an enemy that people should try to conquer and even exploit but an enemy that also sometimes wins. By personifying the "Cold North," the show suggests that nature might not be worth saving. It is something to fight—and perhaps mine—instead. By making it appear that nature has simply won the battle this time, the show also removes any blame for this failure from the crew itself. Despite the crew's lack of preparation, their late departure date, and their insistence on "authentic," ineffective methods, the show allows them to remain just inheritors of an imagined "pioneer" past. When the crew's plane pulls into Dawson City, Parker registers his Yukon claim in the same way, we are told, as people did in the 1890s.

Throughout the early sections of the Schnabel crew's trip, viewers seldom see any other people, giving the impression that Schnabel and his crew are on their own in the "wilderness." However, at one point in episode 1, we visit the cabin of a lady who lives on Bennett Lake and who gives them gear that they had shipped directly to her—a scene that certainly points out quite a lot of "civilization" is present in the form of mail delivery and inhabitants (*Gold Rush: Parker's Trail*, S1E1). The one time the crew encounters many people comes towards the end of episode two. At that point, the crew is supposed to carry their canoes and supplies around a modern hydroelectric dam at Whitehorse—a city of 25,000. The narrator insists that this spot is the only true sign of "civilization" along the trip (*Gold Rush: Parker's Trail*, S1E2). As historian Traci Brynne Voyles puts it, mining regions labeled as uncivilized often become "wastelanded," made to look even more marginal and hence worthy of exploitation. This series does the same for the Klondike and Yukon. As far as *Gold Rush: Parker's Trail* is concerned, the Yukon remains the foreboding "wilderness" that miners in the 1890s encountered.

This spinoff series also directly ties the past to the present—giving us a direct line between white people braving the elements in the 1890s to white people in the 2010s. The opening titles to each episode remind the viewer that the crew of four are following "in the footsteps of legends." We are told that this crew will recognize the sacrifices of the men who "pioneered" through northern North America by re-enacting their colonial mining adventure. When the crew heads into Miles Canyon, for instance, the narrator tells us that 150 boats smashed into its walls during the original Klondike Rush (*Gold Rush: Parker's Trail*, S1E2). At another point, Rick Ness injures his foot. Viewers then hear a heartwarming story about perseverance as the crew member explains that his own relative once hurt a foot out in the backcountry but had to walk for miles so that he could get treated before going into shock. Hence, even a recent foot injury gains a sentimental connection to the frontier (*Gold Rush: Parker's Trail*, S1E2).

Because of Ness's injury, the crew is "forced" to make an unscheduled stop at an urgent care facility in the city of Whitehorse, which they follow up with stops at a bar and a hotel. Both the narrator and Schnabel tell us that this stop does not actually qualify as "cheating" because, during the original Klondike rush, men would often stop at Whitehorse to enjoy whisky, eateries, hotels, and perhaps even houses of prostitution. The narrator and Schnabel make sure to tell white male viewers of the show that "Donald Trump's pioneering grandfather" began the family's fortune by operating a restaurant, bar, and brothel in Whitehorse (*Gold Rush: Parker's Trail*, S1E2 and E4; Pearson). In other words, even when events skew far from what people would have encountered in the 1890s, viewers are told repeatedly that the men are still being "authentic" and honoring their ancestors by doing so.

Only one tough (and often frustrated) woman can come along, but only because she actually has the skills and training that her companions lack. In interviews after the main episodes, cast members suggest that Karla Charlton was clearly the reason the group made it as far as it did. Charlton consistently caught more fish than the men; however, viewers never see her fish in the main show—we see Schnabel and Ness catching fish. Viewers do briefly see Charlton setting up each campsite and cooking each meal, but her hard work often remains in the background (and unappreciated) so that viewers can focus on the men instead. In one case, viewers spend five minutes watching Schnabel and Lavelle bickering as they try to hunt in the dark while Charlton unassumingly fishes, cooks, and sets up the entire campsite (*Gold Rush: Parker's Trail*, S1E4). Hence, the show continually emphasizes the toughness of men overcoming nature, instead of the aptitude of a woman who understands the tasks at hand. At first glance, Charlton might seem like an equal partner to the others, but a deeper look shows that she serves largely as a nurturing presence, thereby affirming traditional gender roles. Charlton is often even seen "mothering" the men, scolding them for not properly training before the trip and worrying when they stay up late drinking in Whitehorse. She is always the calm one when the men become hotheaded. Women like Charlton therefore get to take part in the extractivist enterprise but only on the traditional, domestic terms that the men are willing to accept (Kaplan 581–606).

Charlton also plays an important role in connecting their trip to a sentimental past. Although it is clear that she is a well-trained wilderness guide, it is just not her training but her connection to the past—what the show labels her "Yukon blood"—that makes her truly qualified for this trip. The series therefore naturalizes the presence of both Karla Charlton, whose great-grandfather came during the 1890s stampede of Klondike "pioneers," and Parker Schnabel, whose grandfather they also count amongst the region's "pioneers" (*Gold Rush: Parker's Trail*, S1E1). In this way, the show erases indigenous people from the Yukon's past. White people like Schnabel and Charlton instead become imagined as the true "natives" to this region. This ethnocentric discourse mimics many colonial adventure stories, which often portrayed white "frontiersmen" like Daniel Boone and Natty Bumpo and even frontiers dogs like Buck as even better at tasks like hunting, fighting, and survival than the indigenous people around them—hence, portraying them as belonging to the land. Yet the show goes even further than this: Instead of suggesting that indigenous people are vanishing, as so many Westerns do, *Gold Rush: Parker's Trail* typically fails to mention them at all. In the show's telling, they have already disappeared. Even though Canada has undergone a recent movement to provide formal land acknowledgements that recognize the original inhabitants of the places where settlers live, *Gold Rush: Parker's Trail* largely fails to acknowledge that anyone lived in these areas before, during, or after enterprising white miners arrived. Yet, the name for the path Parker's team follows—the "Chilkoot Trail"—comes from the Tlingit Nation's name for it, the Tagish Khwáan lived further inland in the Yukon, and the Tr'ondëk Hwëch'in inhabited the area around Dawson City. We also get no mention of the fact that so many of the original white "pioneers" enjoyed many advantages, provided both by indigenous people and modern society. Many of these white people had indigenous guides who assisted them in the worst of circumstances. The original "pioneers" also made an aerial tramway to transport goods up the golden stairway and built the train line at Bennett Lake that Schnabel refuses to use. In other words, the nostalgia of Schnabel's crew blinds them to the fact that the Klondike trail had long featured many improvements and many assistants.

The *Gold Rush*'s crew attempting this new Klondike trip similarly received modern advantages hidden by the show's creators. Although the show pretends that only four people are on the trip, later interviews tell us about the "chase crew" that they meet with when they need to change camera batteries.

When Rick Ness injures his foot, it is this same "support crew" that intervenes. When Parker Schnabel ends the trip, he can pull out a radio to ask for a plane. In other words, the trip, at a longer glance, does not look like just four people versus the elements. The show's creators hide the elaborate staging, preparation, and backup systems that made such a long journey possible. This approach allows viewers to believe that our protagonists are truly re-enacting a nostalgic "frontier" adventure.

Gold Rush: Parker's Trail is therefore a mining adventure story that uses frontier nostalgia to justify both colonial projects in the past and resource extraction in the present.

Nostalgic Extraction

Most of the other mining shows on reality TV fit the Gold Rush model, whether it is Yukon Gold, Bering Sea Gold, Fool's Gold, Curse of the Frozen Gold, or Ice Cold Gold. Small teams of men explore new areas, extract resources, and justify their actions under the banner of the "frontier." One of the few outliers featuring a large working mine with many employees is Spike TV's Coal, which ran for one season in 2011. At first glance, it stands apart as an attempt to engage with a modern industrial workplace and yet it purposefully focuses on a smaller underground mine in Appalachia, not one of the massive, less labor-intensive, surface operations that now dominate the area's coal mining. As historian Bob Johnson points out, it also traffics in hyper-masculinity, emphasizing the dangers men face underground (111–38). Dramatic narration about methane, rock falls, and possible accidents highlights the risks of the enterprise, even as the show hides miners' actual reality, placing white veneers on all the miners' teeth and brand-new trucks on the set. As in other mining shows, the workforce is composed almost entirely of white men and each of them talks about his hard work as an impressive individual effort, not as part of a collective process. Despite some attention paid to the workforce, "the interests of the workers are identified with the interests of the owners without any hint of contradiction or antagonism—all aspects of work are understood purely in terms of productivity and profit," as literature scholar Tetiana Soviak explains (135). Instead, the manager of the operation is the show's hero. Although he spends most of his days safely ensconced in an office, the manager enjoys a portrayal as an entrepreneur fighting against mechanical breakdowns, federal regulations, and an unruly workforce (Coal, S1E1–7).

Therefore, *Coal* largely fits the *Gold Rush* model. It too focuses on a heroic entrepreneur conquering a challenging environment through older mining methods and the efforts of hardworking white men. It also reminds viewers of the long history of coal mining in Appalachia, justifying the mining present through its connections with a nostalgic, extractive past. Appalachia is the extractivist "backcountry," already sacrificed to mining. Meanwhile, some of the show's current miners were the progeny of retired miners; hence, viewers receive a suggestion that they are part of an unbroken line of miners. It is a move somewhat akin to *Gold Rush: Parker's Trail*, which repeatedly tells viewers about miner Parker Schnabel's grandfather, who is also a miner. Extractive work becomes seen as another form of family business—a long accepted tradition in North America. In doing so, U.S. shows continue to naturalize resource extraction in regions that are remote from large urban areas.

As the progenitor of shows like *Coal*, *Gold Rush* and its spin-offs therefore serve as good examples of the ways that North American reality television has hidden modern extraction behind a romanticized past. The effects of this portrayal have varied, but it is hard to see many of them as particularly positive. Instead of a complex present, we get a monochromatic past. The global nature of the industry disappears into a vague idea of frontier. Laborers are not seen as workers, but as "real men"—as embodiments of a supposedly "authentic" masculine lifestyle. Environmental issues do not exist in the frontier's supposedly pristine "wilderness." Whiteness and maleness are seen as mining's default, even as the mining industry itself searches for more women to be involved (Doku; Ellix et al.). Despite pretending that the show is "authentic," *Gold Rush* instead imbues its imagery and narration with frontier mythos, thus absolving viewers from their own complicity in colonial practices and modern-day environmental impacts. It is hard to know what a truly modern mining show would look like, but *Gold Rush* is not it.

References

Alexander, Susan M., and Katie Woods. 2019. "Reality Television and the Doing of Hyperauthentic Masculinities." *The Journal of Men's Studies* 27 (2): 149–68. DOI: https://doi.org/10.1177/1060826518801529.

Bosov, Vladimir. 2021. "Top 10 Largest Gold Mines in Canada in 2020-Report." *Kitco*, March 12, 2021. https://www.kitco.com/news/2021-03-12/Top-10-largest-gold-mines-in-Canada-in-2020-report.html.

Boym, Svetlana. 1992. "Stalin's Cinematic Charisma: Between History and Nostalgia." *Slavic Review*, no. 51, 536–43.

Coal. 2011. Season 1, Episodes 1–7. Produced by Original Productions. Aired March 30, 2011 to June 19, 2011 on Spike TV.

Coates, Ken. 1998. "The Klondike Gold Rush in World History." *The Northern Review* 19 (Winter): 21–35.

DeWitt, Jessica. 2021. "'Most of It's Mental': Extractive Nostalgia, Virtual Adventure, and White Masculinity in the Abandoned Mines Exploration Corner of YouTube." Presentation at *Emergence/y: Association for the Study of Literature and Environment*, Virtual Conference.

Doku, Linda. 2019. "Why the Mining Industry Needs More Women." *Forbes*, May 24, 2019. https://www.forbes.com/sites/woodmackenzie/2019/05/24/why-the-mining-industry-needs-more-women/?sh=5fe905c2585c.

Ellix, Hannah, et al. 2021. "Why Women Are Leaving the Mining Industry and What Mining Companies Can Do About It." *McKinsey & Company*, September 13, 2021. https://www.mckinsey.com/industries/metals-and-mining/our-insights/why-women-are-leaving-the-mining-industry-and-what-mining-companies-can-do-about-it.

Etulain, Richard W. 1996. *Re-Imagining the Modern American West: A Century of Fiction, History, and Art*. Tucson, AZ: University of Arizona Press.

Floyd, Janet. 2012. *Claims and Speculations: Mining and Writing in the Gilded Age*. Albuquerque, NM: University of New Mexico Press.

Gold Rush. 2012. Season 2, Episode 2. "Virgin Ground." Directed by Justin Kelly. Aired November 4, 2011, on the Discovery Channel.

Gold Rush. 2012. Season 2, Episode 17. "Frozen Out." Directed by Max Baring, Gavin Campbell, Tim Dalby, Peter Gauvain, and Matt Nicholson. Aired February 17, 2012, on the Discovery Channel.

Gold Rush. 2012. Season 2, Episode 18. "Judgment Day." Produced by Ronon Browne, Edward Gorsuch, Rob Sixsmith, and Molly Wilson. Aired February 24, 2012, on the Discovery Channel.

Gold Rush. 2016. Season 7, Episode 6. "No Crane, No Gain." Directed by Tom Whitworth. Aired November 18, 2016, on the Discovery Channel.

Gold Rush. 2017. Season 7, Episode 21. "Final Fury." Directed by Edward Gorsuch and Tom Whitworth. Aired March 10, 2017, on the Discovery Channel.

Gold Rush. 2018. Season 9, Episode 1. "Declaration of Independence." Directed by Tom Whitworth. Aired October 12, 2018, on the Discovery Channel.

Gold Rush. 2021. Season 11, Episode 21. "Endgame." Produced by Carter Figueroa, David Lawrence, and Tom Sheahan. Aired March 19, 2021, on the Discovery Channel.

Gold Rush: Alaska. 2010. Season 1, Episode 1. "No Guts, No Glory." Produced by Sam Brown, Meagan Davis, Helen Kelsey, and Tim Pastore. Aired December 10, 2010, on the Discovery Channel.

Gold Rush: Alaska. 2010. Season 1, Episode 11. "Full Disclosure." Produced by Meagan Davis and Tim Pastore. Aired February 25, 2011, on the Discovery Channel.

Gold Rush: Alaska. 2018. Season 8, Episode 23. "American Dreamer." Directed by Edward Gorsuch and Tom Whitworth. Aired March 16, 2018, on the Discovery Channel.

Gold Rush: Parker's Trail. 2017. Season 1, Episodes 1. "Footsteps of Legends." Produced by Louise Drew and Greg Wolf. Aired March 31, 2017, on the Discovery Channel.

Gold Rush: Parker's Trail. 2017. Season 1, Episode 2. "Racing the Freeze." Produced by Louise Drew and Greg Wolf. Aired April 7, 2017, on the Discovery Channel.

Gold Rush: Parker's Trail. 2017. Season 1, Episode 3. "Hypothermia." Produced by Louise Drew and Greg Wolf. Aired April 14, 2017, on the Discovery Channel.

Gold Rush: Parker's Trail. 2017. Season 1, Episode 4. "Trail Tales." Produced by Louise Drew and Greg Wolf. Aired April 14, 2017, on the Discovery Channel.

Green, Aimee. 2011. "Alaska Officials Hope Discovery Channel Show Doesn't Inspire Another Gold Rush." *The Oregonian* (Portland, OR), January 2, 2011. https://www.oregonlive.com/pacific-northwest-news/2011/01/alaska_off icials_hope_discovery_channel_show_doesnt_inspire_another_gold_rus h.html.

Green, Heather. 2018. "The Tr'ondëk Hwëch'in and the Great Upheaval: Mining, Colonialism, and Environmental Change in the Klondike, 1890–1940." PhD diss., University of Alberta.

Hamilton, Devin. 2020. "*Gold Rush* Cast Net Worth and Salary in 2020: How Much Does the Cast of Gold Rush Make?" *Reality Show Casts*, April 25, 2020. https://realityshowcasts.com/gold-rush-cast-net-worth-salary-bio/.

Herbert, Christopher. 2018. *Gold Rush Manliness: Race and Gender on the Pacific Slope*. Seattle, WA: University of Washington Press.

Higginson, Ian N. 1998. "Jack London's Klondike Speculation: Capitalist Critique and the Sled as Heterotopia in 'The Call of the Wild.'" *Polar Record* 34 (191): 317–32. DOI: 10.1017/S0032247400026024.

High, Steven, and David W. Lewis. 2007. *Corporate Wasteland: The Landscape and Memory of Deindustrialization*. Ithaca, NY: Cornell University Press.

High, Steven. 2017. "Brownfield Public History: Arts and Heritage in the Aftermath of Deindustrialization." In *The Oxford Handbook of Public History*, edited by Paula Hamilton and James Gardner, 423–44. New York, NY: Oxford University Press.

Jacobson, Kristin. 2020. *The American Adrenaline Narrative*. Athens, GA: University of Georgia Press.

Johnson, Bob. 2019. *Mineral Rites: An Archaeology of the Fossil Economy*. Baltimore, MD: Johns Hopkins Press.

Johnson, Susan. 2000. *Roaring Camp: The Social World of the California Gold Rush*. New York, NY: W.W. Norton.

Kaplan, Amy. 1998. "Manifest Domesticity." *American Literature* 70 (3): 581– 606. DOI: 10.2307/2902710.

Krakauer, Jon. 1997. *Into Thin Air*. New York, NY: Villard.

Lahti, Janne. 2018. *The American West and the World: Transnational and Comparative Perspectives*. New York, NY: Routledge.

Lasley, Shane. 2019. "Fort Knox Passes 8M oz Gold Milestone." *North of 60 Mining News*, October 11, 2019.

Limerick, Patricia. 1987. *The Legacy of Conquest: The Unbroken Past of the American West*. New York, NY: W.W. Norton.

London, Jack. (1903) 2009. *The Call of the Wild*. New York, NY: Library of America.

Lowenthal, David. 2015. *The Past Is a Foreign Country: Revisited*. Cambridge, UK: Cambridge University Press.

MacCannell, Dean. 1976. *The Tourist: A New Theory of the Leisure Class*. Berkeley, CA: University of California Press.

Mitchell, Lee Clark. 2001. "Violence in the Film Western." In *Violence and American Cinema*, edited by J. David Slocum, 176–91. New York, NY: Routledge.

Mitra, Shraman. 2021. "Who Is the Richest *Gold Rush* Cast Member?" *The Cinemaholic*, April 16, 2021. https://thecinemaholic.com/who-is-the-richest-gold-rush-cast-member/.

Morse, Kathryn. 2003. *The Nature of Gold: An Environmental History of the Klondike Gold Rush*. Seattle, WA: University of Washington Press.

Mountford, Benjamin, and Stephen Tuffnell. 2018. "Seeking a Global History of Gold." In *A Global History of Gold Rushes*, edited by Benjamin Mountford and Stephen Tuffnell, 3–41. Oakland, CA: University of California Press.

Murray, Robin L., and Joseph K. Heumann. 2012. *Gunfight at the Eco-Corral*. Norman, OK: University of Oklahoma Press.

Negra, Diane. 2013. "Gender Bifurcation in the Recession Economy: *Extreme Couponing* and *Gold Rush Alaska*." *Cinema Journal* 53 (1): 123–29.

Nystrom, Eric C. 2019. "Witnessing the Alaska Gold Rush: Finding Mining History in Court Records." *Mining History Journal*, no. 26, 21–34. https://www.mininghistoryassociation.org/Journal/journal2019.htm.

O'Sullivan, Shannon Eileen Marie. 2017. "Frontiersmen Are the 'Real Men' in Trump's America: Hegemonic Masculinity at Work on U.S. Cable's Version of Blue-Collar Reality." PhD diss., University of Colorado.

Pearson, Natalie Obiko. 2016. "Trump's Family Fortune Originated in a Canadian Gold-Rush Brothel." *Bloomberg*, October 26, 2016. https://www.bloomberg.com/features/2016-trump-family-fortune/.

"Picking Up Millions in Alaska." 1898. *The San Francisco Call*, January 23, 1898. In Box 1. Klondike Gold Rush Collection, Acc 97–205, University of Alaska-Fairbanks, Elmer E. Rasmussen Library, Alaska and Polar Regions Collections and Archives.

Porslid, Charlene. 1998. *Gamblers and Dreamers: Women, Men, and Community in the Klondike*. Vancouver: University of British Columbia Press.

Pruitt-Young, Sharon. 2020. "The Real Reason Dave Turin Left Gold Rush." *Looper*, November 10, 2020. https://www.looper.com/276658/the-real-reason-dave-turin-left-gold-rush/.

Queen, Jack. 2018. "Discovery Channel's 'Gold Rush' Is Leaving Park County, but Residents Continue to Fight for More Oversight." *Summit Daily* (Summit County, CO), February 17, 2018. https://www.summitdaily.com/news/regional/discovery-channels-gold-rush-may-be-leaving-park-county-but-residents-continue-to-fight-for-more-mining-oversight/.

Rickenback, Anna J. "Letter to M.S. Jacobson, Ophir, Placer County, California, May 6, 1898." In Klondike Gold Rush Collection, Acc 97–205, box 1. University of Alaska-Fairbanks, Elmer E. Rasmussen Library, Alaska and Polar Regions Collections and Archives.

Rumer, Anna. 2020. "'Gold Rush' Dominates Cable Ratings After 'Parker's Trail' Return, Catch an Exclusive Preview." *Pop Culture*, March 19, 2020. https://popculture.com/reality-tv/news/gold-rush-dominates-cable-ratings-after-parkers-trail-return-catch-exclusive-season-preview/.

Sandlos, John, and Arn Keeling. 2021. *Mining Country: A History of Canada's Mines and Miners*. Toronto: James Lorimer & Co.

Sharpe, E.C. 1897. "The Scaguay Trail." *The Argus* (Seattle, WA) 4, no. 33 (September). In Box 1. Folder 5, E.C. Sharpe Diaries Acc #1983-24. University of Alaska-Fairbanks, Elmer E. Rasmussen Library, Alaska and Polar Regions Collections and Archives.

Sharpe, Ruth C. n.d. "Resume of the Life of Edward C. Sharpe as Recalled by His Daughter, Ruth," Sacramento, California. In Klondike Gold Rush Collection, Acc 97–205, In Box 1. Folder 5, E.C. Sharpe Diaries Acc #1983-24. University of Alaska-Fairbanks, Elmer E. Rasmussen Library, Alaska and Polar Regions Collections and Archives.

Slotkin, Richard. 1993. *Gunfighter Nation: The Myth of the Frontier in Twentieth-Century America*. New York, NY: HarperCollins.

Smith, Henry Nash. 1971. *Virgin Land: The American West as Symbol and Myth*. Cambridge, MA: Harvard University Press.

Solomon, Robert C. 2004. *In Defense of Sentimentality*. New York, NY: Oxford University Press.

Soviak, Tetiana. 2017. *"Visions of Labour: Socialist Realism, American Reality TV and the Politics of Documentary."* PhD diss., University of Toronto.

Spude, Catherine Holder. 2015. *Saloons, Prostitutes, and Temperance*. Norman, OK: University of Oklahoma Press.

Trapani, William C., and Laura L. Winn. 2014. "Manifest Masculinity: Frontier, Fraternity, and Family in Discovery Channel's *Gold Rush*." In *Reality Television: Oddities of Culture*, edited by Alison F. Slade, Amber J. Narro, and Burton P. Buchanan, 183–200. Lanham, MA: Lexington Books.

Turner, Frederick Jackson. 1961. "The Significance of the Frontier in American History." In *Frontier and Section*, edited by Ray Allen Billington, 37–62. Englewood Cliffs, NJ: Prentice-Hall.

Voyles, Traci Brynne. 2015. *Wastelanding: Legacies of Uranium Mining in Navajo Country*. Minneapolis, MN: University of Minnesota Press.

Weaver-Hightower, Rebecca, and Janne Lahti. 2020. "Introduction: Reel Settler Colonialism: Gazing, Reception, and Production of Global Settler Cinemas." In *Cinematic Settlers: The Settler Colonial World in Film*, edited by Janne Lahti and Rebecca Weaver-Hightower, 1–10. New York, NY: Routledge.

Wrobel, David M. 1993. *The End of American Exceptionalism: Frontier Anxiety from the Old West to the New Deal*. Lawrence, KS: University Press of Kansas.

Zanjani, Sally. 1997. *A Mine of Her Own: Women Prospectors in the American West, 1850–1950*. Lincoln, NE: University of Nebraska Press.

Zeller, Suzanne. 1987. *Inventing Canada: Early Victorian Science and the Idea of a Transcontinental Nation*. Toronto: University of Toronto Press.

Sentimentality, Sacrifice, and Oil: Reckoning with Offshore Extractive Trauma[1]

Katie Ritson

As the offshore workers who made their careers in the 1970s and 1980s—the boom years of North Sea oil—have retired or are moving towards retirement, a new generation has started to reflect on what it means to have grown up with oil. It is a moment of introspection shared in particular by people in Norway and Great Britain—two countries whose development has been shaped by offshore extraction—and underpinned by scholarly and public interest in the subject. Besides academic and trade books analyzing the history and impact of North Sea oil and gas (e.g., Marriott/Macalister; Sæther; Hein), the last decade or so has seen the publication of personal memoirs looking back at the oil boom of the 1980s, including those by writer and intellectual Aslak Sira Myhre and artist Sue Jane Taylor. Concurrently produced TV documentaries, novels, poetry, and even a high-budget multi-part TV drama series,[2] indicate a widespread appetite to engage with the memories of the extractive industry during these foundational years and have produced in turn new scholarship on the aesthetic and narrative dimensions of specifically North Sea petroculture (Andersen; Campbell; Furuseth et al.; Furuseth; Leyda; Pitt-Scott; Polack/Farquharson; Ritson). In this article, I will look at intergenerational conflict in

1   Thank you to my friends in the Critical PetroAesthetics Collaboratory at the Oslo School of Environmental Humanities, who have contributed so much to my thinking in our many conversations over the past two years.
2   For example, the NRK TV documentary *Olje!* (2006) and the BBC TV documentary *Crude Britannia: The Story of North Sea Oil* (2009). The NRK TV drama *Lykkeland* (2018) was screened in the UK as *State of Happiness* in 2020 and a second season aired in 2022 in Norway. The film *Oljeunge (Oil Kid)* commissioned by and on show in the Petroleum Museum in Stavanger in 2016 gives an artful interpretation of how oil changed the local community in the 1970s, and what that legacy means now.

North Sea petrofiction from both Norway and Great Britain and explore the affective dimensions of reckoning with the legacy of the offshore boom years.

While the new extractive industry undeniably created employment opportunities, new infrastructure, and varying degrees of personal and national wealth, I will focus on the traumas that accompanied the drive to extract oil in the North Sea, in particular two major accidents of the 1980s: The capsizing of the Alexander Kielland platform in 1980 and the explosion on the Piper Alpha platform in 1988. The former accident occurred on the evening of 27 March 1980. The rig, which was being used as accommodation for offshore workers, initially tilted and subsequently capsized; safety provisions were poor, lifeboats inoperable, and weather conditions made it difficult to retrieve survivors from the icy waters. One hundred and twenty-three men lost their lives. Eight years later, on 6 July 1988, a ball of fire engulfed the Piper Alpha rig, the result of miscommunication and poor safety procedures; one hundred and sixty-seven men died, and many of the survivors were badly injured.

Besides recent books re-examining these disasters some decades later (McGinty; Tungland et al.), personal memories of these tragic events are becoming increasingly written at a generation's remove, replacing the survivor testimonies from the immediate aftermath. An example of this can be found in this 2020 text by the chemist Marc Reid, published in a surprisingly personal paper in the journal *ACS Chemical Health and Safety*:

> In my childhood years, I remember noticing that my father's hands appeared somehow older than they should be. To my young eyes, he had the hands of my grandfather, not the hands of a young man. I would later learn that the curious wrinkles on my father's hands were, in fact, skin grafts: an eternal reminder of the burns he endured during his escape from the burning Piper Alpha rig. In those earliest days of my life, I was too young to understand the accident or the struggles my father would later face. As I grew older and more mature, so too did the forthcoming details of my father's ordeal. (88)

Marc Reid's father survived the Piper Alpha explosion with injuries and later lost his life to alcoholism (as was reported in *The Scotsman*, "Marc Reid"); the paper written by his son introduces a note of sentimentality into an otherwise sober review of safety culture. Reid is not the only recent example of someone from the next generation looking for lessons to learn from the painful events of the 1980s oil and gas industry in the North Sea. Odd Kristian Reme, a trainee priest in 1980 and now a public figure in Norway, lost his brother in the Alexander Kielland disaster and published a book about his search for answers about the accident in 2021 (Omdal).

This engagement with the disasters a generation after they took place is not confined to memoir but is also a feature of recent novels. In the following, I will explore two fictional works that engage with the oil industry during the 1980s, from opposite sides of the North Sea. The two novels are linked not just through their subject of the offshore oil industry but also through their portrayal of the Alexander Kielland and Piper Alpha disasters. Scottish author Iain Maloney published *The Waves Burn Bright* in 2016 and *Puslingar* by Norwegian Atle Berge was published three years later, in 2019.[3] In bringing together these two novels written in two different languages, I want to focus on the elements they have in common. Firstly, they take up the theme of the offshore industry and were written at about the same time. Secondly, they are (so far) unique as literary novels to imagine the real-life disasters of the 1980s; there have not been many—if any—direct portrayals of the Alexander Kielland or the Piper Alpha disasters in fiction before the turn of the millennium, although a few novels do make oblique references to the danger and the risks of offshore work.[4] Thirdly, both novels embed the offshore oil industry in a context of intergenerational conflict. The protagonists are children of offshore workers who were born during the boom years of North Sea oil. The key driver of the narrative in each of the cases is the difficult relationship between the generations of the fathers and those of their children. Fourthly, both narratives resolve through the protagonists overcoming trauma, rebuilding family relationships, and coming to terms with a difficult past. In this last point, the sentimentality of the texts is particularly clear; narrative closure is achieved, serving to assimilate the memory of the traumatic disasters into the lives of the protagonists, and by extension, into the wider culture.

Furthermore, both novels employ sentimentality, in particular in relation to what Alexa Weik von Mossner terms "strategic empathy," on different thematic levels. Indeed, readers are made to empathize with the victims of the accident and with the generation of children who grew up in its shadow, and,

---

3   Since I started writing this article, Maloney's novel has been republished under the new title *In the Shadow of Piper Alpha*; I will however in this essay refer to the original edition and title.

4   Ian Rankin's *Black and Blue* (1997) and Kjell Ola Dahl's financial thriller *Lindeman og Sachs* (2006) are examples of widely read fiction that reference the offshore industry in the North Sea and its safety record.

at least on occasion, with the environmental damage caused by fossil fuel extraction. In the chapter of her book *Affective Ecologies* entitled "Imagining the Pain," Weik von Mossner is concerned with narratives of environmental injustices that arise or endure through "a limitation of personal and communal agency due to class, gender, race, ethnicity and a range of other social markers" (78). The novels I examine in this article focalize on characters who are caught up in the immediate trauma and aftermath of offshore disasters, allowing the reader to identify with them in different positions within the unequal environmental risk culture, as victims, agents, and consumers of offshore extraction. Identification with these characters creates the affective investment that drives the narratives through cycles of conflict and trauma to a point of (healing) resolution. This ultimate narrative closure has implications for the way that environmental trauma is represented.

The fact that these texts were written and published so recently is important because of the context of greater awareness and criticism of the role of the offshore industry in generating not just wealth, but also enormous environmental damage. Graeme Macdonald writes of the "sense of an ending" that permeates North Sea petroculture, haunting efforts to extract the resource from the very moment it was discovered but intensifying along with discussions about climate change (62–3). As parts of the globe become uninhabitable and end of oil seems nigh, a kind of double trauma starts to become visible; the human suffering in the offshore accidents of the 1980s finds a long shadow in the specter of human and ecological suffering on a much longer timescale and across a much larger scope. Remembering the Alexander Kielland and the Piper Alpha accidents raises questions—how could they have happened, who was to blame, how should they be remembered?—that can be extended to the oil and gas industry as a whole, with its record of ecological negligence, poor safety, and human greed. Fiona Polack argues convincingly for offshore accidents as "ecological parables," repurposing a concept developed by Steve Mentz, for their ability to confront the limits to human agency in the North Atlantic (Polack 43). The difficult past that the texts are grappling with is not confined to the accidents that happened on the North Sea, but extends as synecdoche, I argue with Polack, to the business of petrochemical extraction itself.

The generationality of the novels is an important tool in integrating current awareness of the problematic nature of gas and oil extraction with the motivations and knowledge of those who worked offshore in the 1980s. Multiple generations are represented in the two novels: those who remember life before the oil industry in the North Sea began (this generation features only in *Puslingar*); the generation active in offshore work in the 1980s; and those born in the early 1970s whose lives were deeply entwined with the oil industry and its effects. If we take the middle generation of oil workers in the novels—the fathers—as standing for the generation that embraced the offshore industry, then their children want to understand their role in relation not just to the human cost of oil, but also to the ecological cost. The constellation of fathers and children in the novels implies that it is up to a new generation to try and understand why their fathers threw in their lot with oil and to exonerate them or find them guilty.

The doubling of the questions of guilt and complicity, incorporating both human pain and ecological damage, is one of many ways by which contemporary literary novels can address issues of climate change and ecological justice without becoming explicitly "cli-fi," that is to say explicitly concerned with an environmental agenda. Amitav Ghosh has argued that formal aspects of the modern literary novel, in particular its focus on human agencies and timescales, make it an unsuitable vehicle for the deep time, uncontained stories of environmental change both slow and sudden, in particular for the agencies of oil (Ghosh 1992, 34; Ghosh 2016, esp. 98–108). Others, such as Adam Trexler (*Anthropocene Fictions*, 10) and Eva Horn and Hannes Bergthaller (*The Anthropocene: Key Issues for the Humanities*, 109) suggest that a formal innovation is necessary to encompass the multiple scales and challenges of the Anthropocene. While the modern realist novel has certainly played its part in obscuring the ecological dependences of human civilizations (Ghosh 2016, 20–37), I join Reinhard Hennig in expressing doubt that novels that are conventional in form are unable to engage some of the more complex entanglements of the Anthropocene (128). Those skeptical of the novel's form in relation to climate change have allowed little space for the agency of readers in bringing their own knowledge and concern to bear on the world of the novel, and it is in this space, between text and reader, that the novel unfolds its *affective* power. Emotions and feelings triggered by the reading of a novel, such as empathy, pity, shame, or nostalgia, shape responses to it, and sentimentality is an important tool in generating such affective reactions. Awareness of the fossil fuel industry that permeates contemporary society, coupled with strategic empathy with particular characters, allow for a nuanced reading of the novels I will discuss here and situates them as mediators in cultural responses to the Anthropocene.

As novels that center on traumatic experiences, *Puslingar* and *The Waves Burn Bright* can be analyzed with reference to the German concept of *Vergangenheitsbewältigung*, which refers to overcoming a (by implication) difficult or traumatic past. This term has been used in literary studies primarily in the discussion of literary texts that deal with aspects of Germany's role in World War II and the Holocaust, subsequently also in relation to the German Democratic Republic and the West German protest movements from 1968 (Eigler 10). Also in other national contexts, intergenerational conflict is a common feature of narrative fiction that seeks to discuss and assimilate different attitudes to historical trauma and questions of guilt, agency, memory, and forgiveness. *Vergangenheitsbewältigung* interacts with the concept of collective cultural memory advanced by Aleida and Jan Assmann. In their understanding of the way that cultural memory is constructed and conveyed as something distinct from history, texts and media (including novels) play a key role in transforming events from social memories to cultural memories over generations and in creating narratives that are compatible with cultural and national identities and values. Aleida Assmann writes "[c]ollective memory [...] depends on transitions from history into memory that involve the framing of historical events in the shape of affectively charged narratives and mobilizing symbols" (67). The novels here are affectively charged and contribute to the transition from history to an evolving cultural memory of the boom years and the trauma of oil and gas extraction in the North Sea.

The idea of working through the past in literature has until now been applied primarily to social and anthropocentric traumas to explore the difficult histories of totalitarianism and extremism and their ongoing legacy for subsequent generations. I extend its use here to cover both the anthropocentric trauma of offshore accidents and the ecological trauma that is at the heart of offshore extraction. The immediate violence of the accidents themselves is underpinned by the "slow violence" (Nixon) of oil spills, air pollution, and global heating, as the results of processes that started long before the 1980s and will continue for centuries to come across the globe. The diffuse and multigenerational nature of extractive trauma, difficult to comprehend in its entirety, lends itself to being approached through these short moments of crisis; working through these human-centered traumas in narrative form generates emotional responses. Sentimentality is employed as a way of creating narrative closure by means of an affective response on the part of the reader. Tropes of sacrifice and atonement in North Sea petrofictions allow for the exoneration of the fathers whilst leaving open difficult questions about extractive guilt and complicity.

Puslingar

Atle Berge's novel *Puslingar* opens with the news of the Alexander Kielland disaster. The protagonist is Marita; at the beginning of the novel, she is a young child who is waiting for her father, Jonny, to come home to her remote house north of Bergen so that he can help her finish building a Lego pirate ship they started together. But he never returns.

The word *Puslingar* translates roughly as "puny little people" and is drawn from the opening of the 1882 novel *Garman & Worse* by the Norwegian writer Alexander Kielland, which is cited (in modern Norwegian) on page 44 of Berge's novel:

> Nothing is so boundless as the sea, nothing so patient. On its broad back it bears, like a good-natured elephant, the puny mannikins that inhabit the world; and in its cool depths it has place for all earthly woes. It is not true that the sea is faithless, for it has never promised anything; without claim, without obligation, free, pure, and honest beats the mighty heart, the last sound one in an ailing world. (44) [5]

In Berge's novel, this passage serves to link Kielland, the author, to the platform that was named after him, the Alexander Kielland that capsized into the (boundless, patient) sea on a stormy night in 1980. But the reference to *Garman & Worse* also calls to mind the tradition of social realism in Scandinavian novels of the later 19th century, with its intent to shine a light on the inequalities and hypocrisies of contemporary society. Berge's contemporary novel is very much a work of social realism in the Scandinavian tradition of writers such as Alexander Kielland. *Puslingar*'s focus on the social dimension of Norway's oil boom, however, is contextualized by a modern awareness of oil's problematic role in ushering in the Anthropocene.

---

5   "Intet er så rommelig som havet, intet så tålmodig. På sin brede rygg bærer det lik en godslig elefant de små puslinger de bebor jorden; og i sitt store kjølige dyp eier det plass for all verdens jammer. Det er ikke sant at havet er troløst; for det har aldri lovet noe: uten krav, uten forpliktelse, fritt, rent og uforfalsket banker det store hjerte—det siste sunne i den syke verden."

The centrality of the Alexander Kielland platform accident is clearly signaled via this intertext, both through the references to *Garman & Worse* within the world of the novel, and less directly through the choice of title. (The cover design by Øystein Vidnes, showing a stylized platform capsizing into a stormy sea, also marks the accident as a central event in the novel). The historical moment of the accident is the motor that propels Marita through her *Bildungsroman*-esque development as a child and young adult. The narrative starts out from a distanced and uncomprehending perspective of the accident as experienced by Marita and her mother from their home in Nordhordaland. For two days they do not know whether Jonny was on the capsized platform or not, and no body is ever recovered. Subsequently the novel accompanies Marita in her quest to find out more about the father she idealizes, about the industry he worked for, and the accident that killed him. Marita starts to find answers once she is able to build a relationship with her father's best friend, Trygve, who survived the Kielland disaster and is suffering from post-traumatic stress disorder (PTSD).

Conflict between generations appears in various constellations and captures the situation in Norway in the 1980s in relation to a new industry that was part of the transformation of the country from a poor nation largely dependent on farming and fishing to a wealthy and increasingly urban one (Ohman Nielsen 215–7). Marita realizes the extent of the transformation when she starts to feel sorry for her grandfather, Jonny's father: "She was very fond of her grandad, but God help us how old-fashioned he was! In a way it was a pity for him, she thought. Everything he knew was in the process of disappearing" (Berge 109; all translations from Berge my own).[6] The sense of something new arriving in the 1980s is evident in the characters of Jonny and Trygve, both country boys from the historically poor and remote region of Nordhordaland. They are presented as innocents who knew little about the oil industry other than that it offered good pay and prospects. The father of Marita's boyfriend, Vegaard Vaage, of the same generation as Jonny and Trygve, reveals a similar sense of innocence as he says to his son: "When I was your age, I was just confused. The only thing I knew was that I didn't want to be a farmer" (132).[7]

---

6   "Ho var svært glad i farfaren sin, men gud hjelpe meg så gammaldags han var! På en måte var det litt synd på ham, tenkte ho. Alt han kjente var i ferd med å forsvinne."

7   "Då eg va på din alder, va eg berre forvirra. Da einaste eg visste, va at eg ikkje ville bli bonde."

The innocence of the country boys who worked offshore is contrasted with unnamed and faceless Phillips executives who were so keen to restart production after the accident that they began drilling on Edda while recovery work was still ongoing, even dumping mud on the divers who were looking for bodies (147). The greed and negligence of those overseeing drilling operations offshore weighs on Trygve when he gives Marita his account of the accident. His anger gives way to Marita's frustration with the mistrusted official investigation, which ultimately decided that faulty construction work coupled with safety failures was responsible for the accident. Marita, determined to find a clearer cause for the death of her father, conscripts Trygve to speak to the media with her and to challenge the investigation's findings. Trygve tells journalists that he has been unable to work and has little support from the state:

> You can put this in. How little help we survivors got. It's only a couple of years ago that the state recognized that our psychological problems are work-related. I don't know if you know but they've done research, and the results show that a third of the survivors have been out of work since the accident. (187)[8]

Berge's emphasis on Jonny and Trygve as underdogs—uneducated men from Nordhordaland who were badly treated by industry bosses and the state alike—gives weight to the narrative of innocent workers who were sacrificed by state-sanctioned greed. Trygve gives his account of Jonny's last moments to Marita, bearing witness to his friend's near-drowning, the attempts of the half-frozen men in the lifeboat to resuscitate him, the excruciating pain of watching Jonny being winched into a helicopter to safety, only for his lifejacket to open and pitch him back into the sea (157–8). The tense narration of Jonny's death and Trygve's rescue, emphasizing the close bond between the two, draws the reader into empathizing with the pair and their tragedy. Jonny's life and Trygve's health have been sacrificed; implicitly, it is now up to Marita to ensure that the sacrifice was not in vain by fulfilling her childhood dream of getting a good education, becoming an engineer, and succeeding in Norway's new age of prosperity.

---

8   "Det kan du ta med i saka di. Kor lite hjelp me overlevande har fått. Først for eit par år sidan gjekk staten med på at dei psykiske problema våre er ein yrkesskade. Eg veit ikkje om du kjenner til det, men me har faktisk blitt forska på, og resultata viser at ein tredjedel av dei overlevande framleis ikkje er i jobb etter ulykka."

Marita is part of the new generation, but her mother, too, is experiencing a degree of social mobility. Generational conflict between mother and daughter arises along with class conflict when Marita's mother starts a relationship with Einar Sletten, a schoolteacher from Bergen. Upon moving in, Einar fills the house with books and challenges Marita on intellectual matters. Marita, who along with most of the children in her school, has started to speak a more urban version of Norwegian, "the Bergen-inspired dialect she had spoken since she started in first grade" (13),[9] reacts by reverting to the rural *strilamålet* dialect spoken by her mother and grandparents, and by Jonny when he was still alive. The tension between the rural working class and the limitations of relative poverty, and the possibilities of wealth and education brought about by Norway's investment in the oil industry is played out in Marita's family. The changing gender politics are also illustrated through intergenerational conflict: Marita's grandfather, proud of his *stril* background, religious, and prone to both racist and sexist comments, tries to persuade Marita that offshore is no place for a woman. Einar Sletten, urbane and detested by Marita, is the one who steps in to defend her interest in becoming an engineer in the oil industry. Marita, torn between loyalty to her roots and her ambitions as an emancipated young woman, takes her grandfather's side (Berge 110), but his death halfway through the novel clears the stage for Marita to unite both parts of her identity.

The fact that the generation that pioneered offshore extraction in the North Sea is represented by men is hardly surprising given the almost exclusively male workforce in the industry in its early decades. But the choice of a female protagonist in *Puslingar* (and also in *The Waves Burn Bright*) overlays economic and social progress with female emancipation. Marita grows up during a period of activism on behalf of women's rights to paid work outside the home and is able to take advantage of education to train as an engineer. By implicitly linking social and economic justice for women to the greater prosperity generated by oil wealth in Norway the novel adds weight to the narrative that the fossil fuel industry has been (and continues to be) a force for good.

Historian May-Brith Ohman Nielsen, writing about the offshore accidents of the 1980s, notes that the "the human and environmental costs were seen as a tragic price but almost unavoidable for a nation that wanted to live on oil"

---

9   "[…] den bergenskinspirerte dialekta ho hadde snakka sidan ho begynte i første klasse."

(215).[10] Marita struggles with the human cost of the oil industry—the loss of her father—whilst also negotiating her own identity as a member of the rural working class. It was mainly working class men who paid the price with their lives in the Kielland disaster and this awareness is what causes her to hold fast to her dialect and working class roots whilst still embracing the possibilities that oil prosperity afford her.

Conflicts about the environmental cost of the oil industry in the novel take place less along generational lines, and more along those of class. Marita's middle class school friend Settembrini and her de facto stepfather Einar Sletten have an agitated conversation about the greenhouse effect and the hole in the ozone layer and Marita immediately shouts them down: "[b]ut, Jesus Christ, lads! Your whole fucking lives are made of oil."[11] She goes on to list all the things that they depend on oil for:

> clothes, paint, plastic in all its many forms. Fertilizer and preservatives. Mamma's nail polish remover, my lego bricks, the chewing gum in your gob, Einar, the glue that's holding your stupid books together. Insulation, furniture, your cassette tapes and skis, Einar. And asphalt, for heaven's sake! Your father's credit card, William, isn't just full up with oil revenue from Lindås District, it's made of oil! Do you not know that? (Berge 123–4)[12]

Marita understands that the materials of Norwegian modernity—the materials that are building her future and are making others rich—are made of and paid for with oil; shame about this is reserved for those who do not acknowledge this dependence, who profess environmental awareness whilst profiting from oil. Within the text, the logic of both the Alexander Kielland disaster and the environmental costs of fossil fuel extraction and consumption as tragic but seemingly necessary sacrifices are upheld.

The novel steers against a contemporary current of "petro-guilt" in Norway identified by Ellen Rees and expanded upon by film scholar Julia Leyda (Rees

---

10   "Omkostningene i menneskeliv og i miljøbelastning ble sett på som tragiske omkostninger, men nærmest uunngåelige, for et folk som vil leve av olje."

11   "Men, Jesus, guttar! Hele fåkkings livet dåkkars e laget av olje!"

12   "Klær, maling, plast i alle mulige formar. Kunstgjødsel og konserveringsmiddel. Neglelakkfjernaren til mamma, legoklossene mine, tyggisen du har i kjeften, Einar, limet som holdar de jævla bøkene dåkkars sammen. Isolasjon, møblar, kassettar og skiene dine, Einar. Og asfalt, for helvete! Bankkortet til faren din, William, e ikkje bare fylt opp av oljeskattepengar fra Lindås kommune, det e laget av olje! Vet du ikkje det?"

45; Leyda 87) as part of the broader notion of "ScanGuilt" theorized by Elisa-beth Oxfeldt (2016). Oxfeldt's work explores the guilt that Scandinavians feel as a result of their privileged positions globally as wealthy democracies with access to natural resources, generous welfare systems, and relatively conflict-free societies. Berge's novel tempers any guilt by stressing the importance of Norwegian modernization in raising the rural working class out of poverty. Marita's success in being proud of her rural roots and her dialect, her love for her family, coupled with her ambition and drive in pursuing the education and career options that are available to her generation trump any ecological or so-cial concerns about oil amongst the characters in the novel. The novel ends as Marita moves to Trondheim—the location of Norway's primary university of science and technology—to start her studies. Marita experiences a moment of displacement; her dialect marks her, she thinks, as a rural outsider, and when she mentions the Alexander Kielland accident, her new city friends fall silent before changing the subject. She resolves to keep her mouth shut, concluding that her student friends do not want to think about the accident: "People who don't manage to forget, who can't forget, are unbearable. People want to forget, they need to, just like the nation has to forget in order to be able to keep going" (247).[13] In a way, the novel is a snapshot of the climate change paralysis in Nor-way in the early part of this millennium. This paralysis is described so well in Kari Norgaard's study of climate denial in Norway, with increasing awareness of global warming and ecological tipping points translating only into inaction and avoidance ("Prologue").

The novel contends that the sacrifices Norway and its people made for its prosperity and modernity—human *and* environmental—are too painful to dwell on for those who bear the consequences at first hand, but in the cultural memory of the nation, they are no more than a stumble on the irrevocable journey to modernity. Ultimately, the affective closure conveyed by ending the novel with Marita on the cusp of a brighter future in the fossil fuel industries relies on a sentimental and conventional sense of wrongs having been righted. In identifying with Marita, tortured country girl made good, the reader is encouraged to override any doubts about the ecological damage caused by oil. Marita's ability to assimilate the loss of her father and to reconcile within herself her working class heritage with the possibility and prosperity of mod-ern Norway, confirm that the traumas caused by the extractivist offshore

---

13   "Folk som ikkje klarer å gløyme, er uuthaldelege. Folk vil gløyme, må gløyme, slik nas-jonen må gløyme, for å halde ut seg sjølv."

industry, such as the Alexander Kielland disaster, have indeed been mostly integrated—and largely forgotten—in Norway's story of progress.

The Waves Burn Bright

The structure of Iain Maloney's *The Waves Burn Bright* is more complex than that of *Puslingar*, moving both back and forth in time and between different narrative focalizations, alternating between the stories of the main protagonists Carrie and her father Marcus. The novel centers on the relationship between daughter and father and the family ties and obligations within which they negotiate it. While the Piper Alpha accident is alluded to in the novel's original title (and made much more explicit in the republished version), it is less obviously a novel about the disaster itself: Wider themes range across deep-time geology, volcanoes, climate change, sexual politics, betrayals of various kinds, and post-traumatic stress disorder. Marcus' rescue from the burning Piper Alpha is the key crisis in the novel that propels father and daughter away from each other, with Marcus becoming an alcoholic and Carrie embarking on a career as a geologist that will take her as far from home as it is possible to go. To complete her alienation from her parents, the night of the Piper Alpha disaster is also the moment she discovers that her mother is having an affair with her colleague. The Piper Alpha explosion produces a metaphorical explosion within the family, propelling father, mother, and daughter in different directions, and leaving the reader the task of stitching together the chronologically disordered fragments towards the novel's closing pages of (partial) reconciliation and understanding.

The link that continues to unite father and daughter even after the accident is their love for geology, and in particular volcanoes. The novel opens with Carrie as a child, visiting Japan with her parents, where her father allows her to hike up a volcano. While Marcus' geology degree eventually brings him to work in the oil and gas industry, including trips offshore, Carrie becomes a professor of geology specializing in volcanology. She moves between Hawai'i, the USA, and New Zealand, careful to avoid returning to Scotland, while Marcus remains in Aberdeen, struggling with alcoholism, unemployment, and PTSD.

On a human level, generational conflict in *The Waves Burn Bright* is driven by moments of betrayal. Carrie feels betrayed by her parents in their failing marriage, giving her a childhood she describes as "fighting, affairs, divorce, recriminations" (Maloney 121). The Piper Alpha disaster compounds the situation; Marcus refuses offers of help with his PTSD and alcoholism and causes first Carrie's mother, and then Carrie herself to leave him. They both feel guilt for betraying him by not helping him in his recovery. Marcus' sense that he has betrayed his colleagues when he survived the disaster is indicated in the flash-back during which the moment of the accident is recounted, focalized on Marcus but addressing him in the second person, showing his disembodiment at this moment of acute stress:

> It falls apart. Melted metal buckling, dropping into the sea [...] You watch the accommodation block. The galley. All those men you left in there. You watch from the boat as it tilts, it slides into the sea and is gone.
> Were they still alive when it hit the water?
> What killed them?
> Smoke.
> Fire.
> Water.
> You.
> You're alive.
> You're alive.
> You left them. (79)

The intense focalization with Marcus suggested by this present-tense narrative fragment pushes the reader to identify with his immediate situation, employing strategic empathy as described by Weik von Mossner to present the disaster from the perspective of the victim. Marcus, however, does not see himself as a victim but aligns himself with the perpetrators; with his survival, he left the men behind and feels responsible for their deaths. Unlike Jonny and Trygve in *Puslingar*, Marcus is not working class or uneducated and has not gone into off-shore work to lift himself out of poverty. Marcus understands something about the industry he is in. Moreover he is shown to be a drinker and a womanizer: Nothing about him is innocent. As Marcus develops through the novel, starting to overcome his PTSD in part through writing, he begins to see himself as part of the systemic failure to look after those who do the dangerous work on the oil rigs. Carrie discovers his anger at the treatment of workers in the oil industry, including himself, when she reads his account of the disaster: "Decisions about safety, budgets, cuts, were made onshore by people who would never be put in danger. *We treated them like faceless drones there to keep profits up and problems down*" (246; italics in original). Marcus understands that the industry in which he was complicit has a price, and this price has been paid by the Piper Alpha victims.

While Carrie is waiting at the hospital for news of survivors from the Piper Alpha, a man says to her: "[t]here's a decent living to be made out of the North Sea, God saw sure it was well stocked with things we'd find useful, but by Christ He made the cost too high" (59). The cost here refers to the human victims of the disaster, but as with *Puslingar*, it can be read as extending into the environmental and ecological costs of oil and gas extraction, as well as the historic risks involved in another extractive practice, that of North Sea fishing. The environmental damage caused by the oil industry is referenced in the text, both explicitly and implicitly through the portrayal of geological processes and forms. As Carrie flies "somewhere over Russia" in 2013, she ponders on the state of the planet:

> The face of Scotland is scarred by glaciers, geological wrinkles, gouged by rivers of ice advancing, retreating for millions of years. Over enough time these scars will disappear, worn down by weather, wind and rain turning rocks to sand, washing it into the sea, washing Scotland away.
> Given enough time everything erodes. The glaciers are still retreating, global warming melting the permafrost. Each summer more and more of Greenland is exposed. The scars, the wounds.
> Consequences.
> The end of the world. Not that climate change is the end for the planet. We're creating the conditions for our own extinction and no geological scientist would ever confuse the two. (29)

This passage exemplifies the way that the novel links the long processes of deep-time that created the oil deposits with the short moments of human time—such as the explosion on the Piper Alpha or Carrie's flight—during which millions of years of crushed sediment can be turned into carbon. It employs sentimental language in doing so, extending the physical and metaphorical scars that have blighted Carrie and Marcus' relationship to those borne by the Earth over time. The collapsing of victimhood here—from physical burns to second-generation trauma to environmental scarring—underlines the way in which texts like *The Waves Burns Bright* can "use readers' empathy strategically to make a moral argument" not only "about people who have been wronged" (Weik von Mossner 78) but also about the damaged planet.

The closing part of the novel, during which Carrie returns to Aberdeen and approaches reconciliation with her father, takes up explicitly the ecological impact of oil extraction. Carrie is in Aberdeen for a conference where she is due to deliver her paper on geothermal energy extraction and collateral seismic events. It is clearly a moment of reckoning; Marcus recognizes the significance of her return to Aberdeen not just in terms of their personal history, but also in terms of Aberdeen's status as an oil city: "She'd come to Aberdeen to deliver bad news to the oil industry in person" (267). This prompts his reflection on the history of the oil industry over his lifetime: "How much things had changed. When he'd first got into the oil industry a lifetime ago, the only two questions asked about potential oil fields were 'how much oil?' and 'how cheap to extract?'" (168). Carrie's paper, when she delivers it, is direct and confrontational: "What my work shows, what the work of my colleague shows, is that the age of petroleum is over. Geothermal energy extraction is no longer a dream. It's a reality. And that reality means the death of the oil industry" (269).

Carrie's research confronts the double traumas of the oil industry—the human trauma of the Piper Alpha disaster that is represented through her troubled father and their damaged relationship, and the environmental traumas of extraction, pollution, and global warming. Her behavior enacts a form of atonement for the sins of her father by pushing back against the industry that destroys lives both directly and indirectly. Suggesting that her research might bring about the death of the oil industry implies a future break with a history of reckless extraction; Carrie also prepares to break with the history of trauma in her own family by deciding not to have children of her own (121), a decision that has both social and ecological overtones. While the novel does imply a future without oil, it still largely conforms to what Graeme Macdonald terms the "privatization of energy guilt, resting the primary burden of ecological response to the problems s/he sees as causing in the individual, in both their 'choice' of energy consumption and their 'green' ethical behaviour" (2). Marcus' suffering and Carrie's actions are an attempt to atone and absolve them both of their guilt from their continued complicity in petroleum wealth.

The novel ends as Carrie and her father finally approach each other on the shore of a lake in the Scottish mountains. As readers we do not witness the sentimental moment of their ultimate reconciliation, but the novel builds towards this picturesque scene when the two of them are finally making sense of the traumas that have haunted them, standing together "looking out over the shimmering mirror of the loch, the last of the sun blazing on the hills, the ground beneath their feet" (277). It is telling that this pastoral scene plays out inland, in the Cairngorms, and not on the Aberdeen coast with a view out to sea. Here, it seems, at least briefly, and away from the visible infrastructure of the offshore industry, there can be the possibility of a happy ending.

Sentimental Extraction

The two novels use affective strategies to reckon with the trauma of the 1980s offshore industry; in so doing, they engage with the cultural perceptions of both the disasters and the wider ecological consequences of extraction. The short and long-term processes set in motion by events in the North Sea in the 1980s are ripe for a literary reckoning in the form of novels, with generational novels as ideal templates for the kind of *Vergangenheitsbewältigung* that I identify. Both novels use the immediate trauma of the two biggest petroleum industry accidents of the 1980s in the North Sea as a way to examine oil and gas extraction more generally, drawing the ecological and deep-time perspectives as well as the human cost of extraction into the cultural narratives they contribute to.

By and large, the novels do not question the role of oil directly, instead reimagining the traumatic events at the center of the early boom years of North Sea offshore extraction, and memorializing the lives and landscapes sacrificed in pursuit of oil wealth. *Puslingar* is critical of the greed of the oil companies, their disregard for the lives of the men who worked offshore but implies that the oil that fueled Norway's modern prosperity was and continues to be necessary. Berge's novel works to inscribe the pain of the accident into Norwegian literary culture, dwelling on the individual traumas and their long legacies, but the narrative closure effected by ending with Marita's pursuit of a career in the oil industry ultimately underpins the sense of innocent men sacrificed for a greater good. The characters in the novel are aware of the way that the oil industry has transformed Norway, including the ecological damage, but implicitly, ecological sacrifices have also been a necessary condition for the success of Norway's new generation.

The Waves Burn Bright goes a step further, taking a more nuanced perspective on the traumas inflicted by North Sea oil and gas extraction and the complicity of many who profited from oil wealth, while pointing towards a future possibility of atonement for the wrongs committed by the industry. The "end of the oil industry" (and the end of Carrie's family line), together with a move towards safer and greener forms of energy could allow an unburdened generation to come to terms with the pain and damage of the past. The novel is a pre-emptive strike towards a new cultural narrative, of a troubled oil and gas industry that lasted some fifty years before being thoroughly discredited and giving way to a more ecologically friendly and socially bearable energy regime. The fathers in both novels can be exonerated; the forces that are really to blame for the accidents are only hinted at. Any stirrings of guilt or shame on the part of readers sensing their own complicity in an oil-rich society is left largely untapped as the generations of oil workers and oil children are reconciled.

Both novels remain ultimately incomplete attempts to come to terms with the past of oil. The complex ways in which people are complicit in the oil economy are hinted at by the characters and their feelings about the industry and its products but sealed within the world of the text by the (at least implied) happy endings. This is problematic for an industry which itself seems entirely resistant to closure. Simultaneously with the ongoing formation of cultural memory through narratives of human and ecological disaster, oil and gas continues to be pumped up from beneath the seabed. Offshore extraction continues apace in the North Sea and elsewhere, and "offshore petroleum exploration and production in the North Atlantic remain inherently risky" (Polack 41). And both slow and sudden traumas continue to leave their mark in other communities, too, the Deepwater Horizon disaster in 2010 being a case in point. A recent article profiles the PTSD of a survivor of the Deepwater Horizon accident, linking this to the "moral taint" of working in the fossil fuel industry amid the ecological damage caused by drilling in the Gulf of Mexico (Press). As new generations grow up and tackle the legacy of fossil fuel dependence, new narratives and new cultural memories will be required, and new generations of oil workers and beneficiaries will need to be held to account.

The novels are a contribution to the ongoing work of cultural and collective memorialization of offshore extraction on both sides of the North Sea; they represent a second-generation attempt to work through the traumas of the past and engage with their evolving status in cultural memory. The sentimentality of the novels lies in their affective strategies, with the model of intergenerational reconciliation suggesting that traumatic events—individual, collective, ecological—can (and should) be overcome. The generational conflict that drives the novels is resolved by the final pages, allowing the characters to move forward with their lives—even as the traumas at the heart of the industry continue—making it all too easy to overlook the ongoing fallout and intractable problems of continuing oil and gas extraction. As readers, we are invited to remember the disasters, recognize the pain and the trauma—and then shed a sentimental tear, and move on.

References

Andersen, Per Tomas. 2019. "The Future Modernism of No-Oil Norway: Øyvind Rimbereid's 'Solaris Corrected.'" *Humanities*, no. 8, 78. DOI: https://doi.or g/10.3390/h8020078

Assman, Aleida. 2008. "Transformations between History and Memory." *Social Research* 75 (1): 49–72.

Berge, Atle. 2019. *Puslingar*. Oslo: Samlaget.

Eigler, Friederike. 2005. *Gedächtnis und Geschichte in Generationenromanen seit der Wende*. Berlin: Schmidt.

Furuseth, Sissel. 2021. "Bilen som økokritisk utfordring: Carl Frode Tiller og Henrik Nor-Hansen diagnostiserer norsk petroleumskultur." *Edda* 108 (2): 128–41. DOI: https://doi.org/10.18261/issn.1500-1989-2021-02-05

Furuseth, Sissel, Anne Gjelsvik, Ahmet Gürata, Reinhard Hennig, Julia Leyda, and Katie Ritson, eds. 2020. "Climate Change in Literature, Television and Film from Norway." *Ecozon@* 11 (2): 8–16. DOI: https://doi.org/10.37536/EC OZONA.2020.11.2.3468.

Ghosh, Amitav. 1992. "Petrofiction: The Oil Encounter and the Modern Novel." *The New Republic*, March 2, 1992, 29–34.

Ghosh, Amitav. 2016. *The Great Derangement: Climate Change and the Unthinkable*. Chicago, IL: Chicago University Press.

Hein, Carola, ed. 2022. *Oil Spaces: Exploring the Global Petroleumscape*. London: Routledge.

Hennig, Reinhard. 2021. "Anthropocene Aesthetics: Norwegian Literature in a New Geological Epoch." In *Changing Concepts of Nature in Contemporary Scandinavian Literature and Photography* (Special Issue of *NORDEUROPAforum: Journal for the Study of Culture*), 105–30. DOI: http://dx.doi.org/10.18452/23 921.

Horn, Eva, and Hannes Bergthaller. 2020. *The Anthropocene: Key Issues for the Humanities*. New York, NY: Routledge.

Kielland, Alexander. 1885. *Garman & Worse*. Copenhagen: Gyldendal.

Leyda, Julia. 2018. "Petropolitics, Cli-Fi, and *Occupied*." *Journal of Scandinavian Cinema* 8 (2): 83–101. DOI: https://doi.org/10.1386/jsca.8.2.83_1

Macdonald, Graeme. 2013. "Research Note: The Resources of Fiction." *Reviews in Cultural Theory* 4 (2): 1–20.

Macdonald, Graeme. 2022. "Dynamic Positioning: North Sea Petroculture's Backwash." In *Cold Water Oil: Offshore Petroleum Cultures*, edited by Fiona Polack and Danine Farquharson, 61–96. London: Routledge.

Maloney, Iain. 2016. *The Waves Burn Bright*. Glasgow: Freight. (Subsequently re-published under a new title: Maloney, Iain. 2022. *In the Shadow of Piper Alpha*. Perth: Tippermuir Books.)

"Marc Reid: My dad escaped Piper Alpha, a friend who helped him did not." 2018. *The Scotsman*, July 5, 2018. https://www.scotsman.com/news/opinio n/columnists/marc-reid-my-dad-escaped-piper-alpha-friend-who-helpe d-him-did-not-278158.

Marriott, James, and Terry Macalister. 2021. *Crude Britannia: How Oil Shaped a Nation*. London: Pluto.

McGinty, Stephen. (2008) 2018. *Fire in the Night: The Piper Alpha Disaster*. London: Pan.

Myhre, Aslak Sira. 2010. *Herrskap og tjenere*. Oslo: Oktober.

Nixon, Rob. 2011. *Slow Violence and the Environmentalism of the Poor*. Boston, MA: Harvard University Press.

Norgaard, Kari Marie. 2011. *Living in Denial: Climate Change, Emotions, and Everyday Life*. Cambridge, MA: MIT Press.

Ohman Nielsen, May-Brith. 2011. *Norvegr: Norges historie*. Bind IV: Etter 1914. Oslo: Aschehoug.

Omdal, Sven Egil. 2021. "Sterk rapport fra tapt kamp." *Stavanger Aftonbladet*, June 8, 2021. https://www.aftenbladet.no/kultur/i/6zxwbo/sterk-rapport-fra-tapt-kamp.

Oxfeldt, Elisabeth. 2016. *Skandinaviske fortellinger om skyld og privilegier i en globalisierungstid*. Oslo: Oslo University Press. DOI: http://dx.doi.org/10.1826 1/9788215028095-2016

Pitt Scott, Harry. 2020. "Offshore Mysteries, Narrative Infrastructure: Oil, Noir, and the World-Ocean." *Humanities*, no. 9, 71. DOI: https://doi.org/1 0.3390/h9030071

Polack, Fiona. 2022. "Encountering the Nonhuman in North Atlantic Oil Catastrophes." In Polack and Farquharson, 40–60. London: Routledge.

Polack, Fiona, and Danine Farquharson, eds. 2022. *Cold Water Oil: Offshore Petroleum Cultures*. London: Routledge.

Press, Eyal. 2022. "Life after Deepwater Horizon: The Hidden Toll of Surviving Disaster on an Oil Rig." *The Guardian*, January 6, 2022. https://www.thegu ardian.com/news/2022/jan/06/life-after-deepwater-horizon-the-hidden -toll-of-surviving-disaster-on-an-oil-rig.

Rees, Ellen. 2016. "Privilege, Innocence, and 'Petro-Guilt' in Maria Sødahl's *Limbo*." *Scandinavian Studies* 88 (1): 42–59. DOI: https://doi.org/10.5406/s canstud.88.1.42

Reid, Marc. 2020. "The Piper Alpha Disaster: A Personal Perspective with Trans-
    ferrable Lessons on the Long-Term Moral Impact of Safety Failures." *ACS
    Chemical Health and Safety*, no. 27, 88–95.
Ritson, Katie. 2019. *The Shifting Sands of the North Sea Lowlands: Literary and His-
    torical Imaginaries*. London: Routledge.
Sæther, Anne Karin. 2017. *De beste intensjoner: Oljelandet i klimakampen*. Oslo:
    Cappelen Damm.
Taylor, Sue Jane. 2005. *Oilwork: North Sea Diaries*. Edinburgh: Birlinn.
Trexler, Adam. 2015. *Anthropocene Fictions*. Charlottesville, VA: University of Vir-
    ginia Press.
Tungland, Else, Marie Smith-Solbakken, and Ellen Kongsnes. 2020. *Kielland*.
    Stavanger: Kielland-nettverket.
Weik von Mossner, Alexa. 2017. *Affective Ecologies: Empathy, Emotion, and Environ-
    mental Narrative*. Columbus, OH: Ohio State University Press.

On Some Absent Presences of Nuclear Extractivism: Retrofuturist Aesthetics and *Fallout 4*

Kylie Crane

Nuclear projects are extractive. This is true for the processes that come before detonations, like mining, and, as I will argue in this contribution, those processes that extend into the long-term future. Nuclear detonations, either slow and enduring (as in power plants) or sudden and explosive (as in bombs), extract from *both* the past *and* the future, and yet cushion the present, even as material remnants of these processes accumulate all around us.[1]

On the topic of harnessing nuclear energy, Rebecca Solnit suggests that

> [t]here is something wondrous about the fact that humans have managed to make stars, and something horrible about the fact that they, or we, went to the trouble of making stars for no more interesting reason that obliterating other human beings, and the places around them. (43)

The processes entailed by, and the histories written about, this technological marvel amidst abject horror are not the main argument here. For this article, I emphasize how the nuclear renders some spaces and times expendable, and how the nuclear hence extracts from the livelihoods of people (and others) living in those marginal spaces and times. The first part of this piece will look to the nuclear as "ways of being in relation to energy, society, and the world" (Flisfeder 242), with particular attention to the violence towards people and places it entails. My main case study will be a popular computer game,

---

1   That the latter use (as a source of energy) came *after* the first (the bomb) is a function of applicable research funding—the military had the resources—as much, perhaps, as anything else (cf. e.g., Flisfeder or Solnit 108–144). The accumulations, as will become clear, are both the kind that will require storage (cf. e.g., Ialenti) or that are stored in the body (cf. Hecht or Williams).

Bethesda Softworks' *Fallout 4* from 2015. The game employs an aesthetic that externalizes risk in temporal terms, that valorizes technological fixes, and at the same time—somewhat paradoxically—implies that nuclear fallout is containable. The marginalization of risk—historically and still today relegated to colonies—is now and has always been relegated to the future. Despite the best attempts at containment and relegation, nuclear technologies and interventions always have worked to collapse sovereignty, spatial regimes of power and even time, and continue to do so today.

Absent Presents, Absent Presences: Elsewhere & Elsewhen

Extractive relations are present in all manner of (material) relations. For Macarena Gómez-Barris, "the extractive global economy" is the system "installed by colonial capitalism in the 1500s and that converted natural resources such as silver, water, timber, rubber, and petroleum into global commodities" (xvi). In the Américas, according to Gómez-Barris, extractivism is embroiled in capitalism and colonialism, that is, in "thefts, borrowings, and forced removals, violently reorganizing social life as well as the land by thieving resources from Indigenous and Afro-descendent territories" (xvii). Whilst in the context of the Américas (and elsewhere), extraction is intricately connected to capitalism and is imbricated in histories of enslaving people, extractivist mindsets also gird non-capitalist relations, as the example of nuclear entanglements in the former U.S.S.R. illustrate (see the work of Kate Brown for more on this, in particular *Plutopia*).

Nuclear energy relies on specific raw materials, quite literally extracted from the earth, as well as on the extractions figured through complex enrichment projects, through sustained experimentation, and, of course, on human labor. For Anaïs Maurer and Rebecca H. Hogue, the extractive relations of nuclear energy are not unrelated to others: "If you live in the United States," they write, "there is a one in five probability that your light is powered by uranium mined on stolen Indigenous land in Australia, Canada, Kazakhstan, Russia, and the continental United States" (29). The extractive relations do not end there, however. Extraction, in nuclear relations, is not simply the removal of minerals—for example uranium—from lands around the world. It is also evident in what is normally called 'tests' and 'test-sites.' As Solnit reminds us, the U.S. Department of Energy also lists the explosions above Hiroshima and Nagasaki as tests (138–39). Whilst Solnit prefers the term 'rehearsals' to suggest that they "were full-scale explosions in the real world, with all the attendant effects" (5), to emphasize cumulative approximation of war, I think 'detonations' might better stress the explosive and material dimensions of these acts.

Maurer and Hogue also note that the first five countries to develop atomic bombs *all* undertook initial detonations ('tests') on indigenous land, and, crucially, recognize that this constitutes placing indigenous peoples under attack (31–32). "Unlike other forms of imperialism," they argue, "nuclear imperialisms are not only interested in occupying another given territory simply to exploit its resources or merely to pollute it. They annihilate their chosen sites of empire" (33). One of their interlocutors in that piece, antinuclear activist Chantal T. Spitz, presses this point with more urgency: "Nuclear countries do not develop and experiment their weapons of death on their own soils but on their colonies' soils. Nuclear is happening because colonies exist" (qtd. in Maurer/Hogue 26). Sometimes these colonies are far away, sometimes much closer; sometimes they are explicit colonies, sometimes they are unceded lands.

Consequently, nuclear relations do not pattern evenly across the globe (although the Pacific [Rim] figures prominently). Isao Hashimoto's video "Timelapse Map of All 2053 Nuclear Explosions 1945—1998" uses pared down computer generated images to map the detonations through this time period and across the globe. After the initial detonations in Japan, the scale shifts to include the entirety of the globe. Each nuclear 'player'—and the aesthetics are more than a little reminiscent of early computer games—is given a different color upon 'entry' to the 'game,' and the acceleration of detonations proceeds. Minor lapses in intensity of detonations following international treaties (e.g., around 1958) become evident, visually and sonically, by contrast to the accumulation of color and noise that otherwise accompanies each detonation. Through the use of color, the relations between the respective nuclear powers and their preferred sites of detonation are rendered more visible, as is the case with Peter Atwood's static image ("Nuclear Detonations 1945–2019"). The colonial relations[2] that gird these detonation structures would come into their own if the centers of each power were specifically mapped alongside with the use of color to map in the respective empires.

---

2   Both Hashimoto and Atwood employ pink to represent the United Kingdom's detonations and thus reference the relations of empire by taking advantage of that particular color reference.

Mapping the testing sites across an (imagined) background of relations of empire then emerges as an extended exercise in mapping colonialism: Kazakhstan's relations to the Soviet Union come to echo Australia's relations to the U.K., and also what New Mexico (and, later, the Marshall Islands) were and continue to be to the U.S. and what Algeria and Polynesia were and continue to be to France. Each of these relations depicts in and of itself a center-periphery relation. Most critically, imagined atop a map of empire, the detonations are far away from their respective centers of power. The risk—the fallout[3]—of detonations is played down and literally marginalized by being staged on the (respective) geographical margins of the so-called first world. To be sure, these margins are, for other people(s), livelihoods and ancestral lands, not marginal at all.

This marginalization of risk is concomitant with an externalization of resource extraction and other exploitative practices. Several terms have been developed to trace this idea. Georg Borgström's "ghost acreage" points to the externalized lands (and, by extension, lives) that feed the wealthy; Kenneth Pomeranz similarly explores the idea of "ghost acres" and "ghost acreage" as an extractive relation emerging with industrialization (275–83). Borgström's and Pomeranz' terms emerge in thinking about the production of food, with some peoples of the present profiting from other peoples' present lack. Val Plumwood proposes the term 'shadow places' for thinking through the "*material conditions (including ecological conditions) that support or enable our lives*" (her italics), which, she argues, the valorization of place has often neglected to consider: "An ecological re-conception of dwelling has to include a justice perspective and be able to recognise the shadow places, not just the ones we love, admire or find nice to look at" (n. p.). Stefan Lessenich, in the *Externalisierungsgesellschaft* (externalization society, analog, perhaps, to Ulrich Beck's *Risikogesellschaft* which has been translated as risk society), makes a similar point: He observes that to be 'doing well,' one is 'doing above average,' and that this necessarily entails that there are others who are 'doing below average' (cf. e.g., 24). Of particular interest for this essay is the way he evokes a temporal dimension (as well as the spatial externalization common to the above-mentioned critics):

---

3   Joseph Masco, in *The Future of Fallout, and Other Episodes in Radioactive World-Making*, asserts: "Attending to fallout draws attention to emerging forms of violence across the Global North and South divide while challenging the temporal logics of settler colonialism and postcoloniality" (Masco 18).

> In this conjunction [intergenerational equity/justice], we find the evocation
> of 'our children and children's children' in whose interest we forego nuclear
> power (at the same time as offering energy monopolists compensation),
> we limit our individual travel (at the same time as exporting more cars),
> and amortize debt (at the same time as exploiting the social assets of the
> classes who otherwise own nothing). (30, translation mine)[4]

The appeal to 'our children and children's children,' even if Lessenich distances
himself from it, invokes a prevalent form of sentimentality.[5]

The nuclear collapses simple relations of externalization: Whilst the testing
is pushed *outwards* to the boundaries for the technocrats of the respective imperial powers, this is not the direction of the radioactive interference in bodies. In
Slow Violence and the Environmentalism of the Poor, Rob Nixon notes that "[c]hem-
ical and radiological violence, for example, is driven *inwards*, somatized into
cellular dramas of mutation that—particularly in the bodies of the poor—remain largely unobserved, undiagnosed, and untreated" (6, my emphasis). In
"Interscalar Vehicles for an African Anthropocene," Gabrielle Hecht similarly
notes the difficulties for Gabonese laborers in acquiring diagnosis, medical attention, or compensation (even as French laborers were able to), compounded
by the lack of knowledge of the 'baseline' exposure in the Oklo uranium mine.
Here, too, the effects are marginalized through the politics of the colony. As
Nixon notes, "industrial particulates and effluents live on in the environmental elements we inhabit and in our very bodies, which epidemiologically and
ecologically are never our simple contemporaries" (8).

---

4   "Da [bei Generationsgerechtigkeit] geht es dann um »unsere Kinder und Kindes-
     kinder«, in deren Interesse »wir« unter anderem auf die Atomkraft verzichten (da-
     für allerdings die Energiemonopolisten entschädigen), unseren Individualverkehr be-
     schränken (dafür aber mehr Autos exportieren) und die Staatsschulden tilgen (dafür
     aber an das Sozialvermögen der ansonsten nichtbesitzenden Schichten ran) müssten."
     (Lessenich 30)
5   Interpellations to think of the coming generations such as this are often articulated
     in this particular way—that is, invoking children and grandchildren. As Naomi Klein
     points out in "The Right to Regenerate" (in *This Changes Everything*), her personal ex-
     periences with fertility issues led to resistance to these kinds of invocations: "[I]f I was
     going through a particularly difficult infertility episode, just showing up to a gather-
     ing of environmentalists could be an emotional minefield. The worst part were the
     ceaseless invocations of our responsibilities to 'our children' and 'our grandchildren.'
     [...] [W]here did that leave those of us who did not, or could not, have children? Was
     it even possible to be a real environmentalist if you didn't have kids?" (423)

In such cases, the inhabitants are rendered 'uninhabitants.' This is a term that Robert Nixon finds in Rebecca Solnit, and that Solnit draws from an interview with Janet Gordon (Nixon; Solnit, especially 154–55), predated, amongst others, by Terry Tempest Williams in her memoir *Refuge* (287). The term derived from the phrase "virtually uninhabited," which of course means that the lands *are* inhabited: The near-negative relation is tenuous, resting on the qualifier 'virtually.' The fallout—which, following Joseph Masco is inherent in the systems which give rise to it (i.e., it is not accidental), and which "formally links human actions, technological capabilities, atmospheres, and ecologies in a new configuration of contamination" (Masco 20)—produces instabilities. Cellular volatilities giving rise to cancer; intergenerational volatilities leading to infertilities and genetic variations; all in excess of baseline rates.

Nuclear imperialisms are not just *simply* extractive; they are also annihilative. And this extends, crucially, to thinking about extraction as it extends into the future. Masco brings the multiple valencies of the term 'fallout' to think about the future dimensions of nuclear entanglements. Fallout, he writes, is a term which "involves individual actions and lived consequences" that is "understood primarily retrospectively but lived in the future anterior" because, most crucially, "[f]allout comes after the event" designating "an unexpected supplement to an event, a precipitation that is in motion, causing a kind of long-term and unexpected damage" (19). Masco couples nuclear weapons with climate destruction—twinned threats that play out keenly in the (nuclear) Pacific (see for instance DeLoughrey)—as "industrially manufactured problems that [...] colonize the future" (5).

At the same 'time': The duration of nuclear detonations itself (barely) occupies a relation to experienced time. As Masco argues, "all the nuclear detonations in human history—the 2,100 or so nuclear events that constitute an unprecedented human intervention into the biosphere, remaking both geological and human time—do not collectively add up to a single second of linear time" (285). This folding of extensive durations of fallout into events of such short duration that we might barely register them is also a recognition that relations of time and space are complicated by nuclear energy, as the quantum physics upon which nuclear entanglements are based might already suggest (cf. also Barad).

Cheryll Glotfelty, amongst others, has accordingly suggested that the aftereffects of nuclear detonations have been purposefully relegated to the future: "As the United States invested in nuclear power, little thought was given to what to do with the radioactive waste produced as a by-product of nuclear fission, the assumption being that new technology would arise to deal with the waste" (198). The reliance on a speculative, future technological fix is one that is not particular to nuclear incursions: Similar examples include geo-engineering fixes for climate change; faith in plastic-eating bacteria for plastic waste;[6] and, for most of the West, the narration of the early stages of the SARS-CoV-19 pandemic as a 'waiting-for-the-vaccine,' where the possibility of a vaccine was a *given*. As energy safety enters the political climate of Europe in 2022, and in a political climate given to considerations of climate *change* in other places (e.g., in Australia, with respect to coal extraction regimes), the future dimension of nuclear energies is somehow, again, conveniently bracketed out of considerations. Nuclear power(s) extract(s) not only from the 'ghost acres' or 'shadow places,' those marginalized places; its externalization is not only spatial but is, crucially, temporal. The elsewhere of nuclear power(s) thus becomes also an 'elsewhen.'

Mediating Futures in *Fallout 4*

This 'elsewhen' of nuclear extraction is projected onto the future. As Maurer and Hogue observe, "mainstream nuclear discourse has predominantly been interested in the future—specifically, a speculative, totalizing future dependent on the existence of nuclear war" (27). The future imagined in *Fallout 4*, indeed, in all of the games that comprise the *Fallout* series, which I now address, is predicated on a hollowing out of the nuclear present, and dependent on extractions from other times and places.

Attending to the future requires imagination. Our repertoires for the future are images in the speculative mode. This is the remit of SF, of postapocalyptic, utopian/dystopian, fantasy and other narratives and cultural artifacts that depart from more realist modes, of which computer games (set in the future) are one. Particularly the narrative and dramatic moments of some games establish relations to the future by explicitly telling and staging the story; the use of graphic representation and sound tracks embed these imaginations in representative forms; and the role of the player acts as a bridge between the

---

6   As Max Liboiron points out, plastic-eating bacteria would also eat the plastic we find useful: the buttons on my computer and my glasses, or as they suggest "the plastics in bridges, airplanes, automobiles, pacemakers, and buildings. Everyday infrastructure would be crumbling around us, like a B horror movie" (103).

imaginary worlds represented, especially in the reception of shooter games in broader media contexts, troubles any easy distinction between the social intra- and inter-game worlds.

Fallout 4, released in 2015, is the fourth release in Bethesda Softworks' *Fallout* series. To date, it is the most recent release in the main titles segment of the *Fallout* line, though some spin-offs have been launched in the meantime. *Fallout 4* is primarily set around 200 years after a set of nuclear detonations have blasted the world. The player adopts an avatar who can partake in a number of quests—ostensibly to rescue their kidnapped son[7]—and/or can play around in the postapocalyptic landscape around Boston, Massachusetts, U.S.A.

Fallout 4 came to my attention in a seminar on Nuclear Cultures when a student recognized some of the tracks from the soundtrack to *The Atomic Café* (1982), which we discussed in class, as being also used in the computer game. We watched a short advertisement for the game in class: The proto-utopian hope of 1950s U.S. nuclear culture portrayed in some of the historical sequences of the documentary film mapped in interesting ways onto the world of the game. In addition to the soundtrack, the architectural and interior design of the computer game referenced, with little interference, the design choices of the 1950s in the U.S.A. (and elsewhere). Housing and domestic scenes of the game, as well as the billboard and other advertisements, seemed to be sutured with the postapocalyptic landscape, a kind of *The Truman Show* meets *I am Legend*, with sentimental overtones—as the trope of the kidnapped child might suggest. The documentary works through cognitive distancing and cognitive dissonance by, for instance, showing footage of Marshallese singing "You Are My Sunshine" just before showing footage of the bomb being dropped (a 'test'). In the game, such distancing emerges in the temporal marginalizations—at once referencing a past known to most of us[8] only through media and a future we cannot know.

The media used on the TV in the opening sequences of *Fallout 4* to tell stories that are, for most of us, most of the time, always medialized and mediated: war, testing, bombs, etc. For most of us, most of the time, these things happen elsewhere. The TV set that brings news of impending nuclear attack in the game acts as a portal and as a buffer. It transports images and sounds from far-away places, and, in doing so, seeks to contain these to the images and sounds

---

7   I am of the understanding that players can select the gender—binary—of their avatar and use the pronoun 'they' and derivatives to reflect this.

8   Well: to all of us in that particular seminar.

presented on the set. The TV set reporting in *Fallout 4* as well as the radio announcements initially suggest the distance to the threat, and, if/when this no longer holds, its contain-ability. DeLoughrey uses the term 'isolate' to do this work, where she argues "[t]he concept of the closed system or isolate was tied closely to the colonization of islands and render[ed] them into nuclear laboratories" (172).

Contain-ability, or the 'isolate,' is a premise articulated in the opening sequences of the game, specifically through the figure of the vault salesman. A vault promises security, or at least storage (usually of things; in the game this is the body). In *Fallout 4*, this promise is only partially upheld, for the vault is breached by 'Institute' members who kidnap the protagonist's baby and kill their spouse, a sequence the protagonist is awake for but unable, for a time, to fully comprehend. The narrative of the game play is thus motivated by the sentimental topos of child separation. For Lauren Berlant, there is a particular "history of sentimentality around children that sees them as the reason to have optimism—for if nothing else, their lives are not already ruined" (171). The latter comes into its own when, later in game play, the reasoning for the capture is given: to retrieve the unspoiled DNA of the child (with the protagonist acting as a back-up repository in case of mistakes). So, whilst the vault protects the protagonist (and their family) from the effects of nuclear fallout, it is precisely this protection which renders them more vulnerable to biopiracy. Complete security, it seems, is a myth based on a faulty comprehension of containment. Against this—tenuous—premise, the world unfolds 200 years later, when the avatar is unfrozen from their 200-year hiatus.

It is possible to play *Fallout 4* by mucking around as a scavenger in a postapocalyptic future, or as, Megan Condis suggests with reference to *Mad Max* and *The Last Man on Earth*, as part of an "escapist fantas[y] about what it would be like to be entirely free of responsibility for each other, for society, for the planet" (187): The final consequences of misbehavior have already come to be—the apocalypse has come and gone. Thinking about the game in this sense is to entertain a dystopian fragmentation, where the destruction of the nuclear family through the nuclear threat ultimately sets the avatar into a world deplete of meaningful relations. However, this interpretation of the game rests, as Condis suggests, on ignoring the narrative arc. The extent to which this is upheld—by, for instance, forgoing the opportunity to collaborate with other characters of the postnuclear landscape in establishing (wait for it...) *settlements* replete with agricultural projects and energy producing machines—is the extent to which this world is purely a survival in the leftovers of a previous time. This kind of scavenging is a dwelling in and living through the waste of a previous time, without means of production. The absence of cooperation means the absence of production, rendering the avatar's play an entirely scavenged existence (not unlike the perpetual motion of the figures in Cormac McCarthy's *The Road*, or the TV series *The Walking Dead*), subsiding off the past's waste, in a wasted land.

Past Imaginings of the Future and Future Reconfigurations of the Past

As already mentioned, the soundtrack draws on bebop hits like "Atom Bomb Baby," songs of the kind that rhyme bomb with wigwam (exoticism leaning toward racism) or describe women in terms of their hotness (not too different to the lyrics of today, though this hotness is radioactive). At the same time, the visuals recollect the buildings built to test nuclear destruction in the region of Nevada, though transplanted to the normally more verdant northeastern region of the U.S. The 'return' to the 1950s is troubled, though, by other aesthetic/worlding decisions.

In the opening sequences of *Fallout 4*, the player is introduced to the prelapsarian world, a suburban setting of the nuclear family (cf. Flisfeder), replete with robot-butler Codsworth. Codsworth speaks with a decidedly English accent, thus seemingly enacting a strange nostalgia for imperial relations, imagined in a sentimental manner that paints Codsworth as a subservient and caring servant. Codsworth, further, acts as a micro case study in what might best be called 'retro-futurism,' for the robot looks much like what I (today) imagine people of the 1950s might have imagined future robots to look like: a looping of temporal imaginings that side-steps the present (except as the time of reception). Codsworth is not the only instance of "content that highlights nostalgia, irony, and time-bending dislocation" (434) as Elizabeth Guffey and Kate C. Lemay define retrofuturism. The above mentioned suburb, as well as large mainframe computers in the vault and other locations, gas stations or truck stops called "Red Rocket" replete with large signs,[9] even the power armor, similarly seem to recollect bygone imaginations of the future. Indeed, the premise of the quest—cyrogenetic freezing in a safely contained vault unaffected by

---

9   The symbolism somehow also seems to fold Elon Musk's and Richard Branson's fantastical space travel into the fossil fueled futurism of the 1950s.

broadscale societal and environmental collapse—might be more representative of a past speculative future than most imaginations of the future from the
mid-2010s (when the game was released) or the early 2020s (when I am writing
this piece).

In this, the game engages in a lengthy displacement of the immediate past
of the game world to a more distanced future. As Joe P. L. Davidson has argued
of science fiction film,

> Retrofuturism [...] refers to the conscious use of a repertoire of images of
> technology, architecture and design, as well as intertextual references to
> other cultural artefacts, that are indexed in the cultural imaginary to the
> futurism of the mid-twentieth century with the aim of reinterpreting, re-
> contextualizing and reworking the meaning of yesterday's tomorrows in
> the present. (731)

In the context of a game that plays out in a nuclear (past-)future, this has, I
argue, the effect of hollowing out the (gameplay) present. The nuclear threat is
configured as a *past* potential future, which may have come into being in the future depicted by the game world, but that necessarily and absolutely bypasses
the present.

Aside from the renditions of the robot-butler Codsworth, of material goods
(like houses, furniture, even food packaging, and posters), and the incorpora-
tion of a 'matching' soundtrack, a similar gesture of historical reconfiguration
is evident on a different level of the game, namely the groups with which the
player can affiliate the avatar to complete quests. Megan Condis gives a suc-
cinct summary of the directed or narrative gameplay storylines of *Fallout 4* in
her review:

> the player [is supposed to] choose between four possible sets of allies to
> guide the future of the Wasteland: the Institute, who use their futuristic
> technology to hide underground and who have developed (and enslaved)
> a robot army to do their bidding in the world above; the Railroad, a ragtag
> group of spies dedicated to freeing synthetic humans from the clutches of
> the Institute; the Minutemen, an alliance of small settlements providing
> safe haven and protection for residents of the area; and the Brotherhood of
> Steel, a militaristic group who are obsessed with gathering up and hoard-
> ing all the weaponry from the world that was. To complete the game, the
> player must choose a faction to align with and become its leader, work-

ing to fulfil its chosen mission, all while seeking the whereabouts of your kidnapped son. (185)

This is ultimately another, important, way in which historical context is (awkwardly!) folded into the ludic present of *Fallout 4*, itself set in a potential future.

Samuel McCready gives two of these groups (the Minutemen and the Brotherhood) more attention in his account, noting the conflict between the two versions of understanding the world are essentially mutually exclusive. McCready thus reads the imaginations of these groups as demonstrating the contingency of historical accounts of the U.S. more broadly: The speculative future draws on specific understandings of the past, somehow nearly entirely bypassing the present. An insistence on teleology is present in the inclusion of both groups, and, at the same time, as McCready points out, "there is no [United States of] America to salvage, for either group" (30).[10] The counterfactual imaginary at work in *Fallout 4* in the re-imagination of past historical factions reconfigures sets of people from the Civil War to consolidate a sense of U.S. exceptionalism, proliferating a particularly U.S. American version of history by resuscitating it. This aspect of the game insists on the persistence of specifically U.S. American histories that continue to inhabit the post-apocalyptic worlds, suggesting—simultaneously and also counter-intuitively—that these myths, in particular of U.S. exceptionalism, are hardy enough to literally survive the end of the world.

The Minutemen, aside from referencing the New England colonial militia that went by this name, are the group most invested in topside settlement (the Institute, another group, shifts underground).[11] Missions with, and for, this group often entail the construction of housing, farm plots, and securing settlements. The relation to the nuclear embodied by this group is a reiteration of settler myths, now set in the distant future, or as Masco suggests (not specifically of *Fallout 4*): "the American modernist story of self-invention via settler colonialism, the ability to always start over somewhere else, to break with the

---

10   "The world of *Fallout 4* challenges players to think about what has led them here to this nuclear hellscape; this includes considering how it is that myths of progress that so often get written into history actively contributed in making a future that was less stable (and ultimately decimated) precisely because it was ideologically monolithic" (McCready 31).

11   The name might also evoke the Minuteman Project—an anti-immigration group that 'watches' the Southern border. Thanks to Axelle Germanaz for pointing this out.

past and begin anew, to escape fallout by simply relocating to a newly exciting frontier" (39).

The Brotherhood, another group, seems to be a thinly veiled metaphor for the military-industrial complex; convinced that controlling technology and stockpiling weaponry is key to domination. In a game like this, complete domination is desirable (and how you win); and destruction is a tool towards this. Affiliating with this group means dissociating from the violent premise of the game, with its near-complete destruction of the world. It requires a selectively edited understanding of history to pursue affiliation with this group with the goal of completing the game, as their goals perpetuate the problems that the story is predicated on. The violence of the past (and future?) is met with more violence. This storyline thus awkwardly echoes many of the dissonances that characterize living in a post-colonial world in the Anthropocene, entailing the capacity to ignore the externalizations of risk outlined earlier as well as the long-term consequences of material engagements with the world in favor of living the present.

The Railroad, even in their denomination, recollect the history of people working to redress the horrors of slavery, that is, the Underground Railroad. In *Fallout 4*, racial politics give way to species considerations, bringing cyborg or posthumanist thought to the kinds of politics that are entailed in histories of exclusion, domination, and exploitation. This group's aim is to free the Synths, synthesized humans 'grown' by the Institute from the DNA of the avatar's son, and who are kept as slaves. When Synths develop (too much) free will they are subject to a radical restart, a kind of social death; the Railroad seeks to help them to freedom.

The Institute is more amorphous, and at the same time the most retrofuturistic of the groups, with the architectural and fashion choices of this faction referencing (historical) science fiction films and/or futuristic spy movies, with some fans pointing to *Forbidden Planet* (1956) and others to *2001: A Space Odysee* (1968) to trace potential influences. The sometimes 'wooden' dialogue seems, in these sequences, to be deliberately on point, a caricature of the kind of films that portray long-gone versions of by-now outdated futures. The Institute has a much cleaner aesthetic than the desolate ruins 'topside': lots of white, clean lines, sweeping staircases, sleek elevators, and verdant plants. Its retro-futurism is clinical rather than ruinous, underscoring the divides between the cultural and physical worlds the different groups of the game inhabit.

At the same time, the ravaged topside world suggests there are limits to this exceptionalism. Pointing out the insertion of imagined bygone advertisements and billboards into the landscape of postnuclear destruction, McCready argues that "juxtaposition of happy consumer culture with total annihilation serves as its own critique of the kinds of excess that are at least in part responsible for the destruction that has been wrought" (25). For McCready, the counterfactual premise of *Fallout 4* reveals, amongst other things, the shortcomings of consumer culture to buttress individuals against destruction. The image he includes in his article "Playing the Past and Alternative Futures" shows a dull and rusting vending machine with two bright posters plastered on it, next to a "moldy box of illegible files" (25) and a fully articulated human skeleton.[12] *Fallout 4*, he argues, "reveals the tenuousness of the historical trajectory that proceeded from that mid-century moment until the present in its own altered futurescape, and makes a powerful claim against totalizing and revisionist attempts to reconstruct an ordered version of events" (26). In my interpretation, I turn to the very specific ways in which the phrase "the present in its own altered futurescape" (ibid.) skips over the player's present: the ways in which the game recognizes and represents the almost entirely absent presence of nuclear threat. Almost entirely, because one of the detonations is indeed shown, though its duration is comparable, if not shorter, than the countdown presented soon after that accompanies the avatar into their cyrogenetic freeze. Both are a-temporal events compressing radical interventions into the future's liveability (collectively, individually) into a manner of seconds, in a link back to Masco's observation about the accumulative duration of all nuclear detonations.

A Brief Conclusion

Fallout 4 excavates the present and all kinds of presences to locate 'the' nuclear in the past, in the future, in the past's imagination of the future … anywhere but the here and now. In doing so, the game replicates fantasies of contain-ability;

---

12   The existence of fully articulated human skeletons and skeletal trees bereft of signs of life are not necessarily fanciful; they can be seen as indicative of the extent to which the critters that usually do the work of decomposition are not compatible with high levels of radiation. Kate Brown observes some scientists working in the larger region of Chernobyl as theorizing that "microbes, worms, larvae, and insects that normally break down organic matter were unable to work well in high levels of contamination (over 50 microsieverts)." (205)

not a strong claim for a game predicated on the existence of a vault imperme-
able to nuclear fallout but not, it seems, so foreign to the military-industrial
complex that probably built it in the first place. With its sentimental cues to
the nuclear family (locating the kidnapped son is crucial to the narrative, particularly at the outset), and the 'innocent' aesthetics of the 1950s, both in the
'simply retro' and the retro-futuristic modes, the locus of the avatar is cush-
ioned against the ravages of the world. And, yes, games tend to do this: We
can, after all, repeatedly save gameplay and resume before some catastrophic
decision or unforeseen consequence. This cushioning is, however, clearly predicated on an externalization of risk and, crucially, an extraction *from* the future.
The liveability of the future is irrevocably based on our capacity to act ethically
towards human, cyborg, and other livelihoods, both of our present and not.

The extent to which the liveability of 'our' current lives is also the un-live-
ability of other's current lives, and many people's future lives, is one of nuclear
culture's entanglements in the present. Debates about energy crises have
brought attention back to nuclear power. In Germany, this is a debate that also
arises from Russia's invasion of Ukraine, with its various impacts on energy
policy: A center (Russia) seeking to reassert itself in a (former) periphery
(Ukraine) is not a speculative meandering around past problems, but trans-
forms into a debate about the sustainability of energy production. The re-entry
of Chernobyl to medialized debates concerning the potential weaponization
of nuclear facilities, along with the reactors at the Zaporizhzhia plant, alarm-
ingly show how tenuous the stability of nuclear generation can be. And, in
France, the drying up of the Loire River in the summer of 2022 has been met
with concern: The river and its tributaries provide water for the cooling of
several nuclear facilities producing electricity (cf. Crellin). Lines of argumen-
tation that render coal dirty and nuclear somehow clean neglect such very real
(future) material impacts. With climate change, the future is closer than it
once perhaps appeared. Nuclear energy has and continues to extract from the
margins; and one of these margins is temporal: the—our—future.

References

"Atom Bomb Baby." 2005. The Five Stars. 4–8 *Atomic Platters: Cold War Music from the Golden Age of Homeland Security*. Bear Family Records.

Atwood, Peter. n. d. "Nuclear Detonations: 1945–2019." Accessed June 23, 2022. https://peteratwoodprojects.wordpress.com/design-projects/#jp-carousel-403.

Barad, Karen. 2007. *Meeting the Universe Halfway: Quantum Physics and the Entanglement of Matter and Meaning*. Durham, NC: Duke University Press.

Berlant, Lauren. 2011. *Cruel Optimism*. Durham, NC: Duke University Press.

Bethesda Softworks. 2015. *Fallout 4*.

Borgström, Georg. 1972. *The Hungry Planet: The Modern World at the Edge of Famine*. New York, NY: MacMillan.

Brown, Kate. 2015. *Plutopia: Nuclear Families, Atomic Cities, and the Great Soviet and American Plutonium Disasters*. Oxford: Oxford University Press.

Brown, Kate. 2019. "Learning to Read the Great Chernobyl Acceleration: Literacy in the More-than-Human Landscapes." *Current Anthropology* 60 (supplement 20): S198–S208.

Condis, Megan. 2017. "Fantasizing about the Apocalypse: A Review of Fallout 4." *Resilience: A Journal of the Environmental Humanities* 4 (2–3): 185–90.

Crellin, Forrest. 2022. "Warming Rivers Threaten France's Already Tight Water Supply." *Reuters.com*, July 15, 2022. Accessed on August 21, 2022. https://www.reuters.com/business/energy/warming-rivers-threaten-frances-already-tight-power-supply-2022-07-15/.

Davidson, Joe P.L. 2019. "Blast from the Past: Hopeful Retrofuturism in Science Fiction Film." *Continuum: Journal of Media & Cultural Studies* 33 (6): 729–43.

DeLoughrey, Elizabeth. 2012. "The Myth of Isolates: Ecosystem Ecologies in the Nuclear Pacific." *Cultural Geographies* 20 (2): 167–84.

Flisfeder, Matthew. 2017. "Nuclear 1." In *Fueling Culture: 101 Words for Energy and Environment*, edited by Imre Szeman, Jennifer Wenzel, and Patricia Yaeger, 242–44. New York, NY: Fordham University Press.

Glotfelty, Cheryll. 2011. "Reclaiming Nimby: Nuclear Waste, Jim Day, and the Rhetoric of Local Resistance." In *Environmental Criticism in the Twenty-First Century*, edited by Stephanie LeMenager, Teresa Shewry, and Ken Hiltner, 196–215. London: Routledge.

Gómez-Barris, Macarena. 2017. *The Extractive Zone: Social Ecologies and Decolonial Perspectives*. Durham, NC: Duke University Press.

Guffey, Elizabeth, and Kate C. Lemay. 2014. "Retrofuturism and Steampunk." *The Oxford Handbook of Science Fiction*, edited by Rob Latham (online edition, Oxford Academic, October 2, 2014). DOI: https://doi.org/10.1093/oxfordhb /9780199838844.013.0034. 434–48.

Hashimoto, Isao. 2011. "Time-lapse Map of All 2053 Nuclear Explosions 1945–1998." *YouTube*, June 28, 2011. https://www.youtube.com/watch?v=d xyRLvcjVCw.

Hecht, Gabrielle. 2018. "Interscalar Vehicles for an African Anthropocene: On Waste, Temporality, and Violence." *Cultural Anthropology* 33 (1): 109–41.

Ialenti, Vincent. 2020. *Deep Time Reckoning: How Future Thinking Can Help Earth Now*. Cambridge, MA: MIT Press.

Klein, Naomi. 2014. *This Changes Everything: Climate vs Capitalism*. New York, NY: Simon & Schuster.

Kubrick, Stanley, dir. 1968. *2001: A Space Odyssey*. Beverly Hills, CA: Metro-Gold-wyn-Mayer.

Lawrence, Francis, dir. 2007. *I Am Legend*. Burbank, CA: Warner Bros. Pictures.

Lessenich, Stefan. 2015. "Die Externalisierungsgesellschaft: Ein Internalisie-rungsversuch." *Soziologie* 44 (1): 22–32.

Liboiron, Max. 2021. *Pollution is Colonialism*. Durham, NC: Duke University Press.

Masco, Joseph. 2021. *The Future of Fallout, and Other Episodes in Radioactive World-Making*. Durham, NC: Duke University Press.

Maurer, Anaïs, and Rebecca H. Hogue. 2020. "Introduction: Transnational Nu-clear Imperialisms." *Journal of Transnational American Studies* 11 (2): 25–43.

McCarthy, Cormac. 2006. *The Road*. New York, NY: Alfred A. Knopf.

McCready, Samuel. 2019. "Playing the Past and Alternative Futures: Counter-factual History in Fallout 4." *Loading... The Journal of the Canadian Games Studies Association* 12 (20): 15–34.

Nixon, Rob. 2011. *Slow Violence and the Environmentalism of the Poor*. Cambridge, MA: Harvard University Press.

Plumwood, Val. 2018. "Shadow Places and the Politics of Dwelling." *Australian Humanities Review* 44. Accessed on October 29, 2022. http://australianhum anitiesreview.org/2008/03/01/shadow-places-and-the-politics-of-dwelli ng/.

Pomeranz, Kenneth. 2000. *The Great Divergence: China, Europe, and the Making of the Modern World Economy*. Princeton, NJ: Princeton University Press.

Rafferty, Kevin, Jayne Loader, and Piercy Rafferty, dir. 1982. *The Atomic Café*. New York, NY: Libra Films.

Solnit, Rebecca. 1999. *Savage Dreams: A Journey into the Landscape Wars of the American West*. Berkeley, CA: University of California Press.

The Walking Dead. 2010. Frank Darabont, executive producer. 2010. AMC Studios.

Weir, Peter, dir. 1998. *The Truman Show*. Los Angeles, CA: Paramount Pictures.

Wilcox, Fred M., dir. 1956. *Forbidden Planet*. Beverly Hills, CA: Metro-Goldwyn-Mayer.

Williams, Terry Tempest. 2008. *Refuge: An Unnatural History of Family and Place*. 3rd edition. New York, NY: Vintage Books.

"You are my sunshine." 1940. Charles Mitchell and Jimmie Davis. Southern Music Publishing Co., Inc.

"All of That Wealth Underneath": How the Logic of Extraction Blocks Discourses of Sustainability in the U.S.[1]

Heike Paul

> "[T]he physical causes […] which can lead to prosperity
> are more numerous in America than in any other country
> at any other time in history."
> *Alexis de Tocqueville, Democracy in America (327–28)*

> "As for the garden,
> Adam,
> after the Fall.
> Make no mistake, he said,
> We will destroy it all."
> *Thomas King, 77 Fragments (1)*

Introduction

The dictum "land of unlimited possibilities" has been a recurring hyperbole in (self-)descriptions of the United States of America—even *avant la lettre*. The

---

1   This paper first appeared in 2020 in the volume *Imaginationen von Nachhaltigkeit. Katastrophe. Krise, Normalisierung*, edited by Frank Adloff, Benno Fladvad, Martina Hasenfratz, and Sighard Neckel. Frankfurt/New York: Campus Verlag, 91–121.

highly praised unlimitedness either referred to notions of freedom, social mobility, economic success, or, last but not least, the seemingly endless "natural"
resources, which made the former possible in the first place.[2] The narrativiza-
tion and iconization of this abundance of resources reaches back to the colonial
beginnings of the United States. In the late 18th and early 19th century, it became
a central topos in the self-image of the young nation, which further evolved in
the context of the paradigm of a general settler colonialism and a specific notion of a westward moving *frontier* that promised land in abundance to prospective settlers. Many early texts about the United States virtually advertised this
wealth and promised it to willing immigrants (cf. Crèvecoeur; Duden).

Sustainability—in the sense of taking future effects of current actions into
consideration—did not only *not* play a role, but it was also literally beyond
the discursive horizon, as it was in open conflict with the new republic's
fundamental capitalist logics focused on property and profit. Consequently,
the process of westward expansion, which rested on the expropriation and
genocide of the indigenous population, was in part also marked by short-
lived and resource-intensive settlement practices characteristic of "extractive
colonialism," where newly founded towns were abandoned quickly when the
resources were depleted or when the settlers faced better prospects for profit
elsewhere.[3] This is central to the early discourse on ruins in the United States,
to which, for instance, a surprised Alexis de Tocqueville made the following
comment during his travels, when he discovered remains of white settlements
in Upstate New York: "How astonishing! Ruins already!" (328). The familiar
idea of America as a big garden (Eden) (e.g., Smith 138ff.) and the vision of an
agrarian ideal state obscure two aspects: on the one hand, the expansionist

---

2   The "land of unlimited possibilities" formula goes back to German author Max Gold-
     berger and his book *Land der unbegrenzten Möglichkeiten*, published in 1903. While
     Goldberger mainly described the economic upswing in the United States, the title
     of his book soon became a common saying and was applied much more broadly to
     different aspects of American society and history (cf. Klautke 7). Moreover, the pub-
     lisher Henry Luce (135) wrote about "unlimited resources" in the context of "manifest
     destiny" and the "frontier."
3   The land grab by European settlers as described by so-called settler colonialism, is
     typically differentiated from "extractive colonialism," which is mainly concerned with
     the exploitation of resources. However, it is important to bear in mind that the dif-
     ferent "types" of colonialism (Nancy Shoemaker identified 12 different ones) do not
     usually occur in their pure form, rather, "different forms of colonialism might coexist
     or morph into each other." For a history of American ghost towns see Ling.

land grab and, on the other hand, the ruthless extraction of resources (also in reference to human labor and especially the bio-politics of enslaved labor as part of an early "racialized capitalism"). Both forms of unscrupulousness indeed seem boundless in retrospect.[4]

Around the end of the 19th and the beginning of the 20th century, after the Civil War and the "closing of the frontier," notions of unlimited growth shifted to the realms of technological and economic progress. Despite the fact that narratives of progress became increasingly contested, such ideas lived on beyond two world wars and have been revived in the postwar years as well as in more recent times—especially in political discourse. As a topic with affective appeal in election campaigns and political agendas, the fantasy of unlimited resources comes up time and time again and must be analyzed as part of the rhetoric of American exceptionalism.[5] In 1954, amid the economic recovery of the 1950s and at the height of the Cold War, the consensus historian David Potter—in his clearly not uncontroversial socio-psychological study—describes Americans as a "people of plenty," whose character was formed by the prosperity and abundance in the United States ("land of plenty") and whose mentality embodied the constant availability and expenditure of resources. Similarly, the European vision of the United States had, for a long time, been informed by the supposed abundance of resources—and the notion that what is needed from nature can be taken and profitably used for one's own benefit: land, humans, animals, natural resources. The logic of extraction—in part literally, in part metaphorically—underlies representations of these historical processes and developments and is perhaps more relevant at present than it has been for a long time.

It is this notion of extraction that is at the heart of the following analysis. According to the *Oxford English Dictionary*, it is "[t]he action or process of drawing (something) out of a receptacle; the pulling or taking out (of anything) by mechanical means" (*OED* Online). In the "Corpus of Contemporary American

---

4   Satnam Virdee analyzed in detail "the structuring force of racism in the history of capitalist modernity" (ibid. 22).

5   In the past years, this rhetoric has been employed in an exceptionally aggressive way by former president Donald Trump. Previously, Ronald Reagan had repeatedly referred to America's "unlimited resources" at the beginning of his first presidency, and even Barack Obama had promised: "We will not apologize for our way of life, nor will we waver in its defense." And even if Obama talked about having to "end the age of oil," his administration mostly conceded to the oil lobby (LeMenager 9).

English," the most frequent collocate of "extraction"—not surprisingly from to-day's perspective—is the word "oil" (Davies). The extraction of fossil fuels has been a focal point in U.S. history. Consequently, it does not only take center stage in economic ventures and political debates but also in cultural produc-tions.[6] American capitalism is and has always been essentially an oil capital-ism, and the much-lauded "American way of life" would not be possible with-out it, neither with regard to consumer culture in general, nor the automobile culture in particular—the outstanding importance of oil for the military-in-dustrial complex should also be mentioned here.[7]

Oil capitalism has been and continues to be in stark contrast to all ideas of ecological sustainability and resource conservation. Not least of all Donald Trump has been one of the most powerful proponents of this system: During his presidency, he embraced extraction in his energy policies on a grand scale, promoting both the revitalization of coal extraction and the controversial prac-tice of fracking (the extraction of oil from great depths by means of injections of water and chemical substances). This way, Trump invoked—and simulta-neously exploited—the U.S. "petro-imaginary,"[8] which reaches as far back as the 19th century and is linked especially to those regions where Trump had his conservative voter base: Texas, for example, and Western Virginia—a predom-inantly rural region with a history determined by the extraction of oil and coal and which to this very day is strongly marked by the frontier-habitus. Ameri-can studies scholar Donald Pease has pointed out that, during his campaign, Trump chose former "frontier sites" as rally sites to deliver his retrotopic (cf. Bauman) election promises:

---

6   Frederick Buell refers to the "culture of extraction" and the 19th century "oil-extrac-tion culture," respectively (74). In doing so, he resorts to the work of Ida M. Tarbell, who associated a special kind of ruthless individualism with oil exploration and the speculation surrounding it, i.e., an "oil individualism" (75). In Tarbell, this results in a criticism of monopoly-capitalism à la Rockefeller.

7   Cf. Pease (2017, 31): "The 'American way of life' would be unimaginable without an oil economy marked by surplus production, militarism, automobility, unregulated mar-kets, and mass consumption. Oil capitalism shaped significant turns in US national history." See also Rice and Tyner, who highlight the role of oil for American states-manship, and Mitchell, who refers to the U.S. as a "carbon democracy."

8   The term "petro-imaginary" appears to have first been used by Georgiana Banita (151) and has since been established as a concept which, on the one hand, takes up aspects of the cultural and political imaginary and, on the other hand, addresses the specifics of oil-related imaginaries.

Trump channels this colonial settler mentality at his rallies [...] A typical Trump rally site hollows a zone of indistinction between the frontier and the normal political order. At a Trump rally, followers collectively participate in the fantasy of their own regression to a state of desublimated rage at a quite literal restoration of a frontier site where these descendants of settler colonists can experience their ancestors' regeneration through violence. The frontier site a Trump rally opens up is, like the original, the not-yet bounded space on either side of the border, which is beyond clear jurisdiction. This alternative geography figures as a topological rendition of capitalist expansion beyond limits. As the primal scene of capitalist accumulation and contract, the frontier names an as yet uncolonized space upon which the processes by which the proper order of capitalist property and racialized capital gets re-installed through Trump's contract from this relentlessly nativist America (Pease 2018, 164).

This frontier scenario is a fitting match for the logic of extraction. It is also the cornerstone of Trump's campaign program, which rested in equal measure on the extraction and exploitation of resources, the explicit departure from the policies of his predecessor (even if the extraction of oil was also heavily increased under Obama, i.e., there has been no complete reversal), and the undermining of well-established political and administrative processes and institutions.[9] The appointment of the Texan Rex Tillerson, CEO of ExxonMobil, as secretary of state already revealed Trump's affinity for petro-fantasies of all sorts. Tillerson, who learned about his dismissal after 14 months as secretary of state via a tweet by the president on March 13, 2018, did not even belong to the hard-core deniers of climate change in Trump's administration. While he did consider it a problem that ought to be solved by a "techno-fix," he did not take it to be a problem that created an ethical obligation or even a political need for action.[10] For Trump, Tillerson appeared to be the right man in the right place—at least temporarily. The fact, however, that Tillerson as a businessman made deals in Russia and elsewhere rather than simply drill "ultradeep" within

9   Thus, in Trump's speech, analyzed below, he describes his cooperation with the U.S.-Environmental Protection Agency as if the EPA were not a controlling body but rather an ally in fighting against control and regulation. He also praises Andrew Wheeler, former coal lobbyist and head of the EPA, for the creation and maintenance of small refineries in the country and as someone "[who] loves the environment."

10   Cf. Tillerson, cited in Mooney. See also Tillerson's keynote at the Argus Americas Crude Summit in Houston, Texas, in January 2020, summarized in Baltimore.

the United States was met with the president's disapproval, as were Tillerson's positions on various political questions regarding climate issues (for instance, his backing of a CO_2-levy and his support of the Paris Agreement; cf. Egan). As he later revealed, Trump utterly disliked it when he was told that his lofty plans were too simplistic and—on top of that—illegal (Tillerson). This statement appears to substantiate Pease's analysis, according to which Trump used the notion of the frontier site for political purposes, a place quasi-unregulated by law, where extraction is primarily a matter of power, possibly of competition, but certainly not of ethics or even moderation in the sense of sustainable management.

To better illustrate the problems arising from this absence of ecological and economic notions of sustainability in the petro-imaginary of the United States, I will analyze Trump's rhetoric of unlimited and affect-saturated "extraction" in the context of his former energy policies that promised short-term success and quick wealth instead of sustainability. A specific focus in this context is on a speech given by Trump at the *Shale Insight Conference* in Pittsburgh, Pennsylvania, on October 23, 2019, from which the first part of the title of this article is taken.[11] In this almost one-hour long address, which was directed at the work force of the local oil industry, the president celebrated his energy-political "successes" and outlined further plans for the energy sector. It can therefore be described as programmatic and can be identified as an example of Trump's characteristic political style referred to as "authoritarian populism." The speech focusses on the "American energy revolution," which he describes as a kind of successful treasure hunt in America, to the supposed benefit of "the people." The repeated reference to subterranean riches evokes adolescent fantasies of unlimited possibilities, and the semantics of revolution is employed to balance against each other the creative and the destructive moments of energy production. The appreciation of the emotional, even sentimental bond to the land in the sense of a rootedness and the exploitation and destruction of the exact same landscape, i.e., the affirmation of the homeland and the simultaneous production of homelessness, are united in a paradoxical kind of conver-

---

11   The *Shale Insight Conference* is organized by the Marcellus Shale Coalition, the Ohio Oil & Gas Association, and the West Virginia Oil & Natural Gas Association and has been an annual event since 2011. Among the well-known speakers who have supported the consortium's energy agenda in this context are Rudy Giuliani, Sean Spicer as well as Donald Trump.

gence. This can be read as a product of what Fintan O'Toole described as sado-masochistic structures in authoritarian populisms.

Following the analysis of the speech, the second part of the essay focuses on what has been described as "petrofiction," i.e., texts which are concerned, in the widest sense, with oil—its extraction, sale, and impact on society. The term petrofiction functions as an umbrella term for a whole series of cultural productions, and the wide range of semi-fictional and fictional spins on the topic illustrates the historical and spatial variability of the issue, as well as the multitude of competing interpretations of different scenarios (cf. LeMenager 10ff.; see also Ghosh). Similar to sugar, coffee, cotton, and tobacco, oil is the stuff of dreams and nightmares, while the focus in petrofictional texts is usually on aspects that address the effects on humans and the environment. More recent texts often critically address the narrative of progress and success employed by Trump in his speeches and put it in a new perspective concerning questions of sustainability. How the land and its resources are to be used, however, remains controversial, and thus the affirmation of the logic of extraction in cultural productions underlies considerable cyclical fluctuations.

In the historical Hollywood drama *Giant* (1956), the agricultural use of the land as a cattle range is still in competition with its use as an oil field and both are normatively saturated: the pasture as rich in tradition, not estranged, idealized in a nostalgic, romanticized manner, but also backward-looking; the oilfield as nouveau riche, estranged, yet forward-looking (cf. LeMenager 5). The film can be regarded as an example of a variant of petrofiction that emerged in the 20th century and has plainly been categorized by Stephanie LeMenager as "pro-oil propaganda" (94). Upton Sinclair's novel *Oil!* (1927; film: *There Will Be Blood*, 2007) is also part of this corpus, as is the television series *Dallas* (1978–1991). The latter fails to critically discuss the wealth and its origin but rather, quite uncritically, indulges in it. It is worth considering the hero of the series and soap opera, businessman and "oil baron" J.R. Ewing, in analogy to former U.S. President Donald Trump. More recent productions portray the oil business in a more ambivalent and critical way: among them, the film *Promised Land* (2012; for an analysis of the film, see the article by Germanaz and Marak in this volume), separate episodes of television series, for example *Longmire* ("The Calling Back," 2015), and numerous literary texts, such as Linda Hogan's *Mean Spirit* (1990; discussed by Gesa Mackenthun in her contribution to this book) and John Sayles' *Yellow Earth* (2020). The latter provides an approach to the cultural imaginary different from campaign speeches and election pledges. Literature can be seen as a kind of interdiscourse (cf. Link), which takes up symbolizations from the cultural imaginary, adapts, modifies or affirms them in a kind of interplay across established discourse boundaries. In such a vein, a novel is the focal point of the second part of this essay. Jennifer Haigh's *Heat & Light* (2016) is set in rural Pennsylvania, approximately 60 miles from Pittsburgh, and it was published in the same year as Donald Trump was elected president of the United States, not least with the votes of the population of Pennsylvania. The fictional Bakerton is not unlike the town of Barnesboro, where the author herself is from (see my interview with Jennifer Haigh in this volume). Already the novel *Baker Towers*, published in 2005, introduces Haigh's Bakerton-universe and she returns to it in the short stories *News from Heaven: The Bakerton Stories* (2013). My focus on *Heat & Light* is not only to acknowledge it as an outstanding literary text, it also pays tribute to the gender-political dimension of the "petro-imaginary" in light of the topic of sustainability and its affective dimensions and side effects.

Thus, in analyzing the link between extraction, frontier spirit, and populism as represented by Donald Trump, the aspect of gender-specific codes within the discourses and the hegemonic notions of femininity and masculinity involved also need to be taken into account. The settler colonialism described in my introduction and its actual as well as metaphorical occupation of the land and the extraction-related damages and devastations to it have been explicitly examined in various seminal works in the field of American studies. In context of the "critical myth-and-symbol school," Annette Kolodny observes a logic of violent penetration and metaphorical violation of the land in the early sources of American colonization by whites, as the title of her classic work *The Lay of the Land: Metaphor as Experience and History in American Life and Letters* (1975) pointedly suggests. This imagery is not only relevant for gender politics but also from an ecological point of view: Kolodny's "psychohistory" demands a different treatment of both women *and* land, which have been exposed to the "most unbridled and seemingly gratuitous destruction" (27) for a long time. For previous historical periods, Carolyn Merchant has brought together the gender-political and eco-critical dimensions of settlement, referring to the "death of nature," with nature having female connotations and being symbolized accordingly. Merchant's study ends with a reference to the Three-Mile-Island-accident in the Pennsylvanian nuclear power plant in 1979, which had clearly shown the consequences of putting economic interests and profit maximization above the security of the people and the health of the earth: "Three Mile Island is a recent symbol of the earth's sickness caused by radioactive wastes, pesticides, plastics, photochemical smog, and fluorocarbons" (295). This accident also plays an important role in Haigh's novel, as the story is set in different time layers and thus historicizes the connection between the different forms and stages of the extraction of resources, placing them on a temporal continuum linked to one and the same region.

For the representations and fictionalizations supplied by the "petro-imaginary," the interdependencies between gender and violence are obvious. According to Heather Turcotte (200), gender and sexuality are central to the symbolizations and representations of petro-violence, i.e., violence which occurs in and is connected to the context of oil exploration and extraction, a connection that has often been neglected in environmental political discourses up until now (cf. Daggett 28). This also results from a continuing sentimental-ization and mystification, or rather re-mystification, of the resource oil, which obviously still is more effective than ecological considerations of sustainabil-ity and which includes the classical ideas of mystified heroism and rugged masculinity.[12] Cara Daggett used the term "petro-masculinity" for this kind of masculinity construction, marked by misogyny, racism, and the denial of climate change. Accordingly, the semantics of penetration and extraction with their male connotations in the context of "drilling" and fracking hardly require an interpretation. However, it can be shown in a next step, that frontier-sentimentality manifests itself as masculine "petro-nostalgia" (Dagget 31) or "petromelancholia" (LeMenager 102) in yearnings which bear clearly regressive and retrotopic traits. Daggett describes this as a gateway for authoritarian positions, as long as they cater to the "psycho-affective dimensions" (35) of these yearnings. It is not by coincidence that Daggett also refers to *Women, Floods, Bodies, History*, the first volume of *Male Fantasies*—Klaus Theweleit's seminal work on the theory of fascism—, in order to demonstrate how the control of liquid flows of all kinds can go hand in hand with violence and fantasies of annihilation. Here again, we encounter a sadomasochism which facilitates authoritarian structures, flanked by misogyny and a propensity to violence (ibid. 42–44). This connects to a number of current concerns, especially Trump's energy political fixation on the exploitation of fossil fuels, which, according to Daggett, reveals the latter's "nascent fossil fascism" (ibid. 27).

---

12   The term "oil-fetishism" was repeatedly used to analyze and characterize this mysti-
      fication (cf. Huber 296).

"Drill, Baby, Drill": Trump's Energy Policies as Part of His Retrotopic Populism

The fact that Donald Trump's election victory was not due to a majority of votes of all Americans (the "popular vote") but a majority of electors in the electoral college, determined by the winner-takes-all principle in the individual states, has been sufficiently pointed out elsewhere. Analyses of the election have discussed in detail how Trump—as a surprise to many—could win three states which previously had commanded democratic majorities for decades, even if they were often characterized as swing states: Pennsylvania (one of the founding colonies which stretches far into the west), Michigan, and Wisconsin. These three states, of which Pennsylvania is the most populous and accounts for 20 electoral votes (only California, Texas, New York, and Florida have more), represent in a special way the 18th and 19th century history of settlement, settler colonialism, and the frontier experience, retrospectively glorified in countless texts and classical Hollywood Westerns since James Fenimore Cooper's historical novels. In her partly autobiographical novel *A New Home—Who'll Follow?* (1839), Caroline Kirkland made an early attempt at demystifying the frontier-romanticism and its connotations of masculinity by describing the hardships of this life, the loneliness of women, and the quite unexpected absence of Indians and other spectacular ingredients of the white male narrative of "proving oneself." Ironically, the symbol of the adventure in the West for Kirkland is the hardly sensational but even more so unpleasant "Michigan mudhole," in which her carriage gets stuck, and which consequently thoroughly demystifies the myth of the West, right at the beginning of her journey (Kirkland 5ff.). Nonetheless, it is exactly this myth of the supposedly formative American experience at the border between "civilization" and "wilderness" that so firmly established the myth of the frontier in the cultural imaginary of the United States; so much so that it can be conjured up, time and time again, in a highly effective way by American presidential candidates, not so long ago by Donald Trump. The politics of affect in Trump's campaign and governing style also relied on a re-enchantment of extraction—American-style and America first—and on a discrediting and erasure of environmental sustainability considerations in the context of global multilateral projects as simply "un-American." This is possibly the most simplistic "argument" that is currently being made in environmental policy debates. The term retrotopia fittingly characterizes the one-sided nostalgic glorification of bygone times, times which are referenced in a palimpsest-like way: the 1980s (Ronald Reagan's presidency), the 1950s ("economic miracle" and postwar conservatism), the turn of the century (Theodore Roosevelt and his "Rough Riders"), or the 1830s (Andrew Jackson's presidency during the "Indian Wars"). The vagueness of the reference makes it all the more resonant and evokes U.S. Cold War discourses of superiority as well as older imperial discourses and frontier romanticism along with their respective "pioneers."

Trump has never been shy about his economic and energy policy views and thus substantiated previously rather latent contradictions (which had also been characteristic of the policies of the Obama administration). As keynote speaker at the *Shale Insight Conference* in Pittsburgh in October 2019, Trump formulated the principles of his energy policies once more and simultaneously celebrated his first "successes."[13] His populist rhetoric makes use of clear antagonisms and opposition pairs, providing supposedly obvious solutions to the problems involved. The argumentative pattern is evident in five terms Trump employs, in part in a rather idiosyncratic way: *revolution, disaster, treasure, energy workers*, and *dominance*.

First, Trump establishes a clear dichotomy between his presidency and that of his predecessor, arguing that President Obama and his Democrats had been blocking the American economic development and energy political independence and that they had been standing in the way of the "American energy revolution." The latter, according to Trump's stylization and metaphorization, refers to fracking and similar practices in Pennsylvania and elsewhere. In the first part of his speech, he discusses in detail how he has already reversed all previous policies originally issued to protect the environment and to foster ecological sustainability (many of them introduced under Obama), including the "Waters of the United States Rule," the "Clean Power Act," and, of course, on an international level, the Paris Climate Agreement. The semantics of revolution has a nationalist basis and refers to American independence of foreign resources and foreign tutelage and the return to America's own, longstanding strength, also in reference to energy politics ("We believe the United States should never again be at the mercy of a foreign supplier of energy [...] We are committed not only to energy independence but to American energy dominance."). In the speech, Trump also repeats the famous sentence that he "was elected to represent the people of Pittsburgh, not the people of Paris." Revolu-

---

13   For a video and a transcript of the speech, see Trump 2019a and 2019b respectively. In what follows, all quotes are taken from the speech given in these sources.

tion in this case does not go hand in hand with social redistribution but with the consolidation of hierarchy and inequality.

In many of his speeches, Trump employs terminology that is also prominently used in debates about sustainability. However, he criticizes the prioritization of ecological matters as a principally wrong-guided attack on U.S. interests, repeatedly refers to the policies of his predecessor as well as the current continuation of these policies by Democratic politicians as a "disaster," and even talks of "total destruction." Yet in his case, the metaphors of catastrophe and destruction do not refer to environmental damage, climate change, and air pollution but to economic issues—without reference to any notion of sustainability. The environment does not appear to be worthy or even in need of protection—unlike the economy. Jobs need to be created, secured, and protected from "total destruction." The sustainability debate is thus reduced to absurdity. Trump's political campaign promises to save sectors and regions that had been especially hard hit by deindustrialization by means of a short-term "re-industrialization"—for example by reviving "King Coal" (as in the "Trump digs coal" slogan) and by extending fracking—turned out to be anachronistic and are tantamount to a rejection of environmentally friendly technologies that promote sustainability. It seems only apt to acknowledge Naomi Klein's thesis of "disaster capitalism" as a perfidious strategy of profit optimization under the cover of crisis management, which she illustrates with various examples (e.g., the profits of the oil industry following hurricane Katrina [cf. Klein 2007, 2017]). The crises of the "rust belt" and of the cities and states belonging to it, among them Pittsburgh, develop at a slower pace and take place in longer temporal cycles. Nonetheless, they are cases of "disasters," the intended management of which, as announced by Trump, clearly allows analogies to Klein's examples. Besides the Obama administration and Barack Obama himself, there are further individuals who receive a scolding from Trump—all those who do not unconditionally agree with his political course, among them Democratic members of Congress, and former governor of New York, Andrew Cuomo. The latter for the time being provided a fitting foil for comparison with Trump in several aspects: as a Democrat and thus political opponent (Cuomo had also been touted as a potential presidential candidate), as a pipeline opponent (Cuomo, who in the meantime has stepped down due to sexual harassment allegations, was against a gas pipeline across his state and against fracking), as part of the establishment (already his father had been governor of New York), and as part of the East Coast elite (Cuomo is originally from New York City—as is Trump himself, however).

In his speech, Trump distances himself sharply from any kind of hesitation and procrastination and presents himself as the doer *par excellence*. Any skepticism towards extraction, any deliberating policies of sustainability are equated with passiveness and inaction and consequently demonized. The people in Democratic New York were "sitting on a goldmine of energy," while the Democrats were keeping those treasures, the mineral resources, well away from them. The Trumpian treasure hunt in all of its manifestations (drilling, offshore drilling, fracking, mountaintop removal) and by all possible means is praised as a remedy in order to keep in check both supposedly anti-business bureaucrats, who insist on authorization procedures and slow down the "energy revolution," as well as civic protests of various groups. The latter are hardly addressed directly, and when some protesters loudly make themselves heard in the room, they are implicitly threatened by Trump, who taunts them by telling them to go home to their "mama" immediately. This is a well-known strategy: It is the feminization of environmental activists as "tree huggers," which insinuates a loss of "true" masculinity.[14] The closeness to nature and the concern for it (traditionally linked to femininity and passiveness) contrasts with its subjugation, domination, and exploitation and their respective connotations of masculinity and activity. This is also part of a complex that Daggett refers to and analyzes as "petro-masculinity."[15] And this is also where the cultural and ideological difficulty of a turn towards sustainability—roundly rejected and even ridiculed by Trump and his followers—becomes apparent. It would presuppose a rethinking on many levels in order to question hegemonial cultural settings, to accept alternative epistemologies, to recode notions of ecological, economic, and social sustainability as desirable and attractive, and to establish such attitudes in the cultural imaginary.

14   Not only is "treehugger" a relevant term from the perspective of gender politics, but at the same time it insinuates a wrong-guided sentimentality, ridiculous esotericism, and a work-shy detachment from reality (especially in contrast to the physically hard-working people in the energy industry, including fracking) and thus discredits environmental concerns.
15   An alternative model of accepted masculinity is described by Martin Hultman in reference to Arnold Schwarzenegger as "ecomodern masculinity." Schwarzenegger had outgrown the clichés of the male hero as bodybuilder, cowboy, or also Terminator and instead managed to project a new mixture of "toughness and compassion" onto himself with his political career (Hultman 87). It is not by coincidence that Schwarzenegger was often targeted by Trump's snide criticism.

The slogan "Drill, Baby, Drill" which served as a subtitle to this paragraph predates Trump's presidency even though it pointedly characterizes his positions in several respects. The slogan was already introduced in 2008 by the Republican Michael Steele and was intoned with its obviously suggestive undertones at the Republican National Convention in St. Paul, Minnesota, during which John McCain was chosen as the presidential candidate with Sarah Palin as vice-presidential nominee. It was already in this context that the link between fracking practices and explicit "country first"-rhetoric emerged, from which it is only a small step to "America first" (cf. Steele). Palin took up the slogan and used it as the headline of a 2009 article directed at Barack Obama. In it, she aggressively pledged in favor of offshore drilling in Alaska and elsewhere, quite similarly to Trump.

Obama consistently opposed encroachment on the Arctic National Wildlife Refuge (ANWR) and other protected regions of the United States. Consequently, Trump blames the Obama administration for not digging up "America's vast energies and treasures." The inability or unwillingness to unearth America's vast treasures is a recurring accusation throughout his speech. It is indeed quite remarkable that Trump likes to use the term "treasure" (see also 2017a, 2019c), evoking the invitation to a treasure hunt on a grand scale, with its associations of Gold Rush (along with its accompanying atmosphere) as well as the memories of typical classics in film and youth literature, such as Robert Louis Stevenson's *Treasure Island*. Following literary scholar Leslie Fiedler, the regressive aspect of "petro-masculinity" could be identified here in the form of a greedy narcissism with a one-sided view of the world as a place to satisfy one's own libidinal wishes, crying "Pieces of eight! Pieces of eight!" like Stevenson's Captain Flint.

While Trump refers to his political adversaries as "anti-energy zealots," who are "blinded by ideology"—the ideology of sustainability one could add—, he flatters the workers in attendance by attributing positive characteristics to them, calling them "our great energy people." However, he reserves the title "warriors" (which are apparently needed in a revolution) for his Pennsylvanian party comrades and congressional representatives. Trump portrays the former as having been unjustly deprived of the treasure they deserve up until now, thus catering to the resentments of those "left behind" in contrast to the elites and interpellating them as the big winners of his energy policy turnaround. Whilst Trump directly addresses the "great energy people," workers—men and women—appear on stage on either side of the speaker like well-draped extras. Clad in safety vests and helmets as "blue-collar workers," they simultaneously represent fervent adherents of his policies. Three of them are allowed to briefly step in front of the microphone in order to add an appearance of authenticity to the whole choreography. In the course of his performance, Trump seems to already extract the energy from his "energy workers," who greet him with thunderous applause. Their display on stage is meant to validate his policies as politics for the "common people." A wide angle shot of the room reveals that, apart from the workers onstage, it is mainly filled with oil industry officials and lobbyists. This is hardly surprising, given that the conference fees start at $625 and the Shale Insight website describes its participants as the "leaders" and "decision makers" of the branch. Thus, the dramaturgy of the event presents Trump on stage flanked by his blue-collar supporters, while the audience mostly consists of participants in suits and ties who attend the spectacle. The phrase "energy people" obscures the difference between the two status groups, while the term "energy" is repeatedly being linked to "poten-tial"—which in a quite neo-liberal style re-delegates the responsibility for the success of energy production to every single person in the room. If they fail to realize the energy potential, it is not the failure of Trump's politics. Regulatory intermediaries—be they labor unions or government agencies—find no (pos-itive) mention. Any sets of rules and regulations appear a source of annoyance and a hindrance to the exponential "unlocking" of profit potentials, i.e., the energy revolution.

The re-nationalization of Trump's policies directs attention back to certain parts of the country which had been hit hard by deindustrialization (and which Trump idealizes in a rather one-sided way), and it combines notions of national greatness with those of nostalgic memories of the days of coal mining and other extractive practices. Trump's agenda owes its attractiveness for voters, who see themselves as the losers of globalization and its economic consequences, to this type of retrotopic references.[16] The speech ends with Trump reaffirming his energy policies and the superiority and "dominance" of the United States, which according to him is now once more "the greatest energy superpower in the history of the world." Other countries would try to emulate the United States but still never catch up, due to the superiority of the American "energy workers," who—as has already been stated—are objectified multiple times during and after the speech. In the end, diverse topics and slogans superimpose each other, when Trump "supplements" his

---

16   Cf. in this respect the seminal and much discussed empirical studies by Cramer, Hochschild, and Duina.

explanations concerning energy with several other campaign topics: the right to own weapons, the necessity of building a wall at the border to Mexico, and getting rid of "sanctuary cities" in order to "keep America great."

Thus, Trump's speech at the *Shale Insight Conference* turns into an election campaign event—like so many other of his appearances, regardless of place and occasion. On a podium offered by the fossil fuel industry, speaking to the fossil fuel industry, the U.S. president talks in the fashion of a businessman, not a statesman, and he uses the stage mainly to stylize himself as a doer—a "builder" and a boss. To summarize, Trump's speech puts economics and ecology in an antagonistic front-line position, which he correlates with further binary oppositions: masculinity/masculinization vs. femininity/feminization; active domination of nature vs. passive conservation; American independence vs. American dependence and dictation by other nations; prosperity and well-being vs. poverty and unemployment; economic profit maximization vs. ecological sustainability. The front-line between economy and ecology characteristic of authoritarian populisms eliminates forms of mediation and compromise as well as social issues that represent an important dimension of sustainability debates. The social inequality between blue-collar workers with their Trump-pleasing pathos formulas on stage and the industry officials in the auditorium is successfully obscured—as is the fact that the extraction is mostly only short-lived anyways and the jobs in extension of the idea of "extractive colonialism" are not sustainable. This is accomplished by inserting the position of the treasure-seeking president into the crumbling foundation of American exceptionalism, built on 19th century extraction-based settler colonialism and promising a new "golden era of American energy" (Trump 2017b).

"More than most places, Pennsylvania is what lies beneath": Jennifer Haigh's Literary Archeology of a Region in *Heat & Light*

The concept of region is significant for the petro-imaginary in times of globalization. Sustainability debates also emphasize the role of glocality, i.e., the global-local nexus. A reflection on the return of regionalism against the changed backdrop of globalization cuts across disciplines; it can also be found in literary and cultural studies (cf., for example, Mahoney/Katz; Lösch et al.). Jennifer Haigh's novel *Heat & Light*, which was published in 2016—the year Trump was elected president, also by a majority of the residents of Pennsylvania, who associated his promise to reindustrialize the region with hopes for a better life—is set not far from the site of Trump's previously analyzed speech. The novel contextualizes and historicizes the statements of the then incoming president in multiple ways, since it incorporates in its plot different groups of actors and their different perspectives in multiple narrative strands (cf. Michaud), thus unraveling the complexity of extraction practices. Literary critics attest Haigh a great success with her novel. As a chronicler of Western Pennsylvania, the author focusses on a little town close to the metropolis of Pittsburgh. The town Bakerton is a microcosm in which important steps in the region's history but also in that of the nation are condensed: the dispossession of the land of the Seneca; the immigration from southern and eastern Europe in the 19th century; the progressing industrialization; coal mining, which thanks to the jobs in the mines led to the town's modest prosperity while severely damaging the workers' health and from time to time even killing them. Originally, the town was named after the mines, whose name again derives from the Baker brothers, the founders of this "company town" in the 1880s, "who dug the first coal mine in the valley and named an entire town after themselves" (Haigh 2016: 3). Not far from the fictional Bakerton, Titusville, Pennsylvania, is also the site of the first oil boom in American history, when in 1859 Edwin L. Drake discovered oil for the so-called Seneca Oil Company. However, the region was also the site of the biggest reactor accident in the history of the United States, where dangerous amounts of radioactive substances leaked from the Three-Mile-Island-reactor in 1979, about which the population was only inadequately informed and in a piecemeal fashion.

These events are already history when the novel sets in. The earlier history with its focus on immigrant families at the times of coal mining is told in Haigh's previous novel *Baker Towers* and her short stories in *News from Heaven*. In *Heat & Light*, the coalmines have already been closed for a very long time. A tragic mining accident in which a lot of men died has become part of the town's collective memory. Now it is almost a ghost town, partly reduced to ruins, partly run down and neglected—a place in decline, hoping for a different economic future. The construction of a new prison complex has created new jobs in the structurally weak region, agriculture is still practiced in some places, and there is a pub in the town's old noble hotel called "The Commercial" and various public facilities. It has become a town of women and widows ("Only the widows remain," 11). The remaining inhabitants are willing to believe in a new economic miracle, when they receive offers to sell the subterranean lease rights for their land in order to extract natural gas via fracking from the "Marcellus Shale" that expands a mile below the surface of the earth. *"Beautiful property you've got here*" (9–10, italics in original)—this is the first sentence with which Bobby Frame, the sales agent of the energy company from Texas, addresses the land owners in Bakerton, and most of them are easy targets for him. As part of his sales strategy, he uses the language and the typical euphemisms of the energy corporations that also Trump used in his speech: "*Buried treasure*, says Bobby, feeling the poetry" (10). Yet not all of them sell their lease rights, and this leads to tensions among the inhabitants who up until then had been living side by side quite indifferently. Slowly, protest materializes against the practice of fracking, especially after the workers brought in from Texas have already started to work and Bobby Frame's promises and claims do not prove true—neither concerning the financial compensation nor the quality of life of the inhabitants during the fracking process. The statement "We drill a half mile down [...] We're so far down you'll never know we're there" (10) turns out to be plain wrong.

The plot starts in 2010 and ends in 2012, while the story line is interspersed with flashbacks: The one reaching back furthest is to the year 1979, from which the story returns to the present in several time jumps (1988, 1992, 2004, 2005). The text creates a multi-faceted panorama of the people involved, who hold different views on the promised comeback of the town and on fracking as part of the projected "energy revolution." The ensemble of Bakerton's inhabitants consists of Rich and Shelby Devlin and their two children, Braden and Olivia; Rena and "Mack" (Susan Mackey), who practice organic dairy farming on their ranch; and Rena's son Calvin who is serving time in the prison where Rich works as a guard. Rena meets Lorne Trexler, geologist and activist, who organizes protests against fracking, and she starts to support his work. Then there is the Rev. Jess, whose husband Wes, her predecessor as the parish pastor, had died of cancer early on and who had attributed his illness to his childhood in close proximity to the damaged Three Mile Island reactor. Wes' story following the disaster is reviewed retrospectively in a separate section of the book. Jess, who is now single, is drawn to one of the oil workers, Herc, with whom she builds a relationship, while Herc hides his family in Texas from her. Other workers of the drill rig—Brando, Jorge, Mickey—also come into view: Each and everyone of them is uprooted, alone and has left his family temporarily for the strenuous work ("There are no soft jobs on a drill rig," 98), content they have one in the first place; their social relationships are mainly confined to the camp and the pub. Aggression and struggles for recognition and about distribution between workers from Texas and locals are on the rise, while those actually responsible are hiding behind a chain of subcontractors, telephone waiting lines, and "slippery PR flacks" (205) and remain elusive. The state and its agencies appear to be absent—Bakerton has a single "town cop" (Chief Carnicella is chief of police without any employees, 78). The regulatory authorities Trump rails against in his speech do not exist in Bakerton, and the people, lured by the prospects of profit, entirely in line with the vague and ultimately unfulfilled rhetoric of "potential," are defenseless against the profit interests of the companies and the distortions caused by the unscrupulous exploitation practices. The police does not even protect the most vulnerable, Bakerton's women and children, from domestic abuse.

Most workers who come to Bakerton are originally from Texas, and Texas is also the site of the headquarter of the company which operates the frack-ing in Bakerton and which considers the new site a pathbreaking investment, a steppingstone for their expansion in the North East. The CEO of the com-pany, Clifford 'Kip' Oliphant, posing for a cover story with his horse in front of his ranch, is hailed as a "new cowboy" at the "new frontier" of fracking (26). Here, the novel demonstrates the continuity of the cultural imaginary between the old settler colonialism and the new forms of resource extraction as well as between the "old" oil drilling in Texas and the application of the new frack-ing technology in the North East of the country—and this in an almost legal vacuum. Haigh's meticulously detailed description of a shareholder meeting of Dark Elephant Energy clearly points to, in some ways even anticipates, the kind of setting of Trump's speeches in front of officials and lobbyists, as dis-cussed above in an exemplary way. The manner in which the novel details the CEO's preparations in his hotel room, self-indulgently practicing his poses, honing his rhetoric, choosing his clothes, and doing anything to make a good impression and to convince the audience, appears almost like a parody, and the depicted behavior shows clear traits of an authoritarian populist style of leadership. In the short term, he will succeed, but in the long run—and this is part of poetic justice—he will suffer personal and professional damage. At the same time, the novel is equally critical in its portrayal of the protest culture against fracking: The charismatic professor of geology and environmentalist Lorne Trexler makes increasingly condescending remarks about the popula-tion of Pennsylvania, also affronting Rena, when she accompanies him to a protest event in New York, where she experiences a feeling of estrangement with university protest culture. Also, Mack feels out of place when she parks her pick-up on the college campus. Lorne's former student, now advisor for an energy company, makes fun of Lorne's arrogance: "Lorne Trexler, the famous populist, champion of the working classes until they dare to disagree with him"

(375). Hence, also Lorne instrumentalizes the residents of Bakerton for his own ends and dumps them when they are no longer useful to him. With this depiction, the text of course runs a certain risk of reproducing the well-known topos of the seducibility of "honest people" by outsiders, not only found in the Western and in numerous representations of the heartland but also in populist rhetoric.

Several other characters inhabit the fictional world of this novel, yet it is the town itself that constitutes the center of the story, a marginal place for the United States that, for centuries, has experienced nothing but extraction and has periodically been "disemboweled" and then forgotten once more: "Rural Pennsylvania doesn't fascinate the world, not generally. But cyclically, periodically, its innards are of interest. Bore it, strip it, set it on fire, a burnt offering to the collective need. Bakerton understands this in its bones" (11). The imagery of the "entrails," suggesting a kind of slaughter as it is performed in the context of meat production, is drastic, and it goes hand in hand with other practices of violation, ultimately even annihilation—not primarily of jobs but of a habitat that is fit for human beings. Looting nature and sacrificing Bakerton is the downside of the adolescent story of a treasure hunt and the promise of happiness that can be heard in both Dark Elephant Energy's marketing and Trump's speech. The place itself, from which the treasure is extracted by any means available, is virtually a collateral damage in the procedure. In a similar context, Traci Voyles has coined the term "wastelanding," which she uses to describe the process of exposing an ecosystem and its human inhabitants to irreversible environmental pollution—in a calculated manner and without providing any protection. In this, it follows the logic and economy of extraction without a single thought on sustainability and ecological consequences. Many of the characters in Bakerton have internalized this logic, no questions asked, as "knowledge in the bones" (Shotwell 125). The connection between the logic of extraction and the metaphor of violent penetration has repeatedly been polemically explicated in analogies of "fracking" and "fucking": Protest posters say "MOTHERFRACKERS, GO HOME" (370), Bakerton is suffering a "FRACKING NIGHTMARE" (179), and Darren (Rich's brother) wonders: "*Fracking*. The word sounds subliminally obscene, a genteel euphemism for *fucking*" (179). This, once more, brings to mind Annette Kolodny's *Lay of the Land*.

On the occasion of a birthday party for Rich's father, who had been a mine worker himself, the family eventually grasps the actual extent of the encroachment caused by oil extraction on their own land they themselves now no longer have control of:

> They cross the yard together, Dick, Rich, and Braden leading the way, fol-
> lowed by Darren, Shelby, and Olivia. They climb the rise and look down.
> Five acres of pasture have been razed and flattened, spread with gravel and
> marked off with chain-link fence [...] The scale of the operation is shocking,
> but not surprising. Rich knew what he was in for. (193)

Together, three generations speechlessly stare at the huge sealed and fenced
area. Later on, when they are having their barbeque, it becomes noisy and uncomfortable. The situation seems like a reprise of the titular metaphor in Leo
Marx's study on the industrialization of the former agrarian nation, *The Machine in the Garden*:

> An immense truck, larger than any he's ever seen, is climbing the access
> road, or trying to. The thing moves at the speed of a cruise ship, enveloped
> in a cloud of diesel fumes [...] In stunned silence they watch the hulking
> machine inch up the ridge. That it moves at all is a straight-up miracle. It's
> as though an aircraft carrier has run aground in Rich's back yard." (195–96)

Here, Haigh impressively creates a form of what Miles Orvell (2006) has referred to as "destructive sublime": a moment of being overwhelmed, almost a
perverted experience of grace in the face of the presence of technology and its
destructive potential.[17]

The emphasis on the disproportionality of the military-grade high tech of
fracking and the modest size of the farm highlights the disproportionality of
the means of energy extraction themselves and also the asymmetry of power
between the large Texan corporation and the individual landowner whose
dreams of future farming are being shattered by fracking. Rich's aspirations
for an economically viable future on his land and for his family have thus failed.
In a way, Rich embodies the link between the generations and the professions
in the novel—he was in the army (in a war also waged for oil), works in prison,
jobs in his father's bar, goes fishing with his son, and dreams of a future life
as a farmer. Like many in Bakerton, he considers his failure in the face of the
reality of extraction as the result of his own wrongdoing: his greed to get the
money for the lease, his inability to read the small print of the contract, and
his unrealistic hopes to be able to farm the land on his own again. At the end of

---

17   Cf. Orvell's conceptualization of the term as an ambivalent combination of "aesthetic
      excitement" and "ethical response" (2006) and his analysis of the large-format pho-
      tographs of the Canadian artist Edward Burtynsky, especially in the publication *Oil*, as
      an example for the "apocalyptic ruin" discourse (2016, 32–36).

the novel, he reminisces his childhood and how he was interested in the early history of the region before settler colonialism:

> How the world must have looked then, in Indian times: his own corner of the world before roads and bridges, tipples and steel mills, the sprawling strip mines that blackened the earth like char. As a boy he imagined it, vividly. As a man he learned it didn't matter. (427)

This reflection contrasts the visions of re-industrialization and the "technological sublime" of fracking with another kind of imagination, a sketch of a premodern existence, connoted with childlike curiosity and innocence and colored with nostalgia. It seems to me symptomatic that Rich quietly takes refuge in a retrotopia instead of envisioning an ecological utopia, when his private conceptions of the future lie shattered by economic realities. According to Fredric Jameson, "it's easier to imagine the end of the world than the end of capitalism" (xii)—and one could modify this: the end of extraction-based oil capitalism. However, sustainability depends to a considerable degree on whether and how convincingly it can be imagined: "The imagination structures existent practices of sustainability which are carried out in a variety of social fields (politics, economy, civil society, science) and which in turn structure the imagination" (Adloff 292). In a positive light, the above quotation from the novel can also be understood as an indication that unlearning the (neo)colonial views and certainties internalized through socialization represents the first step towards a liberation of the imagination from the well-worn tracks of the logic of exploitation.

What is below the ground, the supposed treasure, remains hidden from the readers of Haigh's novel. The lives of the novel's characters in Bakerton take place above ground. Here they observe the changes to their drinking water and in their animals' behavior, and they sense how the earth is shaking. *Heat & Light* spells out the grave and lasting side-effects of the course Trump advertises in his speech at the *Shale Insight Conference*—and which he has continued to espouse ever since. Haigh's novel is the poetic "package insert" to his promised cure-all, possibly even unmasking him as a fraudulent "miracle healer" who captivates his audience with fantastic prospects (which soon turn out to be false predictions) in order to make them forget their own vulnerability along with the injuries inflicted on them. In Haigh's novel, however, there are no easy causalities and one-sided blame. Rena's realization that it is probably Shelby herself who is harming her daughter to compensate for an attention deficit and that she is not sickened by the quality of the water after fracking (even if it smells bad) does not stop Lorne from exploiting the child's illness for his

own purposes. When the fracking company changes its business model and re-
places its CEO because the market collapses due to oversupply, the workers are
let go and the "drill sites go silent" (405) virtually overnight. Fracking in Bakerton ends, at least momentarily, since it is no longer profitable—and for no
other reason than that. And above it all, a sentence is floating midair, keeping alive the nostalgic desire for meaning and dominance at the entrance to
the town, in pale letters that are hardly legible any more: "BAKERTON COAL
LIGHTS THE WORLD" (180, 425).[18]

Conclusion

The goal of this essay was to examine in an exemplary way Donald Trump's
speech at the *Shale Insight Conference* 2019 (an example of a whole series of
programmatically similar energy political speeches during his presidency and
after) and Jennifer Haigh's novel *Heat & Light* from 2016 in order to identify
and analyze the logic of extraction, "American-style," in different discourses
in their respective culture-specific varieties and ideological orientations. The
programmatic rejection of considerations of sustainability has already been
described as a cornerstone of exploitation in context of the 19th century critique
of capitalism—"Après moi le déluge! is the election cry of every capitalist and
of every capitalist nation" (Marx). Donald Trump's speech delivered 150 years
later on the other side of the Atlantic Ocean seems to confirm this diagnosis.
However, a closer look reveals that the logic of extraction in Trump's rhetoric
is amalgamated with certain mythologems of U.S. history and elements of
American exceptionalism, and it is precisely this combination that guarantees
the kind of resonance in parts of the population that enabled Trump's path
to the White House and secured him astonishing approval ratings. While
the former president propagated an increased exploitation of resources as
a simple solution to the economic problems of deindustrialization, Haigh's
fictional text indicates that the extraction of fossil fuels is responsible for the

---

18   While many of the life plans in Bakerton fail, Mack and Rena's farm possibly remains
      the only positive and viable model for sustainable management. Yet also their busi-
      ness success suffers damage due to the town's association with the practices of frack-
      ing, since the urbanite costumers in Pittsburgh no longer trust the quality of their
      products. Sustainability needs to be commodifiable, too. The novel leaves open to
      what extent their business will recover from this.

crisis of the economic system, that, in fact, the extraction capitalism produces these crises.

The literary contextualization of fracking within historical forms of a depletion of nature sheds light on the long history of unscrupulous exploitation and extraction, which have created social and economic inequality and caused the destruction of nature and continues to do so, ignoring any considerations about sustainability. This historization modifies the simplifying antagonisms and dichotomies proclaimed by Trump and the fracking lobby. Against the backdrop of U.S. self-stylizations, the sustainability discourse is taunted to be fundamentally un-American in that it has little alignment with the hegemonic notions of masculinity, success, and a treatment of nature that prioritizes technological progress over care. This is clearly suggested by Trump's speech in a not-so-subtle way and with an air of authoritarianism. At closer sight, however, Trump's populist practices of performance reveal the division between the workers (who are instrumentalized as extras with only a minor role to play) and the industry officials and lobbyists (who control the means of production). In contrast to this, I consider Haigh's novel—despite all the stark differences between political and literary discourse—as a contribution that adds to the complexity of the energy policy debate and examines the mixed emotions and affective dissonances (Ladino's term) attached to the topic. That both discourses refer to the cultural imaginary constitutes a unifying element. *Heat & Light* challenges the dichotomies that Trump's speech creates, and it shows that contrary to the propagated *frontier*-drunk faith in progress in a neoliberal fashion, there cannot only be "winners" and "potentials" and that the underground treasure hunt demands a high price from many people. Moreover, the novel shifts the focus from primarily economic factors to ecological and social ones. Interpersonal relations—at times violent and exploitative (also in the sense of "petro-masculinity")—recur as the main theme and they reveal profound differences between people and their different socializations and milieus. Many more aspects could be addressed, for example the continuing relevance of the oil crisis, dating back to Jimmy Carter's presidency (an epigraph in Haigh's novel comes from him), or the ongoing resistance of indigenous groups to Trump's energy policies (which includes the construction of controversial pipelines on Indigenous territory), simultaneously pointing to the tragic history of land dispossession and destruction of alternative epistemologies.

The difficulty of anchoring notions of economic and environmental sustainability in the U.S. cultural imaginary in the first place has been diagnosed repeatedly; at times it seems easier to captivate the public's imagination with asteroid mining and the colonization of space as new frontiers of energy production (cf. Abrahamian) than to encourage ecological rethinking towards the use of renewable energies and the protection of the environment. The petro-regime suggests and nurtures notions of a dependence on oil and other fossil fuels, which it portrays as being without alternative. This way, it can fuel even the most far-fetched notions of a successful search for these raw materials and mineral resources time and time again with reference to the frontier spirit.

In an era of globalization, such a petro-regime is of course not only an American phenomenon, as is demonstrated by critical petrofictions of other countries. If we broaden our perspective, we can find literary treatments of the topic also in so-called oil states. As examples, one could refer to Abdal-rachman Munif's novel *Cities of Salt* (1988 [1984]) from Lebanon, the novel of the Egyptian author Nawal El Saadawi *Love in the Kingdom of Oil* (2001 [1993]), the short story "Oil Field" (2011) by Saudi-Arabian author Mohammed Hasan Alwan, and *How Beautiful We Were* (2021) by the Cameroonian-American writer Imbolo Mbue. Some texts by Nigerian author and environmental activist Ken Saro-Wiwa (1995 [1986]) also address the role of oil as a resource in the context of corruption and state failure in Nigeria. Saro-Wiwa paid for his system-critical revelations with his life, especially for his disclosures of neocolonial extraction practices and environmental pollution by Shell in his home region of Ogoniland for which he created international publicity. Two further texts within a Nigerian context are Ben Okri's short story "What the Tapster Saw" (1988) and Helon Habila's novel *Oil on Water* (2010).

An important aspect for analyzing sustainability discourses is the identification of culture-specific patterns that either challenge or promote it. Literature, as well as popular culture, can play a role in making sustainability narratable and imaginable and thus to develop and circulate notions of sustainability. Literature invites reflection on a problem without explicitly calling for action and perhaps has a special role to play here in context of work within/on the cultural imaginary. I have touched on how fundamental a shift in thinking must be in order to prioritize sustainability over other interests, in this case in the United States, in terms of gender discourses, regional differences, structures of feeling, and a long history of habitualized extraction and exploitation of natural resources. To provide a broader perspective, there are elements in the national manifestation of anti-sustainability sensitivities that can be connected to transnational and transcultural discourses. Therefore, it seems possible—and necessary—to anchor the topic of sustainability in a transnational (cultural) imaginary in the long term.

References

Abrahamian, Atossa Araxia. 2019. "How the Asteroid-Mining Bubble Burst: A Short History of the Space Industry's Failed (For Now) Gold Rush." *MIT Technology Review*, June 26, 2019. Accessed on April 23, 2020. http://www.t echnologyreview.com/2019/06/26/134510/asteroid-mining-bubble-burst-history.

Adloff, Frank. 2019. "Sustainability." In: *Critical Terms in Futures Studies*, edited by Heike Paul, 291–97. Cham: Palgrave Macmillan.

Alwan, Mohammed Hasan. 2011. "'Oil Field' by Mohammed Hasan Alwan, translated by Peter Clark." *The Guardian*, April 18, 2011. Accessed on April 23, 2020. http://www.theguardian.com/books/2011/apr/18/oil-field-moha mmed-hasan-alwan-story.

Anderson, Paul Thomas, dir. 2007. *There Will be Blood*. Los Angeles, CA: Paramount Pictures.

Buell, Frederick. 2014. "A Short History of Oil Cultures; or, The Marriage of Catastrophe and Exuberance." In *Oil Culture*, edited by Ross Barrett and Daniel Worden, 69–89. Minneapolis, MN: Minnesota University Press.

Ghosh, Amitav. 1992. "Petrofiction: The Oil Encounter and the Novel." *The New Republic*, March 2, 1992, 29–34.

Haigh, Jennifer. 2005. *Baker Towers*. New York, NY: Morrow.

Haigh, Jennifer. 2013. *News from Heaven: The Bakerton Stories*. New York, NY: HarperCollins.

Haigh, Jennifer. 2016. *Heat & Light*. New York, NY: HarperCollins.

Hochschild, Arlie Russell. 2016. *Strangers in their Own Land: Anger and Mourning on the American Right*. New York, NY: New Press.

Hogan, Linda. 1990. *Mean Spirit*. New York, NY: Atheneum.

Huber, Matthew. 2012. "Refined Politics: Petroleum Products, Neoliberalism, and the Ecology of Entrepreneurial Life." *Journal of American Studies* 46 (2): 295–312.

Hultman, Martin. 2013. "The Making of an Environmental Hero: A History of Ecomodern Masculinity, Fuel Cells and Arnold Schwarzenegger." *Environmental Humanities*, vol. 2, 79–99.

Jameson, Fredric. 1994. *The Seeds of Time: The Wellek Library Lectures at the University of California, Irvine*. New York, NY: Columbia University Press.

King, Thomas. 2019. *77 Fragments of a Familiar Ruin*. Toronto: HarperCollins.

Kirkland, Caroline M. (1839) 1990. *A New Home—Who'll Follow? or, Glimpses of Western Life*. New Brunswick, NJ: Rutgers University Press.

Klautke, Egbert. 2003. *Unbegrenzte Möglichkeiten: "Amerikanisierung" in Deutschland und Frankreich (1900–1933)*. Stuttgart: Steiner.

Klein, Naomi. 2007. *The Shock Doctrine: The Rise of Disaster Capitalism*. New York, NY: Metropolitan Books.

Klein, Naomi. 2017. "Get Ready for the First Shocks of Trump's Disaster Capitalism." *The Intercept*, January 24, 2017. Accessed on April 23, 2020. https://theintercept.com/2017/01/24/get-ready-for-the-first-shocks-of-trumps-disaster-capitalism/.

Kolodny, Annette. 1975. *The Lay of the Land: Metaphor as Experience and History in American Life and Letters*. Chapel Hill, NC: University of North Carolina Press.

Ladino, Jennifer. 2019. *Memorials Matter: Emotion, Environment, and Public Memory at American Historical Sites*. Reno, NV: University of Nevada Press.

LeMenager, Stephanie. 2014. *Living Oil: Petroleum Culture in the American Century*. Oxford: Oxford University Press.

Ling, Peter. 2020. "Ghost Towns of America." Accessed on April 23, 2020. http://www.geotab.com/ghost-towns/.

Link, Jürgen. 1997. *Literaturwissenschaftliche Grundbegriffe*. Stuttgart: UTB.

Lösch, Klaus, Heike Paul, and Meike Zwingenberger, eds. 2016. *Critical Regionalism*. Heidelberg: Winter.

Luce, Henry Robinson. 1969. *The Ideas of Henry Luce*. New York, NY: Atheneum.

Mahoney, Timothy R., Wendy Jean Katz, eds. 2009. *Regionalism and the Humanities*. Lincoln, NE: University of Nebraska Press.

Marx, Karl. (1867) 1962. *Das Kapital, Bd. 1*. Accessed on April 23, 2020, http://www.zeno.org/nid/20009217916.

Marx, Leo. (1964) 2000. *The Machine in the Garden: Technology and the Pastoral Ideal in America*. New York, NY: Oxford University Press.

Mbue, Imbolo. 2021. *How Beautiful We Were*. New York, NY: Random House.

Merchant, Carolyn. 1980. *Death of Nature: Women, Ecology, and the Scientific Revolution*. New York, NY: HarperCollins.

Michaud, Jon. 2016. "*Heat and Light* Is the Best Fracking Novel Ever." *Washington Post*, May 10, 2016. Accessed on April 23, 2020. https://www.washingtonpo

st.com/entertainment/books/heat-and-light-is-the-best-fracking-novel-ever/2016/05/10/ef5199b6–16bb-11e6–924d-838753295f9a_story.html.

Mitchell, Timothy. 2011. *Carbon Democracy: Political Power in the Age of Oil*. New York, NY: Verso.

Mooney, Chris. 2016. "Rex Tillerson's View of Climate Change: It's Just an 'Engineering Problem.'" *Washington Post*, December 14, 2016. Accessed on May 16, 2020. https://www.washingtonpost.com/news/energy-environm ent/wp/2016/12/13/rex-tillersons-view-of-climate-change-its-just-an-eng ineering-problem/.

Munif, Abdalrachman. (1984) 1988. *Cities of Salt*. New York, NY: Random House.

Obama, Barack. 2009. "President Barack Obama's Inaugural Address. Summary: Yesterday, President Obama Delivered his Inaugural Address, Calling for a 'New Era of Responsibility.'" January 21, 2009. Accessed on April 23, 2020. https://obamawhitehouse.archives.gov/blog/2009/01/21/preside nt-barack-obamas-inaugural-address.

OED Online. 2020. "extraction, n." Accessed on April 23, 2020. https://www.o ed.com/view/Entry/67087.

Okri, Ben. 1988. "What the Tapster Saw." In *Stars of the New Curfew*. New York, NY: Viking, 183–94.

Orvell, Miles. 2006. "After 9/11: Photography, the Destructive Sublime, and the Postmodern Archive." *Michigan Quarterly Review* 45 (2): 239–56.

Orvell, Miles. 2016. "Ruins, Places, and Photography: Toward a Cultural Aesthetics of Catastrophe." In *Critical Regionalism*, edited by Klaus Lösch, Heike Paul, and Meike Zwingenberger, 25–37. Heidelberg: Winter.

O'Toole, Fintan. 2018. *Heroic Failure: Brexit and the Politics of Pain*. London: Head of Zeus.

Palin, Sarah. 2009. "Drill, Baby, Drill." *The Guardian*, July 14, 2009. Accessed on April 23, 2020. http://www.theguardian.com/commentisfree/cifamerica/ 2009/jul/14/sarah-palin-energy-obama.

Pease, Donald E. 2017. "America." In *Fueling Culture: 101 Words for Energy and Environment*, edited by Imre Szeman, Jennifer Wenzel, and Patricia Yaeger, 31–34. New York, NY: Fordham University Press.

Pease, Donald E. 2018. "Trump: Populist Usurper President." *Yearbook of Research in English and American Literature* 34 (1): 145–74.

Potter, Daniel. 1954. *People of Plenty: Economic Abundance and the American Character*. Chicago, IL: University of Chicago Press.

Rice, Stian, and James Tyner. 2011. "Pushing On: Petrolism and the Statecraft of Oil." *Geographical Journal* 177 (3): 208–12.

Saro-Wiwa, Ken. (1986) 1995. *A Forest of Flowers*. Harlow: Longman.

Sayles, John. 2020. *Yellow Earth*. Chicago, IL: Haymarket Books.

Shoemaker, Nancy. 2015. "A Typology of Colonialism." *Perspectives on History*, October 1, 2015. Accessed on April 23, 2020. https://www.historians.org/p ublications-and-directories/perspectives-on-history/october-2015/a-typo logyof-colonialism.

Shotwell, Alexis. 2011. *Knowing Otherwise: Race, Gender, and Implicit Understanding*. University Park, PA: Penn State University Pres.

Steele, Michael. 2008. "GOPAC Chairman Michael Steele at RNC." September 3, 2008. Accessed on April 23, 2020. https://www.youtube.com/watch?v=V dSsOnVWhic.

Sinclair, Upton. (1927) 2007. *Oil!* New York, NY: Penguin.

Smith, Henry Nash. 1950. *Virgin Land: The American West as Symbol and Myth*. Cambridge, MA: Harvard University Press.

Tarbell, Ida M. 1905. *The History of the Standard Oil Company*. London: Heinemann.

Tillerson, Rex. 2018. Interview with Bob Schiefsfer, MD Anderson Cancer Center, Houston, CBS News, December 7, 2018. Accessed on April 23, 2020. http://www.cbsnews.com/news/rex-tillerson-bob-schieffer-intervi ew-houston-firing-trump-tweet-tillerson-insult-2018–12–07/.

Tocqueville, Alexis de. (1831) 2004. *Democracy in America*. New York, NY: Library of America.

Trump, Donald. 2017a. "Remarks by President Trump and Secretary of Energy Rick Perry at Tribal, State, and Local Energy Roundtable." June 28, 2017. Accessed on June 1, 2022. https://trumpwhitehouse.archives.gov/briefing s-statements/remarks-president-trump-secretary-energy-rick-perry-tri bal-state-local-energy-roundtable/.

Trump, Donald. 2017b. "Remarks by President Trump at the Unleashing American Energy Event." June 29, 2017. Accessed on June 1, 2022. https://t rumpwhitehouse.archives.gov/briefings-statements/remarks-president-trump-unleashing-american-energy-event/.

Trump, Donald. 2019a. "Remarks by President Trump at 9th Annual Shale Insight Conference X Pittsburgh, PA." October 23, 2019. Accessed on June 1, 2022. https://trumpwhitehouse.archives.gov/briefings-statements/re marks-president-trump-9th-annual-shale-insight-conference-pittsburg h-pa/.

Trump, Donald. 2019b. "WATCH: Trump Speaks at Shale Energy Conference in Pittsburgh." *PBS News Hour*, October 23, 2019. Accessed on April 23, 2020. http://www.youtube.com/watch?v=Xzp1xGFZ2eU.

Trump, Donald. 2019c. "Remarks by President Trump on American Energy and Manufacturing X Monaca, PA." August 13, 2019. Accessed on June 1, 2022. https://trumpwhitehouse.archives.gov/briefings-statements/remarks-president-trump-unleashing-american-energy-event/.

Turcotte, Heather M. 2011. "Contextualizing Petro-Sexual Politics." *Alternatives: Global, Local, Political* 36 (3): 200–20.

Van Sant, Gus, dir. 2012. *Promised Land*. Universal City, CA: Focus Features.

Virdee, Satnam. 2019. "Racialized Capitalism: An Account of Its Contested Origins and Consolidation." *Sociological Review* 67 (1): 3–27.

Voyles, Traci Brynne. 2015. *Wastelanding: Legacies of Uranium Mining in Navajo Country*. Minneapolis, MN: University of Minnesota Press.

"Lots of Troubling Ideologies": A Conversation with Writer Jennifer Haigh about Region, Extractivism, and Nostalgia

Heike Paul and Jennifer Haigh

Jennifer Haigh is a prominent and highly esteemed voice in contemporary U.S. American literature and the author of six novels and numerous short stories to date. She received an MFA from the prestigious Iowa Writers' Workshop in 2002. Among her many literary awards and prizes are a PEN/Hemingway Award (2004) and a Guggenheim Fellowship (2018).

The interview with the author took place on March 9, 2022. It has subsequently been edited for clarity and concision.

Heike Paul (HP hereafter): When I first read your amazing novel *Heat & Light* (2016), I did not know whether Bakerton, the town that is the setting of the novel, actually existed, so I went to look it up. Sometimes you find that writers make up their own geography entirely and yet, such fictional geographies can be very similar to real places. To me, it was intriguing that both seems to be true in the case of the town of Bakerton. It is a place that you seem to be intimately familiar with and very much connected to. Still, it is not a place we can find on a map. In what ways do you consider Bakerton, Pennsylvania, your invention? In what way do you consider yourself producing a chronicle of a certain kind of region or place in the United States?

Jennifer Haigh (JH hereafter): The short answer is that indeed both things are true. Bakerton has its roots in a place that actually exists. It is the town where I grew up, a coal-mining town, in Western Pennsylvania. In many ways, my hometown resembles Bakerton but in other ways, it does not. I invented the name Bakerton. Like the town where I grew up, which was called Barnesboro, Bakerton is named after a coalmine. The mine was there first. Later, there was a critical mass of miners and so it became a town. My town Barnesboro came about in exactly the same way, and I find it significant that the mine was there first. They were towns founded for a particular reason, and that reason no longer exists, they have outlived their reason for existing, and that, to me, is very interesting. A lot of my writing about Bakerton deals with that idea. My short stories in the collection *News from Heaven* focus on how people find a way to continue in this town when its purpose is gone. That clearly reflects my experience growing up where I did. When I was a child, the coalmines were still functioning, and these towns were bustling. They were vibrant little towns. I was probably 11 or 12, when the mine started to fail and by the time I finished high school, it was all over, completely finished. These towns, as they exist now, are kind of ghost towns. My mother still lives there—she is 91 years old and not going anywhere, and I go back there to visit her—but everyone my age and younger has mostly left. It is a hard place to make a living now, as the mines were the only industry. Now that they are gone, there isn't very much to do. Cousins of mine who have stayed in this region are either working as prison guards, like Rich Devlin (a character in *Heat & Light*), or they are working in nursing homes with the elderly. Because the population there is aging, many old people need care. It is very much a transformed place from the town where I grew up, and that transformation has been a subject of my work. My first book is set in Bakerton at a time when the mines were booming. I have no memory of that time as the novel opens in 1944, when I had not been born yet. I grew up hearing these stories about what this place was like when things were good, and I have always had the urge to travel back in time and see what that was like. That was the impulse that led to my writing *Baker Towers*: wanting to time-travel and experience the town when it was supposedly a good place to live. When I was growing up, it was already a very hard place to live, and it has only gotten harder. But when my parents were growing up, it was very much the Bakerton you see in *Baker Towers*: That was their experience, coming of age in this region in northern Appalachia. Many Americans do not even realize that Western Pennsylvania is part of Appalachia. When I travel to Kentucky, or West Virginia, I feel much more at home than I do in Philadelphia. While Philadelphia is the other end of Pennsylvania, it is culturally entirely different. It is much wealthier; it was never predicated on extraction the way Western Pennsylvania is. That has been completely formative, the culture of this place is absolutely influenced by being founded on an extractive economy.

HP: It must have been a traumatic moment, when everything stopped, when you were around 11 years old. While it was an individual experience, it was, as you describe it, a kind of collective experience as well, of things shutting down, this being the end of something, without there being a real plan of what is going to happen next.

JH: Yes, and I was aware of this as a child. My father was a schoolteacher, so he was not in danger of losing his job. But all my friends' fathers were coal miners, and their families were really struggling. Lots of families moved away, because there was no more work. I lost friends at that age, which was my experience of this as a child. This is a true story: When I was 11 or 12, I went back to school in September with a new pair of sneakers. I got them every year and so did everyone else. That year, I was the only kid in my class who had new sneakers. I was so ashamed of having new sneakers, I wouldn't wear them. It was very clear to me that nobody else could have them, but I could because my father wasn't a miner. That was my understanding of what was happening. Nobody understood that this was a permanent change. It turned out to be permanent, but at the time, this wasn't clear. The economy of coal mining or oil drilling or gas drilling had always been cyclical. There were ups and downs, there were slowdowns. Even when the town was booming, the mines would sometimes experience a slowdown and the men would maybe only work three days a week. That would last for a period, and then business would improve, and they would be back to working five days a week. The slowdown was a familiar phenomenon and, I think, that's how people understood it at first. It wasn't clear for some time that they were not coming back.

HP: In your Bakerton-novels and short stories, you describe an interesting mix of emotions amidst changing times. In *Heat & Light*, specifically, you seem to indicate that you see some sort of historical continuum for which extractivism is foundational and that you do extend backwards to settler colonialism and forward to fracking. It seems to be a very ambivalent issue to build a community around logics of extraction, and I was struck by this sentence in the novel: "More than most places, Pennsylvania is what lies beneath." It seems both so powerful, and at the same time mystical. In the way that you critique extractivism, you also seem to talk about some sort of mystery of what is hidden, what we cannot get at. That even if we think we can understand a place, we do not seem to grasp all there is to it.

JH: Yes, and in this way, Western Pennsylvania is similar to Kentucky or Tennessee or all these Appalachian states who have all been determined by extractive economies. This is not universally true in the U.S., but it certainly is a regional truth. In many ways, these places are blessed and cursed by the same thing: It comes down to geology. And the same geology that produced coal, also produced oil and gas. They're all there for the same reasons, it's just that the technology has changed. We've known for a long time that there is an ocean of natural gas in this region. But for a long time, we didn't have the technology to extract it. Geologists had known it was down there, there was simply no way to get at it. That changed in the 1990s and that is why gas exploration has begun there. In a certain way, it appears to be the destiny of that region to be extracted.

HP: In an essay included in this volume I compare your novel and put it in contrast to one of the speeches the former president Trump gave in front of oil lobbyists, because he was always so fond of talking about what I like to call the "treasure hunt narrative" with phrases such as "all that wealth underneath," "why don't you dig it up," "we just have to take it outside, and then we are rich," and "why don't you want to do that." This kind of performance reminds me of a character in your book who is contoured along the same lines. I contrast this speech with the novelistic discourse that you unfold in your book, because I think it provides an interesting antidote to this discourse of finding a treasure, just having to dig, and then everyone being rich.

JH: It's true! Of course, it makes sense to me that the people in that region have been huge supporters of Donald Trump, because it is a narrative that appeals to them, to their sense of nostalgia. I think it is very pertinent to talk about the culture of extraction in the context of sentimentality. There is a kind of mythology that people in this region cling to, this idea that things were much better in the past when you could mine and drill without regulation, without restriction. If you look at the campaigns of Donald Trump: He ran on nostalgia. Think about his campaign promise "Make America Great Again." The implication is that it used to be great, and now it no longer is. That he is going to turn back the clock to the times when things were great. The people in that region who have suffered terribly, economically, have responded very enthusiastically to that appeal. There is a real sentimental attachment to the idea of mining and miners. The miners are almost heroic figures in these communities, because everybody's father or grandfather was a coal miner, and it is inextricably tied to this kind of reverence for family and ancestry. My grandfathers were both coal miners. Six of my uncles were coal miners. Every person there has a connection to this history of mining and people see very keenly the contrast between how things used to be and how desperately hard things are now and have been for a long time now. It has now been 30 years of hard times and more. This nostalgic appeal was very effective there. Even though, of course, Donald Trump knows nothing about coal mining or working class people or people who work with their hands, obviously. Yes, it could not be more obvious. It is enraging to me that people who have this history of hard work, don't see that; that it is not a factor in their thinking. So, this idea of sentimentality that you've put your finger on, I think it's very significant. The difference between sentiment and sentimentality, I think is worth discussing. Sentimentality is not simply feeling. It's an attachment to a romantic idea. There's an element of fantasy to sentimentality that distinguishes it from simple sentiment. In *Heat & Light*, there is a passage, where Darren Devlin, who has come back to Bakerton, is at a barbecue at his brother Rich's house and Rich has leased his mineral rights. There's going to be gas drilling on his property and he's very happy about it, and they're having a conversation about this, and Rich says to Darren, "Look, nothing's perfect. The point is, it's an opportunity. I'm not sitting around waiting for the mines to come back. Unlike some people." And Darren says: "Seriously? [...] That's the dream?" "They were good jobs," says Rich. Darren says, "Define *good*." (200). This gets us to something really important: that the people in this part of the country who yearn for the days of coal mining to come back have a very romantic understanding of what those jobs were really like. My maternal grandfather was a coal miner. He was what was called a pinner. His job was to hammer in these posts that would hold up the ceiling in the mineshaft that they were excavating. It's an incredibly dangerous job, and he spent most of his day on his hands and knees. Now it's unimaginable that workers could labor in these conditions for years on end. Of course, he died of black lung, as a lot of men there did. But that is not part of the narrative now. When people in that part of the country—and I'm generalizing, of course, not everyone thinks this way—, but the Trump supporters in these communities, when they think about coal mining, they're not picturing a grown man on his hands and knees for eight hours. They're thinking of prosperity and stability and this idea that you could have a high school education and raise your family and educate your children and have job security and belong to a union and rely on that way of life. That is what people are nostalgic for—yet it is a very romanticized picture.

HP: Let me take up this ambiguity, because one of the concepts that came to my mind, when I thought about this sort of cognitive or affective dissonance was what Lauren Berlant call "cruel optimism" in their work as a cultural theorist. They say that there are certain American myths—or not only American, obviously global notions—that promise you something, and then you become attached to these myths of this better past etc. However, sometimes you don't realize how harmful this attachment can actually be for your life. I thought that this might also be a way to describe what you unravel in *Heat & Light*. Specifically Rich is a very interesting figure here. He is a very complex character, and, of course, you can dislike him for this or that. Yet on the other hand, he is very vulnerable and helpless in trying to rehearse a certain kind of masculinity that is not really working out so well. Does this idea of a cruel optimism resonate with you?

JH: Yes, it does. Well, I think optimism is one of those American ideals and generally, I think it is considered a positive trait. Part of what I find likeable about the character of Rich Devlin is that he is a doer. That he has a plan. He is trying to make something happen, and he is in these bad circumstances, but he has not resigned. He has a plan. He has an idea. He is going to start dairy farming; he's going to buy these milking machines. And he's going to finance this by selling his mineral rights.

HP: He works two jobs. He is also a man, who is very concentrated on his goal and very engaged in everything he does.

JH: Completely. You know, he is attached to this idea of self-sufficiency. He is not waiting for someone to rescue him. He really believes that he can turn his circumstances around, that it is a question of hard work and having a plan and being smart. In Rich's case, it is not enough. It's a very hard lesson. And it's reflected in people's actual lives: It's in fiction because it's in life. I want to go back to your first question, namely to what degree Bakerton is an invented place and to what degree it actually exists. There is, of course, a lot of invention involved with it, too. It is not an exact replica of my hometown. If it were, I would have kept the same name. The reason I renamed it was to give myself the freedom to modify it as needed, to make my work possible. After having written three books—actually four books now with *Mercy Street*—that connect to Bakerton—, it is a place that really exists to me now. It has a life separate from the real town it was inspired by, and that's because of the people I have invented. At this point, I now have a very long, detailed list of all the characters I have invented, who have a connection to Bakerton. It's an alphabetical list and it gets longer and longer. It's an elaborate form of insanity at this point, like imaginary friends listed alphabetically. When I start to write something new that is set in Bakerton or has a connection to Bakerton, I think immediately, "Well, this character graduated high school in 1990. Who was in his class? Would he know Darren, would he know Gia? He's the same high school class as Darren and Gia. So certainly he would know them." It has made my life more complicated because now I'm writing several generations of the same families. For instance, Rich Devlin's father Dick, who owns the bar, appears very briefly in *Baker Towers*. He was a classmate of Sandy Novak. When they graduated high school, they went to Cleveland together and got jobs in this factory at Fisher

Body, making auto bodies. Dick Devlin is a person who exists in my mind, and I can't, for instance, change his age. I know what year he was born and if I ever want to reference Dick Devlin, he was born in that year; I can't change it now, because I've made it a fact by writing about him. Of course, all these characters are creations, but I feel compelled to be faithful to what I've written before. If I were to write something else about Dick Devlin, I couldn't make him a different kind of person. I couldn't make him younger. I couldn't make him older. I couldn't modify these facts that I've already written. This created Bakerton is a world that exists unto itself now, and it has a population, its citizens have children and grandchildren, and I feel bound by what I have already written. I feel some allegiance to those characters I've already written.

HP: So Bakerton is your own fictional universe, and it has a name that is much easier to pronounce than the town William Faulkner invented in his work.

JH: That's right! Faulkner's invented place Yoknapatawpha was a county in Mississippi and although it is hard to pronounce, it's no more difficult than many of the names in Mississippi. It is in that way quite realistic. But Bakerton as a name is a lot easier.

HP: When you talked about nostalgia earlier, I was also reminded of this book by Zygmunt Bauman, who also uses Trump's campaign slogan as an example to talk about what he conceptualizes as "retrotopia," and he says we're now at this place in time that we think the better things are in the past and we just have to redeem them. So, I thought that retrotopia was a very fitting label for "Make America Great Again," Trump's campaign slogan you mentioned earlier.

JH: It is very fitting, and it is also, as we know, very dangerous, because part of this idea that life in the past was better, is that it was a kind of utopia. When you look at the particulars of that life, well, it's before feminism, before any sort of racial equality in this country, and it has set up people to embrace ideas that they would not otherwise have embraced. Here's another example from my hometown: When I was growing up there, the town was entirely white, and it still mostly is. There were no people of other races at all and that was true of all the small towns in that region. I was not aware of racism growing up and in part, this was because there was nothing to stimulate it, there was never any interaction with people of different races. So, there was nothing to make this an issue. But now, when I go back there, I have seen Confederate flags flying. That never, never happened in all the years of my growing up. Of course, Pennsylvania was not part of the Confederacy, it was part of the Union, so it's historically inaccurate. It is shocking to me now, to see these flags—people will have them on flagpoles outside in their yards, I've seen them on people's trucks. People have really embraced this symbol of racism. There is no pretext that this is our history. It is not. They are embracing this symbol precisely because it is a symbol of racism, and they can do this, and no one can stop them. That is something new. It is historically inaccurate, but it says, if this appeals to you, the past has opened the door to lots of troubling ideologies. I'm not going to say, this place was always racist, and Trump simply enabled people to express that. I'm not convinced that this is entirely true. I think there probably was some racism there, as there is everywhere. But I think a lot of it has been cultivated. And it's partly Trump, it's partly the internet, where people find these online communities where they are introduced to these ideas, where they are validated for expressing these ideas. Those two things operate hand in hand. But I do not accept the argument that "Oh, these people have always been terrible racists and Trump simply enabled them." No, it is more complex than that. There's a grain of truth in that, but it's more complex.

HP: I remember that I met a former student of mine when I was on the campus of the University of Illinois, Urbana Champaign, which is a place in the Midwest. This was in 2018 and she said that her family was now divided because of the President and that they could not have any family reunions, because some people voted for Trump and the others didn't, and there was just no way that the family could get together.

JH: Oh yeah, certainly true. It is a very common American story, that a family's divided about Trump. It was true in my own family and my extended family, not my mother or my brother, but say cousins, more distant relatives. Many of them were Trump supporters and it did become very difficult. I think most American families experienced some version of that.

I'll come back to this question of race, which I think is significant. In my recent book, *Mercy Street*, the character who comes from Bakerton is a white supremacist. He is opposed to abortion precisely because he doesn't want white women to have abortions. He has no problem with women of color having abortions, but he's concerned about the demographic balance in the U.S., this feeling of suddenly facing no longer being in the majority, this kind of white panic that I think is at the root of some of the revival of racism in this country. It is painful to me in a way because this is a place that is dear to me and I've written about it a lot, that I have a long artistic engagement with. It is painful to me that the racist character in *Mercy Street* had to come from Bakerton. I didn't know that when I started writing the book. I live in Boston, I've written two

other novels set in Boston, and when I started to write *Mercy Street*, it was going to be a Boston story. And it is. But when I started to think about an antagonist for my main character Claudia, in the figure of an anti-abortion activist,
and I thought about where would such a person come from? It was very natural to me to make him come from Bakerton. Part of the reason is this: When
I was growing up in that town, it was very common to see these signs along
the roadway. They were handmade signs; they were not mass-produced. Signs
that people actually made with anti-abortion slogans like "It's a Child, not a
Choice" or "Abortion Stops the Beating Heart." What I found interesting about
them is that somebody spent the time and money to buy the lumber, cut the
lumber, paint the signs, and then drive around and plant the signs on people's
land. When I was thinking about what sort of person would be an antagonist
to Claudia, I thought about the kind of person who would make those signs.
They are still there. When I go back to visit my mother in Pennsylvania, if you
drive 10 miles in any direction, you will see them, the signs are still up there.
So, in a way, to my surprise, even *Mercy Street* became something of a Bakerton
story. Not entirely, of course, but it was a surprise to me that those two worlds
connected.

HP: It is a surprise to your readers as well, I think. I didn't expect Bakerton to play a role in the novel and then, all of a sudden: "Oh, okay, here it is,
again," which was nice. I saw that you had this conversation with Stewart O'Nan
about your new book. I once did an interview with him about similar topics,
the family, rural America, but also about the meaning and the role of affective
economies. He told me: "You know, you may think that I'm not sentimental in
my books, but I'm actually a very sentimental person, but in my books I try to
avoid that a bit. You know, *I don't stop at the sentimental*." I actually took this line
as the title for the interview. You already said, you want to differentiate sentimentality from sentiment. There is a certain kind of toxic nostalgia, which
obviously can be very sentimental. Apart from that, do you have any other investment in the term or in the way that you use or avoid sentimentality in your
writing? Because the topics that you deal with, of course, are in specific ways
emotionally over-determined.

JH: Well, certainly I have written characters who are sentimental, but that
is a different matter from the writer being sentimental, and it is an important
distinction. Let us come back to the character of Claudia in *Mercy Street*: All
this sentimentality around the fetus, around motherhood, around traditional
marriage, and family—Claudia seems to be immune to this. Her immunity to
this comes from her own life experience, having been raised the way she was,

growing up with a single mother, living in a trailer in poverty, and, in particular, in a family where foster children would come to stay for a period of time. She is immune to any sentimentality, about motherhood, or family, or childbearing. Because every example in her own life contradicts that. She just does not have any appetite for those mythologies, because she has seen the truth of it.

HP: I thought that she was a very interesting protagonist. Until the very end of the novel, we anticipate some kind of confrontation to come, because you pull up all these different plots, and then we wonder, is there going to be a fatal shooting in front of the abortion clinic?

JH: Right, because it is the U.S.A., after all. These are thoroughly American problems—first, the ongoing controversy over abortion that will simply never go away, and second, the easy access to—and great enthusiasm for—guns of all kinds. The novel could not be set in any other country. Really. It is a thoroughly American novel. It is a thoroughly American problem, this ongoing controversy over abortion that will just never go away here. Certainly, in other countries, there are people who oppose abortion, but there is nothing like this protracted battle we've been having in this country for 50 years now.*

HP: Thank you for the conversation.

* Note: Shortly after this conversation took place, the U.S. Supreme Court overturned Roe v. Wade, the 1973 landmark decision granting women the right to abortion.

"This Is Our Barn": Agrarian Sentimentality and the Fracking Formula in *Promised Land*

Axelle Germanaz and Sarah Marak

With the energy insecurity brought about in large parts of the globe by the Russian war against Ukraine, several states, especially in Europe, reinvigorated discussions about energy technologies that were thought to be phased out or eschewed prior. In addition to debates about prolonging the production and use of nuclear energy in Germany, several nation states also brought hydraulic fracturing (fracking) for the extraction of natural gas back on the table. Fracking is a technology that was introduced in the United States as early as the 1950s and that is now used to extract natural gas and oil from shale rock by "injecting millions of gallons of water, chemical additives, and a proppant (sand and/or silica) at high pressure into the wellbore to create small fractures in the rock" (Finkel xiv). While in the earlier days natural gas was extracted from so-called conventional sources, in the new millennium fracking gained a larger popularity with energy companies due to the successful development and implementation of "horizontal drilling," which made it easier to access shale gas, considered an "unconventional" source of fossil fuels (ibid. 3). Especially in the U.S., fracking was hailed as the technology that would bring about energy independence from foreign oil and gas and that would thereby strengthen the nation's position in the global political arena.[1] But fracking has always been controversial: For some it represented a "bridge technology" to cleaner and more sustainable energy production (Kistler 317) because it was said to produce less CO_2

---

1   Fracking is carried out in many locations, from California through Montana and North Dakota (Bakken Shale) to Texas (Eagle Ford Basin), and Appalachia (Marcellus Shale). The biggest shale gas depot in the U.S. is the Marcellus Shale, which lies underneath Virginia, West Virginia, Ohio, Pennsylvania, and parts of New York. Some U.S. states have banned the practice (Washington, New York, Maryland, and Vermont), some of which do not have natural gas depots.

244 Axelle Germanaz and Sarah Marak

emissions than coal and oil (Plumer; Nunez). For others, the environmental cost was too high—not least because it slowed the development of solar and wind energy (Kistler 317). In the early 2000s, a literal fracking boom brought the methods and risks of this type of fossil fuel extraction to the larger public's attention. Despite the economic benefits that extracting cheap natural gas promised, it also led to questions about environmental safety and the possible damages of this practice, such as poisoned wells and contaminated groundwater. This boom of shale oil and gas extraction also inspired a number of works (documentary films, movies, journalistic and non-fictional texts, and novels) that explored fracking and its possible consequences, positive and negative, for rural communities, the environment, and ultimately the nation itself. The central theme of a broad range of cultural texts is what Colin Jerolmack calls the "public/private paradox" (7), which entails that private citizens' decisions on fracking possibly influence the livelihood of whole communities and ecosystems. This can be described, with John Cawelti, as producing (and following) a specific narrative formula—what we call the "fracking formula," which structures the majority of cultural texts focused on hydraulic fracturing.

This article examines how the first—and to date only—major U.S. American motion picture on fracking portrays the controversial debate and diverging attitudes toward the issue and shows how it relies on "agrarian sentimentality" to challenge the environmentally risky extractive practice. In 2012, Gus Van Sant's film *Promised Land* brought the environmental controversy surrounding fracking and the economic dilemma many communities face(d) to the big screen, starring Matt Damon in yet another version of his well-known all-American good guy as protagonist Steve Butler. Steve, born and raised in rural Iowa, is a highly successful "landman" at the oil and gas company Global Crosspower Solutions, traveling the rural United States with his colleague Sue (played by Frances McDormand) to get people to lease out their land for natural gas drilling. Due to some unexpected complications with the well-informed local high school teacher and former engineer Frank Yates (played by Hal Holbrook) and what Sue and Steve call an "environmental presence" (John Krasinski as fake-environmentalist Dustin Noble), they must prolong their stay in McKinley, a town that Van Sant portrays as the generic U.S. small town. Steve, who is himself from the 'heartland,' ends up re-discovering his rural (family) roots and his love for small-town life during his stay. When it becomes clear that Dustin Noble, the environmentalist, was sent by Global to deceive the locals and make them vote in favor of fracking, Steve ends up turning on his employer and warning people about the dangers of fracking.

Promised Land relies both on the Agrarian Myth, a construction deeply rooted in U.S. American cultural memory, and the sentimentalization of small-town life. Indeed, in taking a new agrarianist stance,[2] the film places a rural town and its people's small-scale family farming lifestyle at the center of the national debate surrounding energy transition and sustainability, the rural/urban divide, (loss of) community, and democracy. In the following, we analyze the film as an exemplary text using the "fracking formula" and a particular brand of sentimentality—what we call "agrarian sentimentality"—to teach audiences how to "think and act in a particular way" (Tompkins xi), and we might add "feel," about the destructive effects of resource extraction, and especially hydraulic fracturing. We read *Promised Land* as a romantic, and at times nostalgic, depiction of the rural as the last stronghold of original U.S. American values (and virtues). In offering a sentimentalized account of rural community bonds and small-scale family farming as a bastion against the fracking industry, the film not only obscures the realities of the contemporary agro-industrial complex and the economic struggles of small farms but also evades an in-depth inquiry into the politics of natural gas extraction.

Promised Land and the "Fracking Formula"

Since the 2010s, there has been a wave of documentary films and novels that have aimed to encapsulate the meanings and consequences of hydraulic fracturing—see, for instance, *Gasland* (2010), *Triple Divide* (2012), *TruthLand* (2012) and *FrackNation* (2013), as well as the novels *Fractures* (Herrin 2013), *The Fracking King* (Browning 2014), *The Fracking War* (Fitzgerald 2014), and Jennifer Haigh's *Heat & Light* (2016; see author's interview and Heike Paul's article on the novel in this volume). Most of these cultural artifacts are infused with the same key themes and stock characters and share a similar setting—so much so that one might speak of a "fracking formula" that would unite these texts into a coherent cultural subgenre.[3] This formula often includes the establishment of a di-

---

2   New Agrarianism is a movement of both scholars and farmers that originated in the late 1970s with, for example, author/farmer Wendell Berry as a leading voice. The movement rests on the agrarian tradition that connects democracy and land-use (Fiskio).

3   Amitav Ghosh has introduced the term "petrofiction" in the 1990s to categorize and examine (literary) texts that have dealt with the impact of oil on societies. For our context, it might be relevant to talk about "frackfiction" to discuss the texts that are

chotomy between the (coastal) metropolis or metropolitan area and the small town in the 'heartland;' a reinforcement of stereotypes of not only 'urban environmentalists' or professional protesters but also those of the uneducated rural population; and references to the United States' (mythologized) agrarian past. Moreover, narratives of the formula tend to stress the cultural specificity of fracking in the U.S., and in particular the "intimacy" (cf. Jerolmack) of the issue. The formulaic fashion of narratives about fracking may simply have to do with the strict sequence of events that fracking usually entails: the 'discovery' of natural gas in a certain region, the company landmen visiting people in their homes, residents having to decide whether to lease or not, ensuing environmental protest, and, sometimes, the actual drilling and its consequences for the area (for example the installment of necessary infrastructure, the building of so-called man camps, as envisioned in *Yellow Earth* [Sayles 2020], the influx of money, and environmental degradation). However, we argue that these recurring themes make up a "fracking formula" that points to a fascination with the phenomenon of fracking and the culturally specific way this drilling technology is at the core of controversy in the U.S.

Formulaic narratives, according to John Cawelti, not only "tend to have a much more limited repertory of plots, characters, and setting" but are also tied to "a particular culture and period of time" (120–22). Before going into more detail about the themes, characters, and setting, a closer look at the cultural specificity of fracking helps clarify why much of the cultural production on fracking is in formulaic fashion. While fracking is certainly a topic of (political) discussion in many countries, there seems to be a culturally specific fascination with the technology in the U.S. that also results in specific tropes and themes in narratives about fracking; not only because it is carried out in the U.S. on a scale that had politicians and pundits talk about "the shale revolution" but also because private citizens are especially involved in the decision-making. The choice of whether to 'frack' for natural gas or not is largely left to private citizens and not the American public to decide (Jerolmack 16–17). Colin Jerolmack therefore describes fracking in the U.S. as a "private," even "intimate" matter (7). The reason for this "intimacy" is a legal peculiarity of the United States, namely that property rights here extend "up to heaven and down to hell" (ibid. 17), meaning that whoever owns the surface land also holds the mineral rights and has thus the power to decide whether to lease the land to gas companies

---

turning to this 'novel' form of resource extraction—as powerful and as destructive as oil extraction.

or not. This is especially true for states east of the Mississippi where the practice of 'split estate' (i.e., mineral rights are separate from surface land rights) is not as common as in the western United States (ibid.18). This peculiarity then results in what he terms the "public/private paradox" (7).

Setting

As indicated by Cawelti, setting is a major aspect of formulaic narratives. Due to the Marcellus Shale lying underneath Appalachian states, the debates about fracking also shed light on the rural areas of this region. The election of Donald Trump as President and publications such as J. D. Vance's *Hillbilly Elegy* (2016), put small-town Appalachian communities in the spotlight and have inspired various stereotypes over the years, most significantly that of "a space set apart from the rest of the nation," "America's 'Other,'" characterized by "economic and cultural marginalization" (Long 84; see also Bell 14–17; Harrison 735).[4] Here, fracking meets "socially and geographically isolated heartland communities most decimated by the postindustrial service and tech economy" and the decision whether to 'frack or not to frack' "is largely in the hands of conservative, working-class whites residing in rural America—precisely the communities that purportedly feel forsaken by beltway politicians and coastal elites" (Jerolmack 18). The split estate rule and public/private paradox may also be the reason why most accounts on fracking are preoccupied with and/or set in Appalachia and regions above the Marcellus Shale, as opposed to Texas (the Eagle Ford Basin is the "most active shale play in the world" [eaglefordshale.com]) or North Dakota (Bakken Shale). As already mentioned, here, private citizens carry the burden of making decisions that not only have an impact on their bank account but also on their environment and by extension that of their neighbors and their communities.

This region offers an interesting contrast to the often 'ugly' sights and sites of extraction: hilly and green pastoral landscapes dotted by small-scale family farms and small towns. The economic hardship in the rural parts of the Appalachian states combined with the monetary potential of the fossil resources in the ground further serve to highlight the dilemma of residents and communities, many of which are seemingly dependent on extractive industries—or used to be, in the case of coal—rather than making a living 'off the land' with

4   See Bell's *Fighting King Coal: The Challenges to Micromobilization in Central Appalachia* for a discussion of Appalachia as "internal colony" or "energy sacrifice zone."

traditional farming. Due to the rurality and small-scale community structure of the locations where gas companies seek to conduct fracking, "[s]hale communities are in the unenviable position of having to confront the public/private paradox face to face, at the fence post, the general store, Little League games, and town hall meetings" (Jerolmack 7). In *Promised Land*, Steve and Sue not only travel through all these spaces—the general store, the town hall, and the children's baseball game—, they also have a particular method of convincing people to lease their land that plays on very private and intimate issues. Sue, herself a mother, stresses the importance of school funding to a potential signatory, while Steve claims he wants people to keep their family farms or live in a luxury they never experienced before. At the McKinley dive bar, Steve antagonizes four local farmers for not leasing out their land by telling them:

> You don't want to apply for college loans for your kid? This money says, "Fuck you" loans. You worried about car payments? "Fuck you" payments. The bank's gonna come and foreclose on your farm? "Fuck you" bank. "Fuck you" money is the ultimate liberator. And underneath your town there is "fuck you" money. (01:05:39–01:05:57)

The quote reveals that Steve cannot understand at first why the community would pass on the opportunity he and Sue supposedly offer them on a silver platter. Steve, who is clearly still affected by the downfall of his own hometown after a Caterpillar plant closed down, finds in fracking a promise of economic success that can resuscitate 'let down' small towns around the country. Fracking narratives thus not only examine fracking as a technology and an extractive practice, but as a more comprehensive societal issue with critical economic, social, cultural, and environmental repercussions.

Themes

Fictions about fracking often present a rural community that is disrupted by the 'discovery' of natural gas underneath it—as it is the case, for instance, in Sayles' *Yellow Earth* and Haigh's *Heat & Light*. The prospect of monetary gain and wealth (or of becoming a "shaleonnaire") that is offered by gas company representatives is mostly portrayed as an outside force potentially threatening the rural idyll, community cohesion, and an agrarian lifestyle, bringing to light latent conflicts and intensifying already existing ones. Rarely, fracking is portrayed as the only way to prolong the existence of the otherwise struggling American farmer (as in the documentary *FrackNation*). *Promised Land* is based on the premise that Steve and Sue's offers trigger changes in the community that could possibly upend people's lifestyles. The depicted communities then struggle with making the decision for or against fracking (as embodied by the town's vote in *Promised Land*), with the decisions of their neighbors (like Rena in *Heat & Light*), or the consequences of their own decision (in *Gasland*, *Heat & Light*, and *Yellow Earth*, for example). In a key scene of *Promised Land*, Steve and science teacher Frank Yates share a heart-to-heart on the old man's porch, looking out on Frank's pastures and miniature horses as the sun goes down. In an impassioned speech, Frank describes the sacrifices that many individuals envision in the prospect of giving up their lands to oil and gas companies:

> You're a good man, Steve. You have so many of the qualities we need more of these days [...] I just wish you weren't doing this. You came here and offered us money, figuring you were helping us. All we had to do to get it is, be willing to scorch the earth under our feet. (01:18:56-01:19:25)

Steve is depicted here as an intruder who disrupted the quiet town of McKinley, despite his seemingly good intentions. It is relevant that this scene appears shortly after Steve's "fuck you money" speech because both make use of the image of the underground in very different ways. While Steve equates the ground, and more precisely what lays underneath it, with wealth and riches, Frank posits it as sacred in itself.

The company-sent landmen are agents in the plots of fracking narratives that readers and viewers accompany to the farms, kitchens, living rooms, and porches of small-town Americans. While they symbolize corporate greed and a capitalist disregard for the environment to some, for others they represent financial independence and the American Dream of upward mobility. Despite the cold calculus of lease negotiations and agreements for mineral rights, much of the plot of fracking narratives takes place in these intimate spaces, and not on gas fields or next to waste-water pits, highlighting the personal matter of the choice. It is often during the landmen visits that the technology of fracking is explained to landowners, and, by extension to readers or viewers. These explanations of fracking tend to be 'dumbed down' and its inconvenient and dangerous aspects are left aside or glossed over. This serves to characterize the rural residents not only as gullible and uneducated, but also as falling prey to corporate deception. Steve, who at the beginning of the film proudly accepts his boss' praise that he is the most productive of Global's landmen, comes to admit in the film's final scene that he lied to people on purpose about the worth of their land: "I've looked a lot of you right in the eye and told you there's a bunch of money under your feet and we can get it out, risk free, guaranteed. Clearly, that's not true."

Another major recurring theme in most fracking narratives is water, which also plays a subtle but symbolic role in *Promised Land*. The film begins and ends with Steve washing his face in crystal clear water—once in the bathroom of a restaurant in New York City,[5] and then towards the end in the local town gym. This opening scene is noteworthy because NYC gets large parts of its water supply from the Delaware River basin, which in part lies in Pennsylvania (approximately 5 million New Yorkers are supported by water from the Delaware River basin, which supplies water to 13.3 million people; cf. Delaware River Basin Comission). Water supply in general is a theme that particularly highlights the consequences the public/private paradox can possibly have for millions of Americans in terms of environmental risk. The Academy Award nominated documentary *Gasland* provided the U.S. American public with one of the most infamous, and iconic, images associated with fracking: a man lighting his tap water on fire due to methane contamination.[6] *Promised Land* reiterates this iconic moment from *Gasland* in a scene where Dustin Noble, in a demonstration of what fracking chemicals allegedly do to the groundwater during his presentation on fracking to a school class, sets his props ablaze and ominously says: "This is all the water that we had, all the water we had to drink, all the water that cows had to drink, all the water that puppies and kittens had to drink, all the water for the fish and the rivers" (00:53:10-00:53:20). Though again the film does not show the consequences of fracking for groundwater and wells explicitly, it does visually connect the practice of fracking with water and its potential contamination throughout.

---

5   Though not explicitly stated, there is a reference that Butler's boss flew in to Teterboro airport, NJ.

6   Especially famous is the case of Dimock, Pennsylvania, a small town in the rural part of the state where inhabitants were filmed lighting their tap water on fire due to alleged methane contamination—a scene that was picked up in both *FrackNation* and *Truth-Land* as well as by anti-fracking activists. Protesters used an image of Smokey Bear, a Forest Service icon for wildfire prevention, and updated his famous slogan ("Only you can prevent forest fires") to "Only YOU can prevent faucet fires." The artist who created the Smokey meme, Lopi LaRoe, later received a cease-and-desist letter from the US Department of Agriculture (USDA), which also includes the US Forest Service. The slogan, the agency claimed, was not to be altered in order not to confuse citizens about wildfire prevention. (Rugh; "About LMNOPI")

Characters

Recurring figures of fracking narratives include the landman, representing oil and gas companies, the farmer, mostly represented as farming 'traditionally' and on a small scale rather than in industrial fashion, well-educated, fracking-skeptic outsiders that moved to the country ("rusticators"[7]) or moved back home, and environmentalists. Steve Butler differs to a degree from other representations of this stock character because he can claim a farming back-ground for himself. However, to him, as "one of two guys of [his] graduating class that went to college and studied something other than agriculture" economic success is more important than "the farming town fantasy" he calls "delusional self-mythology" in the beginning of the film. He views money "as the ultimate liberator" and tells the residents of the town they had "fuck-you-money" in the ground—meaning they could leave farming behind in the future thanks to oil and gas money. Environmental safety, especially regarding water, is not Steve's concern in the beginning, who also celebrates natural gas as "the clean alternative" to oil and coal, reiterating the idea of the "bridge technology." Steve is thus depicted as a career-oriented man pursuing a big promotion at Global—which he ends up receiving— and his upward mobility has after all been largely afforded by the extractive industry.

Next to the stock character of the landman, fracking narratives are usually also populated by environmentalists and anti-fracking activists, who also represent an element of disruption. As in *Heat & Light* and *Promised Land*, environmentalism does not seem to exist within the rural regions where the stories are set but is a phenomenon that is brought into the communities by outside actors—rusticators and well-educated city-dwellers. *Promised Land* features an environmental activist who goes by the telling name of Noble, a young man who arrives in the town alone shortly after the gas company. This portrayal of environmentalism as a phenomenon of the city rather than the countryside is reinforcing stereotypes of an urban population that is "out of touch with the economic struggles of those who work in rural extractive economies" (Sutter vii). Similar to the figure of the rusticator, the environmentalist in fracking narratives is usually a city person that is pitted against the small-town com-munity. *Promised Land* makes clear from the beginning that environmentalism poses a threat to Steve and Sue's endeavors, but they come prepared: Before

---

7   According to Jerolmack, "someone of means who moved from a metropolitan area to the country" (8).

they set out to win over a new town, they are briefed on whether they should expect resistance or if there is an "environmental presence." When farmer and MIT graduate Frank Yates asks a critical question about fracking at the first townhall meeting, Butler immediately asks him: "Are you with an environmental group?," indicating a certain disregard for concerns the locals might have and positioning environmentalists as the ultimate obstacle in Butler's way. Later in the film, when Dustin Noble enters the scene, environmentalism vs. extractivism is established as a central dichotomy of the narrative. Steve projects a range of stereotypes about environmentalists on Noble, who is portrayed as the average nice guy wearing a baseball cap (reminiscent of Josh Fox in *Gasland*), driving around in a Forest Service-green pick-up truck,[8] and singing Bruce Springsteen during a karaoke night in town. Steve calls him a "hippie," talks about his "stoner buddies," and orders him "one of those fancy imported [beers] and a granola bar" at the local dive bar, suggesting that Noble does not fit into the rural landscape as well as Steve because he is supposedly a disconnected urbanite. Sue, moreover, calls him "a really nice kid" showing a belittling attitude towards environmentalists. The fact that Noble is later revealed to be an employee of Global, who was sent to McKinley to 'play environmentalist' in order to get the town to distrust any environmental agenda renders the movie's portrayal of environmental activism rather negative. Thus, while "environmental protection as a value is upheld," "the people in charge of it are identified as untrustworthy" (Moore 242).

Instead of offering an in-depth exploration of fracking and its environmental impacts, *Promised Land* thus turns to what could potentially be lost in the fracking boom: namely the (past) agrarian lifestyle of rural America, the close-knit communities of the U.S. small-town, and with it, the nation's core values. It romanticizes small-town America and offers a sentimental return to the Jeffersonian agrarian ideal as a (non-)solution to the problem of hazardous natural gas extraction and the economic problems of rural regions. Here, "the rural is not only suggestive of a particular national past" but is also "appropriated as an allegory of the nation" in envisioning the future (Kley/Paul 3). In fact,

---

8   Ironically, radical environmentalists have historically viewed the Forest Service as an obstacle and accused the federal agency of catering to corporations and betraying their task of managing public lands through timber sales and the building of roads (Woodhouse 174–175). It should be noted though that in some parts of the U.S., the Forest Service is also in charge of managing designated wilderness areas that are, in turn, viewed critically by those in favor of industrial development.

this agrarian sentimentality could also be defining for the fracking formula we conceptualize. In the following, we examine the ways in which the film sentimentalizes agrarian life and reconfigures it to critique extractivism.

Challenging Extractivism through Agrarian Sentimentality

At its release, *Promised Land* gathered mixed reviews from film critics. While some applauded the director and writers' attempt to treat cinematically a determining issue for the contemporary moment, for others, the film was simply too sentimental. Philip French from *The Guardian* judged the film "sentimental, Capraesque fare" and for *NPR*'s Jeannette Catsoulis, it is a "gentle but knowing natural gas drama" that ends up "cav[ing] to sentiment and stereotype." That 'sentimental' is used here pejoratively to condemn the film's supposedly obvious manipulation of viewers' emotions is noteworthy because it reflects a broader cultural suspicion towards the sentimental as something inauthentic, exaggerated, disingenuous, perhaps even, futile. Yet, the sentimental, or sentimentality, "as a communicative and relational code" ("DFG Research Training Group"), performs important cultural and political work on the audience. *Promised Land*'s agrarian sentimentality is geared toward both a political mobilization against fossil fuel extraction and a stabilization of the agrarian ideal at a time of economic and environmental uncertainty. The only way to keep fossil fuel in the ground, it seems to argue, is to care for the land and the communities above it.

To this day, the Agrarian Myth is one of the most enduring and elastic national myths in the United States. Briefly defined, it encapsulates the belief that rural spaces, populations, and lifestyles are the quintessence of the U.S. nation. Attached to this myth is a set of qualities, which are supposedly distinctly agrarian yet also define the whole U.S. national character, like virtuousness, self-sufficiency, integrity, and duty to a local community. In *The Age of Reform*, historian Richard Hofstadter describes that "[t]he American mind was raised upon a sentimental attachment to rural living and upon a series of notions about rural people and rural life" (23). He elaborates:

> The agrarian myth represents a kind of homage that Americans have paid to the fancied innocence of their origins. Like any complex of ideas, the agrarian myth cannot be defined in a phrase, but its component themes

form a clear pattern. Its hero was the yeoman farmer, its central conception the notion that he is the ideal man and the ideal citizen. (ibid.)

For Hofstadter, popular literary discourse in the early 19th century participated largely in the development and affirmation of the myth, noting that later on it evolved into "a mass creed, a part of the country's political folklore and its nationalist ideology" (28). The "sentimental attachment" to the rural that the Agrarian Myth is based on long served to obscure the violent expropriation of Indigenous peoples from the land during European settlement. Scholars, like Richard Slotkin, have traced its lineage back to the nation's colonial beginnings in the 17th and 18th centuries as the myth became crucial to the discourse of Westward expansion and the doctrine of Manifest Destiny. Manifestations of the myth can also be found in early republic writings with notably Hector St. John de Crèvecoeur's *Letters from an American Farmer* (1782) and Thomas Jefferson's *Notes on the State of Virginia* (1785). Jefferson's agrarian republicanism envisioned the United States as a democratic nation founded on the virtuous nature of farmers—"the most valuable citizens" and "chosen people of God" (135)—and the 'richness' of the land. Jefferson posited agrarianism as a safeguard against industrialization, urbanization, and supposed national moral decay. Jeffersonian notions of the farmer as the ideal U.S. American citizen and agrarian spaces as settings of democratic experience, self-sufficiency/autonomy, and virtuousness/authenticity continue to be resonating cultural and political symbols (for a national identity) to this day. Indeed, the Agrarian Myth is particularly malleable and has continuously been (re-)shaped for new purposes and ideologies in relation to rural landscapes and the people who inhabit them—from republican politicians talking about a "real America" to Dodge Ram car commercials (Kley/Paul 3–4), and leftist grassroots social movements arguing for sustainable farming and climate justice (Singer/Grey/Motter). The agrarian setting in Van Sant's *Promised Land* is depicted through vast landscapes with flourishing green fields, only sparsely spotted by small-scale family farms, red barns, and rustic houses with white picket fences. Although it does depict U.S. American rural spaces amidst economic hardship, the film rests heavily on a sentimental activism that uses the Agrarian Myth to propose a story of renewal, hope, and resilience.

First and foremost, the film aestheticizes and idealizes rural spaces. The opening scenes of the film are relevant in this context because they play on the dichotomy at the core of the Agrarian Myth: country versus city, metropolis versus small town. While the film posits the rural as a space of "'authentic'

Americanness," this is only fleshed out as a contrast to "urban or metropolitan spaces" (Kley/Paul 5). At the beginning of the film Steve Butler is shown entering the main room of a fancy restaurant in New York. As the camera follows the character on his way to his table, it lingers on the ostentatious architecture of the place, with its massive columns, huge paned windows, and gold ornaments. The frame is crowded with people dining, laughing, drinking, and is constantly split up by wooden panels, waiters passing by, mirrors, and walls. The scene is set in a cool lighting with blue and grey tones. Overall, the composition of the scene creates a dull, almost gloomy, atmosphere in which the character seems to be 'lost' in the crowd and alone. The next scene is constructed in opposition. From inside an empty barn, the camera follows a man in his late '70s opening the door and loading his pick-up truck with a bag of what looks like hay. The scene seems to be shot in the morning, with natural warm light, beaming through the door and the cracks of the barn—a cat sits peacefully in the frame of the door and birds are chirping. A montage follows and alternates between the elderly man driving off his small farm and lush garden and Steve Butler sitting in a bus, looking at the fields outside the window. While we follow the old man from a shoulder level shot, which provides a sense of intimacy between the viewer and the character, we follow Butler's bus from an aerial shot, which captures the expanse of the vast landscape. Accompanying these images is a score by Danny Elfman, an eerie and melancholic choral music (in fact, performed by a boys' choir) that conveys to the audience a quasi-religious experience—connecting therefore the landscape to the sacred. These shots provide pastoral images of rolling hills and rustic barns that contrast starkly to the cold and impersonal atmosphere of Butler's New York meeting. They establish, right from the beginning of the movie, rural and agrarian spaces as idyllic when compared to urban spaces.

The landscape is indeed a recurring element in the film, and viewers are presented throughout with long aerial shots of green meadows, vast fields, open blue skies, barns and farms, and small-town shops and buildings that aestheticize rural life—this is emphasized by the non-diegetic melancholic score overlapping the images. The film casts a nostalgic look on the rural small town life as it catalogs the well-known landmarks of this idealized space. Steve and Sue shop for clothes to "look local" at the general store and gas station "Rob's Guns, Groceries, Guitars, and Gas" (Sue: "up here, they always wear flannel," Steve: "or camo"), they stay at what appears to be the only motel in town, spend their evenings at Buddy's, the local dive bar, and their mornings at the town diner. One hour into the film appears an unexpected montage of images accompanied by a slow-paced folk song that provides a nostalgic look on the rural small-town life. The camera first displays the town from a birds-eye view, then, in slow-motion, a barber shop and a hardware store, a community center where elderly women play bingo and children play baseball, before the camera lingers on a police officer leaning on a vintage Pepsi machine, men working in a rusted factory, and a woman sitting on her porch with the American flag flying in the wind. This montage, along with the end credits that are paired with an aerial shot of the town slowly zooming out, underlines the notion that this town could be any town in the U.S. The universalization of the small town is a common trope in U.S. culture that has its roots in the Agrarian Myth. As Sheila Webb writes, "[t]he small town occupies a mythic place in American life and culture" as it is often portrayed as "the ideal American space" (35). *Promised Land* plays on this notion of the universal small town quite openly, with protagonist Steve explaining to his bosses at Global that he is so successful at his job because: "Well, I'm from Eldrige, Iowa—it might as well be Rifle, Colorado, Dish, Texas, or Lafayette, Louisiana, any of these towns we've sold. I know them, they know me."[9] Even though the experience of fracking may not be universal, as it is usually very much restricted regionally, the film provides a romantic image of the universal small town in the countryside as an idyllic space. It sentimentalizes agrarian spaces and places as sites of both embodiments and reproduction of an idealized (i.e., fantasized) U.S. American identity.[10]

Secondly, the film sentimentalizes solidarity and community among rural folk as a model of democratic society. It depicts a close-knit community in which the self-interest and greed of one person interested in leasing their lands for fracking could disrupt not only the harmony between everyone in the town but also the harmony between them and the land. The people of the small town are portrayed as sharing the same values—this is highlighted by

9   The references to Dish, Texas and Lafayette, Louisiana are interesting here, as both these towns can be linked to fracking-related health hazards and toxicity; Lafayette, in the fictional world of the film, is later revealed to have had a chemical spill that killed cows; the small town of Dish, Texas, on the other hand, actually became more widely known in and outside of the U.S. because of fracking-related lawsuits and protest. Many residents, among them the major, claimed that they suffered from illness and diseases that could be linked to fracking in the vicinity (cf. "Town's effort").

10   Antje Kley and Heike Paul argue that due to this well-established connection of the rural to "a national discourse of 'authentic' Americanness [...] [it] may ultimately appear as unmarked" (5).

the town's meetings and the collective vote for or against fracking in the town. The movie contrasts the lived and strong bonds that connect rural people, who are shown coming together in the town hall, diner, bar, and community center, explicitly with the digital and broken relations that connect Steve and Sue to their employers and relatives—those are mostly taking place via cell phones and computers. The community, despite the private/public paradox and a general divide between those who want to get at "the money under [their] feet" and those that are more cautious, like Frank Yates, is intact. The rural community is also portrayed as authentic, as opposed to the urban, corporate culture, which is portrayed as dishonest and based on prefabricated jokes.

Thirdly, the film idealizes agrarian ethics of work and care, mostly through the characters of Frank Yates—a retired MIT scientist who teaches science at the local school and who raises miniature horses—and Alice, a school teacher (and Steve's love interest) who teaches her students to care for 'nature' on the farm she inherited from her father. Throughout the film, these rural characters, among others, are opposed to and clash with urban Global consultants Steve and Sue. Frank and Alice are depicted as hard-working, honest, and loyal to their community and as living a simple but satisfying life, while Steve and Sue are (first) portrayed as workaholics, eager for success, manipulative (Steve dupes the mayor into leasing some land for cheap), and lacking foresight. Butler, however, remains remotely attached to his agrarian background. To connect with the prospective leasers, he tells them almost ritualistically that he grew up in a farming community in Eldridge, Iowa. Furthermore, his boots, the family heirloom he inherited from his grandfather ("they're made in America," he proudly tells Sue), can be read as a symbolic connection back to his own agrarian past and express a sentimental attachment to a lifestyle that he initially believed to be gone ("the farming town fantasy was just shattered"). This lasting connection to his agrarian past foreshadows throughout the movie that Steve can, and will, be redeemed through a return to agrarian, and by extension rural, values. In depicting Steve's moral and physical conversion from urban, fossil-fuel industry consultant to rural inhabitant/settler, claims the superiority of pastoral and agrarian ideals over corporate and individualist ones. The film depicts Butler's regained innocence right before and during the penultimate scene at the town meeting at the gym, first when he washes his face in the gym toilet in a symbolical rebirth and when he takes the microphone to address the town as part of their community. The final monologue, along with the choral music from the film's opening scenes, and the fact that it is delivered by a misty-eyed and sincere Matt Damon, sentimentalizes agrarian lifeways.

Holding the picture of dead cattle in front of a barn that Noble used to convince the residents to vote against fracking (before his deception was revealed), Steve addresses the town one last time:

> I was looking at this picture for a while last night […] But I found myself staring at this barn. The wood's chipping away and the paint is flaking off there. Probably from all the salt water in the air. It reminded me of my grandfather's barn. That barn was the bane of my existence. It was immaculate. We painted it every other summer. Just him and me. I asked him 'why?' 'Why do we have to do this?' And he'd look at me and say 'This is our barn. Who else is going to do it?' […] I think he was just trying to teach me what it meant to take care of something. […] This is a real farm. […] Look, is this going to happen here? I honestly don't believe that it will. But they know that the only reason we're all gathered here is to ask the question 'what if it did?' […] But where we are now? Where we're headed? We might be betting more than we think. Everything that we have is on the table now. And that's just not ours to lose. But this is still our barn. (01:31:05-01:34:37)

Through the reminiscing of childhood memories, Steve not only paints a sentimental picture of the family farm and his connection to his lost grandfather but also pays tribute to agrarian values of self-sufficiency and hard work. The personal story morphing into a national one, highlights the importance of care and community over private interests and short-term financial gain with potential detrimental consequences. The barn can also be read in a planetary sense—as a metaphor for Earth and a reminder that extractivism is impacting the future of younger generations, who are also present in the gym. *Promised Land* is ultimately constructed around the idea that a return to agrarianism—in the sense of a return to the community, land, and care—will prevent the expansion and domination of resource extraction in the United States, thereby safeguarding the land and a future for upcoming generations.

The film sentimentalizes agrarian life as the last bastion against corporate greed and as a place of regeneration—it argues that we should care for "our barn" rather than selling it. It tells us that agrarian values are ultimately the answer to the failures of late capitalism and extractivism: The town will not yield to Global Crosspower Solutions and their money-making schemes but will stand in defiance, facing even the dire consequences of economic downfall. *Promised Land* inscribes itself as a kind of rural jeremiad, promising that the suffering and sacrifice of the rural community will not be in vain but will allow the nation to be democratically and environmentally intact for the generations to come. *Promised Land* uses the rural as an allegory for the nation and an 'authentic Americanness,' always to be actualized in the future—in fact, the film's title alludes to this notion of infinite actualization through the Puritans' vision of North America.

Conclusion

This article has examined how Gus Van Sant's 2012 *Promised Land* pictured contemporary debates surrounding hydraulic fracturing in the United States, in a context of heightened awareness of the practice's environmental and health consequences. Though the film erases the materiality of fracking operations—drilling rigs, wells, pipelines, and trucks remain absent throughout the film—, it uses several narrative elements that make up what we have called the "fracking formula" to make a point about extractivism in the 21st century U.S. With an exemplary reading of *Promised Land*, this article has shown how formulaic narratives about fracking rely on a set of key themes to portray it, not only as a technology and an extractive practice, but as a comprehensive societal issue with critical economic, social, cultural, and environmental repercussions. In elaborating a formula about fracking in fiction, we want to bring attention to the presence of the practice in the cultural imaginary.

The film centers on questions of moral, economic, and environmental dilemmas propelled by extraction. Its main character's personal identity quest stands for the nation's own quest for identity in the 21st century. Van Sant's film argues that like Steve, the U.S. can reverse the course of its history, stop exploiting poor rural communities and extracting resources from the ground, to instead become a truly democratic nation and secure a healthy and prospering land for future generations to live on and from. To make this argument, the film rests on what we have called "agrarian sentimentality," i.e., the sentimental depiction and idealization of rural peoples, spaces, and lifestyles. Sentimentality, or the sentimental, performs important political and cultural work because it allows viewers (or readers) to put themselves in a character's shoes (in this case, boots) and can generate compassion and solidarity. Agrarian sentimentality is deployed here to convince the public against the destructive potentials of hydraulic fracking, and more generally of extractivism.

The politics of sentimentality, or sentimental fiction, have long been debated by literary and cultural studies scholars. The kind of agrarian sentimentality that is at the core of *Promised Land* renders the film likewise extremely ambiguous when it comes to its politics and the cultural work it performs. Indeed, at a time of climate emergency, the film raises several important themes, notably the idea that community and care for the land are more valuable in the long term than individual monetary gain and the exploitation of resources. The film seemingly relies on new agrarianism's beliefs as it upholds agrarian spaces, peoples, and lifestyles as virtuous, democratic, and regenerative—a (re-)turn to the local and the agrarian in the face of industrialization and globalization. It constantly depicts the democratic possibilities of the small-town community, which thanks to its limited scale and its shared values, can debate and decide collectively about its future. The town is a microcosm in which the national debate about fracking, and more generally about resource extraction, plays out. The film also successfully argues about the multifaceted consequences of individuals usurping the commons and extraction splitting, not only the ground, but also the fabric of communities, and about the vulnerability of the environment—"our barn"—in the face of extraction. However, the film performs this political reversal only in its last fifteen minutes as it fantasizes a return to agrarian values and lifestyle, without proposing any kind of way forward for the rural at a time of economic and climatic disruption. In fact, the film, by its cinematic circularity and lack of closure, does not provide a solution to the debates surrounding energy transition, sustainability, and environmental crisis. Further, the agrarian sentimentality deployed in the film stabilizes a settler-colonialist, racialized, and gendered regime of representation in showcasing scenes of sentimentalized white U.S. American rural life as essence of 'Americanness.' Finally, the film tends to regress in nostalgic depictions of an agrarian and rural small-town, with mom-and-pop shops, small-scale farms, and even miniature horses, that obscures the realities of contemporary agrarian and rural spaces and their relationship to extractivism, capitalism, the environment. In its reliance on the trope of main-street U.S.A., *Promised Land* is a product of the fracking boom that aims at moving the audience to "think and act [and feel] in a particular way" (Tompkins) about hydraulic fracturing, while providing a glimpse of a non-extractivist future through a return to an imagined past.

References

"About LMNOPI." N.d. *Lmnopi.com*. Accessed July 28, 2022. https://lmnopi.com/about/.

Bell, Shannon Elizabeth. 2016. *Fighting King Coal: The Challenges to Micromobilization in Central Appalachia*. Cambridge, MA: MIT Press.

Browning, James. 2014. *The Fracking King*. Boston, MA: New Harvest/ Houghton Mifflin Harcourt.

Catsoulis, Jeannette. 2012. "'Promised Land': A Folksy Take on Fracking." *NPR*, December 27, 2012. Accessed July 26, 2022. https://www.npr.org/2012/12/22/167867139/promised-land-a-folksy-take-on-fracking.

Cawelti, John G. 1972. "The Concept of Formula in the Study of Popular Literature." *The Bulletin of the Midwest Modern Language Association*, no. 5, 115–23.

Crèvecoeur, J. Hector St. John de. (1782) 1981. *Letters from an American Farmer and Sketches of Eighteenth-Century America*. Ed. Albert E. Stone. New York, NY: Penguin Publishing Group.

Delaware River Basin Commission. 2022. "Basin Water Use." Accessed July 29, 2022. https://www.nj.gov/drbc/programs/supply/basin-water-use.html.

"DFG Research Training Group—The Sentimental in Literature, Culture, and Politics: About." N.d. *The Global Sentimentality Project*. Accessed July 28, 2022. https://www.sentimental.phil.fau.de/dfg-graduiertenkolleg-das-sentimentale/ueber-das-kolleg/.

Finkel, Madelon L. 2015. "Introduction." In *The Human and Environmental Impact of Fracking: How Fracturing Shale for Gas Affects Us and Our World*, edited by Madelon L. Finkel, xiii–xxxiv. Santa Barbara, CA: Praeger.

Fiskio, Janet. 2012. "Unsettling Ecocriticism: Rethinking Agrarianism, Place, and Citizenship." *American Literature* 84 (2): 301–25.

Fitzgerald, Michael J. 2014. *Fracking War*. Minneapolis, MN: Mill City Press.

Fox, Josh. 2010. *Gasland*. International WOW Company. 107 min.

French, Philip. 2013. "Promised Land–review." *The Guardian*, April 21, 2013. Accessed July 26, 2022. https://www.theguardian.com/film/2013/apr/21/promised-land-review-matt-damon.

Ghosh, Amitav. 1992. "Petrofiction: The Oil Encounter and the Novel." *The New Republic*, March 2, 1992, 29–34.

Haigh, Jennifer. 2016. *Heat & Light*. New York, NY: HarperCollins.

Hamilton, Jon. 2012. "Town's Effort To Link Fracking And Illness Falls Short." *NPR*, May 16, 2012. Accessed July 29, 2022. https://www.npr.org/2012/05/16/152204584/towns-effort-to-link-fracking-and-illness-falls-short.

Harrison, Summer. 2018. "Mountaintop Removal Mining Fiction: Energy Humanities and Environmental Injustice." *Appalachian Journal* 45 (3/4): 732–62.

Herrin, Lamar. 2013. *Fractures*. New York, NY: Thomas Dunne Books/ St. Martin's Press.

Hofstadter, Richard. 1955. *The Age of Reform: From Bryan to F.D.R.* New York, NY: Vintage.

Jefferson, Thomas. (1785) 1998. *Notes on the State of Virginia*. New York, NY: Penguin Publishing Group.

Jerolmack, Colin. 2021. *Up to Heaven and Down to Hell: Fracking, Freedom, and Community in an American Town*. Princeton, NJ: Princeton University Press.

Kistler, Sebastian. 2018. "'Don't Frack our Mother' oder die Zerstörung unserer Lebensgrundladen—'"Promised Land'." In *Angewandte Ethik und Film*, edited by Thomas Bohrmann, Mathias Reichelt, and Werner Veith, 309–37. Wiesbaden: Springer VS.

Kley, Antje, and Heike Paul. 2015. "Rural America: An Introduction." In *Rural America*, edited by Antje Kley and Heike Paul, 1–11. Heidelberg: Winter.

Long, Rebecca-Eli. "An Appalachian Crip/Queer Engagement." In *Y'all Means All: Emerging Voices Queering Appalachia*, edited by Z. Zane McNeill, 82–95. Oakland, CA: PM Press.

McAleer, Phelim, and Ann McElhinney. 2013. *FrackNation*. Ann and Phelim Media. 77 min.

Moore, Ellen E. 2018. *Landscape and the Environment in Hollywood Film*. Berlin: Palgrave Macmillan.

Nunez, Christina. N.d. "Can Natural Gas Be a Bridge to Clean Energy?" *National Geographic*. Accessed October 4, 2022. https://www.nationalgeographic.com/environment/article/can-natural-gas-be-a-bridge-to-clean-energy.

Plumer, Brad. 2013. "Is Fracking a 'Bridge' to a Clean-Energy Future? Ernest Moniz Thinks So." *The Washington Post*, March 4, 2013. Accessed October 04, 2022. https://www.washingtonpost.com/news/wonk/wp/2013/03/04/is-fracking-a-bridge-to-a-clean-energy-future-ernest-moniz-thinks-so/.

Rugh, Peter. 2013. "Forest Service Seeks to Silence Smokey the Bear over Fracking." *wagingnonviolence.org*, May 7, 2013. Accessed July 28, 2022. https://wagingnonviolence.org/2013/05/forest-service-seeks-to-silence-smokey-the-bear-over-fracking/.

Sayles, John. 2020. *Yellow Earth*. Chicago, IL: Haymarket Books.

Singer, Ross, Stephanie Houston Grey, and Jeff Motter. 2020. *Rooted Resistance: Agrarian Myth in Modern America*. Fayetteville, AR: University of Arkansas Press.

Slotkin, Richard. 1973. *Regeneration through Violence: The Mythology of the American Frontier, 1600–1860*. Middletown, CT: Wesleyan University Press.

Sutter, Paul S. 2019. "Foreword: Old Growth and a New History of Environmental Activism." In *Defending Giants: The Redwood Wars and the Transformation of American Environmental Politics*, by Darren Frederick Speece, vii–xiii. Seattle, WA: University of Washington Press.

Tompkins, Jane. 1986. *Sensational Designs: The Cultural Work of American Fiction, 1790–1860*. New York, NY: Oxford University Press.

Triple Divide. 2013. Joshua B. Pribanic and Melissa A. Troutman, directors. Public Herald Studies Production.

Truthland: Dispatches from the Real Gasland. 2012. TruthlandMovie. https://www.youtube.com/watch?v=iTJaaeiuzSU.

Vance, J.D. 2016. *Hillbilly Elegy: A Memoir of a Family and Culture in Crisis*. New York, NY: HarperCollins.

Van Sant, Gus, dir. 2012. *Promised Land*. Universal City, CA: Focus Features.

Webb, Sheila. 2006. "A Pictorial Myth in the Pages of 'Life': Small-Town America as the Ideal Place." *Studies in Popular Culture* 28 (3): 35–58.

Woodhouse, Keith Makoto. 2020. *The Ecocentrists: A History of Radical Environmentalism*. New York, NY: Columbia University Press.

A Conversation with Cara Daggett about Affect, Sentimentality, and Extractivism

Axelle Germanaz, Daniela Gutiérrez Fuentes, and Cara Daggett

Cara Daggett is assistant professor of political science in the Department of Political Science at Virginia Tech. Her research examines energy politics and environmental justice in an era of planetary disruption. Her latest work, *The Birth of Energy: Fossil Fuels, Thermodynamics, and the Politics of Work* (2019), traces the changing semantics and uses of energy back to the 19th century science of thermodynamics to confront the underlying industrialist and capitalist logics that informs today's uses of energy.

This interview took place on March 22, 2022, and has been edited for clarity and concision.

Daniela Gutiérrez (DG hereafter): The title of this volume is "Affective Economies of Extraction and Sentimentality." What do you think could be the role of affect and emotions in the complex relation between humans and what we call "natural resources"?

Cara Daggett (CD hereafter): I want to start by thanking you for making a book that is devoted to affect. Although there is a growing literature surrounding affect and the environment, it often remains marginalized in energy studies and 'mainstream' environmental studies. I hope that will change. The importance of affect is right in the word: It points to our capacity to *be affected* as bodies, open to the world and in relation with it. Unlike terms such as 'emotions' and 'feelings,' affect also signals that there is a certain lack of control in how humans respond to experiences and things. The world enters our bodies, and our innermost sense of self; the world also enters and helps to compose our thinking and our reasoning. This directly challenges the ideal of the rational man, whose body, while being impacted by outside forces, is governed by a rational mind that can bracket those affective states and compartmentalize them.

Take, for instance, the way certain non-human entities have been categorized as natural resources and thus framed as a collection of objects to be extracted, exploited, and consumed. But 'resources' are not simply objects outside of us. They affect us, cause in us certain feelings—like distress or even love, disgust, or awe—depending upon the context through which we know them, and how they are built into our memories and cultures. Rational man can supposedly keep his mind apart from the non-human world and the emotions it provokes in him, which makes him better at ordering and controlling it for his benefit. According to this logic, rational man has the superior capacity to improve upon the world, which licenses him to govern ecosystems like forests or farms to his benefit, through cold calculation.

For me, the importance of affect lays in its challenge to these binaries (reason versus emotion, mind versus body) and the way these binaries assume that a Western perspective on the world is a universal one, because it is the most 'rational.' Affect, as a concept, allows us to see that there is no thinking or reasoning without a body, and that bodies will inevitably have different memories and world experiences. What is interesting is that leading neuroscientists have confirmed what feminists have long known, which is that affect, emotion, and cognitive reasoning are deeply embedded processes that are inseparable—René Descartes was wrong: There is no reasoning without emotion and affect.

And yet so much of mainstream social science—which informs much of environmental and climate policymaking—continues to assume a Cartesian separation of reason and emotion, and a corresponding distrust of emotions and embodiment. This has serious consequences for environmental politics. For example, by ignoring the importance of affect and embodiment, many policymakers carry on with the expectation that people will support a politics of climate mitigation once they truly understand climate science, or perhaps after they experience more climate disasters, as a rational response to the facts. Instead, it is evident that people interpret the meaning of science and climate disasters in highly variable ways, through many affective registers. Climate disasters might actually provoke people to double down on supporting fossil fuels and violent extraction, as in the U.S. right-wing movement.

Affect led me to appreciate the way identities and certain affects (like anxiety) are part of the defense of fossil fuels. In energy politics, the latter are usually thought of as simple resources that people and states order, control, and use. Focusing on affect helps us understand that the ways in which people relate to fossil fuels are tied up with historical and geographical contexts of their extraction and use. Fossil fuels are both material things that power machines and fuels that metaphorically power certain identities and cultures.

DG: Would you say then that you see people's attachment to fossil fuels through a relationship or some sort of affective bond?

CD: Yes, for example if you think about smells, they have such a powerful connection to our emotions and our memories. A caregiver probably cooked a special dish for you as a child, and now that combination of spices sizzling in a pan can bring you a feeling of comfort, of nostalgia. The smell of gas, on the other hand, is more complex. Someone who has no cultural experience of gas would be affected very differently by it than someone who has spent a lifetime living around cars. I was at the Petrocultures conference in Stavanger, Norway, where Ernst Logar, an artist, had brought different kinds of crude oil for participants to experiment with. He let me smell them, and their odors were strikingly different—I hadn't expected how much crude oil would have a *terroir*. One, however, was immediately familiar. As soon as it entered my nose, I was at an American gas station, on a road trip, sweating in the humid heat, but also free in the way that open road advertising have encouraged me to feel (I often took road trips in the summer as a child). Maybe someone else worked on an oil rig, lived next to a petrochemical facility, or stores homemade liquor in old gas cans, tasting crude while drinking with friends. My point is that the ways in which people are affected by fossil fuels, and fossil-fueled machines and industry, really depend on personal and collective memories as well as cultural experiences.

Axelle Germanaz (AG hereafter): I would like to come back to what you mentioned earlier about this notion of the "rational man" and the dichotomies of mind vs. body, rational thoughts vs. uncontrolled emotions that affect theory scholars have long been working against. There is a scientific consensus around the fact that fossil fuels are becoming nonviable because they are both a major motor of climate change and a finite source of energy that will ultimately run out. In the face of a global climate and energy emergency, the rational thing to do then would be to move away from the extraction and use of fossil fuels to secure a more ecologically viable future for humanity and the planet. Some environmental and energy studies scholars have talked about an "addiction" (cf. Matt Huber) and a "devotion" (cf. Stephanie LeMenager) to describe the detrimental relationship to an ongoing extractivism. What do you make of these metaphors? Are they helpful in overcoming the dependence on fossil fuels and in moving states and individuals to rely on more sustainable options?

CD: I am interested in why the solutions to the problems caused by fossil fuels are deemed unrealistic by many who are in power. I've heard firsthand, many times, from engineers or economists that it is unrealistic to demand broader transformations for climate justice. Elite economic interests are certainly behind this attitude, in that some people will lose trillions of dollars and pour a lot of money into lobbying politicians and propaganda to influence public feelings. However, a narrow economic reading fails to address why these narratives around denial, and the celebration of fossil fuels, are so easily circulated and so widely embraced, well beyond the elites who personally benefit. There is something more going on and this is what the scholars you mention are trying to decipher with the metaphors of "addiction" and "devotion."

Both are helpful metaphors, but I prefer the term "devotion," only because of the way "addiction" is misunderstood and poorly treated in Western culture. The medicalization of the concept too easily lends itself to rationalist arguments—that there is something irrational or beyond our control in our petro-attachments. Furthermore, the blame or accountability for addiction remains a little diffuse as a metaphor, as Western culture tends to individualize the problem of addiction. It can be thought about structurally, like in the case of the opioid crisis currently unfolding in the area around where I am, Appalachia. Here, pharmaceutical companies knowingly pushed addiction on communities they saw would be more vulnerable to it, as former coalfield regions facing the consequences of industry exploitation. Similarly, with fossil fuels, it is critical to keep the focus on the structural and collective dimensions of accountability.

Devotion, on the contrary, is difficult to think about purely on an individual basis because of its religious connotations—devotion is often going to be an experience that you share with a community. The religious connotations of devotion are also apt in understanding fossil fuel cultures. In *The Birth of Energy*, I explore the cosmological dimensions of energy. The moral aspects of energy are more obvious in premodern notions of energy as life force, or Aristotle's *energeia*. The modern notion of energy appears to be much more objective and mathematical, as it emerges as a scientific term in the 19th century science of thermodynamics. However, even in its scientific application, energy continued to have theological dimensions. For example, some of the first scientists of energy were Scottish Presbyterians, and they were not alone in interpreting the science of energy as a new knowledge that justified the imperial project of putting the world to work. This was based, for them, on the sense that only God stood apart from the laws of thermodynamics. Only God could create and destroy energy. Only God could resist entropic increase, or the tendency for energy to diffuse into forms that cannot do work (again we see this separation between the ideal and the fallen world). Therefore, the best activities were those that put energy to work everywhere it could be found. Work, to these men, was already defined through a capitalist lens, as activity that produced commodities, with all other activities subordinated to that aim.

The science of energy seemed to show that the cosmos reflected the goodness of capitalist production. But there is a slippage here between the laws of capital and the workings of nature. The science of energy does not tell people how to value energy, nor what is useful or wasteful energy. That is why the underlying common sense about how energy is valued can be understood in religious terms, despite its veneer of secular neutrality. Productivism is yoked to the sacred, and to the cosmos, by this one logic of energy. There are other ways to value energy, and other notions of the sacred.

DG: It is important to stress this complex relationship that you mentioned, between the individual and the collective, adding to it matters of temporality. Even if, rationally, people are aware of what is better for a collective ecological future, it is extremely difficult to put an end to the public's devotion to extractivism and to the lifestyles it has granted (some of) us. There is a clear conflict between the daily-life pleasures and comforts afforded by extractivism—with, for example, a family road trip, commuting by car every day, or holidays overseas—and the future-oriented decisions that could influence the planet and the generations to come. Of course, this has also important affective ramifications: We tend to find happiness and pleasure in the things afforded by extractivism in the now while dreading its destructive consequences for the future of the planet and humanity.

CD: Definitely. You could also flip this around and think about how, even if you, as an individual living in a high-energy culture, decide to make different choices and change your way of life because your consumerism is causing too much suffering and making you miserable, there won't be any structural support for that. You will have to do this alone and against the tides of social norms—from its infrastructures and expectations to your peers, their own lifestyles, and prospects. While it feels like it might be an individual choice—that you keep on living a consumerist way of life—it is, in fact, the collective devotion of a culture, and all the material infrastructures built around it, that makes it so hard to stop.

AG: Connected to this, we are also seeing a large-scale instrumentalization of this individualized guilt and this desire for change by various kinds of corporations. For example, airline companies, most infamously, now sell to their customers carbon offsets, which promise to 'cancel out' the CO_2 emissions their flights will produce and therefore alleviate their consciousness. Of course, this kind of intervention prevents any kind of incentive towards actually reducing emissions, decarbonizing economies, and changing lifestyles. They instead keep the devotion to emission-intensive resources and polluting practices tightly in place and only a click away for those who can afford it.

CD: Yes, and interestingly enough oil companies were part and parcel of the effort to come up with the idea of a carbon footprint. They invested tremendous efforts to shift the accountability onto individuals, who are cast as these rational market actors making conscious consumer choices. The rational consumer is now responsible for counting and monitoring their own carbon footprints. This is increasingly how neoliberals invite people to practice citizenship in the United States—through consumer choices.

DG: What affective dimensions have you encountered in your work on energy systems?

CD: As a concept, affect can help us think about our bodies, how we feel when we move through environments and relate to other people and the more-than-human world. And by doing so, it can make us think beyond the limits of our human bodies and recognize that not only can other things feel pleasure, disgust, or desire as a result of our infrastructure, but that our own desires are influenced by, and expressed through, the more-than-human world. What we want, in other words, is not determined by a pre-formed personality.

Automobility is a powerful example of this because our desires, jobs, and homes have been built around cars. My experience of riding a bike to work can feel scary because there are sections without a bike lane, on busy roads, and because some U.S. drivers are aggressive toward cyclists. When we have petitioned the town to fix this, the main obstacles cited are automobiles (not wanting to reduce car space) and private property (homeowners opposed to granting easements to expand the road). Both commitments—cars and suburban yards—are relatively recent social constructions built on the basis of cheap fossil fuels. They are not inherent desires of humankind. As virulent as they are, they could change.

Against this, the co-housing community where I live was designed with small lots and homes (relative to suburban America), and with all the cars are parked around the perimeter, so that the homes are close together and the interior paths are completely pedestrian. This was counter to a traditional suburban development, which would have used the 33 acres to build 33, one-acre, single-family homes. The design of our co-housing community entails minor, but unfamiliar burdens for rural Americans, in terms of living in smaller spaces and having to use carts to move your groceries to your house, like many urban dwellers do. The benefits are enormous, though. People spend more time outside and get to know their neighbors better, and children enjoy freedom of movement across the entire neighborhood and surrounding woods, much of which could remain intact because the homes were built in a smaller area.

This might seem banal, but the dangers surrounding cars and roads in the United States actually do shape people's conception and experience of public space as threatening, stressful, and frustrating. The devotion to online shopping can also be understood in this light: The alternative to shopping online in the U.S. is to navigate crowded parking lots and wide expanses of concrete. Thinking about the effects of automobility has exciting political potential: It shows that another way of life, one that is more sustainable, is not only possible, but could also be pleasurable in its own way.

With sustainability, it often feels like people are asked to give up things, like their cars, their travels, their comfort, etc. But seen from another perspective, justice and sustainability could be achieved through infrastructure that contributes greatly to public and community health and well-being, so that these changes could *feel good*, maybe even better, to many people. Infrastructure can be an important affective strategy to make sustainability just and desirable.

AG: The main criticism that we hear from individuals who are reluctant to make the shift to or even imagine a decarbonized society is that this ecological way of life is simply utopian; it might be ideal and desirable, but it is impossible to achieve now. How can we counter this kind of pessimistic, nihilistic view of a post-fossil fuels future?

CD: I think the real utopianism is among ecomodernists—those who believe that technological innovation alone will solve the problem of global warming. Against all evidence to the contrary, and against common sense, in the corridors of power there is still a magical belief that human production and unlimited economic growth can become delinked from environmental harm. I must admit that it makes me angry when those who hold this belief turn around and dismiss calls for social justice as utopian.

But this notion of utopianism is important because it is a widely held feeling, the famous saying that it is easier to imagine the end of the world than it is to imagine the end of capitalism. To say that sustainability can have its own politics of pleasure does not erase the fact that some things will need to be given up by the wealthiest and most privileged, and more broadly in energy-intensive cultures. But many of those things that will have to be sacrificed might, in the end, not even make people feel good, or might only feel necessary in a culture of long and stressful work hours with unfair compensation. The high suicide, addiction, and mental illness rates in the U.S. are revealing in terms of the impacts of the American consumerist dream.

Working people have received a bad bargain with capital in energy-intensive cultures like the U.S., in terms of poor community well-being alongside access to cheap mass consumerism. It's difficult to give up mass consumerism, though, when all the infrastructure for community well-being has been underfunded and destroyed after decades of neoliberal austerity measures. That is why sustainability must be thought of in relation to building these broader structural supports, like access to high-quality food and housing. Environmental movements need to take seriously that cheap consumerism does provide what Lauren Berlant call a "cruel optimism" (2011), a chance to feel good, and to get through the day, even if the thing you desire is also hurting you. Climate mitigation does entail challenging mass consumerism, but in order to do so, the best path is one that pursues social justice and community infrastructure.

AG: In your 2018 essay, "Petro-masculinity: Fossil Fuels and Authoritarian Desire," you describe how feelings of loss and (gender and climate) anxiety can dangerously fuel desires for authoritarian politics. We were wondering if you had ever thought about those feelings in connection to the sentimental. Is sentimentality at play in the narratives of victimization, pain, and resentment promulgated by climate deniers? Or perhaps in the various narratives that make people *feel right* about fossil fuel extraction and consumption?

CD: Because of your project, I have been thinking more about this relationship, between fossil fuels and sentimentality. It could be helpful to compare petro-masculinity to women's "intimate publics" that Berlant study in *Female Complaint* (2008), their work on sentimental women's genres in the U.S. Women's sentimental literature convenes an intimate public, which offers a fantasy of normality and belonging, a connection to others who have suffered as a result of being women. This genre provides a relief from the cold, hard world of politics and oppression, instead finding pleasure in sharing the generic experiences of love and survival. However, Berlant write that this feeling of solidarity can be politically problematic, as bourgeois White women have often expressed their own suffering through consuming stories about Black and working class women's experiences (6). Indeed, the key for Berlant is that although intimate publics *feel* like ethical spaces of emotional connection, the empathy aroused often favors consensus and unity, rather than antagonistic political demands for change. Sentimentality helps to assuage feelings of guilt and complicity. It provides affective tools for sustaining structural injustice.

The sentimentality of petro-masculinity operates through different affects, but it might still be helpful to consider it as an intimate public, in Berlant's terms. Petro-masculinity also appears as a desire for recognition through shared feelings of normative sexuality; it offers relief from a hard reality by celebrating the pleasures of ordinary life; and it also circulates through a sense of suffering and victimhood.

However, where women's intimate publics are formed around a subordinated identity, "petro-masculinity" congeals around a sense of lost entitlement. I write about petro-masculinity as a hypermasculinity, a concept that I adapted from the work of Lily Ling and Anna Agathangelou—two feminist scholars of international relations. They described U.S. politics post-9/11 as 'hypermasculine,' a term to describe what happens when dominant masculine identities feel threatened and compensate by exaggerating those traditional masculine traits. Here, challenges to patriarchal rule are interpreted as victimization, despite the fact that many of these men are powerful elites.

The sense of victimhood is processed in different ways, according to normative gender scripts. Women's intimate publics follow a love plot, but petro-masculinity is lived through a war plot. Berlant tell us that the love plot manages the gap between the fantasy of romantic love and its disappointing reality in late modern capitalism. Even if love is thwarted, the feeling of love attaches one to a generic sense of community, and to a hopeful possibility for happiness, one day. The love plot features scenes for agency and belonging in a world in which one mostly feels powerless and alone. The war plot operates through a similar deflection of desire. It navigates the gap between the ideal of White patriarchal rule and the reality of frustrated traditional masculinity, in light of myriad challenges to it. It promises that proximity to violence will deliver a generic experience of power that *feels* like domination, even if the political reality is unchanged, and the world remains beyond one's control. Petro-masculinity also sustains the *status quo*, in this way. It is expressed through the shared glee of extraction, explosion, or combustion.

I'm interested to hear your thoughts on sentimentality and fossil fuels.

AG: I think that we would argue that the narratives of loss and victimization that you analyze in "Petro-Masculinity" fit really well with what Berlant call "the unfinished business of sentimentality" —"that 'tomorrow is another day' in which fantasies of the good life can be lived" (*The Female Complaint* 2). As you mentioned, sentimentality has long been viewed as a progressive mode to inspire democratic change, but it is helpful to highlight its stabilizing, and maybe regressive, effects, too. The discourse surrounding the maintaining of 'business as usual'—i.e., the continued reliance on fossil fuels—is very often tinged with sentimentality. For instance, we have recently seen a political discourse that has turned fossil fuel industries' workers into national heroes, sacrificed subjects who suffered the injustices of globalization and sustainability policies, who should be rescued or revalidated through a re-turn to a hardcore extractive economy (see Donald Trump's speech analyzed by Heike Paul in this volume). For Berlant, (national) sentimentality in this sense is "too often a defensive response by people who identify with privilege yet fear they will be exposed as immoral by their tacit sanction of a particular structural violence that benefits them" ("The Subject of True Feeling" 62). With the rise of a global climate justice movement that has staunchly challenged extractivism and normalized the idea that a post-fossil fuel world was not only desirable but also feasible, fossil fuel industries and lobbies are doubling down on counter-narratives focused on the meanings of 'the good life.' This is often done by associating fossil fuel energy systems with stories of personal happiness and comfort, national security and 'strength,' and nostalgic accounts of the hey-days of capitalism. Sentimentality in this context is deployed to perpetuate and strengthen extractivism.

CD: Yes, and I think this is where the difference lies between the use of sentimentality among liberal centrists and the far right. Liberal guilt is aroused by the fear that one will be exposed as immoral by their complicity, or their tacit sanction of the status quo. It is interesting to put this in relation to how Berlant understood White women's empathy, as a means for handling the exposure of one's complicity, for processing guilt and yet remaining politically quiet.

On the right, this fear of being exposed as immoral is also there, but it is handled with refusal rather than passive empathy. We can think, for example, of the many debates happening in the U.S. about public education. People on the right are going to school boards to protest the teaching of slavery and White supremacy because they argue that they "should not be made to feel guilty or ashamed." In such a phrase, there is an interesting acknowledgment of the complex feelings that can arise with social change. But instead of finding a way to process feelings of guilt and shame, and route them toward political accountability, there is simply a blunt refusal.

Sentimentality in liberal culture welcomes some of these feelings of suffering and melancholia but makes a point of always being on the good side of it, through a sense of universal humanity. One can feel bad for the plight of the world, and maneuver to ameliorate some harms, but the property and mate-rial relations of capitalism remain fundamentally intact. The right refuses this space of liberal guilt and recognizes it as hypocritical. However, the right also wants to defend a certain distribution of privilege and material power, but with a dramatically different affective style. For some people on the right, it feels good to celebrate consumption and extraction through, for example, rolling coal with your truck or blowing up mountains in mountaintop removal. It feels good to exit that space of moral ambivalence and liberal hypocrisy.

DG: In *Green European Journal* (March 2020), you argued that the far right is deploying "a melodrama of climate change denial." Why do think the term "melodrama" is helpful here?

CD: I draw my understanding of melodrama from Elisabeth Anker's work. The key element of melodrama is its moral clarity: There are heroes and vil-lains, progress or decadence. Melodrama invites the audience to identify with the good side and to feel self-righteous. It is highly effective as a tool of polit-ical mobilization, and has been used by movements on the Left, too. There is melodrama at work, for example, when environmental movements talk about evil fossil fuels companies and the heroes that fight them.

According to Anker, melodrama has been a central genre for narrating American exceptionalism, where the American public is presented as a force of goodness. Bad events are processed as marginal mistakes, often the fault of small groups of villains, and they do not detract from the overall righteousness of the American project. The problem is that when you try to launch a critique of America within the melodramatic mode, the possibilities are reduced to evil or innocence. The quote from Berlant that Axelle mentioned earlier about the fear of being exposed is powerful, because it plays on this notion: If you have been part of something bad, then you are evil.

The genre of melodrama is not inherently fascist, though. As I mentioned, melodrama has been influential in resistance movements; it has its uses as a political tactic. However, melodrama is problematic in that it tends to leap over the complexity, ambivalence, and murkiness of real events and people. When the public only understands a problem in stark moral terms, it becomes easy to discredit social movements if they fail to perform as perfect heroes, or if their demands are not saintly enough. Likewise, it becomes difficult to fight injus-tice when those in power do not appear entirely evil, or when you yourself are complicit in it. Most people do not like to think of themselves as villains. Mod-ern life is characterized by spaces in which people are both victims and perpe-trators, where people can be exploited while simultaneously enjoying benefits that accrue from violence done to other humans, creatures, and ecosystems. Melodrama does not provide a way to navigate such tricky subject positions.

AG: What you say about climate denial, and really climate defiance, relates nicely to Elisabeth Anker's concept of "ugly freedom," which she uses to discuss the ways 'freedom' has been invoked in oppressive and violent projects in the U.S. (and in its spaces of influence). Climate deniers protest environmental and sustainable policies as punitive and burdensome because they desire the freedom to extract, to consume, to pollute, regardless of the consequences. Your work on "petro-masculinity" and "the melodrama of climate change" has mainly focused on conservative and far-right groups. Do you see sentimental narratives—of suffering, loss, nostalgia—relating to the environment and energy at play in other communities or contexts?

CD: The melodramatic genre in the U.S. guides most mainstream approaches to climate change. America is depicted as the hero, and the story needs a villain. The villain might be China, with its leadership in green technology viewed as a threat. The villain can be feminists, communists, climate migrants. The script differs but the genre remains the same. There is little room for self-reflection or humility in melodrama. These stories avoid the more complicated challenge posed by the problem of fossil-fueled industrialization: understanding the causes of climate change inevitably shakes the heroic vision of the U.S., Europe, or industrial capitalism, as beacons of progress in the world.

That is why denial is not limited to the far right. There is also a kind of denial among ecomodernists, who dominate climate policymaking in the global North. Ecomodernism also would like to sideline challenges to global capitalism and to limit historical accountability for its violent unfolding. If global aid is discussed, it is through the lens of development, or as recompense for unfortunate side effects, rather than as reparations, which are demanded by many in the global South.

In the U.S. and elsewhere, new genres are needed for handling the feelings aroused by complicity and the troubled history of industrial imperialism. Sentimental genres can assuage those feelings of complicity, by appealing to a generic human solidarity, unified around feelings of love or a desire for consumer comforts. This is evident, for instance, in some of the Anthropocene narratives, which turn to a universal human agent (*anthropos*), with the emphasis that "we" are all in this together, in a manner that sidesteps accountability for extreme inequality. It reminds me a little of how White women in the U.S. process their own experiences of subordination through consuming salacious

tales of woe that center on Black and working class women. A similar sentimental trap lurks when stories of climate disaster in the global South are used
to spread a message of universal human suffering, to the extent that they may
create a space for feeling ethical, rather than for encouraging antagonistic demands for justice.

DG: With regard to a successful energy transition, do you think that stories
and narratives that speak to people on an emotional level rather than a rational
one can achieve change? Could we and should we think of a sentimentality that
is strategic, perhaps even pedagogic?

CD: Sentimental genres in late capitalism have used generic consumer
pleasures to absorb a great deal of frustration and anxiety that comes from
structural injustice. Fascist movements are also adept at using sentimentality,
routing emotions of fear and anxiety toward war plots, rather than justice. You
ask whether sentimental genres could be used strategically, in an anti-fascist
manner, to bring about justice rather than to forestall it. I think so, but only
in the sense that sentimentality is unavoidable in modern life. Ignoring it, as
liberal technocrats seek to do, merely cedes more of the emotional landscape
to fascist movements in times of crisis.

Sentimental genres reveal the importance of the everyday, and the desire
for simple connection and recognition, which are so often overlooked in high-
level policy talk. I would be less interested in trying to deploy a new sentimental genre, than in appreciating what it teaches me about the public appetite
for finding small pleasures and feelings of community in getting through each
day. This brings me to the feminist emphasis on the political importance of everyday life, care activities, and relations of dependency. Ordinary life activities
feel too small to consider when faced with global warming, yet they hold the key
to understanding the feeling of 'stuckness' when it comes to achieving climate
justice.

That is why I have been an advocate for talking more about pleasure in relation to sustainability and energy transition. First, that means recognizing
that many people in the world need more energy, more food, and more shelter;
those demands need to be met sustainably, and not through narratives of re-
duction or voluntary simplicity. Second, taking pleasure seriously also means
recognizing the 'cruel optimism' of mass consumerism, which does deliver real
pleasures and fantasies when living in a petrocultural system, where most social alternatives are lacking. This means energy transitions might be less about
fuel switches, and more about building infrastructures of all kinds (social, reproductive, technological, financial) that make less energy-intensive ways of

life possible, meaningful, and pleasurable. Not as heroic consumer choices but as shared, generic experiences.

I acknowledge that there's a difficult circularity here in terms of desire and action; the public needs to demand new infrastructure, but infrastructure needs to be in place sometimes before new desires and genres can arise. The tricky reality is that they will take shape through each other. Instead of a love plot or a war plot, perhaps this is an infrastructure plot.

And, of course, there is a pedagogical moment in recognizing how one's feelings are attached to certain stories, even stories we no longer believe. This means having a kind of affective intelligence about our bodies and selves, one that learns how to develop our capacity for new sensibilities.

DG: When preparing this interview and thinking about societies' devotion to fossil fuels, we kept on returning to the same question: How is it that with all the existing scientific evidence and knowledge about the anthropogenic nature of climate change and the hazardous consequences of extractivism, most people do not seem to be ready to make the needed changes to ensure a sustainable and ecological future for all? This is where perhaps affect and emotions can make a difference. There are pockets of territorial resistances around the world, where communities are organizing at the local level and creating, defending, and imagining other ways of relating to the non-/more-than-human world, to each other and our socioeconomic systems. How, in your view, is a planetary transformation possible?

CD: There are two important questions here. The first: Is planetary transformation possible? Yes, I think it is. These alternative practices that you mentioned give me hope, too. From the perspective of liberal modernity, there is this widespread notion that humanity has to come up with new ideas and new ways of being to 'fix' the climate crisis. It is reassuring to think that there are already many ideas, practices, and knowledges in the world that are worth experimenting with. There are vibrant groups of scholars and activists thinking critically about infrastructure. Ultimately, the problem is not necessarily a lack of ideas, or even of a history and experience with other ways of living. J.K. Gibson-Graham, who are feminist economic geographers writing about capitalism, have argued that non-capitalist practices are happening all around us all the time—practices that we already feel and value. The problem is that these ideas are ruled out in advance as utopian or unrealistic because they do not accord with capitalist maxims of productivism, profit-seeking, and the sacredness of private property. Moreover, there have been, and continue to be, active efforts to destroy and block anti-capitalist experiments, and to erase non-capitalist ways of life. So yes, the change required is dramatic and yet, not impossible.

The second part of your question is more difficult. If more just and sustainable ways of life are possible, how can they be brought about, and brought about on a planetary scale, especially considering the forces ranged against such an outcome? Scale is key because capitalism operates globally. Making elite, wealthy corridors green by accelerating extraction in marginalized regions, for example, does not address the root of the problem. Theories of change are not always explicitly acknowledged in the literatures on transition. Berlant, too, becomes a little vague on this point, recognizing the 'potential' or unfinished business of sentimental genres but not speculating much further on what this would look like. Meanwhile, mainstream policymaking has a largely technocratic theory of change: Experts and engineers will figure out smart solutions, and policymakers will enact them. The public's role is to behave rationally, following price signals and our own self-interest, whatever that is.

Achieving more transformational changes in material distribution threatens the concentrated sites of power, wealth, and violence. That is why debates over the role of the state loom large on the Left. States have been instruments of terror, settler colonialism, misogyny, and environmental racism. States also have considerable, existing institutional power in terms of implementing widespread change. A recent book called *Degrowth & Strategy* (Barlow et al.) wades into this debate, and others, recognizing that there is a need for more writing about "how to bring about socio-ecological transformation" (the book's subtitle). The book is organized around a critical engagement with Erik Olin Wright's influential framework of three "modes of transformation." The three modes are: *interstitial* (building new forms on the margins of capitalism), *ruptural* (direct confrontation or breaks with capital), and *symbiotic* (changing existing institutions from within) (57). These modes create a "strategic canvas" (67) with multiple avenues for seeking change that are not mutually exclusive, and that are often highly effective when combined.

What is interesting to me about this 'strategic canvas' is that it moves us away from the notion of singular, heroic breakthroughs, and insists upon the plurality of resistance and transformation. In keeping with our earlier conversation about melodrama, this is an anti-melodramatic understanding of change. The technocratic theory of change looks for heroic inventors and technologies that will swoop in and save the day. Frustration mounts when the Left does not have a comparably heroic, nor simple, savior idea. Part of encouraging new genres of climate change, though, is embracing new plots—plots that have compelling drama, but also more tolerance for complexity, failure, and surprise. Plots that seek change but also take seriously the sentimental need for ordinariness, for the pleasures to be found in surviving everyday life.

A strategic canvas is a nice metaphor that allows people to see how their efforts could fit into a larger set of movements. This could be understood as 'let a thousand flowers bloom,' but there is also room for alliances, strategy, and organization across modes and sites. Now we need more climate stories that take place in such a landscape.

AG & DG: Cara Daggett, thank you for having taken the time to answer our questions.

References

Agathangelou, Anna, and L.H.M. Ling. 2004. "Power, Borders, Security, Wealth: Lessons of Violence and Desire from September 11." *International Studies Quarterly* 48 (3): 517–38.

Anker, Elisabeth. 2014. *Orgies of Feeling: Melodrama and the Politics of Freedom.* Durham, NC: Duke University Press.

Barlow, Nathan, et al. (eds). 2022. *Degrowth & Strategy: How to Bring about Social-Ecological Transformation.* Mayfly Books.

Berlant, Lauren. 2000. "The Subject of True Feeling: Pain, Privacy, and Politics." In *Cultural Studies and Political Theory* edited by Jodi Dean, Ithaca, NY: Cornell University Press, 42–62.

Berlant, Lauren. 2008. *The Female Complaint: The Unfinished Business of Sentimentality in American Culture.* Durham, NC: Duke University Press.

Berlant, Lauren. 2011. *Cruel Optimism.* Durham, NC: Duke University Press.

Daggett, Cara. 2018. "Petro-Masculinity: Fossil Fuels and Authoritarian Desire." *Millennium* 47 (1): 25–44.

Daggett, Cara. 2019. *The Birth of Energy: Fossil Fuels, Thermodynamics and the Politics of Work.* Durham, NC: Duke University Press.

Gibson-Graham, J.K. 2006. *A Postcapitalist Politics.* Minneapolis, MN: University of Minnesota Press.

Oil Ancestors: Relating to Petroleum as Kin

Fereshteh Toosi

The artwork described below was produced on the ancestral lands of the Miccosukee and Seminole people. This place, also known as South Florida, is home to many Indigenous people, as well as Black, Brown, and Caribbean people whose ancestors lived and worked on this land against their will, while enslaved, or under the threat of violence. The work also relies on the extractive and colonial infrastructure of digital computation, which uses electronics and servers, all of which are made possible by occupying places where other beings live, or once lived.

My creative research focuses on designing live experiences for small groups, immersive performances that consist of encounter, exchange, and sensory inquiry. Much of my artwork follows the historical precedents of instructional poetry, conceptual performance, and new music composition that rose to prominence with Fluxus and other related movements in the 1960s and 1970s. Fluxus artists often incorporated domestic objects and quotidian actions into their artwork and sought to challenge the traditional hierarchy of the art world by blurring the lines between artist and audience. They created works that were participatory, often involving the audience with interactive elements.

Writing about Suriname-born Dutch artist Stanley Brouwn's work for the *Prospect 1969* exhibition, performance scholar RoseLee Goldberg describes how this type of conceptual practice evolved from earlier art forms, such as landscape painting:

> [...] those who followed the instructions would supposedly experience the city or countryside with an enhanced consciousness. It was after all with just such a heightened awareness that artists had painted canvases of their surroundings; rather than passively viewing a finished artwork, the ob-

server was now persuaded to see the environment as though through the eyes of the artist.

My creative research is dedicated to cultivating artistic connections to place through a critical social practice, which connects this conceptual and performance lineage to other precedents set by representational landscape art and landscape architecture. This work is informed by and contributes to contemporary multidisciplinary fields such as landscape studies, social geography, and environmental humanities. While I make artworks and installations for galleries and print media, much of my practice involves researching, producing, and performing media and live art, often situated in public spaces and outdoors. Examples from my past projects include a walking performance about lithium, an overnight camp for broadcasting the dawn chorus of birds, and an experimental documentary featuring food heritage stories.

Oil Ancestors, the project I will elaborate on in this essay, is a multimodal body of artworks relating to petroleum. *Oil Ancestors* invites reflections on sentimental relations to oil and the ways in which humans comprehend and feel long time frames: the deep time of fossilized matter and the future of climate breakdown. It is also a project that asks how we could begin to relate to nonliving beings, like petroleum, as kin.

For example, in a piece called *Oil Ancestors: Into the Proofer,* audiences directly interact with petroleum objects by flashing UV light on them and observing their ensuing blueish glow. Displayed on plinths are a jar of Crudoleum®—a hair product composed of crude oil—as well as prints made with pharmaceutical petroleum jelly and a small cluster of quartz crystals with oil that is naturally trapped inside. By foregrounding these objects and creating a visual allure around them, I make explicit the ways in which oil is extracted and glamorized in the production of commodities.

In the *Oil Ancestors* initiative, attention is drawn to petroleum's absolute ubiquity. Humans depend on oil for transportation and mobility; it is found in most consumer goods, from food to clothing to health products. Its extraction has defined global geopolitics and is deeply linked to the violence of imperialism and political corruption. The *Oil Ancestors* project contributes to conversations addressing petroculture by not only highlighting the materiality of oil and its omnipresence, but by also heightening the audience's sensitivity to their relations with oil.

Another of the multifarious artistic projects that comprise the *Oil Ancestors* initiative is an augmented reality (AR) audio experience available to pedestrians in the Mission neighborhood of San Francisco, California (fig. 1). Listeners use headphones and a mobile phone app to listen to a soundtrack which is triggered to play (through the use of GPS coordinates) when their body is in proximity to specific landmarks. In this sound artwork, entitled *Oil Ancestors: Growth*, the practice of creating immersive experiences for participants to engage with the environment shifts from the physical to the virtual or mediated. The project uses verbal directives to guide the audience to contemplate how we are, as political scientist Cara Daggett says, "unavoidably enmeshed in dependency."

Figure 1: The 23rd Street overpass above Highway 101 in San Francisco as captured by Google Street View in January 2021.

Screen photograph by Fereshteh Toosi.

The text passage that follows is an example of a moment from *Oil Ancestors: Growth*. It is an excerpt from the instructions that listeners hear when they are at the bridge where they arrive near the end of the experience:

> We are almost at the end of this journey, as our active transit path is intersected by a busy freeway dedicated to vehicular traffic. The ancestors of the Indigenous people who currently live and work in the Bay Area were quite mobile around the place we now know as San Francisco. To get around the bay, some Ohlone people used a plant named tule to make boats because the airy thin reeds are very buoyant. In 1775, a Spanish man wrote about

how much better the tule boats floated compared to the wooden rowing boats that the early Spanish ships had on board.

After learning about this history, the narrator asks listeners to reflect on their own experiences:

How do you usually get around the city?
What are the sounds of the different types of transportation that you hear around you right now?
In the air and on land?
Take a moment to imagine that all the vehicles fueled by petroleum and fossil fuels were suddenly gone.
What would the city sound like?

Oil Ancestors: Growth asks the audience to contrast their lives to those of previous generations and to consider the volume and presence of the sounds of automobiles and aircrafts as evidence of human dependence on fossil fuels. While we are dependent on oil, it is often taken for granted and rendered hidden—the pipeline being a prime figure in "making oil invisible, naturalizing its presence in our lives and hiding the environmental impacts of extraction from the eyes of concerned publics" (Wilson/Carlson/Szeman 8).

Art, then, can counter the invisibility of petroleum. Art can also encourage an attunement to feeling and sentiment for matter, which is often rendered invisible and unknowable through the obfuscation of industrialization.

Figure 2: A scene from Camp BreakDown Break Down *as photographed by the author.*

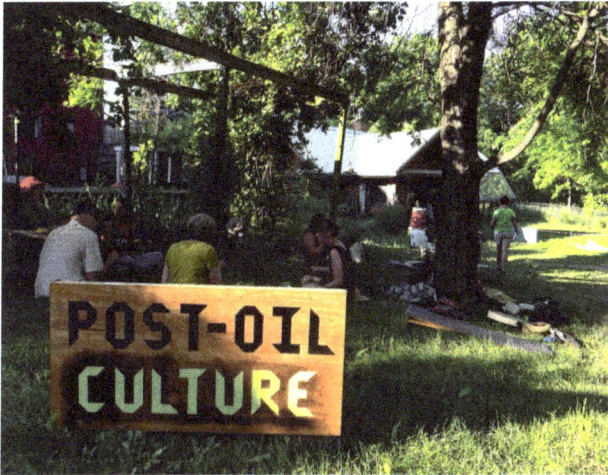

The impetus for the *Oil Ancestors* project began at an event called *Camp Breakdown Break Down*, a gathering of artists in northern Illinois that took place in 2017. It was designed as a place to research, debate, and practice post-oil aesthetics and culture.

The *Camp Breakdown Break Down* mission states:

> One of the biggest challenges to addressing climate breakdown is the fact that we exist primarily in terms of oil use and the relationships it structures, every moment of every day. Constantly relating to the world in this way cauterizes individual and collective petro-subjectivities, a numbing, highly industrialized sense of self and society that can seem impossible to exit. (Bloom/Sacramento)

The *Camp Breakdown Break Down* project uses the phrase "climate breakdown" as a more specific and active description of the crisis of climate change and global warming. The project also introduced me to the notion of "petro-subjectivity," which artist Brett Bloom wrote about in his 2015 book *Petro-subjectivity: De-Industrializing Our Sense of Self*. Illustrated by a visual diagram of the many uses of petroleum, petro-subjectivity is a term that illuminates how a contemporary sense of self cannot exist outside the logic and overwhelming presence of oil.

Embracing the premise that human subjectivity is entwined with oil, *Oil Ancestors* therefore asserts that oil is also an undeniable part of our cultural inheritance. Bloom and I share an interest in environmental action that is grounded in contemplative practice. Our work is based on the understanding that regenerative cultures are rooted in deep relationships beyond the human social sphere. Without regenerative relationships, culture begins to break down.

Eco-oriented contemplative practices are often comprised of somatic and affective activities in which the audience engages in sensory experiences and meditations. People are invited to slow down, reflect, and reconnect to the layers of human and other-than-human life in a landscape. Through creative guided reflections, people learn about the Indigenous history of the land, speculate about ecological futures, and confront climate anxiety, among other outcomes. Drawing attention to the ways in which human culture and geography are entangled shifts the audience's ability to notice, witness, and transform these intersections.

The participatory art practices represented at the core of *Oil Ancestors* and *Camp Breakdown Break Down* utilize mindfulness techniques which emerged from various spiritual traditions, such as Buddhism. I initially incorporated these techniques into my artwork as a result of my own meditation practice and my studies of plant medicine and nature and forest therapy, which focus on the health benefits of plants and nature connection. While I continue to be informed by the wellness movements that I mention above, my artwork distinguishes itself from healing modalities that sometimes serve to reinforce an extractive logic, which prioritizes nature only as far as it serves as a resource for human life.

I am also influenced by the metaphysical traditions of Persianate cultures and southwestern Asia, as well as my study of animism which began while living and working in Japan from 1998 to 2000. Animism explores the relationships between humans and other beings, often through ritual practices. Acknowledging plants, animals, rocks, metals, and bodies of water as persons is the basis of many Indigenous traditions. I prioritize Indigenous philosophy over seemingly similar thought systems such as object-oriented ontology or the legal movement called the "rights of nature" which questions the popular belief that nature is a resource for humans to own, use, and abuse.

The long-term process of consulting traditional ecological knowledges as sources of guidance for my creative research began with listening to the elders of the Onondaga Nation and the Partnership for Onondaga Creek in central New York, where I produced an eco-art project called *Up the Creek!* from 2007 to

2008. *Up the Creek!* examined the history of environmental racism in Syracuse, New York, just as the region was re-evaluating a second multi-million-dollar sewage treatment facility along Onondaga Creek. I name my influences as a form of citation and gratitude, especially because the history of Western and European art includes various artists who have wantonly appropriated Eastern philosophies and Indigenous culture. As a first-generation immigrant based in the United States, I am indebted to myriad sources: from Eastern folk practices to the Western avant-garde tradition of my American art education.

Most notably, American composer John Cage studied Zen Buddhism in the late 1940s and throughout the 1950s. Cage has had a profound influence on American contemporary art. Even though Cage's writings and body of work were a significant aspect of my early studies, I did not recognize and embrace the connection with Buddhism until later in my creative career. I consider the contemplative works of American composer Pauline Oliveros and Brazilian artist Lygia Clark to be more adjacent to my current practice. Oliveros is known for her sonic meditations called "Deep Listening," a concept she coined in the 1980s. Clark transitioned from an art practice to a therapeutic practice in the 1960s and 1970s. As art historian Adrian Anagnost writes of Clark's work: "Rather than contemplation of painting or sculpture, art became an intersubjective practice rooted in affective embodiment."

Though Oliveros died in 2016, her Deep Listening Institute has trained many artists and musicians in the practice of sonic meditation. Musicologist Kerry O'Brien describes Oliveros's work as a form of activism through listening and writes:

> Oliveros's aims were clear: these works were intended to be transformational, even therapeutic, enacting lasting changes on the body and mind. While she spent years immersed in introspective experimentation, Oliveros's "Sonic Meditations" shouldn't be mistaken for escapism or disengagement. The composer described listening as a necessary pause before thoughtful action: 'Listening is directing attention to what is heard, gathering meaning, interpreting and deciding on action [...] Healing can occur [...] when one's inner experience is made manifest and accepted by others.'

Figure 3: Forest immersion guided by Fereshteh Toosi at Pediaios Park in Nicosia, Cyprus for the Urban Emptiness Festival in 2017.

Photograph courtesy of Stefaan van Biesen.

I invite you to have a direct experience of this embodied practice. Please pause reading for a moment to listen to an audio recording. It is available on http://oilancestors.com/device, and a written transcript of the recording follows below.

The best way to experience this meditation is not to read it, but to listen and try it for yourself.

I wrote the meditation below for the *Oil Ancestors* project after experiencing many online webinars and video conference calls during the Covid-19 pandemic. The extreme carbon footprint of the media streaming daily on electronic devices is a result of an intimate reliance on fossilized matter.

As we begin, have your mobile phone or laptop directly within reach.
I recommend sitting in a chair, in a comfortable position, possibly with your feet touching the ground.
Let's go ahead and do that now.
Take a moment to gently settle into your seat. Feel the weight of your body held by gravity.

I invite you to engage with the physical qualities of your device with all your senses.

So if you feel comfortable, you may try to do this meditation with your eyes closed.

Touch your palm to the screen. How does it feel?

Now touch the screen with the back of your hand.

Next, extend your touch to the machine's backside, its underside, and its edges.

What textures are you feeling?

What is the temperature of the different parts of this machine?

Try leaning into your device.

Bring your nose close to your device and consider how it smells.

Think about all the matter that came from underground, now contained inside this machine.

Think of the substances that were mined from the earth.

Imagine all the people who assembled this multifaceted compound mineral stone.

Which of the elements can you name, and which are unknown to you?

Consider all the places they'd been before they came into your hands.

Where will they go when this machine's life ends?

Where will they be, when you're no longer here?

Figure 4: What did you notice while doing the practice?

Photograph courtesy of Stefaan van Biesen.

Figure 5: Fereshteh Toosi's OilAncestry.com website.

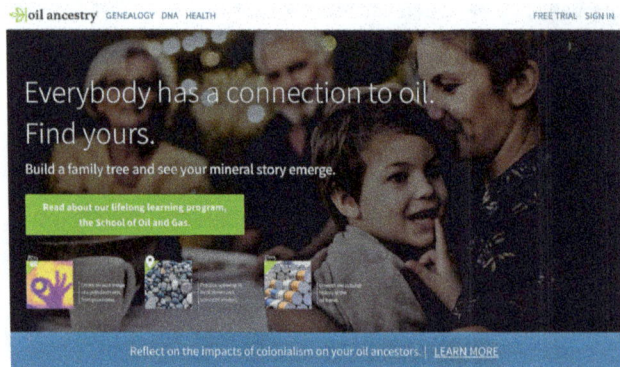

Screen photograph by Fereshteh Toosi.

A spoof of the popular genealogy site Ancestry.com, https://www.oil-ance stry.com/ (fig. 5) is one of the first experiments I made for *Oil Ancestors*.

Oil Ancestors is informed by my experience as an immigrant and artist of the Iranian and Azeri diaspora. Petroleum imperialism has defined the contemporary relationship between my ancestral homeland and the U.S. The legacy of armed conflict and resource extraction also impacts many Caribbean, South and Central American countries that are represented among the immigrant diaspora in Miami, where I live now. In his seminal 1992 book review entitled "Petrofiction," Amitav Ghosh refers to this expansive geographical connection as the "Oil Encounter." In this essay, Ghosh characterizes the history of oil as an embarrassment and reflects on the dramatic possibilities yet to be addressed in literature about the oil industry:

> [...] the Westerner with his caravan-loads of machines and instruments thrusting himself unannounced upon small, isolated communities, deep within some of the most hostile environments on earth. And think of the postmodern present: city-states where virtually everyone is a "foreigner"; admixtures of peoples and cultures on a scale never before envisaged; vicious systems of helotry juxtaposed with unparalleled wealth; deserts transformed by technology and military devastation on an apocalyptic scale. (30)

Perhaps it is a similar discomfort that causes apathy or ignorance about the fact that oil money funded the vacation fantasies that brought railroads to South Florida. John D. Rockefeller became one of the wealthiest people in U.S. American history after founding Standard Oil, which was once the largest petroleum company in the world. Rockefeller's business partner, Henry Flagler, used his oil company earnings to build railroads and hotels throughout Florida. One of these hotels is now a part of Flagler College campus in Florida. During Henry Flagler's development of Florida, swampland and limestone were transformed under the cruel labor systems of convict leasing and debt bondage.

Elia Vargas is an artist and scholar whose recent work centers on the history of early American petroleum industry and refiguring oil as media. Vargas and I share an interest in destabilizing an anthropocentric understanding of oil. Vargas writes:

> As new energy regimes and new critiques of the Anthropocene emerge, it is crucial to continue examining how the ontological status of oil as a fossil fuel persists. Why is it taken for granted that oil—an earth material that exceeds anthropocentric categorization—is represented exclusively as fuel? (n.p.)

Oil Ancestors considers ancient fossils, rocks, and minerals as part of our collective heritage. Although the project is not able to avoid the industrial function of oil, it asks the audience to consider extracted matter, sentimentally, apart from our human use of it as fuel and energy. Rather than theorizing about this categorization, the *Oil Ancestors* project poses the following questions:

> How can we practice relating to petroleum as kin?
> Is oil merely a fuel source and material for humans, or could it have other reasons to exist?
> Who is oil and what does oil desire from us?

The questions listed above serve as the overarching framework for *Oil Ancestors*. But to make these questions accessible to broad audience engagement, it helps to begin with familiar sentiments such as hope, fear, dread, and rage as they constitute different aspects of eco-anxiety. With the goal of encouraging a positively sentimental attitude to ecological history and culture, *Oil Ancestors: Metaphysical Hotline*, is a conversational performance for an audience of one (fig. 6). During the phone performance, the audience is placed in the role of an ancestor to a character from the future. Each call is uniquely shaped by their responses to concerns and questions about the future.

The phone call is approximately 30 to 40 minutes in duration, and it is based on a protocol called "The Work that Reconnects" by Joanna Macy. Macy is a popular author and Buddhist scholar whose research is informed by systems theory and deep ecology. "The Work that Reconnects" is a methodology she developed in response to her experiences as an environmental activist. Impacted by the anti-nuclear movement of the 1980s, Macy designed a series of group workshops to encourage hope as a process for finding, and offering, responses to global issues in times of crisis.

Figure 6: Promotional graphic for Fereshteh Toosi's Metaphysical Hotline, *an immersive telephone theater experience about environmental crisis and climate change.*

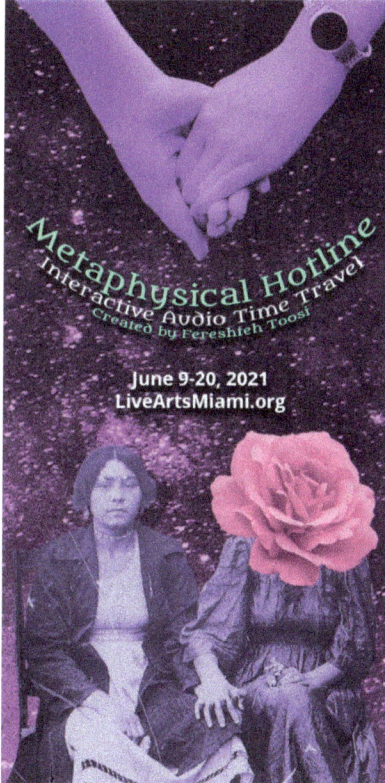

Image courtesy of Kelly Gallagher.

Below is the transcription of a scene from *Oil Ancestors: Metaphysical Hotline.* It was performed live and the participant's spontaneous responses were documented through an audio recording:

Stella, a young person from the far future: There are just so many things about your time that are hard to believe. And so, I just thought it would be good to check in with somebody about them. Like, they tell us that in your time, there are still people building houses on the ocean, in places like Miami and Virginia Beach and New York City, even as the sea level is rising. Of course, we know that history, but they say you know about it, too, just as the high-rise condos are being built. And they say that in your time, there's a small group of people who are richer than all the richest kings, while billions of other people don't have enough food, or houses, or clean water. And they tell us that in your time they keep approving new pipelines, even though they know it's bad for the water. And that plants and animals are going extinct because land is being cleared. And we know about that too. Because gone is gone. But they tell us that you know about all those things while they're happening. Is that true? And if it is true, what is it like for you to be living through this time?

Participant: Yes, it's true. And it's really sad. It feels like that we're alive, but also constantly mourning what we're losing now and what we know our lives are causing to be lost in the future. Yeah, I think it's really difficult, and it feels difficult for those of us who want to change things and to try to participate in ways that challenge and take down these structures. It feels really difficult to be able to do things like that. Because I think the people who are making these decisions and have all the wealth don't really think about future generations, or care about future generations.

Stella: That sounds really hard. But you sound like you care. So when did you first understand that life as you know it with a small group of rich people like Rockefeller and Flagler and all those people just making money off the land wasn't going to be sustainable for future generations? Like how did you realize that humans would have to live in a totally different way for life to continue?

Participant: Oh, gosh, I probably figure this out around when I was in college, and realizing how much waste I create, even though I feel like I am not doing the things that Rockefeller and developers do. But just realizing my own footprint and how that contributed and contributes to these problems, but also starting to understand histories of systemic oppression and how they continue. People like to think … we like to think that they've stopped, but that they're continuing on, and continuing to have these effects on all of us.

The final quote is a reflection shared by someone after they completed the experience:

I loved the very first thing you said that, you know, every living thing, past and future, lives in our DNA. And as then you were sort of talking about the experience—This is this little comment about pandemic times, but like there was a part of me that's like, "wow, I'm going to be connected to the future." And it was a really—it was a sort of heavy emotional concept in parts. Because I don't feel connected to anybody right now. Right? I feel like totally isolated and desperate for community that I don't have right now. And it was very powerful to think about, like a familial connection to some future being.

In imagining themselves as ancestors in a post-oil society, participants enter a relationship with oil wherein they are encouraged to take responsibilities to make such a speculative future possible. Rather than staying in a position of climate devastation, individuals are asked to consider themselves within deep time—an extending stretch of time that can sustainably continue.

In response to the acceleration of ecological destruction and climate breakdown, there is an urgent need to shift away from short-term thinking and develop a greater capacity to understand longer perspectives on human existence.

Oil Ancestors aims to engender affective relations to geological history and the long-term consequences of geological extraction. Many Indigenous philosophies are already grounded in the long-time frames which *Oil Ancestors* evokes. The opening scene of *Oil Ancestors: Metaphysical Hotline* begins with a quote from the Iroquois Constitution, an Indigenous declaration of democratic principles that came long before the U.S. Constitution and Bill of Rights:

Look and listen for the welfare of the whole people
and have always in view not only the present
but also the coming generations,
even those whose faces are yet beneath the surface
of the ground—the unborn of the future Nation. (Murphy)

Inspired by this worldview, *Oil Ancestors* is cultivating care and stewardship for future generations, greater emotional and sentimental connections to non-human matter, and reverence for the long-time frames that are necessary for substances like petroleum to form.

References

Anagnost, Adrian. 2017. "Presence, Silence, Intimacy, Duration: Lygia Clark's Relational Objects." *Pelican Bomb*, May 10, 2017. http://pelicanbomb.com/art-review/2017/presence-silence-intimacy-duration-lygia-clarks-relational-objects.

Bloom, Brett. 2015. *Petro-subjectivity: De-Industrializing Our Sense of Self.* Ft. Wayne, IN: Breakdown Break Down Press.

Bloom, Brett, and Nuno Sacramento. 2020. "Camp Breakdown Break Down–SSW." *Breakdown Break Down*. Accessed February 14, 2021. https://breakdownbreakdown.net/camp%20breakdown-break-down/.

Daggett, Cara. 2021. "Desiring Energy: Toxic Fantasies of Fuel, Freedom, and Work." Keynote lecture at the virtual workshop "Sentimental Extraction," Friedrich-Alexander-Universität Erlangen-Nürnberg, September 29–October 1st, 2021.

Ghosh, Amitav. 1992. "Petrofiction." *The New Republic*, March 2, 1992, 29–34.

Goldberg, RoseLee. 2001. *Performance Art: From Futurism to the Present*. New York, NY: Thames & Hudson.

Macy, Joanna, and Molly Young Brown. 2014. *Coming Back to Life: The Updated Guide to the Work that Reconnects*. Gabriola Island, BC: New Society Publishers.

Murphy, Gerald. 1996. "About the Iroquois Constitution." In *Internet Modern History Sourcebook*, edited by Paul Halsall. Fordham University, January 26, 1996. Accessed December 28, 2022. https://sourcebooks.fordham.edu/mod/iroquois.asp.

O'Brien, Kerry. 2016. "Listening as Activism: The 'Sonic Meditations' of Pauline Oliveros." *The New Yorker*, December 9, 2016. Accessed December 28, 2022. https://www.newyorker.com/culture/culture-desk/listening-as-activism-the-sonic-meditations-of-pauline-oliveros.

Vargas, Elia. 2021. "Field Notes for Future Petropractices: Refiguring Oil and/ as Media." *Media+Environment* 3 (1): n.p. DOI: https://doi.org/10.1525/001c.18931.

Wilson, Sheena L., Adam Carlson, and Imre Szeman. 2017. *Petrocultures: Oil, Politics, Culture*. Montreal, QC: McGill-Queen's University Press.

Contributors

Kylie Crane is Professor of British and American Cultural Studies at the University of Rostock, Germany.

Cara Daggett is Assistant Professor in the Department of Political Science at Virginia Tech, U.S.A.

Katharina Fackler is a lecturer in North American Studies at the University of Bonn, Germany.

Amy Fung is a writer, organizer, and doctoral researcher at the School of Indigenous and Canadian Studies at Carleton University, Canada.

Axelle Germanaz is a doctoral researcher in American Studies at Friedrich-Alexander-Universität Erlangen-Nürnberg, Germany.

Daniela Gutiérrez Fuentes is a doctoral researcher in American Studies at Friedrich-Alexander-Universität Erlangen-Nürnberg, Germany.

Jennifer Haigh is a writer based in Boston, U.S.A.

Sophie Hess is a doctoral researcher in American History at the University of Maryland, U.S.A.

Brian Leech is Associate Professor of History at Augusta College, U.S.A.

Stephanie LeMenager is Professor of English and Environmental Studies at the University of Oregon, U.S.A.

Gesa Mackenthun is Chair of North American Literature and Cultural Studies at the University of Rostock, Germany.

Sarah Marak is a doctoral researcher in American Studies at Friedrich-Alexander-Universität Erlangen-Nürnberg, Germany.

Heike Paul is Chair of American Studies at Friedrich-Alexander-Universität Erlangen-Nürnberg, Germany and Director of the Bavarian-American Academy.

Katie Ritson is a research fellow at the Rachel Carson Center for Environment & Society and an affiliated researcher in the Institute for Scandinavian Studies at Ludwig Maximilian University of Munich, Germany.

Fereshteh Toosi is an artist and Assistant Professor in the Art and Art History Department of the College of Communication, Architecture, and the Arts at Florida International University, U.S.A.

Verena Wurth is a doctoral researcher in American Studies at the University of Cologne, Germany.

Cultural Studies

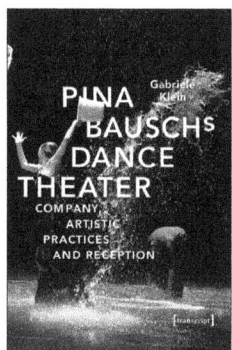

Gabriele Klein
Pina Bausch's Dance Theater
Company, Artistic Practices and Reception

2020, 440 p., pb., col. ill.
29,99 € (DE), 978-3-8376-5055-6
E-Book:
PDF: 29,99 € (DE), ISBN 978-3-8394-5055-0

Markus Gabriel, Christoph Horn, Anna Katsman, Wilhelm Krull,
Anna Luisa Lippold, Corine Pelluchon, Ingo Venzke
Towards a New Enlightenment –
The Case for Future-Oriented Humanities

October 2022, 80 p., pb.
18,00 € (DE), 978-3-8376-6570-3
E-Book: available as free open access publication
PDF: ISBN 978-3-8394-6570-7
ISBN 978-3-7328-6570-3

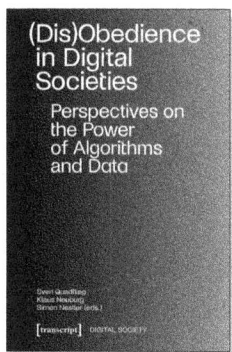

Sven Quadflieg, Klaus Neuburg, Simon Nestler (eds.)
(Dis)Obedience in Digital Societies
Perspectives on the Power of Algorithms and Data

March 2022, 380 p., pb., ill.
29,00 € (DE), 978-3-8376-5763-0
E-Book: available as free open access publication
PDF: ISBN 978-3-8394-5763-4
ISBN 978-3-7328-5763-0

All print, e-book and open access versions of the titles in our list
are available in our online shop www.transcript-publishing.com

Cultural Studies

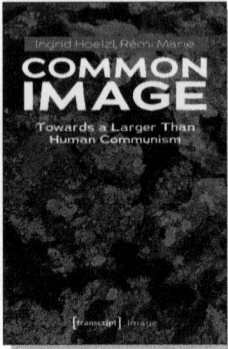

Ingrid Hoelzl, Rémi Marie
Common Image
Towards a Larger Than Human Communism

2021, 156 p., pb., ill.
29,50 € (DE), 978-3-8376-5939-9
E-Book:
PDF: 26,99 € (DE), ISBN 978-3-8394-5939-3

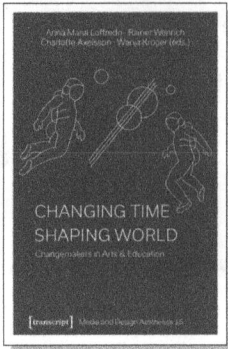

Anna Maria Loffredo, Rainer Wenrich,
Charlotte Axelsson, Wanja Kröger (eds.)
Changing Time – Shaping World
Changemakers in Arts & Education

September 2022, 310 p., pb., col. ill.
45,00 € (DE), 978-3-8376-6135-4
E-Book: available as free open access publication
PDF: ISBN 978-3-8394-6135-8

Olga Moskatova, Anna Polze, Ramón Reichert (eds.)
Digital Culture & Society (DCS)
Vol. 7, Issue 2/2021 –
Networked Images in Surveillance Capitalism

August 2022, 336 p., pb., col. ill.
29,99 € (DE), 978-3-8376-5388-5
E-Book:
PDF: 27,99 € (DE), ISBN 978-3-8394-5388-9

GPSR Authorized Representative: Easy Access System Europe, Mustamäe tee
50, 10621 Tallinn, Estonia, gpsr.requests@easproject.com